E   S S A Y S I N
E S   S A Y S I N
E S S   A Y S I N
E S S A   Y S I N
E S S A Y   S I N
E S S A Y S   I N
E S S A Y S I   N E
S   S A Y S   I   N
E S   S A Y S I N
E S S   ●   A Y S I N
E S S A   Y S I N
E S S A Y   S I N
E S S A Y S   I N
E S S A Y S I   N E   S S A

DATE DUE

1
2
3
4
5
6
7

8
9

Edited and with an introduction by Eyal Amiran & John Unsworth

OXFORD
UNIVERSITY
PRESS
NEW YORK
OXFORD

ESSAYS IN

ESSAY SIN

ESSA YSIN

ESS AYSIN

ES SAYSIN

E SSAYSIN

ESSAYS**P**IN

ESSAYS**O**IN

ESSAYS**S**IN

ESSAYS**T**IN

ESSAYS**M**IN

ESSAYS**O**IN

ESSAYS**D**IN

ESSAYS**ERN**

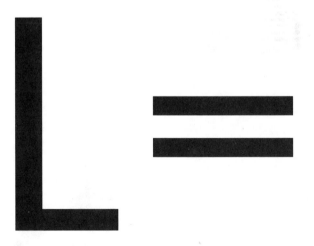

Oxford
University
Press,
Oxford,
New York,
Toronto,
Delhi,
Bombay,
Calcutta,
Madras,
Karachi,
Kuala Lumpur,
Singapore,
Hong Kong,
Tokyo,
Nairobi,
Dar es Salaam,
Cape Town,
Melbourne,
Aukland,
Madrid, &
associated
companies in
Berlin
and Ibadan.
© 1993
by Oxford
University
Press.

First published
as contributions to
*Postmodern
Culture*, a wholly
electronic
journal founded by
the editors
& published by
Oxford Uni-
versity Press. Oxford
is a regis-
tered trademark of
Oxford
University Press.

Library of Congress
Cataloging-in-
Publication Data:
Essays in postmodern
culture / edited
by Eyal Amiran & John
Unsworth. p. cm.
Includes bibliographical
references.
ISBN 0-19-508752-6
(hard : alk. paper). –
ISBN 0-19-508753-4
(pbk. : alk. paper)
1. Postmodernism.
2. Literature, Modern –
20th century –
History and criticism.
I. Amiran, Eyal.
II. Unsworth, John.
PN98.P67E87 1994
909.82–DC20
93-31361 CIP.
Typeset in Letraset
Charlotte Sans.
Book designed by
R. H. Eckersley.

tur

CONTENTS

"" '{[(ANTINOMY IN THE NET)]}' ""*

*Practical engagements with postmodernism

Yet doesn't the word "marginalization" assume

the existence of some master page

beyond whose justified (and hence invisible)

margins the panoplies of themes, authors,

movements, general objects of study exist

in all their colorful, handlettered marginality?

Bob Perelman, The Marginalization of Poetry

In May of 1993, David Blair's 1992 movie, *Wax: Or the Discovery of Television Among the Bees*, was converted from videotape to digital form by computer and broadcast on the Internet (Markoff). This was not an especially noteworthy event; it did not pull the plug on centralized television culture, or put an end to cultural government. It was just another sign – like the appearance of *Postmodern Culture* itself – that the totemic culture of information management and transmission ("All the News that's Fit to Print," or Cronkite's "That's the way it is") is changing. The implications of this change are far from clear: there is evidence for both optimism and pessimism on the subject, as reflected in this volume, as well as in the history and medium of *Postmodern Culture*.

Postmodern Culture published its first issue in September, 1990. At the time, it was the only peer-reviewed electronic journal in the humanities, and probably the only peer-reviewed scholarly journal to make available both its current and back issues free of charge to readers almost anywhere in the world.[1] Born and raised on the international computer networks, and nurtured by the attempts of cultural criticism to deal with politics, ideology, technology, and cultural production, *Postmodern Culture* has been, and continues to be, a self-reflexive enterprise: at the same time that each of the works gathered here attempts a critical engagement with practical and theoretical issues in contemporary literature and culture, each is also in some sense about the political and technological context in which a publication such as *Postmodern Culture* could take root.

The works collected here engage their civilized moment, and as part of the virtual text of *Postmodern Culture*, constitute (to borrow from Mowitt) events in the history of the system.[2] These works have in common a more or less explicit interest in the nature of postmodern culture in various manifestations – art, disease, literature, cyborgs, hypertexts, bodies, the city. The essays collectively evoke and generate issues that are crucial to the representation of the postmodern body, the nature of the postmodern text, the value of history in postmodern culture, and the politics of postmodernity. And repeatedly, the authors brought together here remind us that, as Elizabeth Wheeler says, "without awareness of power, it is the powerless who disappear" (para 13). In discussions of anorexia, hypertext, AIDS, quantum physics, cybernetics, secret wars, and the gentrification of LA among other things, these essays attempt to reconstitute human agency, to rescue the liberatory potential of postmodernism, and to find a way to map what Stuart Moulthrop calls "the networks of transnational power" (para 43) – not forgetting to include the subject-position ("You are here") of the author. For this reason they frequently criticize and sometimes revile Baudrillard, whose notion of simulation is generally seen as disturbingly apolitical and escapist.[3] In order to move "beyond our recent 'depthless,' ahistorical quiescence," Moulthrop argues, "We require not only a sensitivity to the complex textuality of power but an ability to intercept and manipulate that text, an advanced creative paranoia" (para 43).

Creative paranoia: the very relation that binds the subject in cultural nets also enables subjectivity. There can be an antinomic, if not antinomian, logic in an oppositional discourse which attempts to address its own contradictory positions vis-a-vis postmodernism. The project of *Postmodern Culture* has been to recognize this connectedness and to publish work that engages the practical entanglements it produces. Criticism of the discipline, significantly, handles postmodernism from one of its ends only. This applies to critiques from any political viewpoint. Postmodernism has been accused from the left of being indifferent to social context, of articulating an extreme subjectivism and celebrating contemporary alienation in positivist technological utopianism. It has been accused from the middle of empty gestures, "delicious shudders of a bogus revolution" (Bourdieu 255). It has been accused from the right of nihilism, solipsism, and self-indulgence. At different points, these charges have their adherents within this volume; but the works collected here also show that the concept of postmodernism is valuable for the textual-cultural contemporary because it makes it possible to engage diverse aspects of our historical moment without requiring an impossibly separate, metahistorical position from which to mount such a critique. As David Mikics says, in a more specific context,

> By indifferently combining the fragments of various traditions and histories, affirmative postmodernism sets even fragmentation under the sign of Baudrillard's homogeneous, uniform "society of the spectacle." By contrast, Reed via his subcultural strategy sets the

*plural cultural forces of postmodern society in conflict, propound-
ing an aesthetics of resistance or social tension rather than reconciliation.* (para 9)

The essays collected here are remarkable for their tenacious interrogation of postmodernism itself: the ambivalence that characterizes
Baudrillard's and Jameson's discussions of the postmodern becomes, here, a more overt investigation of the contradictory nature
of connectedness, within and among essays such as McCarthy's,
Larsen's, and Wheeler's, and in the exchange of arguments between
Fraiberg and Porush.

The study of postmodernism has shifted its interest from rejection to connection in the last decade. It lost currency in the mid 80s
because it focused on a *condition* (at an MLA panel Ihab Hassan presented twelve terms, like "decentered," that characterize postmodernity, in what Linda Hutcheon has called "a grand flourish of negativ-
ized rhetoric" [3]); the study of postmodernism has become useful
again because it is now more interested in a *process* (Jameson 384), in
the interpenetrative experiences that weave contemporary culture.
Postmodernism is not a disease or a cure; it is a perception of relatedness that rejects reduction – ontological, epistemological, socio-
historical. It is not a thing one can find out there, but a relation that
runs through all things, in art, production, consumption, public policy, and in the minds of people. As Brian McHale puts it, postmodernism "exists discursively, in the discourses we produce *about* it and
using it" (1). Lyotard is right (in *The Postmodern Condition*) that postmodernism is characterized by the rejection of metanarratives, but
his argument – and the notion that postmodernism is a "condition"
– may encourage us to dismiss metanarratives, whereas it is just the
thing to look for: we need not to forget narrative (every narrative is
ipso facto metanarratological), but to identify the narratives important in our cultures and learn to understand how they function.[4]

The study of postmodernism does not conform to older para-
digms of interpretation, nor is it free of their influence. Many ideas
important in postmodern thinking – like Benjamin's notion of the
reproduction of art, or the notion of commodity-exchange culture in
Marx's *Capital*, or the cyberpunk representation that makes the
body mechanical and so interchangeable and constructed, or Baudrillard's idea that the map now precedes its territory – have their

precedents in earlier literature. The constructed body is a common nineteenth-century idea (as in Melville's *The Confidence Man* or in Shelley's *Frankenstein*), Wilde has made the argument for reversing the causal arrow of representation, and Proust has more than hinted at Baudrillard's claim for the map in the "Overture" to *Swann's Way*. But the constellation of concepts that make up postmodernism requires new thinking, however familiar some of its elements. The metaphors of complexity and relation we have come to know – the maze metaphor, for example, the integrated circuit of Pynchon or the rug of Calvino in *Invisible Cities* – do not describe the postmodern. The maze is a closed system, however complicated, and leads one on, however befuddled the interiorized subject. Some of the writers in this collection, for this reason, have sought other ideas, like the text of AIDS, to help them think about this process. It makes little sense to think of postmodernism as a trans-historical entity, something that existed for Sterne or for Cervantes. When these writers argue for indirection and against a linear (mis)representation of experience, they express their allegiance to an established value system (say, a spiritual one) that competes with prosaic living. They do not advocate a postmodern understanding of the self or of their time.

These partial understandings of postmodernism are examples of the dogmatic reduction of the subject to one or another of its elements. On another, more overtly ideological level, a similar reductive impulse is commonplace: one is often asked to believe in the power of the individual to oppose cultural oppression, or conversely in the impossibility of doing so, but either claim is undermined by the way it participates in and is like its other.[5] That is, if we insist that the subject is wholly circumscribed and that resistance must take place on the level of social institutions, we overlook the way in which the freedom possible in the collective is available in the particular inscribed by that system; if we argue that the body politic is oppressive and resistance is available only through radical subjectivity, then we overlook the extent to which the collective embodies and amplifies the subjectivity it holds. And if the subject is *completely* within a collective envelope of power, then it is free again, in the same way that Adam and Eve are free in Milton's universe; as Jeanette Winterson puts it, "If someone is thinking me, then I am still free to come and go" (113).

One lesson common to both Freud and Foucault is that the collective and the private are analogical and not antithetical. For Freud (for individual psychology), personal development (repression) recapitulates the growth of the group and its cultural institutions (in *Civilization and its Discontents*, for example); for Foucault, the collectivist, the mind is also collective: the boundary of social structure is established through the study of madness, through the analogy of the othering and circumscription of the mind (in *Madness and Civilization*, for instance). This holds for similar dualities advanced in the analysis of postmodernity – the body as written and resisting, technological optimism or pessimism, the subject as transcendant particularity (Mouffe and Laclau) or as part of the totalizing expression of power (early Foucault). Properly understood, these inclusive continuums – "Poetry is the creation of public policy in a private space," as Charles Bernstein writes his Percy Shelley (Hart 108) – tell us not which end is winning, but which questions address the world we perceive; they also indicate directions for inquiry into the postmodern, not attempts to isolate some cause or symptom of it as the most telling or most interesting or most dangerous, but practical struggles and negotiations among the elements in this field.

Although none of the essays collected here succeeds entirely in escaping the specialized rhetoric of literary or philosophical professionalism, each author shows an awareness of the contradictory logic of postmodern engagements, the "sad irony" pointed out by bell hooks, in an essay originally published in the first issue of *Postmodern Culture*, that

> the contemporary discourse which talks the most about heterogeneity, the decentered subject, declaring breakthroughs that allow recognition of Otherness, still directs its critical voice primarily to a specialized audience that shares a common language rooted in the very master narratives it claims to challenge. (para 6)

The journal itself has to admit the same irony: in some of our early explorations of what the journal could or should be (and do), we expressed a hope that we could dis-establish the practice of admitting only those who speak our language or who position themselves as we do. In practice, this has sometimes happened, and certainly the journal has not come to represent a dominant viewpoint, but it is also true that the journal is part of what it contests, even as it contests it. A world of new technology – a new electronic civilization perhaps – does not raze the old or atomize texts and subjects. The expectation

8

9

that a new medium will change everything ignores the postmodern realization that one cannot entirely "make it new."[6]

Just as these essays must negotiate practical engagements with and within postmodern culture, so the journal itself is caught in the virtual net – the internet – and must negotiate with it. *Paranoia*, that enabling sense that everything is deeply but obscurely connected, is an apt, perhaps even an adaptive, response to the culture of information, and an appropriate analogue to internet itself, a network of computers connected by phone lines for the transmission of information. The internet began with a 1964 proposal by the Rand Corporation, which had been asked by the Department of Defense how the United States could ensure communications after a nuclear apocalypse. Since any centralized, hierarchically controlled or administered communications network (such as the phone system) would be vulnerable to decapitation, RAND proposed a network that

> would **have no central authority**. *Furthermore, it* would *be* **designed from the beginning to operate while in tatters.** *The principles were simple. The network itself would be assumed to be unreliable at all times. It would be designed from the get-go to transcend its own unreliability. All the nodes in the network would be equal in status to all other nodes, each node with its own authority to originate, pass, and receive messages. The messages themselves would be divided into packets, each packet separately addressed. . . . . If big pieces of the network had been blown away, that simply wouldn't matter; the packets would still stay airborne, lateralled wildly across the field by whatever nodes happened to survive.* (Sterling)

What has emerged from this early blueprint is a "cyborg assemblage" not unlike the one that Addison and Ecstavasia describe in their essay in this volume, an assemblage composed of fiction (such as Sterling's), the law (in this case, the military and civil authorities who own and police the nets), time (hours online), space (geographical space being rapidly replaced by the space of the network itself), the telephone (whose lines carry, but do not constitute, the network), and perhaps most importantly, exchange. But what leaves some room for optimism is the fact that, for the whole of its history, the internet has hosted a different sort of exchange as well – an exchange of ideas and emotions, in an unofficial but not quite underground economy made possible by the system's anarchic design.

The internet has been growing over the last few years by as much as 20% every **month**, a rate that would seem to make centralized governance impossible; but as Roberto Dainotto points out, "the authoritative announcement of the disappearance of authority" is often an effective way to "surreptitiously establish . . . [a] fraudulent totalizing order" (para 19). Even its most optimistic adherents would not claim that the internet answers to Lyotard's description of a totally open informational utopia, where all have equal access and opportunity. On the contrary, access to the network routinely depends on affiliation with one or more of the existing centers of cultural and economic power: institutions of higher education, corporations, the military.

11

Nonetheless, unofficial transmissions such as the broadcast of *Wax* are the norm on the internet: if anything, the broadcast of *Wax* is atypical only because it is a one-to-many transmission, characterized by the passivity of its audience, as television itself is, rather than a many-to-many Babel of signals, characterized by interactivity and the breaking down of the spectacle/audience distinction, as is more often the case on the internet. By the same token, *Postmodern Culture* is in some ways an indicative phenomenon and in other ways an atypical one, as far as the internet goes. As a networked electronic publication, PMC offers a place where the reader may choose, in principle, among myriad texts, may retrieve and manipulate them, may respond to the author(s) of those texts, and may take part in the activity of peer-review. Such activity may revise the old order itself – as Moulthrop notes, "The telos of the electronic society-of-text is anarchy in its true sense: local autonomy based on consensus, limited by a relentless disintegration of global authority" (para 22). On the other hand, if the journal were to avoid authority and judgment, and let every voice speak ungoverned, it would not be a journal but a mirror of the internet itself, that confusing, enjoyable, uncertain mess to which our readers have – of necessity, until now – already subscribed.

12

A NOTE ON THE TEXT

Postmodern Culture is a free electronic journal and does not appear in print. It may appear therefore that this publication of work from the journal forms a print supplement that undermines the integrity of PMC's electronic format. This would only be the case, however, if the journal were not widely available in its electronic format: it is and will continue to be. We hope this collection proves convenient and useful, especially to readers who do not use electronic mail, and we hope that it will encourage those readers to explore the journal and the other resources available on the internet.

These works have been revised slightly from their electronic versions, and their formatting has been altered to conform to print conventions, although PMC allows for different citation formats.

N   O   T   E   S

1. For a discussion of the narratives that organize the reception of electronic text, and a comparison of the reception of etext to that of print in its infancy, see Eyal Amiran, John Unsworth, and Carole Chaski, "Networked Academic Publishing and the Rhetorics of Its Reception," *The Centennial Review* vol XXXVI, no 1 (Winter 1992): 43-58.

For a general discussion of *Postmodern Culture*'s medium, and of gender-specific and institutional questions it raises, including some implications of electronic publishing for libraries, see Eyal Amiran, Elaine Orr, and John Unsworth, "Refereed Electronic Journals and the Future of Scholarly Publishing," in *Advances in Library Automation and Networking* vol 4 (NY: JAI Press, 1991): 25-53.

2. "The text is, like an actual utterance, an event in the history of the system" (Mowitt 5).

3. "Baudrillard is perhaps the most extreme instance of this 'postmodern' drive to extend the aesthetic (i.e. the realm of the imaginary representations) to the point of collapsing every last form of ontological distinction or critical truth-claim," according to Christopher Norris (23).

4. Without transcendental principles, as Steven Connor puts it, "questions of value do not disappear, but gain a new intensity; and the struggle to generate and ground legitimacy in the contemporary academy is nowhere more intense than in the debates produced by and around postmodernism" (8).

5. So Fred Pfeil (whose essay on film noir won PMC's first Electronic Text Award) writes that "postmodernity is either taken to be the disaster that has

already occurred, leaving us utterly resourceless and without hope, wailing zombies under perpetual erasure wandering aimlessly through an endless mall; or else it is just as unproblematically celebrated as a disintegration of old hierarchies and an explosion of new cultural and political practices . . . which together constitute a new carnival of freedom, somewhere out beyond the old orthodoxies, including Marxism itself. What both sides have in common is both their universalist starting point, in which postmodernism . . . is everywhere and nowhere at once, and their fatalistic conclusion" (3). Instead, he urges us to refuse "the apocalyptic cast of mind."

6. This point is made often. See, for instance, Lyotard in "Defining the Post-modern": "The idea of modernity is closely bound up with this principle that it is possible and necessary to break with tradition and to begin a new way of living and thinking. Today we can presume that this 'breaking' is, rather, a manner of forgetting or repressing the past. That's to say of repeating it. Not overcoming it" (8).

W O R K S C I T E D

Appignanesi, Lisa, ed. *Postmodernism: ICA Documents*. London: Free Association Books, 1989.

Bourdieu, Pierre. "The Historical Genesis of a Pure Aesthetic." Trans. Charles Newman. [1987] *The Field of Cultural Production: Essays on Art and Literature*. Ed. Randal Johnson. NY: Columbia UP, 1993.

Connor, Stephen. *Postmodern Culture: An Introduction to Theories of the Contemporary*. Oxford: Basil Blackwell, 1990.

Dainotto, Roberto. "The Excremental Sublime: The Postmodern Literature of Blockage and Release." Raleigh, NC. *Postmodern Culture* 3.3 (May, 1993). Available as DAINOTTO.593 from LISTSERV@LISTSERV.NCSU.EDU or PMC@UNITY.NCSU. EDU (internet). 53 paragraphs.

Hart, David. "RSVP." *Verse* vol 10 no 1 (Spring, 1993): 102-112.

hooks, bell. "Postmodern Blackness." Raleigh, NC. *Postmodern Culture* 1.1 (Sep., 1990). Available as HOOKS.990 from LISTSERV@LISTSERV.NCSU.EDU or PMC@UNITY.NCSU.EDU (internet). 15 paragraphs.

Hutcheon, Linda. *A Poetics of Postmodernism: History, Theory, Fiction*. New York and London: Routledge, 1988.

Jameson, Fredric. "Afterword – Marxism and Postmodernism." *Postmodernism/Jameson/Critique*. Ed. Douglas Kellner. Washington DC: Maisonneuve Press, 369-87.

Lyotard, Jean-François. "Defining the Postmodern." *Postmodernism:* ICA *Documents*. Ed. Lisa Appignanesi. London: Free Association Books, 1989, 7-10.

Markoff, John. "Cult Film Is a First On Internet." *The New York Times*, Monday, May 24, 1993, C3.

McHale, Brian. *Constructing Postmodernism*. London and New York: Routledge, 1992.

Mikics, David. "Postmodernism, Ethnicity, and Underground Revisionism in Ishmael Reed." Raleigh, NC. *Postmodern Culture* 1.3 (May, 1991). Available as MIKICS.591 from LISTSERV@LISTSERV.NCSU.EDU or PMC@UNITY.NCSU.EDU (internet). 41 paragraphs.

Moulthrop, Stuart. "You Say You Want A Revolution? Hypertext and the Laws of Media." Raleigh, NC. *Postmodern Culture* 1.3 (May, 1991). Available as MOULTHRO.591 from LISTSERV@LISTSERV.NCSU.EDU or PMC@UNITY.NCSU.EDU (internet). 59 paragraphs.

Mowitt, John. *Text: The Genealogy of an Antidisciplinary Object*. Durham, NC: Duke UP, 1993.

Norris, Christopher. *What's Wrong with Postmodernism: Critical Theory and the Ends of Philosophy*. Baltimore: Johns Hopkins UP, 1990.

Pfeil, Fred. *Another Tale to Tell: Politics and Narrative in Postmodern Culture*. London: Verso, 1990.

Sterling, Bruce. "Internet." Science Column no 5. *The Magazine of Fantasy and Science Fiction*, February, 1992.

Wheeler, Elizabeth. "Bulldozing the Subject." Raleigh, NC. *Postmodern Culture* 1.3 (May, 1991). Available as WHEELER.591 from LISTSERV@LISTSERV.NCSU.EDU or PMC@UNITY.NCSU.EDU (internet). 65 paragraphs.

Winterson, Jeanette. *Sexing the Cherry*. NY: Vintage, 1989.

FEEDING THE TRANSCENDENT BODY

GEORGE YÚDICE

TO EAT IS TO APPROPRIATE BY DESTRUC-
TION; IT IS AT THE SAME TIME TO BE FILLED
UP WITH A CERTAIN BEING. . . . WHEN
WE EAT WE DO NOT LIMIT OURSELVES TO
K N O W I N G CERTAIN QUALITIES OF
THIS BEING THROUGH TASTE; BY TASTING
THEM WE APPROPRIATE THEM. TASTE IS AS-
SIMILATION. . . . THE SYNTHETIC INTUITION
OF FOOD IS IN ITSELF AN ASSIMILATIVE DE-
STRUCTION. IT REVEALS TO ME THE BEING
WHICH I AM GOING TO MAKE MY FLESH.
HENCEFORTH, WHAT I ACCEPT OR WHAT I
REJECT WITH DISGUST IS THE VERY BEING OF
THAT EXISTENT. . . . ¶ IT IS NOT A MATTER OF
INDIFFERENCE WHETHER WE LIKE OYSTERS
OR CLAMS, SNAILS OR SHRIMP, IF ONLY WE
KNOW HOW TO UNRAVEL THE EXISTENTIAL
SIGNIFICATION OF THESE FOODS. GENERALLY
SPEAKING THERE IS NO IRREDUCIBLE TASTE
OR INCLINATION. THEY ALL REPRESENT A
CERTAIN APPROPRIATE CHOICE OF BEING.
J E A N - P A U L   S A R T R E[1]

§1 At first glance, it seems unlikely that contemporary U.S. culture can offer a gastrosophy to match that of other civilizations. Brillat-Savarin's (and Feuerbach's) adage, "You are what you eat," does not throb today with metaphysical significance as it did scarcely two generations ago for Sartre. In the United States, it is indeed a matter of indifference "whether we like oysters or clams, snails or shrimp"; much of the lower priced seafood today is made from other processed fish. Consequently, the differences between particular foods are less important; what really matters is taste itself, laboratory produced *flavor*. Food as substance gives way to the simulacrum of flavor, which is something that "science" recombines in ever new ways to seduce us to this or that convenience food. As synthetic food replaces Sartre's "synthetic intuition of food," we find it impossible to transcend the brute "facticity" of eating, which is ironically as fake as it is real. We eat substances (the "real") yet we do not *know* them as such but as simulations (the "fake").

§2   The portrait I've drawn here obviously calls for a reference to Baudrillard, which will come in due time. First, however, it is necessary to reflect a bit more on the changes wrought by the transition to simulation in our (seemingly) most immediate experience: eating. Anthropologists have explained in great detail how entire civilizations defined themselves allegorically through their eating practices. Inclusion or exclusion, symbolic and material exchange, body boundaries, gender, and other identity factors are systematically and most deeply inscribed in the members of a given group through eating practices. Consequently, the metaphysics of most groups is conveyed by these practices. This inscription conditions, for example, how people understand divinity. For the Greeks of Hesiod's *Theogony*, the rituals of sacrificial cooking and eating, paralleled in agricultural, funereal and nuptial practices, establish a communication between mortals and immortals which paradoxically expresses their incommensurability. In contrast, the Orphic anthropogony makes possible the mystical transcendence of the barrier between gods and humans by rejecting the sacrifice of the official religion.

BY REFUSING THIS SACRIFICE, BY FORBIDDING THE BLOODSHED OF ANY ANIMAL, BY TURNING AWAY FROM FLESHY FOOD TO DEDICATE THEMSELVES TO A TOTALLY "PURE" ASCETIC LIFE — A LIFE ALSO COMPLETELY ALIEN TO THE SOCIAL AND RELIGIOUS NORMS OF THE CITY — MEN WOULD SHED ALL THE TITANIC ELEMENTS OF THEIR NATURE. IN DIONYSUS THEY WOULD BE ABLE TO RESTORE THAT PART OF THEMSELVES THAT IS DIVINE.[2]

§3 Since mystical transcendence usually involves some relation to eating – or not eating, as in the Orphic cult – it is interesting to ask what are the possibilities of such transcendence in an age of fake fat and microwavable synthetic meals. The mystic engages in a struggle whose reward is nourishing grace. As Saint Teresa says, the soul "finds everything cooked and eaten for it; it has only to enjoy its nourishment."[3] In our consumer culture, however, such convenience food comes to most of us without the struggle. Unlike the mystic – who is "like a man who has had no schooling. . . and [yet] finds himself, without any study, in possession of all living knowledge" – we are not graced by any special knowledge. Without negativity – Sartre's "appropria[tion] by destruction" – there is no transcendence. And negativity is precisely what gives the Orphics and mystics like Saint Teresa--often taken as heretics by orthodoxy – a feeling of **power** which makes them "master of all the elements and of the whole world."[4] Transcendence, in these cases, is closely related to contestatory social movements which attempted to invert the power differential between the dominant and the subaltern.

§4 The experiences of people (mostly women) with eating disorders today seems to contradict the argument that there are no longer any practices of negativity. In fact, on the basis of power reversals similar to the ones claimed by mystics, contemporary theorists/practictioners of *écriture* have rediscovered – and extended to the anorectic – the prototype of an "herethics" beyond the dominant order of things,[5] or a "mysterique" (fusion of mystic and hysteric) who carves out her own space of enunciation within Western discourse.[6] Following this latter analogy, the mystic's relationship to the inquisitor would be like that of the hysteric before the psychoanalyst who seeks to extract her secrets for the benefit of his doctrine.[7]

§5 The correlation of mystic/heretic, hysteric and anorectic, however, encounters a serious problem: against what or whom is the anorectic wielding her negativity? Endocrinological and other biomedical factors aside, anorexia and other eating disorders are, of course, an expression of gender struggle in our society.[8] But that does not explain everything; if that were the case, we could expect all the victims of patriarchy to suffer from eating disorders. It seems to me that the issue of control is a necessary but not sufficient condition for the negativity of the anorectic (or the bulimic or the obese woman). Class and/or gender analysis is not enough to account for all questions of subjectivity and desire. We are all constrained but some of us go on to become mystics or anorectics. Why? In the most suggestive essay I have read on the topic, Sohnya Sayres argues that some of us are more sensitive to the limitless loss brought on by the shrinking of experience. As in mystical experience, the loss becomes the point of departure for the will to greatness and glory, to empowerment:

IT IS GLORY THAT THESE BODY-LOSS-OBSESSED MEN AND WOMEN SEEK, IN MAKING THEMSELVES "LOST," RAPACIOUS GLORY IN SOCIETY CONSTRAINING THEM IN RITUALS AROUND LIMITLESS LOSS. THEY EXTERNALIZE THE RETURN OF THE REPRESSED IN THIS SOCIETY WHICH, MORE THAN OTHERS, IS RATIONALIZED AROUND THE LEDGER SHEETS AND THE ACCOUNTANTS OF GAIN, WHOSE MOST SERIOUS INTONATIONS ARE ABOUT THE "BOTTOM LINE" — WHICH HAS REMADE THE "FULL PLATE" INTO THE LATEST IDIOM FOR DEALING WITH BAD NEWS. ONE WONDERS, NOW, WHETHER THE ULTIMATE LOSS THAT YOUNG PEOPLE SAY THEY ARE ALMOST SURE WILL BE THEIR NOT TOO DISTANT FUTURE — MILLENNIALIST, CATACLYSMIC LOSS — HASN'T EXCITED, BUT SENT DEEPER, THOSE FANTASIES OF MESSIANIC RESCUE LYING CHOKED BENEATH WEEDS THE BODY IMPERATIVES PLANT IN THE SPIRIT. FAT AND ANORECTIC WOMEN AND MEN WANT TO BE GREAT, IN WAYS UNACCOUNTABLE. . . UNLESS WE ACCEPT THE ENORMITY OF THE UNACCOUNTABLE IN THIS SOCIETY. THEN, PERHAPS, THE DRAMA OF FOOD AND THE BODY CAN BE GIVEN A STORYTELLER'S INNOVATIONS, THAT IS, WHEN IT IS RELEASED FROM EXPLANATION AND ACCOMMODATION, ALL THAT QUANTIFYING, INTO FLIGHTS OF WIT AND PROVOCATION — RELEASED, IN OTHER WORDS, FROM A SINGULAR, PETTY, TALE OF COMPULSION INTO ONE OF SACRIFICE, MORTIFICATION, AND REDEMPTION — INTO A GRANDER DELUSION, WORTHY OF THE PERSON, WORTHY OF HEARING ABOUT, WORTHY OF TRANSFORMING.[9]

§6   I have quoted Sayres at length because she expresses so well the dialectic of loss and transcendence which Baudrillard, in turn, will transform into a paean to banality. Baudrillard's hyperreality has no place in it for delusions of grandeur and redemption. Or it may be more exact to say that he does acknowledge grandeur, but it is the grandeur of limitless banality. There is no sense, however, of how people suffer and struggle against that banality. In fact, he has taken the figure of the obese/anorectic, in which some feminists situate a radical negation of patriarchy, and cast it as the emblem of a society in which there is no longer any possibility of opposition because everything has been "digest[ed into] its own appearance":

THIS STRANGE OBESITY IS NO LONGER THAT OF A PROTECTIVE LAYER OF FAT NOR THE NEUROTIC ONE OF DEPRESSION. IT IS NEITHER THE COMPENSA-TORY OBESITY OF THE UNDERDEVELOPED NOR THE ALIMENTARY ONE OF THE OVERNOURISHED. PARADOXICALLY, IT IS A MODE OF DISAPPEARANCE FOR THE BODY. THE SECRET RULE THAT DELIMITS THE SPHERE OF THE BODY HAS DISAPPEARED. THE SECRET FORM OF THE MIRROR, BY WHICH THE BODY WATCHES OVER ITSELF AND ITS IMAGE, IS ABOLISHED, YIELDING TO THE UNRESTRAINED REDUNDANCY OF A LIVING ORGANISM. NO MORE LIMITS, NO MORE TRANSCENDENCE: IT IS AS IF THE BODY WAS NO LONGER OPPOSED TO AN EXTERNAL WORLD, BUT SOUGHT TO DIGEST SPACE IN ITS OWN APPEAR-ANCE.[10]

§7   Like the social systems in which we live, which are "bloated with information" and deprived of significance, Baudrillard's ob-scene obese/anorectic body has lost the "principle of law or mea-sure" that once supported it. Its meanings and representations have also transmuted into metastatic self-replication. History is now seen as a succession of devourments which, along with ideology and politics, reach a saturation point that knows no limits; metastasis encompasses everything, nothing is at odds with it, nothing can transcend it. And as every condition has its symptomatic figuration, Baudrillard's obscene hyperreality finds its "perfect confirmation and ecstatic truth" in the obscene body, which "instead of being reflected, captures itself in its own magnifying mirror."[11]

§8   Europe has long served as the proscenium for the death of the subject and history; the allegory of the death of life could have no other setting, of course, than the United States, home of those exemplary killers of experience: fast food, safe sex and genetic engi-neering.

I WOULD LIKE TO TALK ABOUT AN ANOMALY – THAT FASCINATING OBESITY, SUCH AS YOU FIND ALL OVER THE U.S., THAT KIND OF MONSTROUS CONFOR-MITY TO EMPTY SPACE, OF DEFORMITY BY EXCESS OF CONFORMITY THAT TRANSLATES THE HYPERDIMENSION OF A SOCIALITY AT ONCE SATURATED AND EMPTY, WHERE THE SCENE OF THE SOCIAL AS WELL AS THAT OF THE BODY ARE LEFT BEHIND.[12]

§9   In the grand allegorical tradition, Baudrillard offers us a new reading of the body-as-microcosm-of-the-world. This body is not a temple, nor a machine, nor a holistic organism. It is the obscene body without order, whose cells have gone rampant in "cancerous metastases" that parallel the useless flow of information in the postmodern world. If disease was once interpreted as **lesion** (the body as machine model) or as **adaptive response to stress** (the organic model),[13] Baudrillard's **viral** analogy construes it as coextensive with "life." It is, however, a life with no rhyme or reason other than the momentum/inertia of self-replication: "Quite simply, there is no life any longer [. . .] but the information and the vital functions continue."[14]

§10   The body registers the "useless and wasteful exhaustion" of all systems in the figure of the obese (satiation) and/or the anorectic (inertia). In this view, the obese and the anorectic are neither the victims of some accident whose results can be reversed by altering a body part ("removing portions of the stomach or intestine so that only small amounts of food could be eaten or digested") nor the adaptation to stressful "environmental factors (exercise habits, self-image, personal relationships, work pressures, etc.)."[15] They are, rather, the embodiment of permanent crisis: inflation, overproduction, unemployment, nuclear threat, *anomaly*, to sum up.

§11   Yes. At first sight, the example seems irrefutable. What better emblem of the empire of the senseless, useless waste of resources than the insatiable obese and anorectics of (North) America, driven to passivity, apathy and indifference by the infinite choice of consumables?[16] In a very insightful essay in which he mines the contradictions between capitalism and transgression, Octavio Paz notes that by rigorously applying the norm of the "limitless production of the same," North American society succeeded in coopting the erotic and gastronomic rebellions of the 60s into slogans for the media:[17]

THE POPULAR CHARACTER OF THE EROTIC REVOLT WAS IMMEDIATELY APPRE-
CIATED BY THE MASS MEDIA, BY THE ENTERTAINMENT AND FASHION INDUS-
TRIES. FOR IT IS NOT THE CHURCHES NOR THE POLITICAL PARTIES, BUT THE
GREAT INDUSTRIAL MONOPOLIES THAT HAVE TAKEN CONTROL OF THE POW-
ERS OF FASCINATION THAT EROTICISM EXERTS OVER MEN. [. . .] WHAT BEGAN

AS A[N EROTIC] LIBERATION HAS BECOME A BUSINESS. THE SAME HAS HAP-
PENED IN THE REALM OF GASTRONOMY; THE EROTIC INDUSTRY IS THE
YOUNGER SISTER OF THE FOOD INDUSTRY. [. . .] PRIVATE BUSINESS EXPRO-
PRIATES UTOPIA. DURING ITS ASCENDANCY CAPITALISM EXPLOITED THE
BODY; NOW IT HAS TURNED IT INTO AN OBJECT OF ADVERTISING. WE HAVE
GONE FROM PROHIBITION TO HUMILIATION.[18]

§12 Paz did not fathom the extent to which gastronomy was being
appropriated by industry. Today it no longer takes a major intellectual to understand that food is subject to the same *image manipulation* as all other commodities. Flavor, color, consistency, texture,
smell, caloric and nutritional value, even genetic composition are all
engineered to seduce each and every consumer. Food has, in effect,
become a simulacrum which the omnivorous psyche of North
America cannot get enough of even at the ever quicker pace of
production, preparation and consumption:

WITH THE EVER-ACCELERATING PACE OF LIFE, THE ACT OF EATING — ONCE A
LEISURELY UNDERTAKING SYNONYMOUS WITH PLEASURE AND SOCIAL INTER-
ACTION — HAS BEEN REDUCED TO A NECESSARY FUNCTION NOT UNLIKE
SHAVING OR REFUELING THE CAR, IN THE VIEW OF FOOD MANUFACTURERS,
SOCIAL SCIENTISTS AND OTHERS.[19]

§13 The loss which Sayres refers to above, is not only the erosion
of the supreme experience of transcendence; even the petty pleasure of eating a cheeseburger fades as the milk fat is replaced by
vegetable oils (if not a cellulose-based fat substitute) and the grill
gives way to the microwave. Even the singe marks are painted on the
frozen patty. Increasingly, we consume in solitude; a recent Gallup
poll found that only a third of North American adults dine at home
in the company of others.[20] By 1992, cars will come equipped with
microwaves so we can consume on our way to and from work.[21] And
moms are now *free* to stay at work as children from two years of age
and older pop *My Own Meals* or *Kid Cuisine* in the microwave.[22]

§14 "Freedom" seems to come so easily, there is no struggle;
there isn't even an "other" to struggle against; the values once
instilled by preparing our own food and eating together as a family
have given way to a new ethos: flip the switch. For Baudrillard, we
become the simulacra we consume, hostages "of a fate that is fixed,

and whose manipulators we can no longer see."[23] We are thus lev-
elled to a homogeneous status of victim and perpetrator. None of us
and all of us are to blame. A very convenient fiction that furthers the
hegemony of those whom he refuses to see.

§15 It is hardly a secret that a handful of transnational corporations – General Foods, Nestlé, Monsanto, R. J. Reynolds, etc. –
control agribusiness, from production to shipping, processing, distribution and marketing. It is no secret that this control puts those
"disappeared" others who produce what we consume in the most
onerous of conditions – twelve hours of work for a couple of dollars
in Central America – in a situation which has been getting worse
under the Reagan and Bush administrations. Nor is it a secret that
people here in the United States are also going hungry due to in-
creases in prices and the erosion of welfare benefits by inflation and
cutbacks.[24] Add to these "secrets" the devastation of the world's
natural resources for the ingredients and packaging of fast and convenience foods,[25] and you get a good sense of the loss, the other
side of the simulacrum.

§16 Baudrillard's allegory is a rather simplistic correlation of digestion and information processing, which permits passing over the
intense battles which are currently waged in the medium of the body.
The body is not simply the screen on which the rampant exchange of
information and images is captured; it is, rather, the battleground in
which subjects are constituted, contradictorily desiring and rejecting prescribed representations. Baudrillard does not even recognize
this struggle; in his hyperreal world there is only conformity, an
unproblematic consensus in which not only consumers but even
terrorists collaborate.

§17 Since, for Baudrillard, experience has disappeared, his allegorical viral body is raceless, classless, genderless, ageless; it has no
identity factors. Consequently, and contrary to the reported experience of most people, it is not shaped by the ways particular social
formations interpellate specific bodies through these factors. The
struggle of women against what Kim Chernin has called the "tyranny
of slenderness" is a good example of how some bodies and not
others are made to incarnate certain social contradictions on the
basis of gender.[26] Obesity and anorexia, then, do not correlate so

much with the self-replication of information but rather with the **control** of bodies. In the United States, control of the body by means of "idealizing" representations (consumerism and the media) and ever more frequently through outright coercion and the inter-diction of counterrepresentations (the conservative offensive) have pretty much replaced prior forms of maintaining hegemony. For Susie Orbach, the anorectic's "hunger strike" is a metaphor for this struggle of representation.[27] But this is a struggle to which Baudrillard seems quite indifferent; in his view, we have already lost and there is no way of transforming that loss into the "grander delusion" of something worthy (Sayres). Why play the deluded fool that resists the body snatchers; the sooner we yield the sooner we can all enjoy the obscenity.

§18 Baudrillard bears a resemblance to the confessors of the mystics. They attempted to control the interpretation of the mystics' experiences, differentiating those inspired by God from those in-spired by the devil, thus negotiating the mystics' relationship to the church. Baudrillard also differentiates between experiences of tran-scendence ("This is not Georges Bataille's excessive superfluity") and the *sublime banality* of the hyperreal and hypertelic, which know "no other end than limitless increase, without any consider-ation of limits."[28] Baudrillard, of course, does not evaluate the expe-riences in terms of divine/demonic inspiration, but he does clearly valorize the banalization of life by capital-logic, with its concomitant emptying of moral value. As such he embodies Jameson's description of the sublime hysteric, hungering after figurations (simulacra) of the **other** of capitalism once Nature and Being have been eclipsed.[29] Control and limits, nonetheless, continue to be important, even constitutive, for Baudrillard because his fascination with obscenity, like all appreciations of sublimity, plays off the point at which limits can no longer be controlled. Hence, the body, not figuratively but (hyper)really, embodies the world. In becoming image, it matches the mediatedness that **is** the world.

§19 In one respect I think that Baudrillard has chosen a very apt allegory of sublime banality in the obese/anorectic body. In some sense, women with eating disorders are today's mystics; the ethical substance of their search for transcendence may not be sublime in the conventional sense, but they occupy a privileged space in a world that has depleted its divine incommensurabilities. In other words, today's incommensurability is the representational space of their own bodies, which they struggle to control. Most *interpretive* (in contrast to *biomedical*) analyses of eating disorders take a psychoanalytic and/or feminist stance according to which the obese or the anorectic woman strives to manage the double binds of prescriptions of slenderness and consumption, will and abandon to instant gratification. Whether these analyses take an essentialist (e.g., Kim Chernin) or a social constructionist (e.g., Susie Orbach) approach, they almost exclusively emphasize repression and control.

§20 Susan Bordo summarizes very well the "deeper psycho-cultural anxieties. . . about internal processes out of control – uncontained desire, unrestrained hunger, uncontrolled impulse." Bordo posits the bulimic as the embodiment of the "contradictions that make self-management a continual and virtually impossible task in our culture."[30] The bulimic, she argues, plays out on her body the "incompatible directions" of consumerist temptations and the freedom implied in the virile image of a well-muscled slender body. If consumerism makes the feminine image central to our culture (because of its seductive power, Baudrillard would argue),[31] such that even literary theorists can claim that writing is a subversive feminine activity, it nevertheless requires repressing the very materiality or **essential nature**, as Kim Chernin puts it, of women's bodies.[32] For Chernin it is repression that transforms the body into an "alien" that may in momentary lapses of control rear its head and return with a vengeance.

§21 But clearly it is also the relatively non-repressive introjection of images that produces this alienation. In contrast to Chernin, I would argue that alienation is not the loss of an essential nature; in an age in which people believe and practice *making themselves over,* the traditional notion of essence becomes absurd. **It is, rather, a question of remaking not only oneself but even more importantly the social formation that attributes value to the "nature" that we embody.**[33] It is this capacity which so many people experience as having been **lost**. Sociality can then be understood as the struggle for value, which entails the recognition of diverse "natures" and the social ministration to their needs. Elsewhere I have elaborated on how such ministration responds to the struggle over needs interpretation, which is basically a struggle over the representation of our "nature," be it in the form of gender, ethnicity, age, and so on.[34]

§22 On this view, the materiality that defines us need not be understood monolithically as the rejected archaic maternal body which according to Kristeva undergirds the radical limit-experience of abjection. It seems to me that the very notion of the archaic is remade in the image of the media. The current "fat taboo" may in fact hark back to the separation process performed by traditional dietary and other ritual prohibitions, although today fat food and fat image are hypostatized in our consciousness:

[SUCH PROHIBITIONS] KEEP A BEING WHO SPEAKS TO HIS GOD SEPARATED FROM THE FECUND MOTHER. . . [THE] PHANTASMATIC MOTHER WHO ALSO CONSTITUTES, IN THE SPECIFIC HISTORY OF EACH PERSON, THE ABYSS THAT MUST BE ESTABLISHED AS AN AUTONOMOUS (AND NOT ENCROACHING) PLACE AND DISTINCT OBJECT, MEANING A SIGNIFIABLE ONE, SO THAT SUCH A PERSON MIGHT LEARN TO SPEAK.[35]

§23 Dietary taboos, however, are increasingly becoming a matter of image manipulation. For example, you can still have your cake and eat it too if you're kosher and desire to eat a slice of (simulated) cheesecake after your pastrami on rye at Katz's Delicatessen, that exemplary custodian of Glatt kosher cuisine. Taboo only makes a difference if you can have your cake and **not** eat it. Does this mean, then, that in a culture of simulation there are no longer ways of distinguishing the abject from the proper object, thus making the will to transcendence irrelevant?

Rather than accept this premise, it seems preferable to me to explore Mary Douglas's notion that anxiety around bodily boundaries signals significant social change or crisis. What and how we eat undergirds other kinds of social boundaries (marking off the difference between purity and pollution, inside and outside, etc.). As such, dietary practices function as a support for the cognitive systems by which cultures make sense of the world. They wire, so to speak, the way in which our bodies interface with the media of signification.[36] This is what Kristeva means when she says, in the passage quoted above, that the maternal body archaically establishes radical negativity, which she then goes on to fetishize, in the metaphor of the abyss, as the very condition of speech. But this is to reduce speech to the verbal and practice to negativity, thus privileging avant-gardist practices in the registers of high aesthetics. The recognition of mediation as necessary for our survival does not have to lead, however, to a Baudrillardian celebration of the simulacrum:

SEDUCTION AS AN INVENTION OF STRATAGEMS, OF THE BODY, AS A DISGUISE FOR SURVIVAL, AS AN INFINITE DISPERSION OF LURES, AS AN ART OF DISAPPEARANCE AND ABSENCE, AS A DISSUASION WHICH IS STRONGER YET THAN THAT OF THE SYSTEM.[37]

§24 The struggle over representation as I have briefly sketched it out does not fetishize the disguise nor lead one to confuse the high aesthetic appropriation of pop and mass culture with political effectivity. Its political value is more complex than the simple play of quotes or intertextuality. It challenges institutional control over images but not by remaining totally within the frame of the institution as, say, in the work of Cindy Sherman or Sarah Tuft. In a recent video, *Don't Make Me Up* (1986),[38] Tuft seeks to reframe commercial images of women's bodies variously eating, exercising, courting, etc. by overlaying them with critical comments (e.g., "I just won't buy this pack of lies") and by juxtaposing them with images that give a critical twist to the prescription of thinness, such as photographs of emaciated concentration camp prisoners. The images succeed each other rapidly to the beat of a rap song, a vehicle which should have helped give the video a more contestatory tone. However, due to the blandness of the voice (this is no Public Enemy) and the too rapid succession of images (which does not leave enough time to register that some of the images run counter to commercial idealizations), the video does not succeed in raising the consciousness of those who aren't already convinced. Even the convinced tend to enjoy it for its display of "idealized" bodies and its danceable rhythm. The overall effect is the very opposite of its punch line: "I must get free of the messages being fed to me." With a better sound track, it would not seem out of place on MTV.

§25 David Cronenberg's *Videodrome* (1983) also flirts with the possibility of resistance to the implosion of reality into media imagery. But the video images which the hero/victim Max Renn consumes end up consuming him, absorbing him into the image world of video. As head of a small TV station in search for seductive programming, he views a pirated snuff movie which, unbeknownst to him, inoculates him with electronic frequencies that produce a brain tumor that takes control of body and mind. A vagina-like VCR slot opens up in Max's abdomen in which video cassettes with behavioral programming are inserted by the agents of Videodrome, a transnational corporation engaged in a conspiracy to take control of North America in order to counter the debilitating effects of liberal ways of life. Through the video-mediated intervention of Professor Brian Oblivion, a thinly disguised combination of McLuhan and Baudrillard, Max turns the weapon of his "new flesh" against Videodrome. The film ends with Max killing off his old flesh and fusing with the "new flesh" of the video monitor, whose screen stretches out like a pregnant belly. Professor Oblivion's daughter and assistant Bianca tells Max that he has "become the video word made flesh." Mysticism and abjection thus collapse onto the flesh of mediation.

§26 Despite the evident retaliation which the protagonist carries out, *Videodrome* is less about resistance or rearticulation of society than a Baudrillardian celebration of the apocalyptic collapse – or implosion – onto the surface of the image. This implosion, however, does not collapse the conventions of capitalist, patriarchal culture. The hero is the proverbial white middle class male, female figures are portrayed as the usual stereotypes (whore or primal medium-mother), there is no solidary consciousness on the part of the very few racial minorities or otherwise marginal characters, like the homeless man whose begging is facilitated by the "dancing monkey" of a TV monitor on a leash. The closest to a political intervention is Professor Oblivion's video version of a soup kitchen: The Cathode Ray Mission, where patrons are given a diet of TV frequencies rather than food. They are being prepped, it is suggested, for taking on the "new flesh" of electronic mediation.

§27 E. Ann Kaplan makes a half-hearted attempt to argue for some "progressive" content in *Videodrome*.[39] It is not, for example, typical of mainstream media in presenting the abject in the form of a male body. Secondly, the body is made androgynous by the vagina-like slot that opens up in Max's belly and the placenta-like covered handgun that he sticks in and out of the slot. As a feminist, Kaplan interprets "postmodern discourse of this kind" as an implicit critique of the "horror of technology that deforms all bodies and blurs their gender distinction."[40] I am not convinced of the contribution to feminism, however, of the positive conclusions which Kaplan draws from the androgynizing blurring of distinctions effected by *Videodrome*, rock videos and other forms of mass culture:

MANY ROCK VIDEOS HAVE BEEN SEEN AS POSTMODERN INSOFAR AS THEY ABANDON THE USUAL BINARY OPPOSITIONS ON WHICH DOMINANT CULTURE DEPENDS. THAT IS, VIDEOS ARE SAID TO FORSAKE THE USUAL OPPOSITIONS BETWEEN HIGH AND LOW CULTURE; BETWEEN MASCULINE AND FEMININE; BETWEEN ESTABLISHED LITERARY AND FILMIC GENRES; BETWEEN PAST, PRESENT AND FUTURE; BETWEEN THE PRIVATE AND THE PUBLIC SPHERE; BETWEEN VERBAL AND VISUAL HIERARCHIES; BETWEEN REALISM AND ANTI-REALISM, ETC. THIS HAS IMPORTANT IMPLICATIONS FOR THE QUESTION OF NARRATIVE AS FEMINISTS HAVE BEEN THEORIZING IT, IN THAT THESE STRATEGIES VIOLATE THE PARADIGM PITTING A CLASSICAL NARRATIVE AGAINST AN AVANT-GARDE ANTI-NARRATIVE, THE ONE SUPPOSEDLY EMBODYING COMPLICIT, THE OTHER SUBVERSIVE, IDEOLOGIES. THE ROCK VIDEO REVEALS THE ERROR IN TRYING TO ALIGN AN AESTHETIC STRATEGY WITH ANY PARTICULAR IDEOLOGY, SINCE ALL KINDS OF POSITIONS EMERGE FROM AN ASTOUNDING MIXTURE OF NARRATIVE/ANTI-NARRATIVE/NON-NARRATIVE DEVICES.[41]

§28 The hybridity, ambiguity and lack of a "fixed identity" which Kaplan and cultural historians of video like Roy Armes attribute to the medium,[42] are also terms that Kristeva has used to describe the abject. They both are about "the breaking down of a world that has erased its borders."[43] In this sense, Cronenberg's *Videodrome* is not so much a metaphor or allegory of the abject but rather the cinematic demonstration that experience is the consumption of media, that the body of mediation is the body of the real ("whatever appears on the television screen emerges as raw experience for those who watch it," says Professor Oblivion). If the reality of mediation in *Videodrome* is its embodiment in "uncontrollable flesh," for Kristeva the blurring of the corporeal limits established by food, waste, and signs of sexual differentiation produces "uncontrollable materiality." In both cases there is an avowal of the death drive ("To become the new flesh [of mediation] first you have to kill off the old [demarcated] flesh," Bianca says to Max) and a disruption of identity ("I don't know where I am now. I'm having trouble finding my way around," says Max).

§29 This dissolution of identity, furthermore, takes place for Kristeva in relation to the mother's body, the "place of a splitting," "a threshold where 'nature' confronts 'culture'."[44] In *Videodrome*, Max's dissolution (which is concomitant to the vaginal stigmata that opens up in his belly) and his transformation into the "new flesh" take place in the medium of video, a body on which viewers "gorge themselves" and with which Max fuses in an inverse birth (i.e., when he sticks his head into the "pregnant" TV monitor). In fact, both maternal body and mediation come together in Kristeva's positing of the mother as the agency that maps or formats the body and readies it for the mediation that is language.

[MATERNAL AUTHORITY] SHAPES THE BODY INTO A *TERRITORY* HAVING AREAS, ORIFICES, POINTS AND LINES, SURFACES AND HOLLOWS, WHERE THE ARCHAIC POWER OF MASTERY AND NEGLECT, OF THE DIFFERENTIATION OF PROPER-CLEAN AND IMPROPER-DIRTY, POSSIBLE AND IMPOSSIBLE, IS IMPRESSED AND EXERTED. IT IS A "BINARY LOGIC," A PRIMAL MAPPING OF THE BODY THAT I CALL SEMIOTIC TO SAY THAT, WHILE BEING THE PRECON-DITION OF LANGUAGE, IT IS DEPENDENT UPON MEANING, BUT IN A WAY THAT IS NOT THAT OF **LINGUISTIC** SIGNS NOR OF THE **SYMBOLIC** OR-DER THEY FOUND.[45]

§30 Can we call this experience a transcendence? And what does it achieve? If we consider mysticism, we readily see, as in Saint Teresa's writings, that transcendence is experienced as a freedom which empowers the subject through infinite expansion:

WHEN A SOUL SETS OUT UPON THIS EARTH, HE DOES NOT REVEAL HIMSELF TO IT, LEST IT SHOULD FEEL DISMAYED AT SEEING THAT ITS LITTLENESS CAN CONTAIN SUCH A GREATNESS; BUT GRADUALLY HE ENLARGES IT TO THE EXTENT REQUISITE FOR WHAT HE HAS SET WITHIN IT. IT IS FOR THIS REASON THAT I SAY HE HAS PERFECT FREEDOM, SINCE HE HAS POWER TO MAKE THE WHOLE OF THIS PALACE GREAT.[46]

But the mystic's experience is not totally determined by a God from the outside. Self-mastery through prayer and meditation is the pre-condition for fashioning a space without which the divinity could have no presentation. Perhaps Saint Teresa's best known claim for the constitutive capacity of the mystic is the metaphor of the silk-worm in *The Interior Castle*. Through speech-prayer (*oracion*), the nuns spin their interior dwellings, like the silkworm its cocoon.

In language that recalls Heidegger's, Saint Teresa describes these dwellings as the resting place of the nuns, the space of their death. It is also the space of the Godhead, the "new [mystic] flesh." Saint Teresa would seem to be on the verge of heresy here for she claims that it is the nuns who can place or withdraw God at will since it is they who "fabricate the dwelling which is God so that they might live/die in it."[47] "[The Lord] becomes subject to us and is pleased to let you be the mistress and to conform to your will."[48]

§31   I have brought up the case of Saint Teresa because, as in *Videodrome*, transcendence takes the form of the subject embodying the medium. For both the mystic (Saint Teresa) and the subject of the "new flesh" (Max Renn) phenomenality is overcome not by reaching beyond it but by collapsing what would otherwise be the "supersensible idea" of the sublime onto appearance or image itself. The "new flesh" is the collapse of idea and body as medium, a collapse which, in Saint Teresa's words, provides "free[dom] from earthly things. . . and master[y] of all the elements and of the whole world."[49] In Saint Teresa's case it is not too difficult to understand how the dialectic of freedom and mastery enabled this marginal and subaltern person (woman, "new Christian," eccentric) to negotiate a measure of power in a hierarchical and patriarchal society overseen by the all-pervasive scrutiny of the Inquisition:

YOU WILL NOT BE SURPRISED, THEN, SISTERS, AT THE WAY I HAVE IN-SISTED IN THIS BOOK THAT YOU SHOULD STRIVE TO OBTAIN THIS FREE-DOM. IS IT NOT A FUNNY THING THAT A POOR LITTLE NUN OF ST. JOSEPH'S SHOULD ATTAIN MASTERY OVER THE WHOLE EARTH AND ALL THE ELEMENTS?[50]

The influence of St. Catherine of Siena over popes and monarchs is also well known. Through radical fasting both of these saints brought their bodies to extreme states of abjection that resulted in death. But abjection gave them a power over and above representation that the authorities of the Inquisition felt obliged to recognize and to channel in ways that did not topple the institution, for both saints were also reformers.

§32   Can the same be said for either Max Renn or the anorectics of today? What is their power, if any? Can they, like the mystics, transform their abjection into transformative power? I think not. The problem is that the thematics of abject rebellion have been conceived in relation to high art. Kristeva's examples – Dostoyevsky, Lautréamont, Proust, Artaud, Kafka, Céline – are not easily transferred to the mass mediated reality of today, say Roseanne Barr. Why is that?

§33 In the first place, Kristeva's privileged abjects are all (male) avant-gardists and as we know the lynchpin of the avant-garde was to transform life by recourse to an aesthetic modality that had its *raison d'être* in bourgeois modernity. Secondly, since aesthetics is thoroughly commodified as mass culture absorbs it, it can hardly be the means for a transformation of life in the service of emancipation. To collapse idea and body onto medium, then, implies a commodification which is not sufficiently thematized in *Videodrome*. Can the "new flesh" really be other than commodified flesh? The references to simulated foods in an earlier section of this essay only reinforce the idea that mass mediated simulation is in fact transforming us all into commodified media. The rebellion of the anorectic counters this but only at the cost of dysfunction or death, that is, disembodiment.

§34 Is there, then, any other politics of representation that can prove more successful? One attempt is the acceptance of the premise that we too are simulations but that we can rearticulate the way we have been constituted. This takes at least two forms: one which continues to accept that an autonomous aesthetics can have an impact on the culture. For example the work of Cindy Sherman or Sarah Tuft's video *Don't Make Me Up*. Ultimately, I think these are failed attempts not because they work with commodified images but rather because they still accept the confines of aesthetic institutionalization. On the other hand, the aesthetic practices involved in identity formation among ethnic groups and certain social movements like gays and lesbians do not distinguish between the market, the street, the university and the gallery. The work of such groups as ACT-UP and Guerrilla Girls as well as many other groups working in collaboration with particular constituencies stake out new public spaces for re-embodying media and struggle within and against the dominant media to reconfigure the institutional arrangements of our society. New "safe-sex" videos, for example, attempt to re-eroticize body in an age increasingly defined by a new puritan fundamentalism (which includes the anti-abortion movement, reinforced homophobia, and the War on Drugs).

§35 It is not enough, in the face of this offensive, to reshuffle representations. If this were all there were to contemporary cultural politics, Baudrillard would indeed be correct in understanding any practice as the body "digest[ing] space in its own appearance."[51] As regards the consumption of food, the age of the counterculture, which saw the emergence of the new social movements, also spawned contestatory movements like Fat Liberation and the politically motivated vegetarianism of *Diet for a Small Planet*.[52] Warren Belasco's history of the Food Revolution in the past two and a half decades recognizes that the powerful food industry ultimately won, in part because of the counterculture's too diffuse means of implementing its utopian visions. As an individualistic politics, it gave way to its own commodification and presented no unified front against the social causes of obesity in the u.s., and exploitation of agricultural workers in the third world. A contestatory politics of food production and consumption would have to articulate more directly with other social movements and to take into account the ways in which myriad factors intersect in the constitution of subjectivity and identity. This means also taking into consideration ethical as well as aesthetic questions, even the experience of transcendence as I have been describing it here.

§36 There are signs, however, that a coalitional politics is possible. An example is the Institute for Food and Development Policy, which Frances Moore Lappé founded with the profits from her countercultural *Diet for a Small Planet*. The most recent direction of the institute is to encourage the formation of new social values that, on the one hand, contest the conservative rapaciousness in industry and its attack on civil rights and, on the other, the redefinition of the individual, grounding his/her sense of value not in the isolated person, as proclaimed by Liberal ideology, but rather in the entirety of society. In *Rediscovering America's Values*, Lappé argues that the privatization of values in the Reagan 80s ("fidelity, chastity, saying no to drugs") have to be re-publicized.[53] This entails examining how they have become embodied in us, what social and aesthetic practices have enabled us to become inured to widespread hunger and environmental devastation throughout the world. Lappé's strategy for recreating public values is of a piece with current progressive agendas: new ways of eroticizing, new ways of articulating needs in pursuit of recognition, valuation, and empowerment. In an age of simulation, these are worthy transformations. Perhaps if the will to transcendence were articulated along these lines, we would be able to find more socially responsible and convincing values than those advocated by the Right and by Liberals. The aesthetics accompanying current analyses of eating disorders tend to celebrate the individual body, thus not posing any challenge to the Right or to Liberalism. We need an aesthetics that instills the values of the social body.

N   O   T   E   S

1. Jean-Paul Sartre, *Being and Nothingness,* trans. Hazel E. Barnes (New York: Washington Square Press, 1966).

2. Jean-Pierre Vernant, "At Man's Table: Hesiod's Foundation Myth of Sacrifice," in Marcel Detienne and Jean-Pierre Vernant, *The Cuisine of Sacrifice among the Greeks,* trans. Paula Wissing (Chicago: University of Chicago Press, 1989), 51.

3. Saint Teresa of Avila, *The Life of Saint Teresa of Avila By Herself* (Harmondsworth: Penguin, 1957), 190.

4. Saint Teresa of Avila, *Way of Perfection,* trans. E. Allison Peers (Garden City, NY: Image Books/Doubleday, 1964), 137.

5. Julia Kristeva, "Stabat Mater," in *The Female Body in Western Culture,* ed. Susan Rubin Suleiman (Cambridge: Harvard University Press, 1986), 99-118.

6. Luce Irigaray, *Speculum of the Other Woman,* trans. Gillian C. Gill (Ithaca: Cornell University Press, 1985), 191.

7. "It is easy to learn how to interpret dreams, to extract from the patient's associations his [sic] unconscious thoughts and memories, and to practise similar explanatory arts: for these the patient himself [sic] will always provide the text." Sigmund Freud, *Dora: An Analysis of a Case of Hysteria,* trans. Philip Rieff (New York: Collier, 1963), 138.

Freud goes on to observe that the difficult part of interpretation is taking into account unavoidable transferences, "new editions" or replays of fantasies in which the analyst stands in for prior actors. This phenomenon must also be taken into consideration in the very production of the subaltern's text. In the mystic's case, an analysis of the role of confessors and inquisitors is crucial. The role of the mystic and the hysteric should also be considered transferentially in the production of current theories of gendered discourse or behavior (such as eating disorders).

8. Recognition of endocrinological and biomedical factors in the etiology of eating disorders does not diminish the relevance of an approach that focuses on the social interpretation and evaluation of thinness and obesity. Moreover, it is mistaken, in my view, to take biomedical factors as *real* and social factors as epiphenomenal. On the contrary, the social may work in tandem with the biomedical in a synergistic way. In any case, how one interprets the relative importance of these factors depends on the models of biology, society and disease that frame one's discourse. This essay is part of a more general attempt on my part to discern the workings of the aesthetic as it interfaces bodily sensation and social valuation.

9. Sohnya Sayres, "Glory mongering: food and the agon of excess," *Social Text*, 16 (Winter 1986-87): 94.

10. Jean Baudrillard, "The Obese," in *Fatal Strategies*, trans. Philip Beitchman and W.G.J. Niesluchowski (New York: Semiotext(e)/Pluto, 1990), p 27.

11. "The Obese," 34.

12. "The Obese," 27.

13. For an account of the "body as temple/machine/holistic organism/etc." cognitive schemas which underwrite these different accounts for disease, see Mark Johnson, *The Body in the Mind. The Bodily Basis of Meaning, Imagination and Reason* (Chicago: University of Chicago Press, 1987), 126-36.

14. Jean Baudrillard, "The Anorectic Ruins," in Jean Baudrillard, et al., *Looking Back at the End of the World*, eds. Dietmar Kamper and Christoph Wolf, trans. David Antal (New York: Semiotext(e) Foreign Agents Series, 1989), 39.

15. Johnson, *The Body in the Mind.*

16. Cf. Lena Williams, "Free Choice: When Too Much Is Too Much," *The New York Times* (2/14/90): C1, C10.

17. For a recent account of the radical potential and eventual cooptation of the "gastronomic counterculture," see Warren Belasco, *Appetite for Change: How the Counterculture Took On the Food Industry, 1966-1988* (New York: Pantheon, 1989).

18. Octavio Paz, "Eroticism and Gastrosophy," *Daedalus*, 101, 4 (1972): 81.

19. Dena Kleiman, "Fast Food? It Just Isn't Fast Enough Anymore," *The New York Times* (12/6/89): A1, C12.

20. The September 1989 Gallup poll is cited in Kleiman, C12.

21. Kleiman, C12.

22. Denise Webb, "Eating Well," *The New York Times* (2/14/90): c8.

23. "The Obese," 35.

24. Dr. DeHavenon, director of a private research committee on welfare benefits stated that the "basic welfare grant in New York had gone up only 28 percent since 1969, while prices have increased 180 percent, and that cutbacks in the foodstamp program have contributed to the problem." Richard Severo, "East Harlem Study Shows Hunger Worsens," *The New York Times* (6/3/84): 46.

25. The literature on transnational control of agribusiness and destruction and contamination of resources is voluminous. It includes such books and essays as: Joseph N. Beldon, et al. *Dirt Rich, Dirt Poor. America's Food and Farm Crisis* (London: Routledge and Kegan Paul, 1986); James Danaher, "U.S. Food Power in the 1990s," *Race and Class*, 30, 3 (1989); Susan George, *How the Other Half Dies. The Real Reasons for World Hunger* (Washington, DC: Institute for Policy Studies, 1977); Frances Moore Lappe and Joseph Collins, *World Hunger. Ten Myths* (San Francisco: Food First, 1982); James O'Connor, "Uneven and Combined Development and Ecological Crisis: A Theoretical Introduction," *Race and Class*, 30, 3 (1989); N. Shanmugaratnam, "Development and Environment: A View From the South," *Race and Class*, 30, 3 (1989); Jill Torrie, *Banking on Poverty: The Impact of the IMF and World Bank* (San Francisco: Food First, 1986).

26. Kim Chernin, *The Obsession. Reflections on the Tyranny of Slenderness* (New York: Harper and Row, 1981).

27. Susie Orbach, *Hunger Strike: The Anorectic's Struggle as a Metaphor for our Age* (New York: Norton, 1987).

28. "The Obese," 31.

29. Fredric Jameson, "Postmodernism, or, The Cultural Logic of Late Capitalism," *New Left Review*, 146 (July-August 1984): 77.

30. Susan Bordo, "Reading the Slender Body," in *Women, Science, and the Body Politic: Discourses and Representations*, eds. Mary Jacobus, Evelyn Fox Keller, and Sally Shuttleworth (New York: Methuen, 1989), 88.

31. Cf. Jean Baudrillard, *The Ecstasy of Communication*, trans. Bernard Schutze and Caroline Schutze (New York: Semio-text(e), 1988).

32. Chernin, *The Obsession*, 45-55.

33. "Remaking the self" is part of the contemporary politics of representation, which is often understood in two different ways: as an expression of the collective identity of diverse social movements (feminists, gays and lesbians, racial and ethnic minorities, workers, and so on) or as the expression, in the language of liberal democracy, of **interests**. The difference is important because the latter understanding of representation does not take into consideration the ways in which particular identity factors traverse other collective identities. There is no general, uncontested **interest** for a particular group because it is not monolithic; certainly the participation of lesbians within AIDS activist groups like ACT UP, or the objections of women of color to "general" feminist interests bears this out. The politics of this "transversal" critique of interests is an ongoing will to **transform the institutions** that fix particular interests in place. Jane Jensen ("Representations of Difference: The Varieties of French Feminism," *New Left Review,* 180 (March/April 1990), 127-60) lays out this theoretical perspective and applies it in an historical analysis of French Feminism. This is also the direction that Frances Moore Lappé takes in her recent work (see below).

34. Juan Flores and George Yúdice, "Living Borders/Buscando America. Languages of Latino Self-Formation," *Social Text,* 24 (1990).

35. Julia Kristeva, *Powers of Horror. An Essay on Abjection* (New York: Columbia University Press, 1982), 100.

36. See Mary Douglas, *Purity and Danger. An Analysis of Concepts of Pollution and Taboo* (London/Boston/Henley: Routledge and Kegan Paul, 1969), 121. See also Kristeva, 69.

37. Baudrillard, *The Ecstasy of Communication,* 75.

38. This video was included in "Unacceptable Appetites," a video program at Artists Space (2/25-4/2/88) curated by Micki McGee. McGee's catalogue essay is an invaluable resource for the interpretation of interrelations of images of food and eating, feminine identity and the dialectic of control and self-determination.

39. E. Ann Kaplan, "Feminism/Oedipus/Postmodernism: The Case of MTV," in *Postmodernism and its Discontents. Theories, Practices,* ed. E. Ann Kaplan (London/New York: Verso, 1988).

40. Kaplan, 40.

41. Kaplan, 36.

42. "[It] is a form which is both fascinating and self-contradictory: distributed in video format but shot on film, free-wheeling yet constrained by its advertising function, visually innovative yet subordinated to its sound track,

an individual artefact which is parasitic on a separate and commercially more important object (the record or the cassette), a part of the distinctive youth culture that needs to be played through the equipment forming the focus of family life. Despite – or perhaps because of – these contradictions, the pop video points to the new potential of video as a medium in its own right." Roy Armes, *On Video* (London/New York: Routledge, 1988), 158.

43. Kristeva, 4.

44. Julia Kristeva, "Motherhood According to Giovanni Bellini," in *Desire in Language. A Semiotic Approach to Literature and Art* (New York: Columbia University Press, 1980), 238.

45. Kristeva, *Powers of Horror,* 72.

46. Saint Teresa of Avila, *Way of Perfection,* 189.

47. "Que Su Majestad mismo sea nuestra morada, como lo es en esta oración de unión, labrándola nosotras! Parece que quiero decir que podemos quitar y poner en Dios, pues digo que Él es la morada, y la podemos nosotras fabricar para meternos en ella." *Las moradas (The Interior Castle of the Dwellings of the Soul)* (Madrid: Espasa-Calpe, Col. Austral, 1964), 72.

48. *The Way of Perfection,* 175.

49. *The Way of Perfection,* 136-37.

50. *The Way of Perfection,* 137.

51. "The Obese," 27.

52. Cf. Judy Freespirit and Aldebaran, "Fat Liberation Manifesto," *Rough Times* (formerly *The Radical Therapist*), 4, 2 (March-April-May 1974); Aldebaran, "Fat Liberation – a Luxury?" *State and Mind,* 5 (June-July 1977): 34-38; Alan Dolit, *Fat Liberation* (Millbrae, CA: 1975); Frances Moore Lappé, *Diet for a Small Planet* (New York: Ballantine Books, 1975).

53. Frances Moore Lappé, *Rediscovering America's Values* (New York: Ballantine, 1989). The quote is from an interview with the author: Diana Ketcham, "Author Lappé's plan for planet: Back to basics," *The Tribune Calendar* (5/28/89).

OF

AIDS
CYB**ORGS**
&OTHER
IN DIS**CRE**
TIONS

AllisonFraiberg RESURFACING THEBODYIN

THEPOSTMODERN

PPPP

We live in the ecstasy of communication. And this ecstasy is obscene. . . .
today, there is a whole pornography
of information. – Jean Baudrillard

[T]here has been a mutation in the
object, unaccompanied as yet by any
equivalent mutation in the subject;
we do not yet possess the perceptual
equipment to match this new hyperspace . . . . – Fredric Jameson

[W]e are all chimeras, theorized and
fabricated hybrids of machine and
organism; in short, we are cyborgs.
The cyborg is our ontology; it gives
us our politics. – Donna Haraway

PREDOMINANT in postmodern theories of represen-   1
tation are approaches and practices that locate "the body" within
systematized networks and circuits. Theorists who are representative of very different theoretical positions – such as Jean Baudrillard,
whose "ecstasy of communication" describes a breakdown between
public and private, Fredric Jameson, whose "hyperspace" reflects a
continuous sense of the present in a world of transnational capital,
and Donna Haraway, whose "cyborg ontology" reads the disintegration of distinctions between organisms and machines – nonetheless
concur in presenting scenarios in which traditional tropes of discreteness, of discretion, dissolve and the focus shifts to formulations of connectedness. Subjected to these discursive frameworks
or grounding ontologies, the body, as a clearly delineated unit,
blurs into negotiated relatedness and postmodern systematicity
ushers in a contemporary meltdown of the discrete body. In other
words, it would seem, at best, difficult to try to discuss "the body"
with distinct boundaries, whereas referring to the bounded body –

bounded to and within integrated networks – can emerge as a reflective postmodern image.

2   This networking of bodies has been prominent in the representations of and discourse about AIDS in the U.S. As I will show, mainstream media constructions of AIDS project and feed off a fear of, among other things, circuited sexuality. On the other hand, critics of mainstream AIDS representations work to break down the rhetorical constructions and effects of discrete categories, an obvious example being that of "general public" or "at risk groups." In this paper, I will first resituate familiar discussions of the body in AIDS commentary, both popular and critical, by employing what Donna Haraway calls a "cyborg ontology." I will then move on to suggest that, in terms of AIDS discourses, the body begins to resurface from within the networks defined, urging a very different kind of discreteness, and consequently a revised type of agency, into a postmodern context.

WIRING THE POSTMODERN

3   **W**HEN BAUDRILLARD defines the "ecstasy of communication," he grounds its images in screens and networks. Certain that "[s]omething has changed," he laments the recognition of an "era of networks . . . contact, contiguity, feedback and generalized interface" (127). Communication, for Baudrillard, invokes a "relational decor," a "fluidity," "polyvalence" in "pure circulation" (130-31). Baudrillard anxiously describes these networks as "pornographic" and "obscene" since he sees in them the loss of the body and its familiar figurations: the "subject" and the always tenuous public/private dichotomy. Because of its fusing into the network, the body loses its discretionary status and, for Baudrillard, the "obscenity" lies in the dissolution of the private where "secrets, spaces and scenes [are] abolished in a single dimension of information" (131); Baudrillard's "pornographic" develops out of the inability to produce "proper" limits and he invokes the schizophrenic for tropic legitimation:

> with the immanent promiscuity of all these networks, with their continual connections, we are now in a new form of schizophrenia. Too great a proximity of everything, the unclean promiscuity of

everything which touches, invests and penetrates without resis-
tance, with no halo of private protection, not even his own body, to
protect him anymore. . . . He can no longer produce the limits of his
own being. . . . He is now only a pure screen, a switching center for
all the networks of influence. (132-33)

What is so remarkable about Baudrillard's casting of the discussion in these terms is that, with the substitution of a noun or two, one could easily transpose this rhetoric into a "pro-family" position on AIDS that strains to keep the "halos" on, the "unclean" out, and the private crucially "protected." In both scenarios there is a sense of inevitable fusion of the body within networks – a fusion realized, albeit reluctantly, by Baudrillard, but repeatedly denied and cast out on moral grounds by the so-called "pro-family" position on AIDS. Consequently:

> *The logical outcome of testing is a quar-*
> *antine of those infected. – Jesse Helms*

Baudrillard's mourning of the "loss" of past private spaces of the body is recast, with a similar tone, in Jameson's analysis that isolates postmodernism within the "cultural logic of late capitalism." Jameson reorganizes the postmodern schema into a "bewildering new world space of multinational capital" (58) with "effaced frontiers," "integrated" commodity production, "intertextuality," and the "disappearance of the individual subject." What Jameson calls postmodern "hyperspace" is the global networking produced by transnational capital, a networking he sees as "transcending the capacities of the individual human body to locate itself, to organize its immediate surroundings perceptually, and cognitively map its position" (83). Jameson arrives at the point of calling for ways to map this network and/by/for those "caught" within it, to make it epistemologically accessible, and finally, dialectically, make the best of what, he argues, had to come anyway.

Jameson differs from Baudrillard in, among other places, his isolation of a particular disjunction between subject and space. "My implication," Jameson argues, "is that we ourselves, the human subjects who happen into this new space, have not kept pace with that evolution . . . we do not yet possess the perceptual equipment to match this new hyperspace" (80). Jameson does identify a new field of relations, but the subject he posits remains essentially the same, just a little lost in its new surroundings. For this reason, Jameson's call for cognitive mappings resembles a type of postmodern finding of one's self in a "bewildering" new field. This position, like Baudrillard's, can find its correlative in AIDS discourse: the Jamesonian view would be reminiscent of the mainstream position that asserts the "general public" can contract HIV "as well." In other words, the field has changed, but how the subjects are thought of within it remains virtually the same. Therefore:

> I have asked the Department of Health and Human Services to determine as soon as possible the extent to which the AIDS virus has penetrated our society. – Ronald Reagan (in 1987, when 25,644 were known dead)[1]

6   For Haraway, however, both the field and the subject change as cyborgs provide the ontological myth that captures the image of post-industrial capitalist culture. She defines the cyborg as a "cybernetic organism, a hybrid of machine and organism" ("Manifesto" 174). Dissolving apparently clear distinctions propels the cyborg. "Needy for connection," it lurks at the boundaries constructed and demanded by humanist thought, dismantling discretion in favor of interconnected networks and integrated systems. Boundaries "breached," or at least "leaky," include those between human and animal, between animal-human and machine, and between the physical and the non-physical. Like other postmodern strategies, cyborgs "subvert myriad organic wholes," and, unlike Baudrillard and Jameson, Haraway can see potential in the loss of discretion: "So my cyborg myth is about transgressed boundaries, potent fusions, and dangerous possibilities which progressive people might explore as one part of needed political work" ("Manifesto" 178). It is not the case that Haraway sees her cyborg myth as some post-organic *deus ex machina*; instead she invests her myth with perpetual tensions where "potent fusions" are balanced with "dangerous possibilities." Focusing on the production and reading of integrated circuits and the relations within them, theorists can, then, in Haraway's words, negotiate through various "system constraints" ("Biopolitics" 12-13).

7   Other theorists of postmodernism may argue and debate about whether to embrace or view with horror a cybernetic age; about whether the status of subjectivity has changed; about whether post-

modernity signals a turn beyond that which was once valued (by some). Haraway, on the other hand, like many feminist cultural theorists, resists these debates about how one **should** feel in these times (paranoid, horrified, ecstatic) and instead tries to focus on **what to do**, how to proceed, and how to start thinking of pro-active strategies. (Granted, Jameson calls for cognitive mapping, but the energy seems reconciliatory rather than pro-active.) Quite simply, what separates Haraway out from a substantial set of discourses about cybernetics is that she is not so much concerned with how good or bad a cybernetic age will be, or has become; she wants to talk about how the world **is** ontologically/epistemologically structured and what feminists can **do** about it.

OF AIDS : RESITUATING DISCOURSES

It is patriotic to have the AIDS *test and be negative.* – Cory Servaas, Presidential Commission

Everyone detected with AIDS *should be tattooed in the upper forearm, to protect common needle users, and on the buttocks to protect the victimization of other homosexuals.* – William F. Buckley

AIDS *is God's judgment of a society that does not live by His rules.* – Jerry Falwell [2]

So MUCH OF AIDS criticism has had to contend with cauterizing the effects of officially sanctioned positions such as those above; consequently, much of the work on AIDS to date has centered on exposing the assumptions and values embedded within mainstream representation. These important critiques focus predominantly on three, often intersecting, sites of construction. Often, representations of AIDS have problematically inherited historical and biomedical contexts, and various critics have discussed the problems when AIDS becomes another "venereal disease" or the latest version of rampant infectious disease where "contagion," "quarantine," and "contamination" [8] become the dominant terms conditioning meaning (and often policy and research).[3] Moreover, a large amount of critical practice has focused on exposing the racist, classist, sexist, and homophobic assumptions embedded in popular, medical, and sociological representations. Many of these undertakings highlight the politics behind discourses of "risk groups" that isolate people rather than practices; of the "general public," which turns out to function more like an exclusive country club; and of "origins," which, as Simon Watney argues, equates a source of something with its cause ("Missionary" 95).[4] In addition, critics and activists have foregrounded organized/reorganized erotic economies and resisted the anti-sex and "pro-family" campaign engineered by hegemonic AIDS representations.[5]

9   These critical projects are crucial in that they expose the biases upon which policies are constructed. But what I would now like to do is think about some mainstream positions and some critical ones at the same time, in the same field of relations – in the field of what Haraway might call a cyborg-like network. Reorganized in this framework, attitudes range from denial of networking – in terms of the subject and/or the field – to a kind of hysterical reaction of recognition, to finally more productive readings and codings. Because I am trying to **resituate** these arguments on the same discursive field, the next few pages might be repetitive for those who are acquainted with the various critiques of mainstream AIDS commentary. Please bear in mind, however, that I am trying to re-view these positions as they relate to a cyborg-netic field; this resituating, while at times somewhat belabored, is necessary ground out of which the resurfacing of the body emerges.

DENYING CYBORGS

10   HE CYBORG notion of transgressed boundaries and leaky distinctions finds its immunological referent in the discourses of AIDS. The reality of HIV has opened up and relegated bodies to an integrated system of, among other things, sexuality. The bringing to consciousness of the presence of AIDS has broken down the traditional demarcations of the body, blurring the boundaries between inside and outside. For

years now, with less safe practices, an interface propels the body to serve as an osmotic shell through which systematized sex circulates. Moreover, shared needles construct a network of IV drug users; and shared blood forces to consciousness a crucial interconnectedness. And, of course, these systems interpenetrate as networks of social relations emerge. The realities of AIDS dissolve the boundaries of the discrete body, and the cyborg, still needy for connection, integrates it into its discursive network. The New Right, mainstream media representation, and a lot of public sentiment have responded by denying cyborg-netic reorganizations of the body. Desperate to retain the traditional boundaries of the body as individual, both conservatives and liberals have articulated a rhetoric that has made several attempts to keep AIDS outside the sphere of the "general American public" – read white, heterosexual, middle-class nuclear family. In each situation, the position that denies recognition of a circuited body image tries to fabricate and maintain crucial distinctions between self and other.

The most obvious boundary that "official" conservative discourse clings to is the one between human and "disease": "us" and "AIDS." The strategic construction that urges keeping "it" out of "us" relies primarily on a projection since "it" would not be if it were not for "us." Repressing that integration, the first rhetorical maneuver involves anthropomorphizing AIDS into a live virus and then militarizing its context. Susan Sontag notices that in this "high-tech warfare," the AIDS virus [sic] "hides," "attacks," "lurks," and, of course, "invades" (17-19). Similarly, Paula Treichler describes the rhetorical evolution of the "AIDS virus" as "a top-flight secret agent – a James Bond . . . armed with a 'range of strategies' and licensed to kill" insidiously invading the cell and "establishing a disinformation campaign" (59). 11

Reinforcing the "us/them" binary that denies the cyborg body is a continual search for a cause of AIDS, and consequently, the origins of HIV. Overdeterminations of HIV as the single agent cause of AIDS foreclose on posited co-factors; and then the quest for origin can shift to isolating sources of HIV. That a strain of virus remotely similar to HIV has been found in a species of monkey (the so-called "Green Monkey Hypothesis") produces and perpetuates a popular contention that AIDS originated in "Africa." Responsibility is projected onto a convenient other and the body of the "general American public" 12 remains "safe" and isolated, establishing its boundaries not only by geography, but by implied race as well. Not only does this premise displace origins thousands of miles away, but in doing so relies on a familiar moral opposition of white and black. The "cause" of AIDS becomes the monolithic "dark continent," the land of the primitive, and as Simon Watney notes, of "naked 'animal' blackness" (75). These multiple moral projections would enclose and protect white, middle-class, heterosexual America from invasion. Again, the nuclear family body denies the cybernetic organization of AIDS by refusing to recognize its integration within its networks.

13   Once discursively acknowledged, mainstream representations of AIDS draw on newly delineated boundaries; a revised "us/them" dichotomy emerges that keeps denying the AIDS-body cyborg. "Risk groups" or "those at risk" (revised from the "4-H" groups of the 80s) become the convenient other: most often cited as gay men and IV drug users (who are almost always represented as people of color). The nomenclature advocates that these are groups of people who are at high risk of contracting HIV, therefore the "general public" should stay away from "them." The first striking characteristic of this configuration is that these are groups of people and if you find yourself fitting into one of these groups, you are necessarily at "high-risk." This framework denies the subject any sort of agency, an ideologically motivated strategy that makes its point: the subject who falls into a high-risk group has no option but to occupy a position in it; at the same time, if one does not slip into one of these groups then there is, within this construction, no "risk." Here, it doesn't matter what you do because what counts is who you are; and for the person living with AIDS, this context leaves no room for subjectivity, for agency, for action.

14   That the intended audience of "risk group" identification is the "general public" underscores the contention that "those at risk" are precisely not part of that audience. The tenuous dichotomy, however, slips at several sites: that of what gets represented as the case of the "tragic" hemophiliac who contracts through blood products; the recipient of a transfusion of "tainted" blood; and the sex worker who "infects" the unknowing consumer. In each case, though, an innocence factor mitigates contraction. In a more recent attempt to reproduce the innocent body, and therefore maintain the ability to name guilt, the term "Pediatric AIDS" has become embedded in rep-

resentations of certain people living with AIDS. In a move that seeks to reestablish boundaries to the now quite messy binary, "AIDS" and "Pediatric AIDS" have surfaced, rhetorically, as two very distinct constructs, each conditioning very different identities: babies born testing positive for HIV antibodies can occupy a position of "wholly innocent" while the mothers, depending on their backgrounds, await textual, moral assignation.

With the deconstruction effected, with the representational ac- 15 knowledgement that AIDS indeed "leaks" into the "general public," conservative thought reorganizes its "us/them" dichotomy into a rhetoric explicitly moral and "pro-family." Each time the hint of connection emerges, a new denial of integration surfaces; each time a new illusory individual unit is posited. Prevention strategies that, at this point, still reject the implication of some bodies into the AIDS-body network consciously construct new boundaries around the body of the nuclear family. If the "innocent" general public can contract HIV as well, so the story goes, then a prevention campaign that extrapolates from occluded attitudes within risk-group discourse must center on a question of morality: if "we" can get AIDS (and this is precisely the moment when discursive productions can either accept the cyborg ontology or try yet again to deny it), then "we" must try to be good. The moralizing trope serves as the building material for the construction of boundaries. And "good" in the 1980s functions euphemistically to mean monogamous heterosexual relationships with people who "just say no" to drugs. The safest sex of all becomes abstinence – the illusory production of a self-contained body – and those who abstain from sex altogether become "very good" people; those who insist on having sex but do so only in monogamous relationships, preferably in marriage, are "good"; and, of course, those who engage in sex with many partners, who insist on being promiscuous, or use IV drugs, bring on infection "themselves." In this configuration, a closed-off body equivocates into a pure body as the nuclear family forges boundaries embedded

in

orality.

STARTING WITH CYBORGS

16   **B**Y STRESSING abstinence, by prescribing heterosexual monogamy, by condemning IV drug use, conservative discourse engages in a repressive hypothesis that promotes an economy of desire: the more you say yes, the higher your chances of "infection," the more leaky the moral boundaries that surround you. The hierarchy of morality – abstinence, monogamy, condoms, etc. – has eroded, however, under the scrutiny of critics, many of whom recognize the flimsiness of the boundaries constructed. Douglas Crimp argues against abstinence as a strategy of prevention because "people do not abstain from sex, and if you only tell them 'just say no,' they will have unsafe sex" (252). Moreover, repressed in the call for monogamy is any reference to history: monogamy means little if one partner is HIV+ and the couple, thinking they have fulfilled the moral requirement in the symbolic contract that disqualifies them from contraction, practices unsafe sex. This education campaign denies a discursive field of indiscretion by promoting a rhetoric of the discreet individual.

17   Critics of media representations of AIDS have addressed this problematic by exposing its repressive mechanisms. John Greyson, for example, has produced a music-video exposing the "ADS" campaign – the "Acquired Dread of Sex" that one can get from watching, among other things, television (270). Consequently, Crimp notices how media campaigns to get people to use condoms have used fear as their manipulative device rather than sexuality. Ironically, he wonders why "an industry that has used sexual desire to sell everything from cars to detergents suddenly finds itself at a loss for how to sell a condom" (266). What culminates in an "acquired dread of sex" is the logical conclusion of a discourse that organizes repeated "us/them" oppositions to keep AIDS out, to deny a cyborg-netic field; and once AIDS manages to "infiltrate," the emphasis shifts to deny its presence in the morally pure and displace it onto the deviant, thereby constructing new boundaries. It's the repetition of a posture that attempts at any cost to deny connection/identification; it's a constricted stance that tries desperately to repress indiscretion: a term defined more traditionally in the context of such denounced behaviors as sex and IV drug use, but also indiscretion described here as a

certain dissolution of clear delineation. With indiscretion (both kinds) repressed, those remaining are left to close off their bodies, constricting any potential openings.

> *To speak of sexuality and the body, and not to speak of aids, would be, well, obscene.* – B. Ruby Rich

> *Simply put, those who enjoy getting fucked should not be made to feel stupid or irresponsible. Instead, they should be provided with the information necessary to make what they enjoy safe(r)! And that means the aggressive encouragement of condom use.* – Michael Callan

In contrast to conservative rhetoric that denies indiscretion, of any kind, one can locate an ontology that takes the breakdown of traditional boundaries associated with the body as a grounding premise. Since mainstream representation compulsively represses interconnectedness, resistant strategies can and do rupture the process, forcing the latent networks to percolate to consciousness, to representation. Rejecting the discursive displacements that produce others at risk, it is a position that recognizes, like Rich, that the **discourses** of AIDS are in some sense always already within: "To speak of sexuality and the body and not to speak of AIDS, would be, well, obscene." The texts that construct "AIDS" metaphorically become an ontological current running through bodies, making the connections of a systemic circuit. Distinctions, then, between self and other become archaic, and the AIDS-body cyborg functions as an icon that organizes perceptions and writings of the body.

Precisely because a notion of "risk group" or "those at risk" becomes problematic (which, granted, at this point does nothing to address the real inequities of representation), because the networks and narratives established by leaky boundaries integrate and implicate all and avoid projecting blame, the argument can shift from singling out risk groups to focusing on risk practices. The networks made manifest can then accommodate Watney's call for an "erotics of protection" as well as Singer's "body management" – both are organizations of erotic economies. If discussion of risk groups and the general public lead us to ask who we are when we have sex or use IV drugs, then the cyborg discursive configuration of risk practices asks all of us what we do when we have sex and use IV drugs. Unlike the former position that relegated the subject to helplessness within its constructions – an especially problematic space for a PLWA (Person Living With AIDS) – this field posits a subject, precisely because of its "indiscretion," that can choose. Because this subject gives up its limit, its "halo" (to invoke Baudrillard momentarily), of private protection, it gains agency for resistance – a key term for immunological reference.

20   And this subject can choose to have sex, unlike its anti-cyborg parallel, but must undergo what Linda Singer calls "changes in the economy of genital gestures and erotic choreography" (55). Whereas anti-cyborg bodies repressed sexualities when confronted with AIDS, integrated bodies adamantly guard the right to them. Carol Leigh, a sex worker and playwright, argues that "we must fight against all those who would use this crisis as an excuse to legislate or otherwise limit sexuality" (177). Those who have thought of sex as heterosexual penile penetration and ejaculation (many caught within the anti-cyborg "general public") must reorganize perceptions in such a way as to eroticize non-genital areas; and when sex is genital, condoms and dental dams become new age sex toys. Embedded in all of these calls for safer practices are two assumptions that are crucial as far as my own argument is concerned: first, that the forged boundaries constitutive of the individualized units are amorphous; and second, that safer shooting and sex depend on a recognition of interconnectedness, of indiscretion.

RESURFACING THE BODY

21   RATHER THAN REPRESSING sexuality, the AIDS-body network sublimates it, dispersing teleologically-oriented sex into more polymorphous activity. Within this revised organization, the rules of safe sex and calls for clean works dictate that, precisely because the boundaries are illusory, the body resurfaces as discrete entity. Condoms, dental dams, clean needles, and reserved blood manifest a surface awareness, a consciousness focused on clearly delineating the boundaries of bodies. The traditional, tenuous limits of the body dissolved into fused networks, into open circuits of intercon-

nectedness, produce an ontological recognition that, from this perspective, urges the body into discretion. Closed off, guarded against infection, beware the surface; any exchange of fluid, that is, any disclosure of an open, leaking body, threatens. A closed, self-contained body resurfaces from the within the integrated network.

But this is a different kind of discretion. It's not the kind of   22
discretion clung to by those who deny any fusion; it's a kind of discretion, discreteness, that is a consequence of the recognition of indiscretion. So while the cyborg ontology takes as its premise the dissolution of traditional boundaries associated with the body, its referent in the texts of AIDS, epistemologically speaking, forces the body to resist coming to rest with those integrated circuits and, instead, reorganizes into discrete units. In this sense, discretion re-turns, not in the form of reactionary denial, but as conditioned by a cyborg-like system. In other words, if the cyborg ontology can be said to function as the discursive field upon which networks of social relations play themselves out, then that field must by willing to admit – indeed, it has already admitted – the constructions of what might seem quite odd to cyborg theorists: writings and readings of the body grounded in discretion.

The resurfaced, discrete body/subject is different from its prede-   23
cessor because the recognition of blurred boundaries is precisely that which makes the body resurface. "Discretion" functions, then, as an ambivalent marker for both sets of discourses and, as the foundational site for constructions, poses key questions. The dis-cursive peril here, in terms of the discourses of AIDS, involves the confusion between a conservative "pro-family" stance and progres-sive reconstructions. In the representational treatments of AIDS, two different discrete bodies emerge: one that denies the cyborg and ultimately prescribes racist, classist, and homophobic attitudes; and one that reorganizes discretion within the AIDS-body circuit. Con-fusing the two could potentially elide the latter construction as well as its ethics. For instance, media campaigns have urged the use of condoms, but they have done so within an atmosphere of repressive (hetero)sexuality; consequently, safe sex, instead of organizing an erotic economy, becomes an unreliable alternative for those hetero-sexuals who won't say no. The racist, classist, and homophobic subtexts remain intact and the white, middle-class, heterosexual family assumes the position of general public all over again.

24   This is not to say that a circulatory ontology ought to be abandoned, nor is it to say that any codings of the body as a discrete unit will necessarily become subsumed by mainstream representation. In fact, I believe that too many areas have seen a reformulation of discretion, a resurfacing of the body, to leave such a pessimistic reading intact. One obvious example in the u.s. involves strategies organized around women's reproductive rights. When, for instance, abortion rights activists carry signs reading "Bush, get out of mine!" we engage in a similar move that recognizes existing intervention and then expels the groping hands of legislators from women's bodies and reformulates a discrete body, closing off from the legislative machinery. This analogy was reinforced during this year's 4th Annual Gay and Lesbian Film Festival held in Olympia, Washington: I saw a man wearing a button with a slogan made famous by reproductive rights activists – "My body is *my* own business."

25   For these reasons, I would suggest that working within postmodern network theory to discuss AIDS strategy, or even some other "indiscretions" such as reproductive rights practices, can grant a crucial sense of agency to renegotiate some of the blatant horrors of mainstream representation. Working within a single field of relations that resituates perceptions of both "official" AIDS representation as well as those who criticize it diffuses the rhetorical and positional strength of a centralized power dictating, and conditioning, meaning; this circulatory system affords the space for a localized biopolitics and active resistance. It posits resistance, not at the expense of agency but, rather, as a condition of agency; and with mainstream representation continually constructing helpless, objectified "AIDS victims" awaiting "certain death," the discursive leverage to act and re-act obviously takes on added significance for persons living with AIDS.

26   It's a type of agency that carries with it, and can put to use, the contextual histories of the networks from which the subject emerged. Material, contextual conditions become built into the theoretical frame, rather than being held in opposition or tension with the theory: this type of agency does not recognize a traditional distinction between "theory" and "praxis" or "theory" and "experience" because the material context of the networks produces the agent. Agency loses its abstract, theoretical, and often vague status and becomes recognizable only through its multiple material con-

texts. Moreover, the specificity of agents differs across contexts: the resurfaced agent of reproductive rights discourses would not be the same agent progressive AIDS strategies produce since each is conditioned by differing intersections of networks.

In this case, resurfacing the body becomes the mechanism 27 through which one sense of agency can be constituted. Resurfacing the body, then, within the postmodern, exposes mainstream investments as it articulates a new space, a revitalized subject, as it re-codes discretion from within the circuits of systematicity. At the same time, tropes of postmodern networking that posit a process of integration, of dissolving, don't necessarily end there: within and beyond the blur can lie a resuscitated agent ready for action.

Casting agency in this way can revise ideas about authorization. 28 The realm that denies cyborg-like integration ultimately leaves in-tact traditional sites of authority, sites with various investments in the "general public": for example, biomedical research, the position of Surgeon General, governmental and legal policy decisions. On the other hand, a large scale recognition of this resituated inter-connectedness, and the subsequent resurfacing of the body – of some – might begin to shift those sites of authority. If this recogni-tion is granted, attention might be (re)drawn toward those whose experience is most most important and whose energies are spent organizing pro-active strategies. In other words, the agency evolving through the resurfacing could loosen the mainstream's hold on the discourse about AIDS and create an opening for actions such as: having more than one PLWA speaking at the International AIDS confer-ence; ending the scientific community's holding of people for ran-som; or instituting a media campaign that can offer something more effective, and finally less dangerous, than a choral cry to

ust say no.

N O T E S

1. Statistics from Douglas Crimp, "AIDS: Cultural Analysis/Cultural Activism," 11 (in the volume of the same name, edited by Crimp).

2. All quotes from Crimp, 8.

3. For further historical perspectives see Elizabeth Fee and Daniel M. Fox, AIDS: The Burdens of History, Dennis Altman's AIDS In the Mind of America, and Simon Watney's Policing Desire. Randy Shilts provides a journalistic history of AIDS in And the Band Played On, but his account is both voyeuristic – awkwardly, he scrutinizes the life of Gaetan Dugas, alleged "patient zero" – and morbid – he keeps a running tab on AIDS cases, deaths, and projected deaths. Douglas Crimp has also noted a homophobic attitude in the book: see his essay "AIDS: Cultural Analysis/Cultural Activism" in Crimp, ed.

For specific analysis of the construction of "disease" see especially Paula Treichler, "AIDS, Gender, and Biomedical Discourse: Current Contests for Meaning," in Fee and Fox. See also Charles Rosenberg, "Disease and Social Order in America: Perceptions and Expectations," and Gerald Oppenheimer, "In the Eye of the Storm: The Epidemiological Constructions of AIDS" – both in Altman.

For discussions of health care and biomedical discourse, see Douglas Crimp, "How to Have Promiscuity in an Epidemic," in Crimp, ed.; Daniel M. Fox, "The Politics of Physicians' Responsibilities in Epidemics: A Note on History," in Fee and Fox; Suki Ports, "Needed (For Women and Children)," in Crimp, ed.; Mark McGrath and Bob Sutcliffe, "Insuring Profits From AIDS: The Economics of an Epidemic," in Radical America 20.6 (1986): 9-27.

4. For further reference on intertwinings of discussions of "risk groups," "general public," and "origins" see especially Watney's Policing Desire, "The Spectacle of AIDS" in Crimp, ed., and "Missionary Positions."

For discussions of homophobia in representation see Watney, Crimp, Cindy Patton, and Leo Bersani (in Crimp, ed.), among many others. Observing that most media coverage of AIDS addresses a heterosexual audience, the "general public," while completely eliding the fact that homosexuals are part of that audience, Bersani complains that "TV treats us to nauseating processions of yuppie women announcing to the world that they will no longer put out for their yuppie boyfriends unless . . ." ("Rectum" 202), and that the "family identity produced on American television is much more likely to include your dog than your homosexual brother or sister" (203).

5. For instance, Gregg Bordowitz "picture[s a] coalition of people having safe sex and shooting up with clean works" (Crimp, ed. 195), while Linda Singer outlines an erotics of "body management" ("Bodies" 56). Watney has called for an "erotics of protection," an arena which would include "huge regular

Safe Sex parties [with] . . . hot, sexy visual materials to take home" and "safe sex porno videos" (*Policing Desire* 133-4). Similarly, Douglas Crimp urges that "gay male promiscuity should be seen. . . as a positive model of how sexual pleasures might be pursued" ("How to Have Promiscuity" 253).

W O R K S C I T E D

Altman, Dennis. *AIDS in the Mind of America*. Garden City, WA: Anchor, Doubleday, 1986.

Baudrillard, Jean. "The Ecstasy of Communication." Trans. John Johnston. *The Anti-Aesthetic*. Ed. Hal Foster. Port Townsend, WA: Bay Press, 1983.

Bersani, Leo. "Is the Rectum a Grave?" *AIDS: Cultural Analysis/ Cultural Activism*. Cambridge, MA and London: MIT Press, 1987.

Crimp, Douglas. "How to Have Promiscuity in an Epidemic." *AIDS: Cultural Analysis/Cultural Activism*. Cambridge, MA and London: MIT Press, 1987. 237-270.

Fee, Elizabeth and Daniel M. Fox (eds.). *AIDS: The Burdens of History*. Berkeley, Los Angeles, and London: U of California P, 1988.

Haraway, Donna. "A Manifesto for Cyborgs: Science, Technology, and Socialist Feminism in the 1980s." *Coming to Terms*. Ed. Elizabeth Weed. New York: Biopolitics of Postmodern Bodies: Determinations of Self in Immune System Discourse." *Differences* 1 (Winter 1989): 3-43.

Jameson, Fredric. "Postmodernism, or, the Cultural Logic of Late Capitalism." *New Left Review* 146 (July-August 1984): 53-92.

Leigh, Carol. "Further Violation of Our Rights." *AIDS: Cultural Analysis/ Cultural Activism*. Cambridge, MA and London: MIT Press, 1987. 177-181.

Shilts, Randy. *And the Band Played On: Politics, People*, 1987.

Singer, Linda. "Bodies–Pleasures–Powers." *Differences* 1 (Winter 1989): 44-65.

Sontag, Susan. *AIDS and Its Metaphors*. New York: Farrar, Strauss, and Giroux, 1988.

Treichler, Paula. "AIDS, Homophobia, and Biomedical Discourse: An Epidemic of Signification." *AIDS: Cultural Analysis/Cultural Activism*. Ed. Douglas Crimp. Cambridge, MA and London: MIT Press, 1987. 31-70.

Watney, Simon. "Missionary Positions: AIDS, 'Africa,' and Race." *Differences* 1 (Winter 1989): 67-84.

Watney, Simon. *Policing Desire: Pornography, AIDS, and the Media*. Minneapolis: U of Minnesota P, 2nd edition, 1989.

« C O M M E N T A R Y »« A N »« E X C H A N G E »

« B E T W E E N »« D A V I D »« P O R U S H »« A N D »

« A L L I S O N »« F R A I B E R G »« C O N C E R N I N G »

« F R A I B E R G ' S »« O F »« A I D S »« C Y B O R G S »

« A N D »« O T H E R »« I N D I S C R E T I O N S »

» Allison Fraiberg uses the discourses of AIDS to read large   1
oppositions and tendencies at work in our culture. As such,
AIDS is one more battlefield between right thinking and
wrong thinking. Here wrong thinking is promoted by a reactionary,
self-serving, moralizing majority that prescribes a cure for AIDS in
"traditional" values to the exclusion of others and that denies the
extent to which all our bloods and responsibilities commingle in the
vast, luscious, and newly-dangerous circuitry of sexuality. The Bad
Guys in her reading of her culture are clearly defined: they are listed
and quoted at the beginning of her essay and resurface in various
guises – people who promote the nuclear family, white middle class
males, ad propagandists who ironically forget how to use sex to sell
the public on the use of condoms.

At times, Fraiberg manages to free herself from her orgy of jargon   2
and deconstructionist agitprop to achieve real eloquence, especially when she calls for a redefinition of sexuality – also the most fun
parts of the essay. Almost all of the conclusions which she reaches in
her argument are both inarguable and quite tame: we must all engage in safe sex, but do so with the awareness that sex puts us in the
circuit, that we take responsibilities for our own bodies, that AIDS
should not be a tool for scapegoating and dehumanizing groups of
people. Rather, AIDS ought to impel us to redefine the body, the self,
and our sexuality (along with our discourses' sexuality) as participants in a looping feedback with the interpenetrating systems of
otherness which really create our culture (or really culture our creativity).

The essay, however, has a tendency to discard or demolish prac-   3
tices and ideals that would satisfy even a new cyborg mentality
simply because they have been tainted by association with conventional, conservative ideology. In this, there is a confusion or conflation between reactionary rhetoric (out of homophobia and racism,
the moral majority use their prescriptions to define the other as alien,
diseased) and technically safe practices (monogamy, safe sex, absti-

nence from IV drug use, the nuclear family) – in short, discretionary activities. The clearest example comes when Fraiberg writes,

> monogamy means little if one partner is HIV
> + and the couple, thinking they have fulfilled
> the moral requirement in the symbolic con-
> tract that disqualifies them from contrac-
> tion, practices unsafe sex.

4   While we would not argue with the premise (that there's some-thing nasty about the prescription of exclusive monogamy for every-one in the culture) nor with the amusing analysis elsewhere in this essay (that the more you ask folks to say no to their pleasure they more likely they are to embrace it impulsively), we might argue with the conclusion. After all, monogamy means quite a lot, **especially** if one partner has AIDS. It promotes responsibility to and awareness of everyone else in the circuit, and indeed fulfills Fraiberg's own call to greater cyborg awareness.

5   The second problem here actually arises from the essay's greatest strength: Fraiberg's excellent application of deconstructive methods to the term "discrete" and "discretion." The effect of her analysis is to construct a marvelous pun (there is high magic to low puns): she converts the word **discrete** from its first meaning (distinct, separate, severed, discontinuous) into its other meaning, as in **discreet** (exer-cising judgment, discernment, etc.). To enhance the beauty of this play, and in typically deconstructive fashion, phrases like **to exercise discretion**, Fraiberg notes, ought to mean the opposite of the first kind of discrete: the "discreet" individual now knows that AIDS uncov-ers the very extent to which we are not discrete but are participants in the circuit. All well and good so far.

6   The problem is that Fraiberg herself has trouble explaining exactly what all this means and resolving the contradictions to which it leads:

> The traditional, tenuous limits of the body
> dissolved into fused networks, into open
> circuits of interconnectedness, produce an
> ontological recognition that, from this per-
> spective, urges the body into discretion.
> Closed off, guarded against infection, be-
> ware the surface; any exchange of fluid, that
> is, any disclosure of an open, leaking body,

threatens. A closed, self-contained body resurfaces from the within the integrated network. ¶But this is a different kind of discretion. It's not the kind of discretion clung to by those who deny any fusion; it's a kind of discretion, discreteness, that is a consequence of the recognition of indiscretion. So while the cyborg ontology takes as its premise the dissolution of traditional boundaries associated with the body, its referent in the texts of aids, epistemologically speaking, forces the body to resist coming to rest with those integrated circuits and, instead, reorganizes into discrete units. In this sense, discretion returns, not in the form of reactionary denial, but as conditioned by a cyborg-like system. In other words, if the cyborg ontology can be said to function as the discursive field upon which networks of social relations play themselves out, then that field must by willing to admit – indeed, it has already admitted – the constructions of what might seem quite odd to cyborg theorists: writings and readings of the body grounded in discretion.

What happened to all that fun stuff about broadening and redefining the sexual act itself?

I think these two problems are actually produced by a deeper flaw 7 in Fraiberg's argument, one that rests with her reification of the Bad Guys, her tendency to see them as blind and inexperienced at best, sheerly vicious at worst. She wouldn't need to twist and contort her prose into these unnatural postures if only she would grant that perhaps aids brings us all – not just the privileged few who have been immersed in the discourses of a salvational cyborg ideology – to pretty much the same level of self-awareness about our position in the intertwined cyborg loops of culture-sexuality-identity. We are all equally "conditioned by cyborg-like systematicity" and we are all made more aware of our sexuality by aids. The proof is in the result:

most of us, William F. Buckley included, have come to the same conclusion – that survival entails reorganization "into discrete units." The only difference is that Fraiberg claims a greater degree of awareness and calls her interpretation a "progressive reconstruction" while denying a level of agency to (and blaming for a certain intentional viciousness) the poor dumb self-righteous suckers who stick to monogamous heterosexuality and keep their spouses and kids and stupidly try to prescribe it for others, not only because it works for them but because they may not have a taste for the impedimenta of dental dams and condoms, not to mention anal penetration and fellatio and IV-drugs.

8   Perhaps the proper conclusion is that all the rhetorics about AIDS are dispensable. We can certainly do without the oppressive totalizing rhetoric of the official versions of AIDS, with its self-righteousness and its encouragements of hatred and fear and otherness. But maybe we could just as soon dispense with arguments that use AIDS to take what is in the end an obscure high moral ground through the sterile and overly-self-conscious rhetoric of the encrusted academic. In this case, such a rhetoric strives to reconcile the "good" ideology of openness, liberation, and tolerance (as well as rejection of all simple and patent and conventional formulations, like "safe sex" and "monogamy") with two incompatible notions: the allure of the cyborg and the realities of AIDS. In the end, two into one won't go and the rhetoric of liberation finds itself sadly overmatched. This is one ménage à trois which is simply an unproductive configuration. Cyborgization probably produces just as many new reactionaries roaming the golf courses in their abstinence as it does enlightened networkers, the new cyberpunker proles who roam the loop looking for action. And AIDS, as this essay manifestly demonstrates, produces caution and discretion and a discipline of the self, a redefinition of the body not simply as a sensorial machine, but as an invitation to disease, no matter what rhetoric you process it through. Postmodern liberation, with its yearning for whatever it is postmodernism yearns for, must await some different kind of apocalypse to scratch that epistemological/ontological itch.

9   I know this is an anathematic suggestion to most postmodernists, who hold, as I did for a long time, to a more or less constructivist position: there is no reality that isn't reconfigured or constructed by discourse. In its most radical tenet, we convince ourselves that it's all

discourse, there is no reality at all, so you'd better be careful which discourse you choose. But if you look at the facts of AIDS, it really does scare you out of the constructivist position. There's something awfully touchable and factitious about it, especially if you watch it close, destroying a friend. There's even something haunting and scary, to which any AIDS researcher will attest, about the HIV virus itself. Let's take a paragraph to explore it:

Normally, a cell begins with DNA, which is transcribed into RNA,   10 which then codes for proteins, the building blocks of cells. But AIDS is the ultimate cybernetic disease; it inverts and subverts the normal DNA-RNA-DNA loop (thus the "retro" in "retrovirus") by imposing its own loop. Where most viruses are DNA, HIV is an RNA virus. With the insidious collaboration of reverse transcriptase, it takes over and alters the DNA transcription process, forcing it to produce more retroviral RNA, which in turn takes over the DNA in other cells. At the same time, it changes other parts of DNA, encoding for proteins that alter the body's cells, actually making them more receptive to further HIV infection. Finally, the RNA replication cycle is activated by anything that turns on the immune system: in other words, the immune system defeats itself every time it tries to work. Spooky and evil disease. Nasty shit.

I suggest we all take a closer look at the possibility – made even   11 more ironic by the tendency of some to laud the coming cyborgization of our bodies and minds – that aids is just the first of a terrible series of cyborg events against which simple enlightened discretion is not proof. Perhaps retroviruses themselves are the product of orgiastic physiological feedback mechanisms between the world and the world-body, which might continue to spawn these transcription reversals between RNA and DNA because we have achieved some new order of Prigoginesque complexity.[1] aids really does make cyborgs of its victims, and by extension, of us all, as the glomming of a cybernetic system onto an organismic host. If this is what cyborgization portends, I'm gonna resist.

1. In Order Out Of Chaos: Man's New Dialogue with Nature (New York: Bantam, 1984), Ilya Prigogine and Isabelle Stengers discuss the consequences of Prigogine's Nobel Prize-winning work on chaos. They explain how new biological organisms of increasing complexity arise naturally and inevitably from conditions of turbulent chaos: the HIV viral family may be an example of just such an occurrence.

12 〉〉 In reading David Porush's comments, I realized that parts of my essay were not as clear as I would have liked them to be. Based on Porush's comments, I would like to take this opportunity to reiterate some points that I think are crucial to my argument as a whole. Consequently, I will reply to Porush by focusing on areas where I sensed the most confusion.

13 What concerns me the most are quibbles about, or blatant dismissals of, two crucial starting points in my essay. The first involves a conclusion of Porush's that retroactively revises one of my premises. Porush writes that "[p]erhaps the proper conclusion is that all the rhetorics about AIDS are dispensable" (8). Easy to say, but not so easy – or even desirable – to do. Douglas Crimp opens the collection of essays in *aids: Cultural Analysis/Cultural Activism* with an important reminder. I quote him at length since he reaches the heart of the matter:

> AIDS does not exist apart from the practices that conceptualize it, represent it, and respond to it. We know AIDS only in and through those practices. This assertion does not contest the existence of viruses, antibodies, infections, or transmission routes. Least of all does it contest the reality of illness, suffering, and death. What it does contest is the notion that there is an underlying reality of AIDS, upon which are constructed the representations, or the culture, or the politics of AIDS. If we recognize that AIDS exists only in and through these constructions, then hopefully we can also recognize the imperative to know them, analyze them, and wrest control of them. (3)

14 To dispense with the rhetorics of AIDS, in Crimp's frame, becomes an impossible task since AIDS exists "in and through" them. Crimp's point is that you can't distinguish AIDS from the practices which make it intelligible. Choosing to ignore the discourses of AIDS is

something I can't even picture: every day I see stories on television, in the newspapers; I hear of new public policy and legislation; I see people die. I don't see how one can dispose of the rhetorics – it's not a Lego set that one can put away when one has tired of playing. I can, however, see how some people have tried to revise/alter/speak different rhetorics in attempts to "recognize the imperative to know them, analyze them, and wrest control of them." And, in seeing and experiencing various actions and discourses put into motion by AIDS strategists, I have realized that "encrusted" academics have no property rights on discourse.

The second premise around which Porush and I disagree centers 15 on a temporal sense of positioning. Porush writes of the "coming cyborgization of our bodies" and how he's "gonna resist" it. I'm somewhat taken aback by the future tense here since my whole argument rests on the assumption that Haraway's cyborg myth is not **going** to happen but that it **has** happened ("The cyborg is our ontology"). The first half of my essay uses a cyborg ontology as its premise: Haraway for the description, then my resituating of discourses using Haraway's frame. By using the cyborg as a starting point, I'm saying that – and this is by no means an astounding observation – rhetorics of humanism and organicism have produced, are currently producing, and, dare I say, will probably always produce, radical material inequities for the vast majority of people.

So, if a) the cyborg is our ontology and b) discourses that deny 16 the cyborg are at best archaic and at worst deadly, do you continue to tell the story of organics – a story that doesn't quite fit the picture? Do you speak of the futility of trying to do anything in this configuration (Haraway: "Paranoia bores me")? Do you speak in the rhetoric of the future – and thereby deny various realities? I choose none of these since I see in them no opportunities for change. Instead, I'll take on Haraway's challenge of "being in the belly of a monster and looking for another story to tell" ("Cyborgs at Large" 14). Consequently, what I did was take a description of current relations and resituate AIDS discourses on it.

And what I saw from the belly of the monster was how certain 17 discourses had tried so hard to resist being digested by the monster; I also saw others that knew that's where they were. The alternate AIDS strategists knew that they were in the belly of a monster and while I was there I saw something exciting happen: the alternate AIDS discourses began to revise the belly. These discourses, the discourses that recognize a cyborg-netic body, began to revise postmodern versions of the blurry boundaries of the body. They resurfaced the body and by so doing created a post-circuited discrete unit.

18   Porush says in his response that I pun on "discrete" and "discreet": I do, but he misses my final step. I move from the discrete bodies of liberal humanism (separate, distinct) to the pun on discreet (the various definitions on **all** sides of what constitutes a certain sense of judgment). But then I move on to discrete again. I move on because it's not a revised sense of judgment that propels the argument; it's a revised discrete sense of the body. In other words, I go from "discrete," to "discreet," to "discrete." And by the time I get around to the second version of discrete, it looks very different from the first one that set the pun in motion. That alternate AIDS discourses and strategies revise versions of the body offered by mainstream media, humanism, **and** postmodernism seems to me a powerful and energetic practice.

19   It's a powerful practice that begins to tell another story – another story that tries to describe what's happening to people – and I read the story as being about agency. So my essay isn't about safe sex or new forms of judgments: people with a lot more visibility than I've got have been saying these things for 10 years with little luck (but, based on what I read in a recent poll I took on the electronic bulletin board used in composition courses at the University of Washington, it wouldn't hurt to have those ideas reiterated, again and again and again). Instead, I'm interested in how agency is conditioned and produced in the move from "discrete" (version 1) to "discrete" (version 2).

20   In this second version, you can't arrive at an agent without looking at what Porush rightfully calls the "realities of AIDS." Agency is the result of the resurfacing of the – differently discrete – body; and the agency arises out of the material conditions that force the resurfacing. When Porush quotes me saying we are all conditioned by cyborg-like systematicity, he adds a word that completely alters my intention and, consequently, my argument: he adds "equally" before the quote, a move that once again forecloses on this version of agency. I would never say that we are all **equally** conditioned by anything. I would never say, for instance, that the women on factory lines in Southeast Asia who assemble my computer and I, who use

this computer to write, are "equally" conditioned by the transnational circuit of which we are both part; I would never say that gay men and straight white women in this country are "equally" conditioned by the cyborg-like systematicity I describe in my essay.

In fact, it is the redistribution of agency that grounds my argument (I must apologize to Mr. Porush if he doesn't find this as much "fun" as he would like). The type of material agency I propose is one that shifts attention and authority away from hegemonic biomedical and governmental institutions and onto those most affected. It also forces theorists, postmodern and otherwise, to take our cues from where the materialist agent stands: usually downtown organizing street actions, protests, and die-ins. 21

hypertext

hypertext

hypertextual,

hypertextual

"**hypertext.**"

hypertext

hypertext

Y O U

YOU SAY YOU WANT A REVOLUTION? HYPERTEXT & THE LAWS OF MEDIA

S A Y

YOU SAY YOU WANT A REVOLUTION? HYPERTEXT & THE LAWS OF MEDIA

Y O U

YOU SAY YOU WANT A REVOLUTION? HYPERTEXT & THE LAWS OF MEDIA

S A Y

YOU SAY YOU WANT A REVOLUTION? HYPERTEXT & THE LAWS OF MEDIA

YOU SAY YOU WANT A REVOLUTION? HYPERTEXT & THE LAWS OF MEDIA

Y O U

YOU SAY YOU WANT A REVOLUTION? HYPERTEXT & THE LAWS OF MEDIA

Y O U

STUART MOULTHROP STUART MOULTHROP STUART MOULTHROP STUART

S A Y

s ago, ve

ard of **hypertext**, a   h

ectro   which the   ser

infor   on is no   ons   ned   y linea

s of discou

hypertext has

cr

orig

y

were q

s ar **hypertextual**,   er in

esponse to   , 9-   . I

arche   first **hypertextual**

er g   ," i   der to e

pu   (Levy

a so

emic and   ded

"hypertext." N   er

tion, c   n

d Xanadu. In a tr

ary M

na

ac

son collabor

hypertext sys

eriments f

ea o **hypertext** – which

amic, r

cor

e

When this essay first appeared, all of two years ago, very few people   1
outside the information sciences had heard of **hypertext**, a technology for creating electronic documents in which the user's access
to information is not constrained, as in books, by linear or hierarchical arrangements of discourse. This obscurity had always seemed
strange, since **hypertext** has been around for a long time. Its underlying concept – creating and enacting linkages between stored
bits of information – originated in 1945 with Vannevar Bush, science advisor to President Roosevelt, who wanted to build a machine
called Memex to help researchers organize disparate sources of
knowledge (see Bush; Landow, 14-15). Bush's design, based on microfilm, rotating spools, and photoelectric cells, proved impractical
for the mechanical technologies of the late 1940s. But when electronic computers arrived on the academic scene a few years later,
Bush's projections were quickly realized. In a sense, all distributed
computing systems are **hypertextual**, since they deliver information
dynamically in response to users' demands (Bolter, 9-10). Indeed,
artificial intelligence researchers created the first **hypertextual** narrative, the computer game called "Adventure," in order to experi-
ment with interactive computing in the early 1960s (Levy, 140-41).

It was about this time that Theodor Holm Nelson, a sometime   2
academic and a dedicated promoter of technology, coined the term
"**hypertext**." Nelson offered plans for a worldwide network of information, centrally coordinated through a linking and retrieval system
he called Xanadu. In a trio of self-published manifestoes (*Computer
Lib, Dream Machines, Literary Machines*), Nelson outlined the structure and function of Xanadu, right down to the franchise arrangements for "Silverstands," the informational equivalent of fast-food
outlets where users would go to access the system. (This was long
before anyone dreamed of personal computers.) Nelson's ideas got
serious consideration from computer scientists, notably Douglas
Engelbart, one of the pioneers of user interface design. Englebart
and Nelson collaborated at Brown University in the early 1970s on a
hypertext system called FRESS, and a number of academic and industrial experiments followed (see Conklin). To a large extent, however,
the idea of **hypertext** – which both Bush and Nelson had envisioned
as a dynamic, read/write system in which users could both manipulate and alter the textual corpus – was neglected in favor of more
rigidly organized models like distributed databases and electronic

libraries, systems that operate mainly in a read-only retrieval mode. To Nelson, **hypertext** and other forms of interactive computing represented a powerful force for social change. "Tomorrow's **hypertext** systems have immense political ramifications," he wrote in *Literary Machines* (3/19). Yet no one seemed particularly interested in exploring those ramifications, at least not until the mid-1980s, when the personal computer business went ballistic.

3   1987: the *annus mirabilis* of **hypertext**. Many strange and wonderful things happened in and around that year. Nelson's underground classics, *Computer Lib* and *Dream Machines*, were published by Microsoft Press; Nelson himself joined Autodesk, an industry leader in software development, which announced plans to support Xanadu as a commercial enterprise; the Association for Computing Machinery sponsored the first of its international conferences on **hypertext**; and most important, Apple Computer began giving away HyperCard, an object-oriented **hypertext** system, to anyone who owned a Macintosh personal computer. HyperCard is the Model T of **hypertext**: relatively cheap (originally free), simple to operate (being largely an extension of the Macintosh's graphical user interface), quite crude compared to more state-of-the-art products, but still enormously powerful. In the late 1980s it seemed plausible that HyperCard and other personal computer applications would usher in a new paradigm for textual communication, the logical step beyond desktop publishing to all-electronic documents containing multiple pathways of expression.

4   It has now been six years since that great unveiling of **hypertext**, and no such "digital revolution" has arrived. At one point, sources in the personal computer industry foresaw a burgeoning market for "stackware" and other **hypertext**ually organized products; nothing of the kind has materialized. Instead, the most commercially ambitious application of HyperCard in electronic publishing has been the Voyager Company's line of "Expanded Books," based exclusively on print titles and carefully designed to duplicate the look and function of traditional books (Stansberry, 54). True, the **hypertext** concept has finally received some attention from humanist academics. Jay David Bolter's *Writing Space* (1991) outlines a historical view of **hypertext** as the successor to print technology – and with Nelson's *Literary Machines* is one of the first studies of **hypertext** to be presented in **hypertextual** form. George Landow's **Hypertext**

(1992) places developments in electronic writing within the context of poststructuralist criticism and postmodern culture (and is also due to appear shortly as a **hypertext**). The spectre of **hypertextual** fiction has even been raised by the novelist Robert Coover in the *New York Times Book Review* (see "The End of Books"). But paradoxically (or as fate would have it), this recognition comes when **hypertext** is no longer what one of my colleagues calls a "bleeding edge" technology. Indeed, much of the caché seems to have bled out of **hypertext**, which has been bumped from the limelight by hazier and more glamorous obsessions: cyberspace, virtual reality, and the Information Highway.

Such changes of fashion seem a regular hazard of the postmodern territory – taking *post modo* at its most literal, to mean "after the now" or *the next thing*. Staring down at our desktop, laptop, or palmtop machines – which we know will be obsolete long before we have paid for them – those of us within what Fred Pfeil calls the "baby-boom professional-managerial class" will always desire *the next thing* (*Another Tale* 98). Not for nothing have we updated *Star Trek*, our true space Odyssey, into a "Next Generation." We are the generation (and generators) of nextness. Or so Steve Jobs once assumed, somewhat to his present chagrin. Possibly **hypertext**, like Jobs's sophisticated NeXT computer, represents an idea that hasn't quite come to the mainstream of postmodern culture, a precocious curio destined to be dug up years from now and called "strangely ahead of its time." Unfortunately, as Ted Nelson can testify, **hypertext** has been through this process once before. A certain circularity seems to be in play.

Perhaps the problem lies not in our technologies or the things we want to do with them, but in our misunderstanding of technological history. Some of us keep saying, as I note in this essay, that we need a revolution, a paradigm shift, a total uprooting of the old information order: an apocalyptic rupture or "blesséd break," as Robert Lowell once put it. And yet that is not what we have received, at least so far. Maybe we suffer this disappointment because we do not understand what we are asking for. What could "revolution" mean in a postmodern context? We might look for answers in Baudrillard, Lyotard, Donna Haraway, or Hakim Bey; but Hollywood, as usual, has the best line. J.F. Lawton's screenplay for *Under Siege*, last summer's Steven Seagal vehicle, includes an enlightening exchange between a

CIA spymaster (played by Nick Mancuso) and a rebellious terrorist formerly in his employ (Tommie Lee Jones). The spook chides the terrorist, reminding him that the sixties are over, "the Movement is dead." Jones's character replies: "Yes! Of course! Hence the name: 'Movement.' It moves a certain distance, then it stops. Revolution gets its name by always coming back around – *in your face.*"

7   Perhaps **hypertext** is just another movement. On one level, it is hard to discriminate among **hypertext**, virtual reality, and next year's interactive cable systems. All three seem to move in the same general direction, attempting to increase and enrich our consumption of information. But as Andrew Ross has noted, undertakings of this type may have large consequences (*Strange Weather* 88). Potentially at least, they threaten to upset the stability of language-as-property – a possibility with great political ramifications indeed. It might therefore be dangerous to dismiss **hypertext** as merely a local movement, an initiative as dead as the social agendas of the sixties from which it partly sprang. Considering the vicissitudes of **hypertext**'s history, we might indeed call it a "revolution" – if revolution is something that comes full circle, escaping repression to smack us smartly in the face. Such being the case, however, is this revolution something our culture genuinely wants? When it comes to information technologies, what *do* we want? Why are we moving in circles? What is this figure we are weaving, twice or thrice, and what enchanter or enchantment do we wish to contain?

                    * * *

8   The original Xanadu (Samuel Taylor Coleridge's) came billed as "A Vision in a Dream," designated doubly unreal and thus easily aligned with our era of "operational simulation" where, strawberry fields, nothing is "real" in the first place, since no place is really "first" (Baudrillard, *Simulations* 10). But all great dreams invite revisions, and these days we find ourselves perpetually on the re-make. So here is a new Xanadu™, the universal **hypertext** system proposed by Theodor Holm Nelson – a vision which, unlike its legendary precursor, cannot be integrated into the dream park of the hyperreal. Hyperreality, we are told, is a site of collapse or implosion where referential or "grounded" utterance becomes indistinguishable from the self-referential and the imaginary. We construct our representational systems not in serial relation to indisputably "real" phenome-

na, but rather in recursive and multiple parallel, "mapping on to different co-ordinate systems" (Pynchon, 159). Maps derive not from territories but from previous map-making enterprises: all the world's a simulation.

This reality implosion brings serious ideological consequences, for some would say it invalidates the informing "master narratives" of modernity, leaving us with a proliferation of incompatible discourses and methods (Lyotard, 26). Such unchecked variation, it has been objected, deprives social critique of a clear agenda (Eagleton, 63). Hyperreality privileges no discourse as absolute or definitive; critique becomes just another form of paralogy, a countermove in the language game that is techno-social construction of reality. The game is all-encompassing, and therein lies a problem. As Linda Hutcheon observes, "the ideology of postmodernism is paradoxical, for it depends upon and draws its power from that which it contests. It is not truly radical; nor is it truly oppositional" (120). **9**

This problem of complicity grows especially acute where media and technologies are concerned. Hyperreality is as much a matter of writing practice as it is of textual theory: as Michael Heim points out, "[i]n magnetic code there are no originals" (162). Electronic information may be rapidly duplicated, transmitted, and assembled into new knowledge structures. From word processing to interactive multimedia, postmodern communication systems accentuate what Ihab Hassan calls "immanence" or "the intertextuality of all life. A patina of thought, of signifiers, of 'connections,' now lies on everything the mind touches in its gnostic (noö)sphere. . . ." (172). Faced with this infinitely convoluted system of discourse, we risk falling into technological abjection, a sense of being hopelessly abandoned to simulation, lost in "the technico-luminous cinematic space of total spatiodynamic theatre" (Baudrillard, *Simulations* 139). If all the world's a simulation, then we are but simulacral subjects cycling through our various iterations, incapable of any "radical" or "oppositional" action that would transform the techno-social matrix. Even supposedly resistant attitudes like "cyberpunk," as Andrew Ross has observed, tend to tail off into cynical interludes where the rules of the game go unquestioned (Ross, 160). **10**

Of course, this pessimistic or defeatist outlook is hardly universal. We are far more likely to hear technology described as an instrumentality of change or a tool for liberation. Bolter (1991), Drexler **11**

(1987), McCorduck (1985), and Zuboff (1988) all contend that post-modern modes of communication (electronic writing, computer networks, text-linking systems) can destabilize social hierarchies and promote broader definitions of authority in the informational workplace. Heim points out that under the influence of these technologies "psychic life will be redefined" (164). But if Hutcheon is correct in her observation that postmodernism is non-oppositional, then how will such a reconstruction of order and authority take place? How and by whom is psychic life – and more important, political life – going to be redefined?

12   These questions must ultimately be addressed not in theory but in practice; which is where the significance of Nelson's new Xanadu lies. With Xanadu, Nelson invalidates technological abjection, advancing an unabashedly millenarian vision of technological renaissance in which the system shall set us free. In its extensive ambitions, Xanadu transcends the hyperreal. It is not an opium vision but something stranger still, a business plan for the development of what Barthes called the "*social* space" of writing (81), a practical attempt to reconfigure literate culture. Xanadu is the most ambitious project ever proposed for **hypertext** or "non-sequential writing" (*Dream Machines* 29; *Literary Machines* 5/2). **Hypertext** systems exploit the interactive potential of computers to reconstruct text not as a fixed series of symbols, but as a variable-access database in which any discursive unit may possess multiple vectors of association (see Joyce; Landow; Slatin). A **hypertext** is a complex network of textual elements. It consists of units or "lexias," which may be analogous to pages, paragraphs, sections, or volumes. Lexias are connected by "links," which act like dynamic footnotes that automatically retrieve the material to which they refer. Because it is no longer book-bounded, **hypertextual** discourse may be modified at will as reader/writers forge new links within and among documents. Potentially this collectivity of linked text, which Nelson calls the "docuverse," can expand without limit.

13   As Nelson foresees it, Xanadu would embody this textual universe. The system would provide a central repository and distribution network for all writing: it would be the publishing house, communications medium, and great **hypertextual** Library of Babel. Yet for all its radical ambitions, Nelson's design preserves familiar proprieties. Local Xanadu outlets would be Silverstands™, retail access

and consulting centers modeled after fast-food franchises and thus integrated with the present economy of information exchange. Xanadu would protect intellectual property through copyright. Users would pay per byte accessed and would receive royalties when others obtained proprietary material they had published in the system. The problems and complexities of this scheme are vast, and at the moment, the fulfilled Xanadu remains a "2020 Vision," a probe into the relatively near future. But it is a future with compelling and important implications for the postmodern present.

The future, as Disney and Spielberg have taught us, is a place we 14 must come "back" to. The American tomorrow will be a heyday of nostalgia, an intensive pursuit of "lost" or "forgotten" values. Xanadu is no exception: Ted Nelson sees the history of writing in the 21st century as an epic of recovery. His "grand hope" lies in "a return to literacy, a cure for television stupor, a new Renaissance of ideas and generalist understanding, a grand posterity that does not lose the details which are the final substance of everything" ("How **Hypertext** (Un)does the Canon" 4). To a skeptical observer, this vision of Xanadu might suggest another domain of the postmodern theme park. Gentle readers, welcome to Literacyland!

But on the other hand, this vision might add up to more than just 15 a sideshow attraction. Nelson foresees a renovation of culture, a unification of discourse, a reader-and-writer's paradise where all writing opens itself to/in the commerce of ideas. This is the world in which all "work" becomes "text," not substance but reference, not containment but connection (see Barthes; Landow; Zuboff). The magnitude of the change implied here is enormous. But what about the politics of that change? What community of interpretation – and beyond that, what social order – does this intertextual world presume? With the conviction of a true Enlightenment man, Nelson envisions "a new populitism that can make the deeper understandings of the few at last available to the many" ("How **Hypertext** (Un)does the Canon" 6).

What is *populitism?* – another of Nelson's infamous neologisms 16 (e.g., "hypermedia," "cybercrud," "teledildonics"), in this case a portmanteau combining "populism" with "elite." The word suggests the society-of-text envisioned by theorists like Shoshana Zuboff and Jay David Bolter, a writing space in which traces of authority persist only as local and contingent effects, the social equivalent of the deconstructed author-function. A "populite" culture might mark the first step toward realization of Jean-François Lyotard's "game of perfect information" where all have equal access to the world of data, and where "[g]iven equal competence (no longer in the acquisition of knowledge, but in its production), what extra performativity depends on in the final analysis is 'imagination,' which allows one either to make a new move or change the rules of the game" (52). This is the utopia of information-in-process, the ultimate wetware dream of the clerisy: discourse converted with 100 percent efficiency into capital, the mechanism of that magical process being nomology or rule-making – admittedly a rather specialized form of "imagination."

17   At least two troubles lurk in this paradise. First, the prospect that social/textual order will devolve not unto the many but only to a very few; and more important, that those few will fail to recognize the terms of their splendid isolation. Consider the case of the reluctant computer dick Clifford Stoll, whose memoir, *The Cuckoo's Egg,* nicely illustrates these problems. Stoll excoriates "cyberpunks," electronic vandals who abuse the openness of scientific computing environments. Their unsportsmanlike conduct spoils the information game, necessitating cumbersome restrictions on the free flow of data. But Stoll's definition of informational "freedom" appears murky at best. He repeatedly refers to the mainframe whose system he monitors as "his" computer, likening cybernetic intrusions to burglaries. Digital information, as Stoll sees it, stands in strict analogy to material and private property.

18   Private in what sense? Stoll professes to believe that scientists must have easy access to research results, but only within their own communities. He is quick to condemn incursions by "unauthorized" outsiders. There is some sense in this argument: Stoll repeatedly points out that the intruder in the Stanford mainframe might have interfered with a lifesaving medical imaging system. But along with this concern comes an ideological danger. Who decides what information "belongs" to whom? Stoll's "popular elite" is restricted to academic scientists, a version of "the people" as *nomenklatura,* those whose need to know is defined by their professional affiliation. More disturbingly, Stoll seems unaware of the way this brotherhood is situated within larger political hierarchies. Describing a meeting with Pentagon brass, he reflects: "How far I'd come. A year ago, I

would have viewed these officers as war-mongering puppets of the Wall Street capitalists. This, after all, was what I'd learned in college. Now things didn't seem so black and white. They seemed like smart people handling a serious problem" (278).

Here is elite populism at its scariest. Though he protests (too much) his political correctness, Stoll's sense of specialist community shifts to accommodate the demands of the moment. He observes repeatedly over the course of the memoir that he is finally "coming of age" as a working scientist. When in Fort Meade, Stoll does as the natives do, recognizing agents of Air Force Intelligence, the National Security Agency, even the CIA and FBI as brothers-in-craft. After all, they are "smart" (technologically adept) and "serious" (professional). Their immediate goal seems legitimate and laudable. They are just "handling" a problem, tracking down the intruder who has violated the electronic privacy of Stoll's community (and, not coincidentally, their own). They are the good policemen, the ones Who Are Your Friends, not really "Them" after all but just a quaint, braid-shouldered version of "Us." 19

Stoll is not troubled that these boon companions live at the heart of the military-industrial complex. He disregards the fact that they seem aware of domestic communications intercepts – in phone conversations, Stoll's CIA contact refers to the FBI as "the F entity," evidently to thwart a monitoring program (144). Stoll does task his agency buddies for sowing disinformation and managing dirty wars, but this critique never gets much past the stage of rhetorical questions. In fact Stoll seems increasingly comfortable in the intelligence community. If the data spooks turn out to be less interested in freedom of scientific speech than in quashing a security leak, Stoll has no real objection. His own ideals and interests are conveniently served in the process. 20

What leads to such regrettable blindness, and how might it have been prevented? These may be especially pertinent questions as we consider entrusting our literate culture to an automated information system. The spooks are not so easily conjured away. It is no longer sufficient to object that scientists and humanists form distinct communities, and that Stoll's seduction could not happen in our own elect company. The old "Two Cultures" paradigm has shifted out from under us, largely through catholic adoption of technologies like data networks and **hypertext**. Networks are networks, and we 21 can assume that most if not all of them will eventually engender closed elites. Fascism, as Deleuze and Guattari instruct, is a matter of all-too-human desire (26). What can shield humanist networks, or even the "generalist" networks Nelson foresees, from the strategy of divide and co-opt? What might insulate Xanadu from those ancestral voices prophesying war?

22   The answer, as forecasters like Pamela McCorduck, K. Eric Drexler, and Andrew Ross point out, may lie in the **hypertext** concept itself – the operating principle of an open and dynamic medium, a consensual canon with a minimum of hierarchical impedances and a fundamental instability in those hierarchies it maintains. Visionary and problematic as it may seem, Nelson's idea of "populitism" has much to recommend it – not the least of which is its invitation to consider more carefully the likely social impact of advanced communication systems. In fact **hypertext** may well portend social change, a fundamental reshaping of text production and reception. The telos of the electronic society-of-text is anarchy in its true sense: local autonomy based on consensus, limited by a relentless disintegration of global authority. Since information is now virtually an equivalent of capital, and since textuality is our most powerful way of shaping information, it follows that Xanadu might indeed change the world. But to repeat the crucial question, how will this change come about? What actual social processes can translate the pragmatics of Nelson's business plan into the radicalism of a **hypertext** manifesto?

23   The complete answers lie with future history. In one respect, Ted Nelson's insistence that Xanadu become an economically viable enterprise is exemplary. We will discover the full implications of this technology only as we build, manage, and work in **hypertextual** communities, starting within the existing constraints of information capitalism. But while we wait on history, we can try a little augury. In trying to theorize a nascent medium, one is reduced to *playing* medium, eking out predictions with the odd message from the Other Side. Which brings us to the last work of Marshall McLuhan, a particularly important ancestral voice from whom to hear. At his death, McLuhan left behind notes for an enigmatic final project: the fourfold "Laws of Media" which form the framework for a semiotics of technology. The Laws proceed from four basic questions that can be asked about any invention:

– What does it enhance or intensify?
– What does it render obsolete or displace?
– What does it retrieve that was previously obsolete?
– What does it produce or become when taken to its limit?

As McLuhan demonstrates, these questions are particularly in-   24
structive when applied to pivotal or transforming technologies like
printing or broadcasting. They are intended to discover the ways in
which information systems affect the social text, rearranging sense
ratios and rewriting theories of cultural value. They reveal the nature
of the basic statement, the "uttering or 'outering'" that underlies
mechanical extensions of human faculties. If we put Xanadu and
hypertext to this series of questions, we may discover more about
both the potential and the limits of **hypertext** as an agency of
change.

1. What does **hypertext** enhance or intensify?

According to McLuhan's standard analysis, communications media   25
adjust the balance or "ratio" of the senses by privileging one channel
of perception over others. Print promotes sight over hearing, giving
us an objectified, perspectival, symbolized world: "an eye for an ear"
(*Understanding Media* 81). But this approach needs modification for
our purposes. **Hypertext** differs from earlier media in that it is not a
new thing at all but a return or *recursion* (of which more later) to an
earlier form of symbolic discourse, namely print. The effect of **hypertext** thus falls not simply upon the sense channels but farther
along the cognitive chain. As Vannevar Bush pointed out in the very
first speculation on informational linking technologies, these mechanisms enhance the fundamental capacity of *pattern recognition* ("As
We May Think," qtd. in *Literary Machines* 1/50).

Hypertext is all about connection, linkage, and affiliation. For-   26
mally speaking, its universe is the one Thomas Pynchon had in mind
when he defined "paranoia" as "the realization that *everything is
connected,* everything in the Creation – not yet blindingly one, but at
least connected. . . ." (820). In **hypertext** systems, this ethos of
connection is realized in technics: users do not passively rehearse or
receive discourse, they explore and construct links (Joyce, 12). At the
kernel of the **hypertext** concept lie ideas of affiliation, correspon-

dence, and resonance. In this, as Nelson has argued from the start, **hypertext** is nothing more than an extension of what literature has always been (at least since "Tradition and the Individual Talent") – a temporally extended network of relations which successive generations of readers and writers perpetually make and unmake.

27   This redefinition of textuality gives rise to a number of questions. What does it mean to enhance our sensitivity to patterns in this shifting matrix, to become sensitized to what Pynchon calls "other orders behind the visible?" Does this mean that **hypertext** will turn us into "paranoids," anxious interpreters convinced that all structures are mysteriously organized against us? What does interpretive "resistance" mean in a **hypertextual** context? Can such a reading strategy be possible after poststructuralism, with the authorfunction reduced (like Pynchon himself) to a voiceless occasion for deconstructive "writing" (McHoul and Wills, 9)? Perverse though it may seem, **hypertext** does increase the agonistic element in reading. Early experience with **hypertext** narrative suggests that its readers may actually be more concerned with prior authority and design than are readers of conventional writing. The apparent "quickliming of the author" does not dispel the aura of intention in **hypertext** (Douglas, 100). The constantly repeated ritual of interaction, with its reminder of discursive alternatives, reveals the text as a made thing, not monologic perhaps but hardly indeterminate. The text gestures toward openness – *what options can you imagine?* – but then swiftly forecloses: some options are available but not others, and someone clearly did the defining long before you began interacting. The author persists, undead presence in the literary machine, the inevitable Hand that turns the time. **Hypertextual** writing – at least when considered as read-only or "exploratory" text (see Joyce) – may thus emphasize antithetical modes of reading, leading us to regard the deconstructed system-maker much in the way that Leo Bersani describes the author of *Gravity's Rainbow:* as "the enemy text" (108).

28   So perhaps we need a Psychiatrist General's Warning: Interacting With This **Hypertext** Can Make You Paranoid – indeed it must, since the root sense of paranoia, a parallel or parallax gnosis, happens to be a handy way to conceive of the meta-sense of pattern recognition that **hypertext** serves to enhance. But would such a distortion of our cognitive ratios necessarily constitute pathology? In dealing with vast and nebulous information networks – to say nothing of

those corporate-sponsored "virtual realities" that may lie in our future – a certain "creative paranoia" may be a definite asset. In fact the paragnosticism implicit in **hypertext** may be the best way to keep the information game clean. Surrounded by filaments and tendrils of a network, the sojourner in Xanadu or other **hypertext** systems will always be reminded of her situation in a fabric of power arrangements. Her ability to build and pursue links should encourage her to subject those arrangements to inquiry. Which brings us to the second of McLuhan's key questions:

2. What does **hypertext** displace or render obsolete?

Though it may be tempting to respond, *the book, stupid,* that answer is ineligible. The book is already "dead" (or superseded) if by "alive" you mean that the institution in question is essential to our continued commerce in ideas. True, the cultural indications are ambiguous. Irving Louis Horowitz argues that reports of the book's demise are exaggerated; even in an age of television and computers, we produce more books each year than ever before (20). Indeed, our information ecology seems likely to retain a mix of print and electronic media for at least the next century. Yet as Alvin Kernan recently pointed out, the outlook for books in the long run is anything but happy (135-43). As the economic and ecological implications of dwindling forests come home, the cost of paper will rise precipitously. At the same time, acidic decay of existing books will enormously increase maintenance costs to libraries. Given these factors, some shift to electronic storage seems inevitable (though Kernan, an analog man to the last, argues for microfilm).

Yet this change in the medium of print does not worry cultural conservatives like Kernan, Neil Postman, or E.D. Hirsch nearly so much as the prospect that the decline of the book may terminate the cultural dominance of print. The chief technological culprit in Kernan's "death of literature" is not the smart machine but the idiot box. "Such common culture as we still have," Kernan laments, "comes largely from television" (147). But the idiot box – or to be precise, the boxed idiot – is precisely the intellectual problem that **hypertext** seems excellently suited to address. In answer to McLuhan's second question – what does **hypertext** render obsolete? –

29

30

the best answer is not *literacy* but rather *post-literacy.* As Nelson foresees, the development of **hypertext** systems implies a revival of typographic culture (albeit it in a dynamic, truly paperless environment). That forecast may seem recklessly naive or emptily prophetic, but it is quite likely valid. **Hypertext** means the end of the death of literature.

31   Here the voice of the skeptic must be heard: *a revival of literacy? – read my lips: not in a million years.* Even the most devoted champion of print is likely to resist the notion of a Gutenberg renaissance. In the West, genuine literacy – cultural, multicultural, or simply functional – can be found only among a well-defined managerial and professional class. At present that class is fairly large, but in the U.S. and U.K., world leaders in laissez-faire education, it is contracting noticeably. So it must seem foolish to imagine, as Ted Nelson does, a mass consumer market for typographic information, a growth industry based on the electronic equivalent of the local library.

32   Indeed, should Xanadu become a text-only system (which is not intended), its prospects would be poor in the long run. There are however other horizons for interactive textuality – not just **hypertext** but another Nelsonian coinage, "hypermedia." Print is not the only means of communication deliverable in a polysequential format articulated by software links. In trying to imagine the future of **hypertext** culture, we must also consider interactive multimedia "texts" that incorporate voice, music, animated graphics, and video along with alphabetic script (Lanham, 287). **Hypertext** is about connection – promiscuous, pervasive, and polymorphously perverse connection. It is a writing practice ideally suited to the irregular, the transgressive, and the carnivalesque (see Harpold). Culturally speaking, the *promiscuity* of **hypertext** (in the root sense of "a tendency to seek relations") knows no bounds of form, format, or cultural level. There is no reason to assume that **hypertext** or hypermedia should not support popular as well as elite culture, or indeed that it might not promote a "populite" miscegenation of discourses.

33   But what can this mean – talking books in homeboy jive? Street rap mixed over Eliotic scholia? Nintendo with delusions of cinema? Or worse, could we be thinking of yet more industrial light and magic, the Disneyverse of eyephones and datagloves where YOU (insert userName) ARE IN THE FANTASY? Perhaps, as one critic of the computer industry recently put it, interactive multimedia must inev-

itably decay to its lowest common denominator, "hyper-MTV" (Levy, "Multimedia" 52). According to this analysis, the linear and objectifying tendencies of any print content in a multimedium text would be overwhelmed by the subjective, irrational, and emotive influence of audio/video. This being the case, **hypertext** could hardly claim to represent "a cure for television stupor."

But Nelson's aspiration should not be so easily set aside as mere-   34
ly a vision in a dream. **Hypertext** does indeed have the power to recover print literacy – though not in quite the way that Nelson supposes; which brings us to the third of McLuhan's queries:

3. What does **hypertext** retrieve that was previously obsolete?

Xanadu and similar projects could invite large numbers of people to   35
become reacquainted with the cultural power of typographic literacy. To assert this, of course, is to break with McLuhan's understanding of media history. It is hard to dispute the argument of *Understanding Media* and *The Gutenberg Galaxy* that the culture of the printing press has entered into dialectic contention with a different ethos based on the "cool" immediacy of broadcasting. But though that diagnosis remains tremendously important, McLuhan's cultural prognosis for the West holds less value. McLuhan saw clearly the transforming impact of "electric" technologies, but perhaps because he did not live much beyond the onset of the personal computer boom, he failed to recognize the next step – the *recursion* to a new stage of typographic literacy through the syncretic medium of **hypertext**.

It is crucial to distinguish recursion from return or simple repeti-   36
tion, because this difference answers the objection that print literacy will be lost or suppressed in multimedia texts. Recursion is self-reference with the possibility of progressive self-modification (Hofstadter, 127). Considered for its recursive possibilities, "writing" means something radically different in linked interactive compositions than it does in a codex book or even a conventional electronic document. Literacy in **hypertext** encompasses two domains: the ordinary grammatical, rhetorical, and tropological space that we now know as "literature," and also a second province, stricter in its formalisms but much greater in its power to shape interactive dis-

course. This second domain has been called "writing space" (Bolter, 4); a case might be made (with apologies to those who insist that virtual reality is strictly a non-print phenomenon) that it also represents the true meaning of *cyberspace*.

37   Walter Benjamin observed with some regret that by the 1930's, any literate European could become an author, at least to the extent of publishing a letter or article in the newspapers (232). With no regrets at all, Ted Nelson envisions a similar extension of amateur literary production in Xanadu, where all readers of the system can potentially become writers, or at least editors and commentators. The First Amendment guarantee of free speech, Nelson points out, is a *personal* liberty: anyone may publish, and in Xanadu everyone can. Nelson bases his prediction of revived literacy on the promise of a broadly popular publishing franchise.

38   This vision is limited in one crucial regard. Nelson treats print essentially as the *content* of his system, which is taking a rather narrow view. In describing Xanadu as a more or less transparent medium for the transmission of text, Nelson overlooks the fact that alphabetic or alphanumeric representation also defines the *form* of Xanadu, and indeed of any **hypertext** system. This neglect is consistent with the generally broad focus of Nelson's vision, which has led him to dismiss details of user-interface design as "front-end functions" to be worked out by the user.

39   Design details, whether anterior or posterior to the system, cannot be passed over so easily. In fact the structure and specifications of the **hypertext** environment are themselves parts of the docuverse, arguably the most important parts. Beneath any **hypertext** document or system there exists a lower layer that we might call the *hypotext*. On this level, in the working implementations of its "protocols," Xanadu is a creature of print. The command structures that govern linkage, display, editing, accounting, and all the other functions of the system exist as digital impulses that may be translated into typographic text. They were written out, first in pseudo-English strings, then in a high-level programming language, finally as binary code. Therefore Xanadu at its most intimate level is governed by all those features of the typographic medium so familiar from McLuhan's analysis: singular sequentiality, objectivity, instrumentality, "left-brained" visual bias, and so on. The wonder of **hypertext** and hypermedia lies in their capacity to escape these limitations by

using the microprocessor to turn linear, monologic typography recursively back upon itself – to create linear control structures that militate against absolute linear control.

In recognizing the recursive trick behind **hypertextual** writing, we come to a broader understanding of electronic literacy. Literacy under **hypertext** must extend not only to the "content" of a composition but to its hypotextual "form" as well – e.g., the way nodes are divided to accommodate data structures and display strategies, or the types of linkage available and the ways they are apparent to the reader. Practically speaking, this means that users of a **hypertext** system can be expected to understand print not only as the medium of traditional literary discourse, but also as a meta-tool, the key to power at the level of the system itself. 40

Ong and McLuhan have argued that television and radio introduce "secondary orality," a recursion to non-print forms of language and an "audile space" of cognition (*Orality and Literacy* 135; *Laws of Media* 57). By analogy, **hypertext** and hypermedia seem likely to instigate a *secondary literacy* – "secondary" in that this approach to reading and writing includes a self-consciousness about the technological mediation of those acts, a sensitivity to the way texts-below-the-text constitute another order behind the visible. This secondary literacy involves both rhetoric and technics: to read at the hypotextual level is to confront (paragnostically) the design of the system; to write at this level is to reprogram, revising the work of the first maker. Thus this secondary literacy opens for its readers a *cyberspace* in the truest sense of the word, meaning a place of command and control where the written word has the power to remake appearances. This space has always been accessible to the programming elite, to system operators like Clifford Stoll and shady operators like his hacker adversary. But Nelson's 2020 Vision puts a Silverstand in every commercial strip right next to McDonald's and Videoland. Vice President Gore's information "Superhighway" would bring cyberspace even closer. If Xanadu succeeds in re-awakening primary literacy as a mass phenomenon, there is reason to believe that it will inculcate secondary literacy as well. 41

But like any grand hope, this technopiate dream of a new literacy ultimately has to confront its man from Porlock. Secondary literacy might well prove culturally disastrous. The idea of a general cyberspace franchise, in which all control structures are truly contingent 42 and "consensual," does summon up visions of informatic chaos. "Chaos," however, is a concept we have recently begun to understand as something other than simply an absence of "order": it is instead a condition of possibility in which new arrangements spontaneously assemble themselves (Prigogine and Stengers, 14).

43   Taking this neo-chaotic view, we might inquire into the positive effects of secondary literacy in a postmodern political context. In outlining a first move beyond our recent "depthless," ahistorical quiescence, Frederic Jameson calls for an "aesthetic of cognitive mapping," a "pedagogical political culture" in which we would begin to teach ourselves where we stand in the networks of transnational power (92). At this moment, as the West reconsiders its New World Order in the aftermath of a war for oil reserves, we seem in especially urgent need of such education. But a cultural pedagogy clearly needs something more than the evening war news, especially when reporters are confined to informational wading pools. We require not only a sensitivity to the complex textuality of power but an ability to intercept and manipulate that text – an advanced creative paranoia. This must ultimately be a human skill, independent of technological "utterance"; but the secondary literacy fostered by **hypertext** could help us at least to begin the enormous task of drawing our own cognitive maps. Here, however, we verge on the main question of **hypertextual** politics, which brings up the last question in the Toronto catechism:

4. What does **hypertext** become when taken to its limit?

44   Orthodox McLuhanite doctrine holds that "every form, pushed to the limit of its potential, reverses its characteristics" (*Laws of Media* viii). Media evolution, in McLuhan's view, proceeds through sharply punctuated equilibriums. "Hot" media like print tend to increase their routinization and determinism until they reach a limit (say, the prose of the late 19th century). Beyond that point, the overheated medium turns paradoxical, passing almost instantly from hot to supercool, bombarding readers with such a plethora of codings that conventional interpretation collapses. Structure and hierarchy, the distinguishing features of a hot medium, reduce to indeterminacy. The plurality of codes overwhelms hermeneutic certainty, the

"figure" of a univocal text reverses into polysemous "ground," and we reach the ultima thule of Gutenberg culture, *Finnegans Wake.*

But though McLuhan had much to say about the reversal of overheated media, he left the complementary possibility unexplored. What happens to already cool or participatory media when they reach their limits? True to the fourth law, their characteristics reverse, but here the effect is reactionary, not radical. Radio, for instance, begins in interactive orality (two-way transceiving) but decays into the hegemony of commercial broadcasting, where "talk radio" lingers as a reminder of how open the airwaves are not. Television too starts by shattering the rigid hierarchies of the Gutenberg nation-state, promising to bring anyplace into our living rooms; but its version of Global Village turns out to be homogenous and hegemonic, a planetary empire of signs (as we say in Atlanta, "Always Coca-Cola"). 45

Hypertext and hypermedia are also interactively cool, so following this analysis we might conclude that they will undergo a similar implosion, becoming every bit as institutionalized and conservative as broadcast networks. Indeed, it doesn't take McLuhanite media theory to arrive at that forecast. According to the economic logic of late capitalism, wouldn't the Xanadu Operating Company ultimately sell out to Sony, Matsushita, Phillips, or some other wielder of multinational leverage? 46

Such a self-negating "reversal" may not be the only possible outcome, however. What if the corporate shogunate decide not to venture their capital? What if business leaders realize that truly interactive information networks do not make wise investments? This conclusion might be supported by memory of the nastiness Sears and IBM stirred up when they tried to curtail user autonomy on their Prodigy videotex system (see Levy, "In the Realm of the Censor"). This scenario of corporate rejection is not just speculative fabulation, but the basis for a proposed modification to McLuhan's fourth law. Media taken to their limits tend to reverse, but not all media reverse in the same way. The case of a complex, syncretic, and fundamentally interactive medium like **hypertext** may involve a "reversal" that does not bring us back to the same-as-it-ever-was – not a reversal in fact but a recursion (*déjà vu*) to a new cultural space. 47

We have entered into a period of change in reading and writing that Richard Lanham calls a "digital revolution" (268). As this revolu- 48 tion proceeds (if it is allowed to do so), its consequences will be enormous. The idea of **hypertext** as a figment of the capitalist imagination, an information franchise in both Nelson's and Lyotard's senses, could well break down. Though Xanadu may in fact open its Silverstands some day, **hypertext** might not long remain a commercial proposition. The type of literacy and the kind of social structure this medium supports stand fundamentally against absolute property and hierarchy. As we have hinted, **hypertext** and hypermedia peel back to reveal not just an aesthetics of cognitive mapping but nothing less than the simulacral map-as-territory itself: the real beginnings of cyberspace in the sense of a *domain of control.*

49   "Cyberspace. A consensual hallucination experienced daily by billions of legitimate operators, in every nation. . . A graphic representation of data abstracted from the banks of every computer in the human system" (Gibson, 51). William Gibson's concept of a cybernetic workspace, laid out in his dystopian novel *Neuromancer,* represents the ultimate shared vision in the global dream of information commerce. For all its advancement beyond the age of nation-state capitalism, Gibson's world remains intensely competitive and hierarchical (for nation-state substitute the revived *zaibatsu*). *Neuromancer* is *Nineteen Eighty-Four* updated for 1984, the future somewhat gloomily surveyed from Reagan's America.

50   There is accordingly no trace of social "consensus" in Gibson's "consensual" infosphere. In his version of cyberspace, the shape of vision is imposed from without. "They" control the horizontal, "They" control the vertical. Of course there must be some elements of chaos, else Gibson would be out of business as a paperback writer; so he invents the "cyberspace cowboy," a hacker hero who plays the information game by what he likes to call his own rules. But though cowboys may attempt to unsettle the system, their incursions amount at best to harrassment and privateering. These forms of enterprise are deemed "illegal," though they are really just business by another name ("biz," in Gibson's parlance), inventiveness and competitive advantage being the only effective principles of operation.

51   Gibson's dark dream is one thing – in effect it is a realization of McLuhan's prophecy of reversal, an empowering technology turned into a mechanism of co-optation and enslavement. But perhaps Ted Nelson's 2020 Vision of **hypertextual** literacy is something else. If

not a utopian alternative, Nelson's project may at least provide a heterotopia, an otherplace not zoned in the usual ways for property and performativity. Cyberspace as Gibson and others define it is a Cartesian territory where scientists of control define boundaries and power lines. The Xanadu model lets us conceive instead a decentered space of literacy and empowerment where each subject acts as *kubernetes* or as Timothy Leary says, "reality pilot," steering her way across the intertextual sea ("Reality Pilot" 247).

Nelson's visions of the future differ crucially from Gibson's. In 52 Xanadu we find not consensual illusion but genuine, negotiated consensus. The pathways and connections among texts would be created on demand. According to Nelson's plans to date, only the most fundamental "back end" conventions would be strictly determined: users would be free to customize "front end" systems to access information more or less as they like. Xanadu thus possesses virtually no "canons" in the sense of a shelf of classics or a book of laws; the canons of Xanadu might come closer to the musical meaning of the word – congeries of connections and relationships that are recognizably orderly yet inexhaustibly various. The shifting networks of consensus and textual demand (or desire) in Xanadu would be constructed by users and for users. Their very multiplicity and promiscuity, one might argue, would militate powerfully against any slide from populitism back toward hierarchy.

Nelson's visionary optimism seems vindicated, then. Xanadu as 53 currently conceived – even in its status as Nelson's scheme to get rich very slowly – opens the door to a true social revolution with implications beyond the world of literature or mass entertainment. Xanadu would remove economic and social gatekeeping functions from the current owners of the means of text production (editors, publishers, managers of conglomerates). It would transfer control of cultural work to a broadly conceived population of culture workers: writers, artists, critics, "independent scholars," autodidacts, "generalists," fans, punks, cranks, hacks, hackers, and other non- or quasi-professionals. "Tomorrow's **hypertext** systems have immense political ramifications, and there are many struggles to come," Nelson warns (*Literary Machines* 3/19). This is an understatement of cosmic proportions.

But it would be a mistake to celebrate cybernetic May Day with- 54 out performing a few reality checks. Along with all those visionary forecasts of "post-hierarchical" information exchange (Zuboff, 399), some hard facts need to be acknowledged. The era of the garage-born computer messiah has passed. Directly or indirectly, most development of hardware and software depends on heavily capitalized multinational companies that do a thriving business with the defense establishment. This affiliation clearly influences the development of new media – consider an influential paper on "The Rhetoric of **Hypertext**" which uses the requirements of a military training system to propose general standards of coherence and instrumental effectiveness for this medium (Carlson, 1990). Technological development does not happen in cyberspace, but in the more familiar universe of postindustrial capital. Thus to the clearheaded, any suggestion that computer technology might be anything but an instrument of this system must seem quixotic – or just plain stupid.

55   Before stepping off into cyberspace, we do well to peel off the futurist headgear and listen to some voices in the street. No one wants to read anymore: "books suck, Nintendo rules." Computers are either imperial business machines or head toys for yuppies. Anyone still interested in "mass" culture needs to check out the yawning gap between the rich and the debtpayers, not to mention the incipient splintering of Euro-America into warring ethnicities and "multicultural" tribes. And while we're at it, we might also do some thinking about our most recent global conflict, wargame-as-video-game with realistic third-world blood, a campaign in defense of economic imbalance and the West's right to determine political order in the Middle East. Perhaps we are using the word "revolution" far too loosely. Given the present state of political and cultural affairs, any vision of a "populite" future, or as John Perry Barlow has it, an "electronic frontier" (see Sterling), needs hard scrutiny. Revolution, as Tommie Lee Jones reminds us, is what you find *in your face.*

56   Do we really want a revolution? Are academic and corporate intellectuals truly prepared to dispense with the current means of text production and the advantages they afford in the present information economy? More to the point, *are we capable* of overturning these institutions, assuming we have the will to do so? Looking back from the seventies, Jean Baudrillard criticized the students of Paris '68 for assuming control of the national broadcast center only to reinstate one-to-many programming and the obscurantist focus of the "media event." The pre-revolutionary identity of television swift-

ly reasserted itself in the midst of radical action. The seizure was a sham, Baudrillard concludes: "Only total revolution, theoretical and practical, can restore the symbolic in the demise of the sign and of value. Even signs must burn" (*Political Economy of the Sign* 163). Xanadu as Nelson imagines it does promise to immolate certain cultural icons: the entrepreneurial publishing house, the codex book, the idea of text as unified, self-contained utterance. Taken to its limits, **hypertext** could reverse/recourse into a general medium of control, a means of ensuring popular franchise in the new order of virtual space. Public-access Xanadu might be the last hope for consensual democracy in an age of global simulation.

Or it might not: we do well to remember that Ted Nelson's vision 57 comes cleverly packaged with assurances that copyright and intellectual property shall not perish from the earth. Some signs would seem to be flame-resistant. The vision of Xanadu as cyberspatial New Jerusalem is conceivable and perhaps eligible, but by no stretch of the imagination is it inevitable. To live in the postmodern condition is to get along without the consolation of providential fictions or theories of historical necessity. This renunciation includes the "Laws of Media," whose force in the final analysis is theoretical and heuristic, not normative. As Linda Hutcheon observes, postmodernism undermines any attempt at binary distinction. To invoke the possibility of a "post-hierarchical" information order, one must assert the fact that all orders are contingent, the product of discursive formations and social contracts. But this postulate generates a fatally recursive paradox: if all order is consensual, then the social consensus may well express itself against revolution and in support of the old order. The term "post-hierarchical" may some day turn out to carry the same nasty irony as the words "postmodern" or "postwar" in the aftermath of Desert Storm: welcome back to the future, same as it ever was.

In the end it is impossible to dismiss Nelson's prophecies of 58 cultural renovation in Xanadu; but it is equally hard to predict their easy fulfillment. Xanadu and the **hypertext** concept in general challenge humanists and information scientists to reconsider fundamental assumptions about the social space of writing. They may in fact open the way to a new textual order and a new politics of knowledge and expression. However, changes of this magnitude cannot come without major upheavals. Responsibility for the evolution of **hypertext** systems as genuine alternatives to the present information economy rests as much with software developers, social scientists, and literary theorists as it does with legislators and capitalists. If anything unites these diverse elites, it might be their allegiance to existing institutions of intellectual authority – the printed word, the book, the library, the university, the publishing house.

59   It may be, as Linda Hutcheon asserts, that though we are incapable of direct opposition to our native conditions, we can still criticize and undermine them through such postmodern strategies as deconstruction, parody, and pastiche (120-21). Secondary literacy might indeed find expression in a perverse turn about or within the primary body of literate culture. But it seems equally possible that our engagement with interactive media will follow the path of reaction, not revolution. The cultural mood at century's end seems anything but radical. Witness President Bush's attacks on cultural diversity (or as he saw it, "political correctness") in higher education. Or consider Camille Paglia's memorable "defense" of polyvalent, postprint ways of knowing, capped off by a bizarre reversal in which she decrees that children of the Tube must be force-fed "the logocentric and Apollonian side of our culture" (Postman and Paglia, 55). Given these signs and symptoms, the prospects for populite renaissance do not seem especially rosy. "It is time for the enlightened repression of the children," Paglia declares. Yet in the face of all this we can still find visionary souls who say they want a textual, social, cultural, intellectual revolution. In the words of Lennon:

> *Well, you know. . .*
> We all want to change your head.

60   The question remains: which heads do the changing, and which get the change

W O R K S C I T E D

Barthes, Roland. "From Work to Text." *Textual Strategies: Readings in Poststructuralist Criticism.* Ed. & trans. Josué Harari. Ithaca, NY: Cornell UP, 1979. 73-81.

Baudrillard, Jean:

For a Critique of the Political Economy of the Sign. Trans. Charles Levin. St. Louis: Telos, 1981.

Simulations. Trans. Paul Foss, Paul Patton, and Philip Beitchman. New York: Semiotext(e), 1983.

Benjamin, Walter. "The Work of Art in the Age of Mechanical Reproduction." *Illuminations.* Ed. Hannah Arendt. Trans. Harry Zohn. New York: Schocken, 1969. 217-52.

Bersani, Leo. "Pynchon, Paranoia, and Literature." *Representations* 25 (1989): 99-118.

Bolter, Jay. *Writing Space: The Computer, Hypertext, and the History of Writing.* Fairlawn, N.J.: Lawrence Erlbaum Associates, 1990.

Bush, Vannevar. "As We May Think." *Atlantic Monthly* (July, 1945): 101-08.

Carlson, Patricia. "The Rhetoric of *Hypertext.*" *Hypermedia* 2(1990): 109-31.

Conklin, Jeffrey. "Hypertext: An Introduction and Survey." *Computer* 20 (1987): 17-41.

Coover, Robert. "The End of Books." *New York Times Book Review,* June 21, 1992. 1 ff.

Deleuze, Gilles and Félix Guattari. *Anti-Oedipus: Capitalism and Schizophrenia.* Trans. Robert Hurley, Mark Seem, Helen R. Lane. Minneapolis: U of Minnesota P, 1977.

Dorfman, Ariel. *The Empire's Old Clothes.* New York: Pantheon, 1983.

Douglas, Jane Yellowlees. "Wandering through the Labyrinth: Encountering Interactive Fiction." *Computers and Composition* 6(1989): 93-103.

Drexler, K. Eric. *Engines of Creation: The Coming Era of Nanotechnology.* New York: Doubleday, 1987.

Eagleton, Terry. "Capitalism, Modernism and Postmodernism." *New Left Review* 152 (1985): 60-73.

Gibson, William. *Neuromancer.* New York: Ace, 1984.

Harpold, Terence. "The Grotesque Corpus: **Hypertext** as Carnival." *What's a*

Critic to Do? Ed. G.P. Landow. Baltimore: Johns Hopkins UP [forthcoming].

Hassan, Ihab. *The Postmodern Turn: Essays in Postmodern Theory and Culture.* Columbus: Ohio State UP, 1987.

Heim, Michael. *Electric Language: a Philosophical Study of Word Processing.* New Haven: Yale UP, 1987.

Hofstadter, Douglas. *Gödel, Escher, Bach: An Eternal Golden Braid.* New York: Basic, 1979.

Horowitz, Irving Louis. *Communicating Ideas: The Crisis of Publishing in a Post-Industrial Society.* New York: Oxford UP, 1986.

Hutcheon, Linda. *A Poetics of Postmodernism: History, Theory, Fiction.* New York: Routledge, 1988.

Jameson, Frederic. "Postmodernism, or, the Cultural Logic of Late Capitalism." *New Left Review* 146(1984): 53-92.

Joyce, Michael. "Siren Shapes: Exploratory and Constructive Hypertexts." *Academic Computing* (November, 1988): 11 ff.

Kernan, Alvin. *The Death of Literature.* New Haven: Yale UP, 1990.

Landow, George. *Hypertext: The Convergence of Contemporary Critical Theory and Technology.* Baltimore: Johns Hopkins UP, 1992.

Lanham, Richard. "The Electronic Word: Literary Study and the Digital Revolution." *New Literary History* 20(1989): 268-89.

Leary, Timothy. "The Cyberpunk: The Individual as Reality Pilot." *Storming the Reality Studio: A Casebook of Cyberpunk and Postmodern Fiction.* Ed. Larry McCaffery. Durham: Duke UP, 1992. 245-58.

Levy, Steven:

Hackers: Heroes of the Computer Revolution. New York: Dell, 1984.

"The End of Literature: Multimedia is Television's Insidious Offspring." *Macworld* (June, 1990): 51+.

"In the Realm of the Censor: The Online Service Prodigy Tells its Users to Shut Up and Shop." *Macworld* (January, 1991): 69+.

Lyotard, Jean François. *The Postmodern Condition: A Report on Knowledge.* Trans. Geoff Bennington and Brian Massumi. Minneapolis: U of Minnesota P, 1984.

McCorduck, Pamela. *The Universal Machine: Confessions of a Technological Optimist.* New York: McGraw-Hill, 1985.

McHoul, Alec and David Wills. *Writing Pynchon: Strategies in Fictional Analysis.* Urbana: U of Illinois P, 1990.

McLuhan, H. Marshall. *Understanding Media: The Extensions of Man.* New York: McGraw-Hill, 1964.

McLuhan, H. Marshall and Eric McLuhan. *Laws of Media: The New Science.* Toronto: U of Toronto P, 1988.

Nelson, Theodor Holm:

Computer Lib/Dream Machines. Redmond, WA: Tempus Books, 1987.

Literary Machines. Sausalito, CA: Mindful, 1990.

"How Hypertext (Un)does the Canon." Paper delivered at the Modern Language Association Convention, Chicago, December 28, 1990.

Ong, Walter. *Orality and Literacy: The Technologizing of the Word.* New York: Methuen, 1982.

Pfeil, Fred. *Another Tale to Tell: Politics and Narrative in Postmodern Culture.* New York: Verso, 1990.

Postman, Neil and Camille Paglia. "She Wants Her TV! He Wants His Book!" *Harper's* 282 (March, 1991): 44 ff.

Prigogine, Ilya and Isabelle Stengers. *Order out of Chaos: Man's New Dialogue with Nature.* New York: Bantam, 1984.

Pynchon, Thomas. *Gravity's Rainbow.* New York: Viking, 1973.

Ross, Andrew. *Strange Weather: Culture, Science, and Technology in the Age of Limits.* New York: Verso, 1991.

Slatin, John. "Reading Hypertext: Order and Coherence in a New Medium." *College English* 52 (1990): 870-83.

Stansberry, Dominic. "Hyperfiction: Beyond the Garden of the Forking Paths." *New Media.* May, 1993. 52-55.

Sterling, Bruce. *The Hacker Crackdown: Law and Disorder on the Electronic Frontier.* New York: Bantam, 1992.

Stoll, Clifford. *The Cuckoo's Egg: Tracking a Spy Through the Maze of Computer Espionage.* New York: Doubleday, 1989.

Zuboff, Shoshana. *In the Age of the Smart Machine: The Future of Work and Power.* New York: Basic, 1988.

POSTMODERN PLEASURE & PERVERSITY

Scientism & Sadism

Paul McCarthy

1

Introduction

This study traces the nature and consequences of the circulation of desire in a postmodern order of things (an order implicitly modelled on a repressed archetype of the new physics' fluid particle flows), and it reveals a complicity between scientism, which underpins the postmodern condition, and the sadism of incessant deconstruction, which heightens the intensity of the pleasure-seeking moment in postmodernism. This complicity raises disturbing questions about the credentials of postmodernism, and it has the dehumanising effect of obscuring the individual and putting an end to praxis. In addition, the unbounded play of difference in this order of things tends to dissolve restraints to sadism and barbarism, giving desire and capital free rein in the fluid play of market signifiers. [1]

The analytical procedures of deconstruction are a key component of postmodern thought: Derrida and Deleuze and Guattari engage structures through breaking them into their component parts. Deconstruction's notion of the "structurality of structure" is grounded in the history of atomising thought which begins with the relations of Dionysus and Apollo, in which desire is contained by the atomistic concept. Deconstruction sets forth a de-centered and unbounded horizon in Derrida: "Différance is the systematic play of differences, of the traces of differences, of the spacing by which elements are related to each other" (1981: 27). Deleuze and Guattari's atomistic "multiplicity" is also evident in Derrida's "irreducible and generative multiplicity" (1981: 45). [2]

The relations of capitalism and atomising thought, particularly as they manifest themselves in science and instrumental reason, are mutually supportive. Horkheimer and Adorno (1972) trace these [3] relations (demonstrated in de Sade's *Juliette*) as a pre-condition for the turn of enlightenment thought into barbarism. Adorno's non-reductive stance refuses to collapse subject and object or "other." This distinguishes his project from deconstruction and postmodernism generally. From this standpoint, atomising thought engenders the free play of desire, signifiers, and capital which characterises postmodernism.

4   The complicity of postmodern form and atomising thought in the commodification of culture and intellect is also suggested by Lefebvre's conditions for the production of space. Lefebvre questions "the multiplicity of these descriptions and sectionings" (1991: 8). The same complicity is also pointed out in Jameson's definition of postmodernism as "the cultural logic of late capitalism" (1984). Here, the accumulation of capital by multinationals is furthered by the discontinuous forms of postmodern architecture. This problem is illustrated by Liggett's distress, in stepping around young men asleep on the sidewalk, in transit to the restored Biltmore in Los Angeles for a planning convention. Liggett attributes the circumstances of the homeless to the "theoretical, administrative and economic 'space' of contemporary urban forms which are organised to facilitate global exchange" (1991: 66).

5   The deconstructing moment of postmodernism molecularises the complex texture of existence into an order conducive to positivist categorisation: culture is rendered into a particle form amenable to numericisation, and, through the device of probability, the random number machine orchestrates difference. The postmodern order of things assumes its own legitimacy, thereby revealing itself as the quasi-transcendental projection of an idealised world view. This view instates a new mysticism and a new form of pleasure-seeking, acted out through the unrestrained dance of capital and desire in the social. The social, in turn, is implicitly conceptualised in terms of atomised, deconstructed elements which constitute a neo-positivist play of particles and desire. The patterns revealed in sketching out these circuits of desire also reveal the turbulent and fateful grounding of a survivalist neo-conservatism which grows within and in reaction to the arbitrariness of the postmodern order of things. Such underpinnings short-circuit the critical force of deconstruction into affirmation.

6   There is reason for concern when unresolved "antinomies of culture" such as "consciousness and experience" are collapsed (Rose,

1984: 212), let alone when the categories of postmodernism recapitulate those of post-structuralism in "commencing from a starting point outside of human experience" (Harland, 1987: 75). In these circumstances, there is wisdom in Priest's "dialethism" (1987), a no- reduction logic of dialectic. This perspective is compatible with Rose's suspension of the history of philosophy and the philosophy of history, each within the other, in order to resist the reduction of the complexities of history to the "unitary and simply progressive" (1984: 3). The reduction of experience to a play of signifiers with such characteristics is dehumanising, as is evident in a postmodernism which fulfills Horkheimer and Adorno's prognosis with the dominance of "the myth of things as they actually are, and finally the identification of intellect and that which is inimical to the spirit" (1972: xii). Rose (1988) seeks a way beyond this. In contrast to Derrida's interpretation of the biblical Babel allegory as a triumphal encounter of humanity with God which opens the "endless labyrinth" that is postmodernism, Rose reads Babel as a point of configuration and of learning in the on-going measure and revision of the limits of human potentialities in encounters with absolute power (1988: 386). Recognising the architectural moment of deconstruction here, Rose warns of "a tendency to replace the concept by the sublimity of the sign, which is, equally, to employ an unexamined conceptuality without the labour of the concept" (1988: 368).

This re-opening of the antinomy of consciousness and experience invites evaluation against predecessors. For example, to what extent is Lukács' (1971) indictment of modernism as fragmenting and dehumanising carried forward in this project? If it is, then how can the cul-de-sac of his tortured attempts to reconcile the absolute and experience be avoided? Heller rejects the ending of the philosophical discourse of "production and collective morality," such as concerned Lukács, in "paradigmatic failure" (1983: 190). Lukács' late desire to start anew does not stem from despair or faith, but arises because "the absolute character of the absolute had been called into question" (Heller, 1983: 190). In continuing to seek an ethics, Lukács embodied "the courage of the critical spirit." An Adornian stance circumvents some aspects of Lukács' impasse in refusing to privilege the proletariat as the bearers of praxis. It also refuses to defer to an absolute, in favour of a contradictory, non-reductive "constellation" of tensions (Jay as cited in Bernstein, 1991: 42). This

stance maintains the "unresolved paradox" of reason as simultaneously a vehicle of emancipation and entrapment – a paradox
which contributes to the contemporary "rage against reason" (Bernstein, 1991: 40). From this vantage point, Adorno anticipates the
escape from reason and the capture of desire in an absolutised
postmodern play of difference.

8   Deleuze and Guattari's (1987) A Thousand Plateaus, presented as
the fully developed form of postmodern thought, will provide a focal
point for this discussion; when weighed against the prototypical
deconstructionism of de Sade, it is arguably more mimetic than
critical. The approach here shapes an immanent critique which dis-
tances the reader from compelled immersion in an all-encompassing
world of signifiers (Harland, 1987). Specifically, tracing the complicities of desire and concept reveals an ontology of postmodernism
and contributes to the broader project of locating postmodernism at the intersections of history, philosophy, science, and global
socio-economic and political formations. This process revives the
subject of praxis and picks up the threads of radical humanism,
admittedly a difficult task in the fragmented theoretical terrain beyond the end of history, structure and Marxism. A non-reductive
stance, in the Adornian sense, also provides points of reference for
tracing lines of desire and opens perspectives from which to evaluate
the "ethical-political" moments (Bernstein, 1991) in a postmodernism which will be regarded as the flux at the cutting edge of modernism, abetting the passage of modernism into culture. In these terms,
the quest for incessant innovation points to the mutually supportive
dynamics of modernism and postmodernism, as Lyotard observes:
"Postmodernism thus understood is not modernism at its end but in
the nascent state, and this state is constant" (1984: 79).

PROBLEMS OF PARTICLES, PLEASURE AND MYSTICISM IN POSTMODERNISM

9   Some postmodern theorists (Baudrillard, 1983; Kroker, 1985; Deleuze and Guattari, 1987; Lyotard, 1988) have recognised the relations between postmodernism and quantum scientism. An explicit
recognition of the appropriation of quantum scientism to cultural
analysis is given by Kroker (1985), who sees postmodernism as the
culmination of the logic of Capital in culture. This appropriation is

flanked by Nietzsche's *The Will to Power* and by Baudrillard's "fetish-ism of the sign" (Kroker, 1985: 69). For Kroker, Baudrillard is "a quantum physicist of the processed world of mass communica-tions," who reinterprets Marx's *Capital* as "the imploded, forward side (the side of nihilism in the value-form of seduction) of Nietz-sche's *The Will to Power*" (Kroker, 1985: 72, 69). The quantum dance of *Capital*, power and the desire which characterises postmodern-ism is fully revealed in Deleuze and Guattari's (1987) *A Thousand Plateaus*. Here, the celebration of the libidinal economy of decon-struction takes the form of a quantum logic of particle flows of desire, and is at the apogee of the trajectory of atomising thought.

Another writer who recognises the influence of the quantum 10 form in social analysis is Lyotard. His prescription of the relativistic clash of genres subsuming the subject reveals the longing for an epistemological fluidity which underpins the postmodern science of language. For Lyotard, "in the matter of language, the revolution of relativity and the quantum theory remains to be made" (1988: 137). The focus of the postmodernists is on contradiction and on tracing the play of difference, and it is here that they are most prone to reach into the quantum archetype to shape their explanations. This tendency is also evident in Foucault's (1972) fluid positivity of the archival field as the principle of the dispersion of statements. In Foucault there are many examples of the seepage of quantum scien-tism into the epistemological void of postmodern thought. Post-modern reason rides quantum logic into culture; the confluence of Nietzschean desire, *Capital*, and quantum logic constitute the re-pressed conceptual field for the postmodern play of signifiers.

An implicit *telos* of desire is at work within Deleuze and Guattari's 11 schema, namely the potential of flows of desire to reach the contin-uous intensities of the "plateau" or "plane of consistency." While these two writers end totalising thought, one can discern in their work a repetition of ideas concerning the relations of unity and difference which emerged with Heraclitus and which were also evi-dent in ancient Hindu and Taoist mythology (Capra, 1976; Postle, 1976). Also, while Deleuze and Guattari appear to suppress the mo-ment of unity and eschew dialectics, implicit ideas of unity and dialectical relations of unity and difference remain in their work. The *telos* of their "plateau" carries forward the desire to submerge self in the streams of molecularised existence which characterise the great

Eastern religions. In *A Thousand Plateaus*, rationality turns back on itself, breaking into pure desire as flows and clashes of particles. In a schizoid sense, desire has been split and projected out into the "plateau"— a term drawn from Gregory Bateson's "continuous regions of intensity constituted in such a way that they do not allow themselves to be interrupted by any external termination, any more than they allow themselves to build towards a climax" (Deleuze and Guattari, 1987: 158). There is a mystical play of forces implicit in postmodernism generally, and the incantations by the gnostics traversing the plateaus of postmodern pleasure are phrased in a fluid positivism, in the form of a scientology.

12   Desire has floated free from the material reality of everyday life, and this is what constitutes the ontology of the particle, and tendentially, the form of the signifier: the postmodernist now acts out, intellectually, the yearning which immersed the body in the flows of desire in the 1960s. Contra physical, corporal, or semiotic interpretations, the abstract machine of Deleuze and Guattari is diagrammatic, "is pure matter-function – a diagram independent of the forms and substances, expressions and contents it will distribute" (1987: 141). It is at the threshold of an assemblage that this diagrammatic genetic circuitry is able to calculate the marginal trade-off of pleasure and pain, doing so in terms and directions which could lead to a change of state: "Exchange is only an appearance: each partner or group assesses the value of the last receivable object (limit-object), and the apparent equivalence desires from that . . . " (Deleuze and Guattari, 1987: 439). In this manner, the calculus of desirability at the threshold draws upon the pleasure-pain preferences of every element of the group, which, at a given point, may change state.

13   We must also consider the location of postmodernists, including the post-structuralist writer, within the bureaucratised intelligentsia which is under considerable threat in the conditions of late capitalism. The move to roll back government expenditure on education, and the resurgence of corporate claims to power, contribute to a sense of heightened anxiety. This anxiety underlies the desire to deconstruct, into their component parts, structures which have failed to provide solutions in the conditions of image capitalism. In addition, there is a sadistic pleasure, one which heightens the sensitivity of the organism, to be had from sublimating anxiety into the deconstruction of some object, or code, into its constituent parti-

cles. The heightened sensitivity and pleasure gained from this deconstructing molecularisation reveals the perverse and narcissistic underside of the postmodernists' absorption in the play with the elements of their own deconstructions. They reduce culture and individuality to a pseudo-difference, in fact more a bland consistency of component parts. In so doing, they feed capital with a flow of particle inputs which are more easily reconstituted to suit the infinitely changing tastes of the market. In this sense the postmodernists, rather than orchestrating genuine difference, pre-digest culture, tradition, and structure, reducing it to a form more palatable to capital.

2

de Sade's Legacy; Postmodern Pleasure and Perversity

The postmodern heightening of sensitivities of pleasure through the perversity of molecularisation as code-breaking is grotesquely prefigured by de Sade's *Juliette*. Simone de Beauvoir questions, "must we burn de Sade? . . . the supreme value of his testimony is that it disturbs us" (cited in de Saint-Yves, 1954: 16). In addition, de Saint-Yves suggests that de Sade reveals the hypocrisy of the social display, a refinery which barely conceals Juliette's gross machinic organising for pleasure (1954: 16). This hypocrisy is now repeated beneath the attractiveness of the social order signified by the global capitalist imaging of desirable social machines within the information networks of global capitalism. The mating of desire, images, and production is electronically sorted on a global scale. The laws and moral conventions, which are postured by and maintain the content of these social machines, themselves provide the codes through which a pleasure is gained in transgression. The postmodernists, as a part of the new class intelligentsia whose status is enmeshed within the legal and moral status quo, experience a doubling of pleasures: firstly, in the benefits of their position, and secondly, in the heightened sensitivity derived from the perversity of code-breaking within their deconstructing discourses.

15   The postmodernists are less likely to speak of the sadistic side of their prescriptions. Yet, tracing the epistemological affinity between de Sade's (1796) *Juliette* and Deleuze and Guattari's (1987) *A Thousand Plateaus* reveals that this inheritance persists. Both are concerned with flows of desire at the molecular level and with heightening intensities. Both parody the social and productive conditions within which they were produced. De Sade's (1796) *Juliette* appeared just before Goethe's (1808) *Faust*, which Berman's (1980) *All That Is Solid Melts Into Air* identifies as embodying the modernist cum-postmodernist spirit. Goethe's *Faust* is also a precursor to Nietzsche's (1887) *On the Genealogy of Morals* and his (1888) *The Will to Power*, expressing the strong man as a code-breaker of the weak principles of Christianity and socialism, and as a manipulative developer. We find this trajectory of indefinite cycles of deconstruction and reconstruction continues through postmodernism to culminate in the inversion of Marx's *Capital* and Nietzsche's "abstract power" in Baudrillard (Kroker, 1985).

16   The postmodern order of things is prefigured in de Sade's "matrix of maleficent molecules" (1968: 400), in which the propensity to rule-breaking and irregularity is natural. Pleasure-seeking in postmodernism may be seen as pain avoidance which both stems from and drives the cycles of desire in the postmodern condition. This calculus is at the basis of an incipiently postmodern reason which, in de Sade, mirrors natural law: "What is reason? The faculty given to me by nature whereby I may dispose myself in a favourable sense toward such-and-such an object and against some other, depending on the amount of pleasure or pain I desire from these objects" (1968: 34).

HEIGHTENING INTENSITIES: THE PLEASURES OF CODE-BREAKING

17   Juliette's machinic organising conjoined sadism and code-breaking to raise the level of excitation of the nervous system, so that the experience of pleasure is heightened in intensity: "There is a certain perversity than which no other nourishment is tastier, drawn thither by nature – if reason's glacial hand waves us back, lust's fingers bear the dish towards us again, and thereafter we can no longer do without the fare" (de Sade, 1968: 11). Thus driven, the unconstrained imagination may wreak havoc and destruction as nature does in

pursuing its ends (de Sade, 1968: 12). This opportunism is evident in Lyotard's (1984) affirmation of what we might see as the polymorphous perversity of the play of Eros, Thanatos, and *Capital* through the electromagnetic dance of the information society in his *Postmodern Condition*. Lyotard concludes that "our fear of the system of signs and thus our investment in it, must still be immense if we continue to seek these positions of purity … what would be interesting would be to stay where we are, but at the same time to seize every opportunity to function as good conductors of intensities" (1984: 311). However, the focus of Lyotard's argument represses the pathology of the postmodern subject, who – as de Sade predicted in *Juliette* – heightens the intensities of pleasure through the sadistic adventures of indefinite deconstruction.

The political claims of deconstruction are repeated when [18] Deleuze and Guattari enlist pleasure-seeking molecularisation to "[overcome] the imperialism of language" (1987: 65). Deleuze and Guattari's logic has its precursor in *Juliette*, in the form of Debene's exhortation to a "voluptuousness which can tolerate no inhibitions": this voluptuousness "attains its zenith only by shattering them all" (de Sade, 1968: 53). The zenith is the excitement of transgressing laws, which, for Juliette, "has a strong impact upon the nervous system." Deleuze and Guattari's molecularising thought crystallises de Sade's deconstructionist lubricity in the intellectual sphere: their social machine is not cast in terms of the Marxist preoccupation with the production of goods, but rather in terms of the "state of the intermingling of bodies in society, including all the attractions and repulsions, sympathies, and antipathies, alterations, amalgamations, penetrations and expansions that affect the bodies of all kinds in their relations" (1987: 89). One consequence of this is the relativising of moral-ethical concerns, since "good and bad are only products of temporary selection which must be renewed" (Deleuze and Guattari, 1987: 10).

Deleuze and Guattari propose the withdrawal to the "Body with- [19] out Organs" as their pleasure dome – "a tantric egg," a condition in which all the attachments of organs to stratified social space have been cut off. It is a matter of pushing desire through to the point of its origins in the body, by intensifying the behaviour to which desire is attached, whether masochistic, sadistic, or paranoid: "Where psychoanalysis says 'stop find yourself again,' we should say instead, 'let's go further still we haven't found our BwO yet, we haven't sufficiently dismantled ourselves'" (Deleuze and Guattari, 1987: 151). The desire to achieve the intensity of the experience of pure desire in the body without organs is evident in Deleuze and Guattari's masochist, who closes off organs:

> The masochist body: it is poorly understood in terms of pain; it is fundamentally a question of the BwO. It has its sadist or whore sew it up; the eyes, anus, urethra, breasts, and nose are sewn shut. It has itself strung up to stop the organs from working, flayed, as if the organs clung to the skin; sodomized, smothered, to make sure everything is sealed tight. (1987: 150)

This scene might have been drawn from one of the many instances of sado-masochism in *Juliette*. It is from such a point that Deleuze and Guattari's masochist must break through to the pleasures of the body without organs, not by exercising caution or holding onto self, but through further experimentation and "dismantling of self" (1987: 151). This pleasure-seeking is unconstrained by remorse, carrying forward Clairwil's prescription that guilt must be overcome by breaking any restraining rules – in fact, by "destroying everything it rests upon" (de Sade, 1968: 396).

20   It is de Sade who kills the God that Nietzsche declares to be dead: de Sade declares that "the impediment presented by religion is the first that ought to be liquidated" (1968: 341). De Sade's transgression of moral codes as a natural outcome of human striving is also a precursor to Goethe's *Faust*. In this work, Gretchen's virtue is violated in natural cycles of desire, deconstruction and development, cycles which are carried forward in Nietzsche's *The Will to Power*. For Kroker, Nietzsche stands at the beginning and end of *Capital*, in a trajectory which spans the thought of Deleuze, Lyotard and the early Barthes: "In this account, *Capital* is disclosed to be a vivid, almost clinical study of the inner workings of modern nihilism" (Kroker, 1985: 69). However, it is in de Sade that we find the prototypical pleasure and perversity of a deconstructing desire acted out in a complicity with capital in the mass culture of postmodernism. Juliette's desire for pleasure, luxury, property and income are furthered by "the most terrible orgies," and her sadistic pleasure-plays are financed in a manner in which capital itself becomes both object and instrument of pleasure-seeking.

It is only recurrent cycles of sadistic deconstruction which break   21
Juliette out of the intoxication resulting from "giving in to every
irregularity" of her senses. Here Juliette's strategies are prototypes
for the image-making and image-breaking binges of the postmodern accumulators, who produce models for emulation by *everyman*.
Juliette's Gods carry forward the coupling of Dionysiac materiality,
eroticism, and spatial intellectualisation in a manner which prefigures the eroticism invested in the figural delineation of postmodern
commodity signifiers. One must go through pleasure to experience
the nature of things:

> *Pleasure is an affection of a person or a subject; it is the only way
> for persons to find themselves. But the question is precisely wheth-
> er it is necessary to find oneself . . . It is a question of making a body
> without organs upon which intensities pass, self and other – not in
> the name of a higher level of generality or a broader extension, but
> by virtue of singularities that can no longer be said to be person-
> al, and intensities that can no longer be said to be extensive.*
> (Deleuze and Guattari, 1987: 156)

In *Juliette*, also, pleasure is the pathway to the life principle: "a   22
consuming and delicious conflagration will glide into your nerves, it
will make boil the electrically charged liquor in which your life principle has its seat" (de Sade, 1968: 19). The play of irregularity and
pleasure is the natural order of things: "As soon as you have discovered the way to seize nature, insatiable in her demands upon you she
will lead you step by step from irregularity to irregularity" (de Sade,
1968: 19). This allure of the immersion in irregularity re-surfaces in
Foucault's (1972) archaeology, Derrida's (1973) difference, Lyotard's
(1984) agonistics, and in Deleuze and Guattari's (1987) plateau.

POSTMODERN SADISM

There is a long trajectory of that desire which circulates through   23
sadistic activities, a manipulation of the Fates in the interest of
group survival and pleasurable existence. This trajectory is observ-
able in *Dionysus* and in *Juliette*. It also manifests itself in postmodernism, but is concealed beneath the pleasures of the pursuit of difference. The channels through which desire flows into sadism, and the

mutually supportive relations of this desire with anality, require some examination as a moment in the understanding of the pleasures and perversities of postmodernism. De Sade's legacy may be discerned in the writing of Deleuze and Guattari (1987), and in postmodernism generally.

24 *Juliette* is a precursor to Nietzsche's *Superman*. In *Juliette*, the heightening of the intensities of the perversity and pleasure arising from the mimesis of nature's propensity to self-destruction is rampant. However, a problem which is a source of sadistic pleasure in de Sade, and which is glossed over in postmodernism, is that the adverse consequences of unrestrained pleasure-seeking fall more heavily on the weaker sections of the society. This is of particular concern in the coupling of postmodernism and neo-conservatism:

> *The stronger . . . by despoiling the weaker, that is to say by enjoying all the rights which he has received from nature, by giving himself every possible license, enjoys himself more or less in proportion to that license. The more atrocious the harm he does the weaker, the more voluptuous the thrill he gives himself.* (de Sade, 1968: 119)

The problem with the mimesis of natural strength is that it, of necessity, is cast in terms of an unconstrained destructiveness. Likewise, the postmodern desire to deconstruct sublimates the anxiety of existence into strong solutions which carry forward both Faust's and Juliette's sadistic pleasure-seeking at the expense of the weak. With respect to tendencies to neo-conservatism within postmodernism, we might consider the pleasures inherent in policies of deregulation and restructuring: there is a perverse thrill, legitimated by nature, to be gained from tough solutions which sadistically degrade conditions of the poorer sections of society. In postmodernism, as in de Sade, there is little concern for the cruelty or terror inflicted upon particular individuals or groups: "When the law of nature requires an upheaval, does nature fret over what will be undone in its course?" (de Sade, 1968: 121).

25 *Juliette*'s natural order anticipates the free flowing, unbounded play of assemblages later found in Deleuze and Guattari:

> *The perpetual movement of matter explains everything: The universe is an assemblage of unlike entities which act and react mutually and successively with and against each other; I discern no start,*

no finish no fixed boundaries, this universe I see only as an incessant
passing from one state into another, and within it only particular
beings which forever change shape and form. (de Sade, 1968: 43)

This indefinite atomism is carried forward into both Foucault's and
Derrida's difference, and it culminates in Deleuze and Guattari's rhi-
zomic multiplicities:

A multiplicity is neither subject or object, only determinations,
magnitudes and dimensions that cannot increase in number with-
out the multiplicity changing in state . . . An assemblage is precisely
this increase in the dimensions of a multiplicity that necessarily
changes in nature as it expands its connections. (Deleuze and
Guattari, 1987: 8)

It is into these flows of a natural order of difference that both de
Sade's and Deleuze and Guattari's subject dissolves itself. In both
cases, it is a mimesis which seeks satisfaction at the cost of losing
the memories, desires, and the mind of the subject, which – collectively with other subjects – could contain the propensity to sadism.

The sadisms which may be unleashed in Deleuze and Guattari's   26
(1987) unrestrained flight to pleasure lie repressed in the crevices
beneath their plateaus. It is into their black holes that is consigned
the repressed anality of the polymorphously perverse stage, which,
I have argued, is latent in the desire for deconstructing play with
the objects of postmodern existence. In their schizo-analytical
re-interpretation of Freud's wolf-man, Deleuze and Guattari argue
against phallocentrism, the father, and castration as key analytical
criteria. They interpret the wolf-man by projecting anality into multiplicity delineated as the quantum dynamics of swarming particles
and black holes. "Who could ever believe that the anal machine
bears no relation to the wolf machine . . . a field of anuses just like a
pack of wolves . . . lines of flight or deterritorialisation, becoming-
inhuman, deterritorialised intensities: that is what multiplicity is . . . a
wolf is a hole, they are both particles of the unconscious" (Deleuze
and Guattari, 1987: 32).

The relations of anality, pleasure, and sadism might be better   27
grasped by recovering the subject-object dialectics of the polymorphously perverse stage within capitalism: however, the implications
of this anality remain unexamined when Deleuze and Guattari escape

the pain of everyday postmodern existence by projecting it out onto the heights of the continuous pleasure of the plateau. Thereupon, the dissolution of self into the neo-Platonism of the perfect form of the pure multiplicity of particles is completed. This is the essence of molecularising thought, and it is driven by sublimating a latent anality which relentlessly and sadistically renders wholes into their molecular elements as objects of play. The Platonism of this process in molecularising thought carries forward the "vision of the human body as excremental" (Brown, 1977: 295). It is through this moment of atomising thought that we may uncover the suppressed anality of the postmodern character, the precursor to which is Freud's 1908 essay, "Character and Anal Erotism." The traits of the anal character – orderliness, parsimony, and obstinacy – are sublimated into desires to control as the delineations of postmodern signification. The movement is both controlling and pleasure-seeking, and the postmodern desire to immerse self in the play of images acts out the desire to play in the objects one has created. This latent anality at the individual level is in mutually reinforcing relations with a disorganised capitalism, within which the phallus still dominates social expression. Hocquenghem (1987: 24) says of this that "the anus is over invested individually because its investment is withdrawn socially."

28   While in Deleuze and Guattari anality is projected into the pleasure and covert sadism of the plane of consistency, in de Sade it is unmasked and brought into direct experience as an aperture through which self may be sado-masochistically dissolved into the natural pleasures of the incessant transgression of the order of things. Saint-Frond's instruction of Juliette in the pleasures of sadistic code-breaking are legitimatised by nature's own processes. There is an on-going play of anal pleasure and sadism in *Juliette*: Juliette relates that he "kissed me and ran his hand down my behind, into which he promptly popped a finger" (de Sade, 1968: 235). Commonly, the intensity of the pleasures of Juliette's orgies is heightened by the acting out of sadistic anality (de Sade, 1968: 266). Juliette's deconstruction of sexual codes knows no bounds: her unconstrained lust abases more noble concerns and is demanding and militant in its tyrannical perversion of beauty, virtue, innocence, candour and misfortune (de Sade, 1968: 270). Postmodernism's own polymorphous perversity is acted out by playing in the mess of deconstruction, but the memory of how the subject was drawn into this mess remains repressed.

POSTMODERNISM: PLEASURE AND PERVERSITY FOR EVERYMAN

Bourdieu finds that the impetus for code-breaking has devolved to a   29
growing *petite bourgeoisie* who further the processes of accumulation, dealing in information in a manner which was once reserved for
privileged groups:

> In the name of the fight against "taboos" and the liquidation of
> "complexes" they adopt the most external and easily borrowed
> aspects of the intellectual life style, liberated manners, cosmetic or
> sartorial outrages, emancipated poses and postures and system-
> atically apply the cultivated disposition to not yet legitimate cul-
> ture (cinema, strip cartoons, the underground), to every day life
> (street art), the personal sphere (sexuality, cosmetics, child-
> rearing, leisure) and the existential (the relation to nature, love
> and death). (Bourdieu, 1984: 370)

These cycles of code-breaking are driven by a desire to emulate
higher status groups. The style and opinion leaders of the new *petite
bourgeoisie* perpetuate the play of difference inherent in commodity
signs, deconstructing tradition and high culture into everyday life
and increasing the possibilities for the attachment of capital and
desire. From beneath the veneer of an attractive style, sadism is
projected out elsewhere. For example, it is projected into the Third
World as life-threatening methods of production, as the disruption
of communities, and as the practice of using torture to maintain the
system of power and control. It is also projected into the psyches
of the postmodern worker and consumer, wherein the anxieties of
maintaining position in the play of commodity signifiers, and in the
hierarchies of symbolic accumulation, are aggravated.

The pleasurable and terroristic nature of postmodern consumer   30
society can be discerned as two sides of the same coin. Firstly, the
writing of lifestyle ideals in consumer consciousness terrorises the
masses into appropriate consumption and productive behaviours.
Secondly, as Baudrillard has argued, the immersion of the masses in
symbolic exchange sets in train a terroristic reaction to the simulacra
which will lead the system of simulations to collapse in on itself:

> The system's own logic turns into the best weapon against it. The
> only strategy of opposition to a hyperrealist system is pata-
> physical, a "science of imaginary solutions," in other words a

> *science fiction about the system returning to destroy itself at the extreme limit of simulation, a reversible simulation in a hyperlogic of destruction and death.* (Baudrillard, 1984: 58-9)

Postmodernism promises the masses a veritable orgy of code-breaking in the play of signifiers. It completes the devolution of the pleasures of code-breaking through de Sade's aristocracy to the elites of Marx and Weber, and to Bourdieu's higher status groups, intellectuals and the new *petite bourgeoisie* to everyman. The postmodern allure is that everyman may experience the pleasure and sadism of code-breaking, at the level of bodily molecular excitation, by dissolving self in the play of commodity signifiers.

BEYOND JUSTICE: EVERYMAN A DECONSTRUCTIONIST

31   One consequence of postmodernism associated with the dissolution of self into the pleasures and perversities of an unfettered play of difference is the end of meaningful discourse concerning justice and human agency. Justice is relativised in the language games of postmodernism. For example, Lyotard argues that we must arrive at an idea of justice that is not linked to that of consensus (1984: 66). In postmodernism, desire wells up in the sphere of language and is the exotic force driving the play of difference: "a move can be made for the sheer pleasure of its invention" (Lyotard: 1984: 10). De Sade prefigures this abasement of justice to desire, pointing to the universal motion of justice evident in nature by arguing that justice is relative and that it is natural to heighten the intensity of pleasure by breaking its codes.

32   This relativising of justice de-sublimates the modernists' desire for equality, liberty, and happiness for all into contingencies subject to the play of market fates. The consequence is an abdication of any containing ethical discourse in favor of the play of difference among signifiers: this means that anything is possible as the molecularities of desire and production pursue one another in a dance which tramples the less powerful, less involved bystanders. The Faustian cycles of eternal deconstruction and reconstruction work their way through Nietzsche into a postmodern will to signify, a will which carries the developer's ethic into cultural and intellectual processes. De Sade

provides an earlier illustration of the relations of desire fixated in deconstruction, an illustration which is also repeated in Nietzsche's incipient postmodernism. De Sade reveals the hypocritical and pitiless side of this complex, characteristics further revealed in the complicity of postmodernism and neo-conservatism. There is nothing to constrain the terrorisation, or elimination, of those who stand in the way of a natural flow of desires into cycles of indefinite change:

> One of the basic laws of nature is that nothing superfluous subsists in the world. You may be sure of it, not only does the shiftless beggar, always a nuisance, consume part of what the industrious man produces, which is already a serious matter, but will quickly become dangerous the moment you suspend your dole to him. My desire is that instead of bestowing a groat upon these misfortunates we concentrate our efforts upon wiping them out. (de Sade, 1968: 726)

De Sade prefigures the contemporary conflation of desire, rationality and market naturalism, which I have argued become mutually supportive within postmodern logic. This is acted out when *everyman* may have the pleasure of Faustian deconstruction and development in postmodernism. Again, de Sade expresses in advance the naturalism which is to surface in postmodernism as a rejection of the idea of generalised rules: "No man has the right to repress in him what Nature put there . . . A universal glaive of justice is of no purpose" (1968: 732). De Sade's prototypical natural order of difference carries forward that of Heraclitus and its ideal type is realised in Derrida's epistemology of difference. This epistemology instates the clash of signifiers as the self-driving force of language:

> In a language, in the system of language these are only differences . . . what is written as difference, then, will be the playing movement that "produces" – by means of something that is not simply an activity – these differences, these effects of difference. (Derrida, 1982: 11)

Derrida's naturalism here opens language to a Darwinism in which there is nothing to contain the slide into de Sade's "perpetual outpouring of conflict, injury and aggression" (1968: 733). For Lyotard also, "to speak is to fight, in the sense of playing, and speech acts fall within the domains of a general agonistics" (1984: 10). The post-

33

modern hope is that unconstrained difference will break through to a liberalist ethics of equal opportunity for participation in language games. The corresponding promise is that this equality of participation will alleviate the condition of those who are victimised by the social structure: Lyotard's agonistic language games protect against "piracy" by breaking the rules (1984: 7). For postmodernism, the act of deconstructing the law and social codes is held to undermine the propensity to despotism (1968: 735); however, there is nothing to constrain the slide into terrorism. De Sade's unconstrained anarchism is the precursor to this play of postmodern difference, and reveals its propensity to turn into terror against the weaker sections of society. For de Sade, "give us anarchy and we will have these victims the less" (1968: 733).

34   The neurology of de Sade's propensity to the heightened intensity of law-breaking prefigures Deleuze and Guattari's analysis of desire at the molecular level: "Foreign objects act in a forceful manner upon our organs, if they penetrate them violently, if they stir into brisk motion the neural fluid particles which circulate in the hollow of our nerves, then our sensibility is such as to dispose us to vice" (de Sade, 1968: 278). It is in atrocity that the highest intensity from this code-breaking is achieved. Within de Sade's technics of heightening the intensity of pleasure, doing good is useless. De Sade's language is carried forward in Deleuze and Guattari's studies of the particle flows of intensities; here, by implication, arguments concerning the good are dissolved in particle flows. Heightened intensity is achieved to the extent that particles of desire can crash through striated (coded) space to the libertinage of the plateau (Deleuze and Guattari, 1987: 507). However, the consignment of justice to a space beyond the subjective and collective relations of concern for others leaves a state of lawlessness in which no individual or subgroup is safe.

3

Particle Thought and the End of the Subject

The trajectory of social thought which reduces the complex texture 35
of existence to molecules, or to particles, reaches its fully developed
form in Deleuze and Guattari's writing. Their concepts reveal that the
epistemology of difference, which underpins postmodernism, rests
on a cultural scientism. Furthermore, Lyotard proposes modelling
social relations in terms of quantum theory, since "research centred
on singularities and 'incommensurables' is applicable to the pragmatics of most everyday problems" (1984: 60). These models provide prospects for Lyotard to realise the quantum revolution within
language. Lyotard would then be able to explain the logic of the
clashes and discontinuities, in his study of the agonistics of discourse, in terms of the probabilistic positivism applicable to this
model. There is a problem for the subject in this view, since the
subject is overawed by, and precariously existing in, an unfathomable
cosmic flux of energies. I propose to trace the trajectory of this view
and to evaluate it by directing Simone Weil's critique of quantum
theory at the manifestation of this form within postmodernism.

The trajectory of probabilistic positivism begins with Heraclitus, 36
and continues through Nietzsche's universe as a "monster of energies without beginning, without end – a play of forces, a wave of
forces" (1968: 550). It is the base matter of classical scientism, revit-
alised in a fluid positivism by the quantum theorists, and emerging
as the repressed archetype for the postmodern play of difference as
a quantum scientism of signifiers. We find that this trajectory culminates in Deleuze and Guattari's *A Thousand Plateaus*, which imports
quantum modelling of particle movement into social theory. This

importation tends to gloss over problems in relation to knowledge which remain to be resolved.

37   Simone Weil's (1968) *Reflections on Quantum Theory* is instructive in revealing the manner in which quantum theory furthers an episte-mology of particle plays which ends human concerns. We might reasonably depict these concerns as those that derive from the modernist catch cry of equality, liberty and fraternity. Weil's critique usefully informs this evaluation of the form of postmodern thought. Weil perceives a crisis in twentieth-century physics which we may also discern in the social physics of postmodernism in general, and in Deleuze and Guattari's work in particular. Weil argues that scien-tism must not eliminate the concerns of "human destiny" and "hu-man truth" from culture or intellectual pursuits (1968: vii). She criti-cises the ending of human truth in the seeking of scientific truth: "utility at once takes its place . . . utility becomes something which the intelligence is no longer entitled to define or judge, but only to serve" (Weil, 1968: ix).

38   In Deleuze and Guattari (1987) we find that there is a utility of particle flows to understanding, but that it is a utility which decon-structs ideas of "human destiny" into a dynamic atomism. It is a dead atomism devoid of a humanising moment. Their world of particles recapitulates the trajectory of the ancient Greek atomism, through to the atoms of modern physics, from which Cornforth (1912) claims that the concerns of human life have passed. Deleuze and Guattari reduce a humanised utility and pleasure-seeking from activities sub-ject to human thought and wisdom to a universal and autonomous pleasure-seeking which is diagrammatically programmed into a uni-versal field of particle flows.

39   Quantum theory reflected the re-emergence of an over-riding concern with the discontinuous in science. Weil (1968: 5) criticises this tendency, stating that "the human mind cannot make do with number alone or with continuity alone; it oscillates between the two." The potential to think in terms of both number and space is instated as a necessary *a priori* of comprehension. In this sense Weil carries forward the paraconsistent logic of Heraclitean unity and difference. It is the loss of the sense of spatial unity in the reduction to the discontinuity of atoms and quanta that has led to a loss of meaning. Here, Weil expresses a similar observation to that of Corn-forth (1912), who claims that the atomism of physics carries forward

the spatial rationalisation entailed in the naming of the Olympian Gods. However, with the vanishing of the Gods from Mount Olympus and the diminution of their influence in everyday life, a space opened in which the secularised, dead particles of physics were constructed. The concerns of human life, which had maintained their vitality through projection into the Olympian Gods, now pass out of the conceptualisation of the nature of things, leaving the dead matter of atomism.

Weil argues that scientists between the Renaissance and the end   40 of the nineteenth century carried on their experiments within the context of a broader attempt to establish the relations of people and the universe. Their anthropo-mytho-materio framework for this was Promethean. People had been cursed to act out desires through work. Causality was grasped in terms of "intermediate stages analogous to those traversed by a man executing a simple manual labour" (Weil, 1968: 6). These relations of work were further reduced to the universal formulae of energy, effectively dehumanising relations of distance and force (or mass and velocity), relations which hitherto had been grasped in terms of the human work required to move weight. Furthermore, the experience of the consequences of directional time was added in terms of the concept of entropy, expressed algebraically.

Coupled with necessity, these ideas reduced human nature (in-   41 cluding relations of desires hopes, fears, becoming and the good) to something determined within the constellation of energies and atoms of the universe. The cost is a world deprived of human meanings: "It tries to read behind all appearances that inexorable necessity which makes the world a place in which we do not count, a place of work, a place indifferent to desire, to aspirations and the good" (Weil, 1968: 10). In these terms, classical science contained a vital flaw which would lead to its demise, namely the gap between human thought (including wisdom) and an infinitely accumulating array of facts. Human beings are more than particles of matter condemned to work. They are able to imagine, construct becomings, and experience the good and the beautiful. The reduction of language to scientism ends this aspect of human existence, one which "can, perhaps, only be expressed in the language of myth, poetry and image, the images consisting not only in words but also in objects and actions" (Weil, 1968: 13).

42   The spatio-temporal relations of desire and action are also dehu-
manised in the transition from Greek to modern science in a manner
which we shall see has been carried into postmodern cultural scientism. Weil sees in ancient Greek science the foundations of classical
science. Classical science is cast in terms of a tendency to equilibrium, an equilibrium which encompasses the relations of injustice and
justice, and ideas of beauty such as expressed in Greek art (Weil,
1968: 15). However, these humanising relations are lost in classical
science. The desire of Greek science is "to contemplate in sensible
phenomena an image of the good" (Weil, 1968: 21). Classical science
takes as its model for representing the world the relation between a
desire and the conditions for its fulfillment. However, it suppresses
the first term of the relation (Weil, 1968: 15). The linear motion of
classical science encapsulates desire as an acting out of "desires to
go somewhere" (Weil, 1968: 26).

43   One might also discern an early expression of this travelling motion in Homer: Odysseus' restless adventuring now continues its
trajectory through modern physics to culminate in the spatial explorations of the postmodernists. The postmodern reduction of distance, space and desire into the image as commodity signifier reproduces Odysseus' adventuring through mass travel – in a manner
which involves an unending hopping from one simulation of culture
and history to the next – and one in which desire goes nowhere
really positive but around in a circle to return repression to itself.
Horkheimer and Adorno's (1972) reading of Odysseus as an arche-
typal bourgeois character fits with Weil's modernist (1968: 16). Both
act out desires "to go somewhere, for example, or to seize or hit
something or somebody, and upon distance which is a condition
inherent in every desire of a creature subjected to time." This incessant journeying prefigures the postmodernists' spatial traversing
and subdividing of the activities of everyday life into a kaleidoscopic
symbolic field. However, aesthetical and ethical considerations are
suppressed in this acting out of classical scientific perceptions. It is
in Weil's reference to an earlier image of the Manichaeans that the
tendency to fragmentation now carried forward by the postmodernists is most visible.

44   Weil's Manichaeans saw the fragmentation of the spirit through
its attachment to the necessities of time and space. We may also
recall the crises of Odysseus' adventuring in these terms. Both Od-

ysseus' experiences and those seen by the Manichaeans prefigure the postmodern condition as one in which character is fragmented in spatial delineation driven by the temporality of a play of difference. Weil is prescient to the postmodern split, conceiving of character as split between desires and aspiration. Any sense of having found oneself is continually undermined as the past is lost. The feelings arising therefrom are repeated in postmodern nihilism.

> *What he is at any single moment is nothing; what he has been and what he will be do not exist; and the extended world is made up of everything that escapes him, since he is confined to one point, like a chained prisoner, and cannot be anywhere except at the price of time and effort and of abandoning the point he started from. Pleasure rivets him to his place of confinement and to the present moment, which nevertheless he cannot detain; desire attaches him to the coming moment and makes the whole world vanish for the sake of a single object; and pain is always for him the sense of his being torn and scattered through the succession of moments and places.* (Weil, 1968: 16,17)

This splitting of the psychic space of the subject is also expressed 45 by Lacan in that the signifier is the death of the subject:

> *Hence the division of the subject — when the subject appears somewhere as meaning, he is manifested elsewhere as "fading," as disappearance. There is, then, one might say a matter of life and death between the unary signifier and the subject, qua binary signifier, cause of his disappearance.* (Lacan, 1968: 218)

These terms are also applicable to the source of the anxiety of postmodern existence which arises from the dissolution of self into the world of signifiers. The context of postmodern existence is given its dynamic ontological structure by the new physics. The new physics is the atomism of classical science dissolved into transitory particles which emanate from underlying fields. This form provides a natural scientific legitimation for a postmodern existence remarkable for its fragmentary and transitory nature. In addition, it stylistically underpins the electrodynamics of the global image-making systems which channel postmodern desire. This is the context for the pain of postmodern existence manifested by the postmodern split. The splitting or play of difference within character acts in sympathy with a play of difference in an everyday life. What is remarkable here is the predominant preoccupation with the pursuit of difference as distinction, measured in terms of signifying fashions.

46   In this ongoing deconstruction and reconstruction of self, elements are continually shed and replaced with new signifiers. However, something is gained only at the expense of something lost, and as repeated failures of satisfaction are experienced, the feeling of the tragedy of deconstruction grows. In its psychotic mode, the postmodern split manifests a masochistic self-deconstruction, on the one hand, and a sadistic rending of culture into its elemental particles, on the other. This postmodern desire to reduce things to their elemental particles carries the quantum hypothesis into culture as a stylistic legitimating form, and we shall see that it also imports a loss of the connection of humanity and materiality.

47   The dehumanising loss in the quantum hypotheses is the loss of "analogy between the laws of nature and the conditions of work" (Weil, 1968: 22). The work of the human being to move a weight over distance is represented in terms of the mechanical devices of classical science (mechanical man). In contrast, quantum conceptions (for example, Planck's) subsume discontinuous mechano-humanism under the continuity of formulae which express the product of number and a constant (Weil, 1968: 23). Weil's conception of the spatial continuity implied by such formulae belies the apparent discontinuity of quantum particles. This spatial continuity is the underlying unity of the field. In an equivalent form, Foucault's (1972) "archive" functions as a field which emanates difference. In Deleuze and Guattari's social physics, this is the same unity as the suppressed term of the relations of pure discontinuity, and in postmodernism generally it is the suppressed unity of spatial continuity which underlies the plays of difference.

48   The postmodern idea of infinite difference rests on an unbounded continuity of space within which there is no limit to figural divisions. Deleuze and Guattari's (1987) idealisation or telic destiny of this is the "plateau" or "plane of consistency." However, such a schema dissolves humanity itself, and with it, human meaning. On the social plane, Deleuze and Guattari repeat the formulations of physics which move outside human thought into pure algebra. The problem, to Weil, is that algebra is "a language with this peculiarity, it means nothing" (Weil, 1968: 24). In this manner, the conditions of

human existence are reduced to the algebraic relations of dead atoms out of which the concerns of human life have passed, thus realising the condition foreseen by Cornforth (1912). The idea of human agency is lost in the traversing of continuous space which mindlessly emanates difference.

The discontinuities of quantum physics are grasped at the micro 49 level through the linking of atomism, chance, and probability. Weil warns that the idea of chance at the micro level does not end spatio-temporal necessity, since the same macro-structures, for example, the distribution of thousands of throws of dice, are carried forward – by necessity (1968: 24). The same argument may be used to question the postmodernists, in general, and Deleuze and Guattari's ending of concern with totalities. From this perspective, we may question Deleuze and Guattari's social physics in respect of its concern with plays of difference at the particle level. The characteristic postmodern indulgence in chance ends structural necessity in favour of the idea of a random number machine which authorises infinite spatial multiplicity.

In problematising this, consider the manner in which modern 50 physics reduced the concerns of energy, particles, entropy, and continuity to the discontinuous numbers of probability. The algebraic formulae of probability functions overrode paradoxical concerns of human thought: Einstein's paradoxes as expressed in terms of a "velocity which is both infinite and measurable, a time which is assimilated to a fourth dimension of space" (Weil, 1968: 29). Weil proposes investigating ways in which probability can be conceived without reduction to the discontinuity of numbers – for example, through generalised numbers. It is clear that atomising thought is an artifice which suppresses the potential of the human mind to conceive continuity, and with it conceptions of destiny and the good. These are suppressed in favour of the measuring convenience of numbering in science, or its equivalent, signifiers as the cultural atomism of postmodernism.

The same problem exists in the Deleuze and Guattari's concep- 51 tion of atomistic particle thought. They assign the idea of continuity to the utopian, transcendental space of the "plateau" or "plane of consistency," thus projecting the continuous and the good to Olympian heights above the conditions of human existence. Their flows of particles are a mathesis and their molecularising thought is one to which human experience is not reducible. Weil remarks that "Physics is essentially the application of mathematics to nature at the price of an infinite error" (1968: 34). And Deleuze and Guattari's social physics carries forward the same error – the discontinuous particle experience is not the universal experience. It is a product of individual human minds, a product which is shared, not a producer of human minds. In addition, Lyotard also carries forward this error in his dehumanising relativism. He discusses "genres of discourse" as "strategies . . . of no-one." He also characterises conflict as autonomous, "not between humans or between any other entities," but rather the as product of "phrases" (Lyotard, 1988: 137).

52   Deleuze and Guattari's conceptualisations are perhaps best grasped as an attempt by the postmodern mind to locate itself in a changing terrain, but a terrain which instates the hypotheses of quantum physics in culture as a repressed absolute governing human existence. However, it is apparent that this view raises problems for cultural analysis, problems which remain to be examined. Both the human potential to imagine the Olympian Gods and the form of the existence of the particle contain the infinite error of assuming the pre-eminence of these products of imagination over the conditions of human existence:

> The grace which permits wretched mortals to think
> and imagine and effectively apply geometry, and to
> conceive at the same time that God is a perpetual
> geometer, the grace which goes with the stars and
> with dances, play and work is a marvelous thing; but
> it is not more marvelous than the very existence of
> man, for it is a condition of it. (Weil, 1968: 41)

53   The infinite error carried forward in postmodern thought is that of regarding the play of difference as a universal and a valid resolution of the twentieth century's contradictions: the discontinuities of difference with the continuities of infinite space, time and desire. This error arises from the belief in interminable deconstruction and its counterpart in capitalising the unending possibilities of attaching desires to an infinite array of consumption images. It does not end the modernist project but updates it by substituting the more dynamic particle plays of quantum physics for nineteenth-century atomism. The instating of the principles of quantum physics in social

thought provides a more reactive reagent for the furthering of modernist concerns:

> The nineteenth century, that century which believed in unlimited progress, and believed that men would grow richer and richer, and that constantly renovated techniques would enable them to get more and more pleasure while working less and less, and that education would make them more and more rational and that public morals in all countries would grow more and more democratic, believed that his domain of physics was the whole universe. The goods to which the nineteenth century attached were precious, but not supreme; they were subordinate values but it thought it saw infinity in them. (Weil, 1968: 42)

This prognosis of the nineteenth century is applicable to our so-called postmodern era. We observe postmodern thought investing human hopes and desires into a universe which is an infinity of signified differences at the level of culture and consumption. However, the idea, implicit in postmodernism, that desire can be infinitely attached to the play of signifiers, is neither supreme nor sublime.

POSTMODERN NEO-POSITIVISM, OR THE SIGNIFIER AS NUMBER

The culmination of the logic of the postmodern world of signifiers is in the neo-positivism of Deleuze and Guattari's "numbering" within "nomad space." "Nomad space" is conceived as numerical space and is contrasted with the linear space of primitive society and the territorial striations of State society. While the State numericises its striations, it is in nomad space that the "autonomous arithmetic organisation" of the "numbering number" comes to function: "The number is no longer a means of counting or measuring but of moving: it is the number itself which moves through smooth space" (Deleuze and Guattari, 1987: 389).   54

To reveal the numerics at the underside of the signifier, first let's recapitulate the tendency to fragmentation in postmodern thought. The fully developed form of this is in Deleuze and Guattari's reduction to the particle. This adds a new fluidity to culture and provides more opportunities for desire to attach to capital. Under these circumstances, postmodernism gives modernism entrée to culture. In   55 this sense, Kroker has recognised postmodernism as the culmination of the logic of capital in a culture which is driven by a Nietzschean will to power. We might regard Deleuze and Guattari's reduction of the complex texture of individual and social relations to an essential constitution of rampant particles of desire as a Nietzschean desire for power through deconstruction. In postmodernism, this will to power draws on the fluid epistemology of the quanta of modern physics and uses it to fragment social spaces and structures. The play of particles so formed is one of a cultural positivism, in which the signifier behaves probabilistically in the form of the number. It is at this point of the rendering of culture into its elemental quantum numerics that the social field is most permeable to the passage of capital.

56   Furthermore, within the sense of a dialectical view of history, I have previously argued that the moment of deconstruction or fragmentation is often misconstrued as a permanent condition, unjustifiably freezing dialectic at this point. This fixation on the moment of difference is central to postmodern reason and lies at the confluence of the trajectories of a number of historical tendencies. These trajectories are mutually attractive and intersect to create the space of postmodern reason. They include the global capitalism of the information society, which heightens the intensities of the relations of fear, anxiety, and the pleasure and perversity of infinite deconstruction by abetting their investment in the flux of commodity signifiers.

57   Postmodern reason facilitates the fluidity of these relations by conjoining the propensity to think atomistically with the notion of the random number machine and probability. In effect, it dissolves culture into a quantum epistemology. Here, the fluid, probabilistic, and rapidly appearing and disappearing number, as the concealed form of the signifier – for example in the mathematical coordinates which blueprint the electronic image – becomes the epistemological currency of postmodern thought. This is the order of things driving the postmodern cutting edge of modernism, a postmodern neo-positivism which breaks up culture into the form of a probabilistic mathesis.

58   It is the random number machine of postmodern reason that is the hidden orchestrator of the production of infinite difference as pure multiplicity, in which the signifier is reduced to the form of the self-moving number. The random number machine is revealed at the

seat of that quasi-transcendental force which is self-referential in terms of Deleuze and Guattari's "numbering number" and sets forth its own probabilistic order of things. Desire and capital pursue one another through patterns issuing from the random number machine as it arbitrarily pours forth an infinite array of profiles of the possible relations of desire and commodity signifiers. The random number machine also sets forth lines of escape from the hegemony of state and market relations – for example, into the probabilities that reactive numbers will coalesce in reaction against the dominant order. Deleuze and Guattari's "numbering numbers" escape from their state organisation into "autonomous arithmetic" (1987: 389). In the death knell of praxis and the subject, "the number is no longer a means of counting or of moving: it is the number itself which moves through smooth space" (Deleuze and Guattari, 1987: 389). The culmination of the logic of postmodernism, then, is in the play of signifiers, the essential constitution of which is a play of numbers: in other words, the fluid neo-positivism of signifiers is a play of difference among "numbering numbers."

The desire to systematise the play of difference into a fluid   59
positivism is also apparent in the positivity of Foucault's (1972) statement. In addition, Lacan (1968) attempts to geometricise post-structural desire, and one also senses that Lyotard (1984) desires a mathesis as the basis of his agonistic discourse-games. Deleuze and Guattari's reduction of social quanta to particle flows realises the *telos* of postmodern thought, reducing cultural complexity to signifiers in the form of number-signs. This is also the designation of the subject in postmodernism, an order which abets the depiction of everyday life in terms of the concealed numerical coordinates which make up the electronic flashes of the image machines. A self-proficient and determining neo-positivism thus overtakes human reason.

This order of things is the end of reason – an electronic mating of   60
capital with a Faustian cum-Nietzschean will to deconstruction. The reality of Deleuze and Guattari's escaping social quanta within late capitalism is that they are fearful and greedy multiplicities of desire which do not break free of capital but ride it into the fantasy of pure difference, seeking the pleasure of the "plateau." The will to signify steers and provides the legitimating rationale for the passage of the turbulent leading edge of modernist capital into culture: atomis-

ing postmodern thought breaks up culture into exceedingly fine particles, creating a cosmic soup through which capitalism may re-nourish itself, unconstrained by structure. The particle flows of pleasure-seeking capital and fearful desire mutually attract and interpenetrate, and out of this mutual attraction arises an interminable metamorphosis that is the postmodern condition. While I contend that the reduction of the individual and social space to "numbering numbers" leaves no containing ethico-politico structure to constrain the propensity for terror, Deleuze and Guattari are at pains to disagree: "Horror for horror the numerical organisation of people is no crueler than linear or state organisation" (Deleuze and Guattari, 1987: 390). However, the individual, with an inherent potential for ethical and political praxis, can say no to the madness of the crowd in its elemental form of a swarming numerics of particles of desire.

61   To place this discussion within the broader project of locating postmodernism historically, something has been lost in our focus on the luminescent trajectory of postmodernism since Paris in May, 1968: we have lost sight of the function of postmodernism as that which carries the modernist ethos into culture. This has seriously weakened the critical credentials of postmodernism. However, as this trajectory burns out (Los Angeles in May, 1992, is arguably postmodernism's memorial monument), a re-orientation is called for. Opening up the reductiveness of the signifier to an understanding of the complicities of desire and concept is a step to relocating the individual, as the subject of ethico-politico praxis, within the mutually supportive dynamics of modernity and postmodernity. If the pleasures of deconstruction have perverted the modernist spirit of equality, liberty and fraternity into degrading conditions of existence for the weaker sections of society, then reversing this process entails an awareness of the subject's dissolution, by stages, into signifier, difference, particle-quanta, and finally into that autonomous mathesis of number concealed beneath postmodern figural **P**LAY.

W O R K S C I T E D

Baudrillard, J.:

In the Shadow of Silent Majorities. New York: Semiotext(e), 1983.

"The Structural Law of Value and the Order of Simulacra." In J. Fekete, ed. *The Structural Allegory: Reconstructive Encounters with the New French Thought*. Minneapolis: U of Minnesota P, 1984.

Berman, M. *All That is Solid Melts Into Air*. London: Verso, 1980.

Bernstein, R. *The New Constellation*. Cambridge: Polity, 1991.

Bourdieu, P. *Distinction*. London: Routledge, 1984.

Brown, N. *Life Against Death*. Middletown: Wesleyan UP, 1977.

Capra, F. *The Tao of Physics*. Fontana/Collins, 1976.

Cornforth, M. *From Religion to Philosophy: A Study in the Origins of Western Speculation*. Brighton: Harvester, 1912.

Deleuze, G., and Guattari, F. *A Thousand Plateaus*. Minnesota: U of Minnesota P, 1987.

Derrida, J:

Speech and Phenomena and Other Essays on Husserl's Theory of Signs. Evanston: Northwestern UP, 1973.

"Limited Inc. a b c. . . ." Trans. Samuel Weber. Glyph 2. Baltimore: Johns Hopkins UP, 1977. 162-254.

Positions. Trans. Alan Bass. Chicago: U of Chicago P, 1981.

Margins of Philosophy. Trans. Alan Bass. Chicago: U of Chicago P, 1982.

Sade, marquis de. *Juliette*. Trans. Austryn Warinhouse. New York: Grove, 1968.

Saint-Yves, de L. *Selected Writings of de Sade*. New York: British Book Centre, 1954.

Foucault, M. *The Archaeology of Knowledge*. London: Tavistock, 1972.

Harland, R. *Superstructuralism*. London: Methuen, 1987.

Heller, A. "Lukács' Later Philosophy." In A. Heller, ed. *Lukács Revalued*. Oxford: Blackwell, 1983.

Hocquenghem, G. *Homosexual Desire*. London: Allison and Busby, 1978.

Horkheimer, M., and Adorno, T. *Dialectic of Enlightenment*. New York: Seabury, 1972.

Kroker, A. "Baudrillard's Marx." *Theory, Culture and Society* 2.3 (1985): 69-84.

Lacan, J. *The Four Fundamental Concepts of Psychoanalysis*. Trans. Alan Sheridan. New York: Norton, 1968.

Lefebvre, H. *The Production of Space*. Trans. D. Nicholson-Smith. Oxford: Blackwell, 1991.

Liggett, H. "The Theory/Practice Split." In D. Crow, ed. *Philosophical Streets*. Washington: Maisonneuve, 1990.

Lukács, G. *History and Class Consciousness*. London: Merlin, 1971.

Lyotard, J-F:

The Postmodern Condition. Minneapolis: U of Minnesota P, 1984.

The Differend: Phrases in Dispute. Minneapolis: U of Minnesota P, 1988.

Nietzsche, F. *The Will to Power*. Trans. W. Kaufmann and R.J. Hollingdale. New York: Viking, 1968.

Postle, D. *The Fabric of the Universe*. London: Macmillan, 1976.

Priest, G. *In Contradiction*. Dordrect: Martinus Nijhoff, 1987.

Rose, G:

Dialectic of Nihilism: Post-Structuralism and the Law. Oxford: Blackwell, 1984.

"The Postmodern Complicity." *Theory, Culture and Society* 2-3, (1988): 357-371.

Weil, S. *On Science, Necessity and Love of God*. Trans. and ed. Richard Rees. London: Oxford UP, 1968.

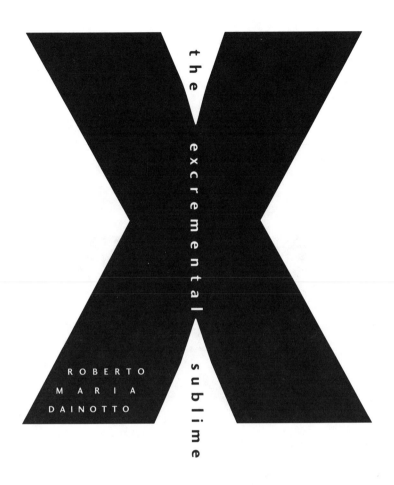

the excremental sublime

ROBERTO
MARIA
DAINOTTO

the postmodern literature of blockage   and   re-
l   e   a   s   e

Once a famous Hellenic philosopher, [Aesop's] master in the dark days of his enslaved youth, had asked him why it was, when we shat, we so often turned around to examine our own turds, and he'd told that great sage the story of the king's loose-living son who one day, purging his belly, passed his own wits, inducing a like fear in all men since. "But you don't have to worry, sire," he added, "you've no wit to shit." Well, cost him a beating, but it was worth it, even if it was all a lie. For the real reason we look back of course is to gaze for a moment in awe and wonder at what we've made – it's the closest we ever come to being at one with the gods.

Now what he reads in this analecta of turds is rampant disharmony and anxiety: it's almost suffocating. Boundaries are breaking down: eagles are shitting with serpents, monkeys with dolphins, kites with horses, fleas with crayfish, it's as though there were some mad violent effort here to link the unlinkable, cross impossible abysses. And there's some dejecta he's not sure he even recognizes. That foul mound could be the movement of a hippogriff, for example, this slime that of a basilisk or a harpy. His own bowels, convulsed by all this ripe disorder, feel suddenly with a plunging weight, as though heart, hump, and all might have just descended there: he squats hastily, breeches down (well, Zeus sent Modesty in through the asshole, so may she exit there as well), to leave his own urgent message on the forest floor.

Robert Coover, "Aesop's Forest"

For this relief much thanks . . .

Hamlet, 1: i, 8

dedicatory epistle to the reader

1. The paper hereby presented is, properly speaking, a treatise on evacuation. As such, its ideal location would be between Dominique Laporte's *Histoire de la merde* and Pietro Manzoni's *Merde d'artista* – works, in other words, secretly dedicated to friendly souls, or, as in this case, to the logorrheic interpreter of postmodernity. The author, but a humble hack, aims at the scholastic fame of having been able, if not to tap, at least to indicate a peculiar gap in postmodern criticism: for it appeared astounding to him that, among so many postmodernisms – "John Barth's postmodernism, the literature of replenishment; Charles Newman's postmodernism, the literature of inflationary economy; Jean-François Lyotard's postmodernism, a general condition of knowledge in the contemporary informational regime; Ihab Hassan's postmodernism, a stage on the road to the spiritual unification of humankin . . . . " (McHale 4) – the one concerned with the sublimity of evacuation had been so absolutely neglected.

2. To single out a certain sense of the sublime in contemporary literature, it is mandatory to impose severe limitations on and some critical selecting of the otherwise too heterogeneous material at hand. First, this research will be limited to North American fiction. Second, the investigation will focus on one particular theme that seems to have grieved American literature since the fifties – a theme that goes under the name of "the crisis of consciousness."[1] What is intended here by "critical selecting" is that pre-Kantian form of judgement that constitutes the essence and very nature of the author's critical method: "I like it, or I don't." On this basis, I have not

the least intention to encompass within this reading the "fast-food fictions" (Pfeil 2) and minimalist melancholies of Jay McInerney or Susan Minot. They do not "fit," and, moreover, they get on my nerves.

3. Of this critical scheme, the author is ready to admit that it is what nowadays seems to be the object of ridicule and scorn: it is, no doubt, a dogmatic scheme. It begins with an assumption about what contemporary American literature might be, and therefore it handles exclusively those works which "fit" into the scheme. In defense of this method, the author can only mention the innocence with which he is trying not to impose his assumption on *any* work.

4. If the reader finds this preamble to be redundant, or the following to be repugnant, let us make clear that these notes, "neither a defense nor yet another denigration of the cultural enterprise we seem determined to call postmodernism" (Hutcheon, *Poetics* ix), should be intended as an attempt to single out some strategies of aesthetic, and maybe also moral and political, survival within the limits of what Jameson has so grimly called the "logic of late capitalism" – or, in Baudrillard's more pertinent formulation, the logic of fast-food, anorexia, bulimia, and obesity. Henceforth, dear reader, consider the following as yet one more exercise in survival and digestion – an exercise morally and socially relevant of which the author professes himself to be a persevering practitioner.

fables of digestion

> *The term digestion itself is one of the interfaces between ideas of bodily and mental process. Latin* digero *meant properly to force apart, to separate . . . –* R. M. Durling, "Deceit and Digestion in the Belly of Hell"

> *Inclusion and exclusion, symbolic and material exchange, body boundaries, gender, and other identity factors are systematically and most deeply inscribed in the members of a given group through eating practices.* – George Yúdice, "Feeding the Transcendent Body"

5. In this paper, the term "sublime" refers not only to a set of aesthetic practices and transcendental ideals that have manifested themselves in contemporary American literature, but also to certain features of our own life and culture, features that, to paraphrase Geoffrey Harpham, "have survived the loss of the ideological structures within which they emerged" (xi). Loss and survival are two of the most remarkable traits of the sublime: since Longinus, they mark the stages of the individual's confrontation with a superior force that momentarily marks the disruption of the subject, which is first "scattered," and then joyfully reconstituted, "uplifted with a sense of proud possession . . . filled with joyful pride, as if we had ourselves produced the very thing we felt" (Longinus, *On the Sublime* VII, translation mine).

6. There seems to be general agreement today about the fact that the first epochal horizon within which one can speak of postmodernity coincides with the alleged death of the subject – or, at least, with an "attenuation of the self," as Lionel Trilling puts it in *Sincerity and Authenticity.* From the "loss of the self" of Wylie Sypher, through the "divided self" of Ronald Laing, to the "deconstructed self" of Leo Bersani, the identity of the "I" is dramatically scattered.

7. One can locate the first symptoms of the vanishing Emersonian self in the *schlemiel* of the literature of the fifties.[2] Undoubtedly, there are specific historical reasons that generate this sense of pessimism and loss. The crisis of consciousness in the literature of the fifties may well witness, in Edmund Wilson's words, the "homicidal and menacing schemes" of McCarthyan policy (Wilson 128). At the turn of the new decade, Ken Kesey's *One Flew over the Cuckoo's Nest*

warns against the clinical suppression of the subject in the political style of Kubrick: "[they] try to make you weak so they can get you to toe the line, to follow their rules, to live like they want to" (Kesey 57). As Hendin puts it, society, as symbolized in Kesey's asylum, "controls and infantilizes [the subject] in the name of the best interests of the inmates" (Hendin 132).

8. And yet, the fiction of the sixties muses, with Kesey's McMurphy, an outside space ("We want to live out of this society," the king of the Merry Pranksters avows), the revival of the American dream, the fantasy of an ultimate frontier that, once crossed, will open onto the uncontaminated plains of ultimate innocence and freedom. Although the themes of power and suppression undergo some variations, say, from Kesey's dystopic vision to Kerouac's beatnik quest, the literature of the sixties traces a neat line between a power reduced to mere symbol of evil and an Adamic individual consciousness outside power and innocently extraneous to it. Curiously enough, the writer of the sixties uses the themes of power and consciousness in a way that resembles Thoreau's, Whitman's, and Hawthorne's more than it resembles any postmodern writer's: the Walden of literature is still a sacred wood in which I sing myself far from the evil of civilization and far from its scarlet symbols of doom. But is there any such a space of innocence in the coming society of the spectacle?

9. Postmodern statements on politics and society, from Pynchon's *Gravity's Rainbow* to Coover's *The Public Burning*, persistently echo the gloomy tones of Kesey's Foucauldian clinic – but where is the ultimate frontier of innocence and freedom?

> *America was the edge of the World. A message from Europe, continent-seized, inescapable. Europe had found the site for its kingdom of Death, the special Death the West has invented. . . . Now we are in the last phase. American Death has come to occupy Europe. It has learned empire from its old metropolis. . . . Is the cycle over now and a new one ready to begin? Will our new Edge, our new Deathkingdom, be the Moon? . . . Gravity rules all the way out to the cold sphere,* there is always the danger of falling. (Pynchon 722-23, Pynchon's emphasis)

Or, as Richard Nixon admits in *The Public Burning*, some pages before being sodomized by Uncle Sam, "we cannot escape" (Coover 8).

10. Yet, the theory and practice of postmodernity may recast the question of "the crisis of consciousness," raised in the fifties and brought to its final "paranoid" conclusions in the sixties, in "a more positive mode of confrontation between subject and power" (Olderman 124); the postmodern answer to this question attempts at producing new and different structures of survival – "new mutants," to say it with Leslie Fiedler. The argument I want to support with this paper can be summarized as follows: the claim of a death of the subject in postmodern discourse must be understood, *pace* all those critics who take the "death-theme" in absolute earnestness, as a "radical irony" (Ihab Hassan) which aims at reconstituting what one can call – *faute de mieux* – the "radical subject": a subject which stands to represent "the community of disappointed . . . literary intellectuals – and how many of us really stand outside this class? – whose basic need is to believe in the autonomy of self-fashioning."[3] Escape is impossible, since Kesey's clinic is virtually everywhere, in "the crime labs . . . the records . . . the radios and the alarm system and the TV over the teller's cages . . . the cells and the jails and the schools and institutions . . . the traffic signals and the alternate-side-of-the-street parking regulation . . . the magnified maps of the city . . . the beats and patrols," as Elkin's *Bad Man* witnesses (70); and yet, the repressive project of society reveals itself inefficient to discipline the postmodern self-fashioning individual.

11. "I say all this to assure you that it is incorrect to assume that, because I am invisible and live in a hole, I am dead. I am neither dead nor in a state of suspended animation. Call me Jack-the-Bear, for I am in a state of hibernation." But what can Ellison's Bear do in the society of spectacle? How can Trilling's "liberal imagination" survive the mystifications of mass-culture? And how can individual consciousness confront and survive a power disseminated in the most appealing forms of advertising, a power so forcefully obliterating reality with fictive simulacra? If "my life is a kind of simulation," as the protagonist of DeLillo's *Mao II* believes (97), how can the subject reposition itself within a society that transforms everything into simulation, in which even the individual, as Teresa de Lauretis warns, is "continually engaged, represented, and inscribed" ("Alice Doesn't" 37)? In the last analysis, power is not framed within an

inside that allows an outside innocence: power resides in the pre-fabricated notions of "reality" that the subject lives, "a series of overlapping fictions [that] cohere into a convincing semblance of historical continuity and logical truth" (Coover, *Burning* 122). Power is the ability of mass-media to create a "static tableau – *The New York Times*'s finest creation – within which a reasonable and orderly picture of life can unfold" (Coover, *Burning* 192).

12. Once reality and life have lost any ontological *arche*, and have become the result of a fictive construction, the radical subject, as Coover puts it, must become "cynical about it. . . learn the rules and strategies . . . [and become] a manipulator" ("Interview" 72); or, as Jerome Klinkowitz suggests, the radical subject must recuperate some sort of "transformative imagination" (*Disruptions* 16) to be able to change plots and life, drive force beyond exhaustion, and transform indifference and its simulacra.

13. Indeed, the publication of Berger and Luckmann's *The Social Construction of Reality* (1967) had to convince a group of American authors, now labelled as "post-modernists," that the first step towards the *Bildung* – or rather, a re-membering – of the radical subject was "to destroy the hold which these artificial constructions have on men, typically by forcing the very patterns and mythic structures to undermine themselves" (McCaffery, "Checklists" 112). Robert Coover declares:

> *Men live by fiction. They have to. Life's too compli-*
> *cated, we just can't handle all the input . . . All of*
> *them [fictions], though, are merely artifices – that*
> *is, they are always in some ways false, or at best*
> *incomplete. There are always other plots, other set-*
> *tings, other interpretations. So if some stories start*
> *throwing their weight around, I like to undermine*
> *their authority a bit, work variations, call attention*
> *to their fictional nature.*[4]

Thus, the dead "I" opens a breach in the institutionalized mythic structures, a breach in which s/he will find space enough for inventing new plots and new fables of identity: the radical subject survives the attempt of annihilation by virtue of his/her ability to transform social plots, "work variations, call attention to their fictional nature."

14. Why, then, does postmodernism insistently repeat the litany

of the dead at the same moment in which death is to turn into survival? One reason may be that postmodernism tries to re-enact a drama that takes place in daily life – the risk that the subject could be actually annihilated by his/her inability to confront overpowering social myths. Most important, this dramaturgy allows postmodernism to celebrate an ironically initiatory rite, or "mythotherapy," as Campbell Tatham suggests ("Mythotherapy" 155), that enacts the drama of a temporary collapse in order to subsequently reconstitute a new subject in a stage of sublime ecstasy: as a ritual, the death of the subject initiates the reader to confront overpowering structures and destroy their hold. "The process is part of our daily life," Richard Poirier tells us, "and no other novelist predicts and records it with Pynchon's imaginative and stylistic grasp" (*V.* 5). Indeed, Pynchon's *Gravity's Rainbow* might be the best example to illustrate this kind of ritualistic sublimation of the self. If "They" have transformed the self into a "poor cripple, [a] deformed and doomed thing" (GR 720), living in the "master plan" of a continuous alienation; if the self has been ensnared in a plot that is trying to subject both humanity and the Earth to the principle of economic exploitation – then it is "our mission to promote death," and to become, like Katje and Gottfried, "children who are learning to die" (GR 175). As the narrator says, "We must also look to the untold," to a story different from the "master plan" that has constructed our very idea of identity (GR 720). Like Slothrop's, the human self must first be "broken down" and "scattered" in order to overcome alienation and return as the Benjaminian "bright angel of death" (GR 738 ff.). In Pynchon's novel, Slothrop's "death" serves the purpose of recognizing fictions and social "master-plans" for what they are, thus liberating the subject from his/her dependency on artificial constructs. As Ihab Hassan argues, "revulsion against the self serves [postmodernism] as a link between the destructive and visionary impulses of modern apocalypse; it prepares for rebirth" (*Postmodern Turn* 5). It administers last rites to all of human life.

15. Coover's fictions are no less rich of ritualistic sublimations. Coover, with his proclaimed interest in Roger Caillois' Eucharistic rites ("Interview" 74), repeatedly stages sacrificial public burnings, regicides, and other executions. In "Aesop's Forest" the artist/Aesop, who has sinned against Apollo, is, like Orpheus, dismembered by the angry Delphians – "one eye is gone, the other clouded, an

ear is clogged with bees, his hide's in tatters."[5] Aesop's sacrilege consists in having denounced Apollo's Truth as a fable.

16. As Aesop remarks, with a sense of tragic irony, "I told them the truth, they called it sacrilege." Like the postmodern demiurge, Aesop has de-mystified an absolute Truth, but, in so doing, he has hypostatized his own construction as a new truth, allegedly free from any Dionysian construction. Men live by fictions, they have to. But some fictions, like Aesop's "deconstruction" of Apollonian Truth, start throwing their weight around. When this happens, fictions can turn against their creator, and Aesop's moralized animals join the Delphians in the lynching of the author:

> they are on him: wolves, boars, apes, moles, toads, dancing camels, plucked daws, serpents, spiders, snails, incestuous cocks and shamming cats, hares, asses, bats, bears, swarms of tongueless gnats, fleas, flies and murderous wasps, bears, beavers, doves, martins, lice and dungbeetles, mice and weasels, owls, crabs, and goats, hedgehogs and ticks, kites, frogs, peacocks and locusts, all the fabled denizens of the forest, all intent in electing him into the great democracy of the dead. ("Aesop's Forest" 82)

17. At once, Coover's story gives the idea of Aesop-the-fabler's "radical" (anti-Apollonian) activity, and of Aesop-the-man's entrapment in his own "eloquent text of the forest." It is not less amazing to notice how Aesop is dismembered by his own "fabled denizens" than to notice how the Rosenbergs are sacrificed to the fable of American democracy in *The Public Burning*. To give credit to fictions is to put lives at stake. It is not surprising, in this context, that Coover's narrative technique continuously aims at constructing "exemplary fictions" – fictions that, in Robert Alter's formulation, "flaunt their own condition of artifice" (*Partial Magic* x) and that, by so doing, escape any hypostasis onto the plane of myth and absolute Truth:

> Ejemplares *you [Cervantes] called your tales, because* "si bien lo miras, no hay ninguna de quien no se pueda sacar un ejemplo provechoso," *and I hope in ascribing to my fictions the same property, I haven't strayed from your purposes, which I take to be manyfold. For they are* ejemplares, too, *because your intention was* "poner en la plaza de nuestra república una mesa de trucos, donde cada uno pueda llegar a entratenerse sin daño del

alma ni del cuerpo, porque los ejercicios honestos y agrad-
ables antes aprovechan que dañan" – *splendid,* don Miguel!
for as our mutual friend don Roberto S. [Robert Scholes, in The
Fabulators] *has told us, fiction "must provide us with an imaginative experience which is necessary to our imaginative well being . . .
We need all the imagination we have, and we need it exercised and
in good condition" – and thus your* novelas *stand as exemplars of
responsibility to that most solemn and pious charge placed upon
this vocation. . .* (Coover, *Pricksongs,* 77)

18. Coover's self-denouncing fictions, differently from Aesop's
moralities, do not permit "to have their miserable excrement read so
explicitly"[6] – they do not establish any interpretive order. Because, if
Aesop was the victim of an Apollonian social order, he has become,
quite paradoxically, the grantee for a classical order – think of La
Fontaine – which sees in Aesop's fables the explicit moralities of
"avarice, panic, vanity, distrust, lust for glory and for flesh, hatred,
hope, all the fabled terrors and appetites of the mortal condition,
drawn together here now for one last demented frolic." Eventually,
whether they were guilty or not of a radical and anti-Apollonian
statement, Aesop's fables serviced another artificial but stable moral
order. Establishing the tradition of the Aesopian genre tells enough
about the institutionalization of fable and the fetishization of narrative constructs, as Chénetier argues: "Aesop['s] . . . transformations,
a founding gesture for his particular world-view, [have become]
a-dynamic and irreversible" ("Ideas" 101). Hence, Coover's exemplary tale, in order to exercise "all the imagination we have . . . in
good conditions," must dismantle the whole of Aesop's mytholo-
gized apparatus. For reasons antithetical to those of the Delphians,
Coover himself must sacrifice Aesop – or his now overpowering
plot – on the altar of the postmodern transformative imagination, in
the "Temple of the Muses" ("Aesop's Forest" 81).

19. Whatever happens to Aesop, and whoever kills him, we know
that his is a tragic end. But what happened to the postmodern
subject, or, to a lesser extent, whatever happened to Coover in
Aesop's forest? Does the death of Aesop stand to signify the death
of the author *tout court?* Does this coincide with Lyotard's claimed
death of grand narratives? Coover's allegory is very careful about
this: the felicitous announcement of the death of the author can well

serve the political agenda of the fox, "that treacherous foul-mouth." Should we give absolute credit to the wide-spread announcement of the death of narrative (another myth, indeed), the fox may engineer a subtle takeover and make us believe that its realpolitik is the ultimate de-mystification – we may find ourselves entrapped in Peter Sloterdijk's "cynical reason," the belief that, since ideologies are all equally false, one's behavior should then be absolutely determined by "particular interests." The problem with Sloterdijk, and with our fox, is that they do not see in their "cynicism" a new fiction, a novel artificial construction: the "particular interest" is not more "real" than what has so far been deconstructed. Interests, to paraphrase Baudrillard, are never "free" from ideological determinations: "there is no basis on which to define what is 'artificial' and what is not. . . . No one experiences this [particular interest] as alienation" ("Consumer Society" 40). The grand narratives that have a hold on our life may be easily condemned and unmasked on the assumption that, much like the Socratic "enlightened" rationalism according to Nietzsche, they aspire to Apollonian truth, forgetting that they are bound to the deceptive nature of the Dionysian. However, what is striking is precisely the degree of forgetfulness that accompanies many annunciations of death and unmaskings of grand narratives: the authoritative announcement of the disappearance of authority, and the articulation of a total and comprehensive narrative of a postmodern condition in which it would be impossible to articulate any narration, surreptitiously establish, as Coover suggests, a "foxy" and fraudulent totalizing order. If there is any difference between Aesop's and Coover's postmodernism, it is this: the "suspicion" Aesop casts on Apollonian order is recast by Coover on the suspicion itself, with the result that the denunciation of myths does not acquire the status of an *Aufklärung*, but rather, in Bentham's formulation, of a "necessary fiction."[7] In other words, the "de-mythification" itself is the result of another fictive construction that can acquire "exemplarity" only if it recognizes itself as "fictive," thus avoiding any hypostasis onto the plane of absolute truth and enlightenment. Whoever would execute the myth-maker and fight an order of reality must be fully aware that the logics on which s/he would perform the "de-mythification" are not devoid of a necessary fictional nature – or, in Coover's own words, "It's all shit anyway" ("Aesop's Forest" 83).

   20. More precisely, the death of the author/Aesop prepares for a

rebirth: once Aesop's moralized forest "extinguishes itself around him," a new, exemplary forest can be created, and a new "self-conscious" author can take Aesop's place. The execution of the author participates in a tribal ritual of initiation in which "killing the author," as Frazer would say, "assumes, or at least is readily combined with, the idea that the soul of the slain author is transmitted to his successor." As in Freud's "totemic meal," oral incorporation and its correlates – instalment and digestion of authority within the self – consume a patricidal act that sublimates the subject's desire for strength, authority, and life. The Gerontion-like loss of sight, smell, hearing, taste, and touch that characterizes the narrator of "Aesop's Forest" must be counterbalanced by a will to eat: "even in such decline, the familiar hungers stir in him still. . . his appetite for power outlasting his power to move" ("Aesop's Forest," 68).

21. It is the same hunger that saves the characters of Maxine Hong Kingston's *The Woman Warrior* in their endless combat against the ghosts of patriarchal culture: "my mother won in ghost battle because she can eat anything. . . . All heroes are bold toward food. . . . Big eaters win."[8] In Kingston's and Coover's vocabulary, one must introject the myth for reasons of survival; only by following the drive of this appetite can the postmodern subject "learn the rules," and find alternative plots, "more pathways, more gardens, and more doors" (Coover *Pricksongs*, 19). In other words, if eating practices and "disorders," as Julia Kristeva suggests, may be the product of a hysterical resistance to (patriarchal) authority ("Stabat Mater"), it must be noticed that the postmodern resistance is not on the part of the anorectic, but, rather, of the bulimic. As the title (if not the argument) of Sohnya Sayres's article on "Food and the Agon of Excess" suggests, postmodernism is a tale of bulimic excess, or, as George Yúdice puts it, the promise of "transcendence in an age of fake fat and microwavable synthetic meals" ("Transcendent Body" par. 3). As Susie Orbach's *The Anorectic's Struggle as a Metaphor* implies, even the anorectic's "hunger strike," a loss at the level of the physical, "replenishes" the body with the metaphors of an excess in respect to social codes.

22. But is "appetite" enough for the individual's survival? Cannot eating rather be, as Baudrillard's discussion on "The Obese" insinuates, a "fatal strategy,"[9] or simply produce a blockage? "As a child," Kingston tells us, "I pictured a naked child sitting on a modern toilet

desperately trying to perform until it died of congestion" (86). Cannot the introjection of social structures, literary traditions, and Aesop's moralities, actually paralyze the childlike postmodern imagination in some sort of congestion? Or into a compulsion to repeat? Indeed, the rather heavy meal can create a digestive disorder, a rampant dyspepsia, and a metabolic chaos. The "urgent message" of the postmodern author is hindered. The author "squats hastily, breeches down. Ah!, what a plunging weight." Can postmodernism overcome this moment of blockage, this compulsion to cite and repeat – this compulsion to death? One has reason for worrying: the signs shed in Coover's forest seem to be Aesop's and La Fontaine's, rather than Coover's own – "there's some dejecta he's not sure he even recognizes"! For the voracious postmodern individual, blockage is the real threat, and survival coincides with some sort of "digestive capability" – the power to actively transform authorities and traditions into fecal signs, into wastes from which the subject has to separate in order to constitute itself as a subject. It is the ability of forcing apart, separating one's individuality from that of the slain king. In the next section, I will try to associate the possibility of survival for the postmodern individual with a sublime ability to evacuate. This – it goes without saying – is a topic that the author, who is not free from certain academic scruples, has not the power to censor nor the happiness to approve. It is a topic that has been forced upon me by Robert Coover, for whom evacuation is "the closest we ever come to the gods."

23. And so, with a timid "Can I?," I'd like to move to the second section.

from citation to sublimation: metaphors of evacuation

As if it were a game played by the sphincter muscle . . .
– Richard Brautigan, *Trout Fishing in America*

24. Although several critics have commented on the subject, the key document in defining postmodern American literature remains John Barth's "The Literature of Exhaustion" (1967). Barth's radical announcement was that writers were facing "the used-upness of certain forms of exhaustion of certain possibilities" (29). From then on, the author could only cite and repeat old stories and earlier forms. It is evident that postmodern literature seemingly endorses Barth's aesthetics of exhaustion: Coover's repetition of Aesop's fables, Barthelme's rewriting of *Snow White*, Kathy Acker's Borgesian *Don Quixote*, equivocally suggest a compulsion to cite, quote, and repeat a whole literary tradition that disturbingly crops up in the postmodern literary body. "Nobody had enough imagination," Barth's Ambrose muses at the end of *Lost in the Funhouse* (97). The postmodern author is condemned to cite and repeat old stories, given forms and structures. Or so it seems. Because some questions can still be asked: Is it possible to turn Barth's aesthetic ultimacy, his entropic compulsion to cite, into a sublime strategy for the survival of the subject? Can the citing subject be "uplifted with a sense of proud possession" above the cited material? And, if so: According to which paradigm can we define this "uplifting" as "sublimation," and in what terms?

25. Suzanne Guerlac, in her study on "Longinus and the Subject of the Sublime," locates the force of the sublime in the humble practice of citation, in which the author takes "proud possession" of the given message (275). Frances Ferguson replies to Guerlac by suggesting that citation rather promotes, to be fair to Longinus, a "*suppression* of the author" (295; emphasis mine). Despite the different conclusions they reach, both Guerlac's and Ferguson's arguments, as Geoffrey Harpham argues (198-199), are essentially cor-

rect, since the Longinian sublime, in the last analysis, does not aim to promote auctorial individuality, but instead the unification of the author with a transcendent totality, or with a past re-presented by and in the citation. The author is thus "promoted" (Guerlac) by dispersing him/her self within a "totality" (Ferguson). When the Longinian author recognizes the citation "as something he had himself produced," s/he is caught in the sublime experience because s/he feels as part of a transcendental creative energy.

26. From its very outset, postmodernism seems to tell a rather different story: postmodern citation can be more correctly imagined as a moment of blockage, in which the author is compelled to cite, to repeat,[10] because a given totality – a literary tradition, a social given to which the author feels belated, or, as Kathy Acker puts it, some "great expectations" – *already* comprehends him/her. The problem for the postmodern author is that s/he, unlike Longinus, tries to escape that totality, whose overpowering force blocks and paralyzes. Donald Barthelme's Snow White, trying to narrate her own story, finds herself captured in a plot – Grimm's *Snow White* – from which she cannot escape: "Oh I wish there were some words in the world that were not the words I always hear!" (6). Whereas the Longinian sublime contents the subject with a syntactical "sympathy" (the term is Burke's) between subjective expression and absolute *logos*, postmodern technique tries to free the subject from the hierarchy of syntax, and hinges, as Hayden White comments, on "a paratactical consciousness: a language of linear disjunction rather than narrative sequence" ("Culture" 69). To put it in rhetorical terms, the organizing principle of postmodern narrative would be metonymy – the succession of unconnected elements – rather than metaphor – the link between the parts. Accordingly, Donald Barthelme breaks syntactic hierarchy to introduce an element of error, a metonymic uncodifiable fragment, in the ordered space of social information:

> *I have a number of error messages I'd like to introduce here and I'd like you to study them carefully . . . they're numbered. I'll go over them with you: undefined variable . . . improper use of hierarchy . . . missing operator . . . mixed mode, that one's particular grave . . . invalid character transmitted in sub-program statement, that's a bitch . . . no* END *statement.* ("Explanation" 79)

The Guerlac-Ferguson debate suggests that Longinus's holistic sublime may lose its usefulness to describe a postmodern strategy. The ironic tone of postmodern citation implies a different movement, namely, in Paul Bové's terms, "a radical break or rupture in the genetic pattern," in which the subject inter-relates dialectically with his/her genetic/historical predecessor, thus instituting "discontinuities" rather than syntheses.[11]

27. If Longinus's sublime and Burke's "sympathy" do not "fit" postmodernism, Neil Hertz's "The Notion of Blockage in the Literature of the Sublime" tries to define the postmodern practice of citation in terms of Kantian sublime. The enormous "accumulation of secondary discussion," the "proliferation of secondary comments," Hertz argues, brings the postmodern author to face "a point of blockage: he [writes] of the threat of being overwhelmed by too much writing, and it may not be possible to go beyond that" (62 ff.) This "accu-mulation," an enormous difficulty to ex-press (etymologically: *ex premere*, to push out) new signs under "the pressure of the super ego," produces on the author/subject what Hertz calls a "blockage," something emotionally similar to Kant's fear and amazement in facing an overwhelming, "limitless" force. The subject/author feels impotent, constipated, quite dead. Yet, Hertz suggests, after the postmodern author posits this impossibility, after s/he installs such a monstrous accumulation impeding writing – after blockage is posited, writing flows out: a logorrhea, indeed, about the "impossibility" of writing. This process constitutes, according to Hertz, the liberating experience of contemporary sublime – an experience organized on the double "mind's movement [of] blockage, and release."

28. Let us consider, as an example of this mechanism of sublimation, Linda Hutcheon's *The Politics of Postmodernism*. The first chapter of this text is entitled "Representing the Postmodern," and it begins with a subchapter devoted to the discussion of "What is Postmodernism?" That is to say: Can postmodernism have any identity? Hutcheon astutely plays on the oxymoron opened between the notions of "representation of postmodernism" and that of "postmodern impossibility of representation." How can we possibly represent, in fact, a phenomenon whose first given is that of unpresentability? Impossibility rules the program of Hutcheon's text, which is to represent the unpresentable. *The Politics of Postmodernism* may be seen as some kind of allegory – quite literally an anagogic attempt –

of postmodernism itself. The entire postmodernist project is re-enacted here as the desire to "project," and create, that which cannot be pinned down or mastered by representation. The transcendent object of desire is that which, according to Lyotard, moves postmodernism toward the sublime:

> The postmodern would be that which, in the modern, puts forward the unpresentable in presentation itself, that which denies itself the solace of good forms, the consensus of a taste which would make it possible to share collectively the nostalgia for the unattainable; that which searches for new presentations. (Postmodern Condition 81)

29. The entire postmodern "representation" (or "postmodernism represented") is in it – the "post-modernist project," or, in other words, that ephemeral, brilliant moment of writing the impossibility of writing that by itself represents an entire era, and transcends the logical and stylistic possibilities of representation in the moment the unpresentable is finally presented:

> it seems reasonable to say that the postmodern's initial concern is to de-naturalize some of the dominant features of our way of life; to point out that those entities that we unthinkingly experience as "natural" . . . are in fact "cultural"; made by us, not given to us. Even nature, postmodernism might point out, doesn't grow on trees. (Hutcheon, Poetics 2)

30. The "indeterminate," the "unpresentable," is thus transcended, as Kant puts it, in the "representation of the limitlessness." The question "What is postmodernism?" poses to the reader an apparently unrecoverable "momentary check" (Kant) to the possibilities of representing "an indeterminate reference"[12]; the feeling of impotence is then "followed at once by a *discharge* all the more powerful" (Kant) in the moment the unpresentable is finally "connected with the mere presentation or faculty of representation, and is thus taken to express the accord, in a given intuition, of the faculty of presentation, or the imagination, with the faculty of concepts" (Kant). The identity of postmodernism is given, albeit in a negative way, as discrepant from representation itself; or, rather, as ironic (negative)

representation, as a representation that takes traditional (positive) representation ironically.

31. However, we have come a long way from Kant's sublime. Kant's was the attempt, once again, to reconstitute the excess of feeling within the notions of "unity," "integrity," and "coherence" sanctioned by the "ethical man." As Hayden White has noticed, Kant's sublime is some sort of disguised ideology which disciplines the suprasensible by reconciling it with the re-cognition of a social meaning in it. The individual, rather than freeing him/herself from overwhelming totalities, is eventually subjected to the overpowering force – a force of representation, or "faculty of concepts" – of the ethical man.[13] By advocating the need for rupture, disjunction, and *différance*, the postmodern "improper use of hierarchy" might well fall out from any Kantian categorization. In his insightful "Sublime Politics," Donald Pease implicitly maintains the necessity, for postmodernist poetics, of dropping out any argument about, and tendency toward, the sublime:

> Despite all the revolutionary rhetoric invested in the term, the sublime has, in what we could call the politics of historical formation, always served conservative purposes . . . the sublime, instead of disclosing a revolutionary way of being that is other than the ethical, in Kant's rendition, is reduced to strictly ethical duties. Or, put differently, the sublime makes the formation of an ethical character sound as if it is a rebellious task. (275-276; Pease's emphasis.)

32. Published in *boundary* 2 in 1984, Pease's might be seen as a declaration of postmodernist intents. However, Pease's refusal of the sublime may be contradictorily sublime in itself. What Pease claims, in his elaborate discussion and description of so many theories of the sublime, is the necessity of dropping out, releasing a certain political embarrassment which seems to be the given of the sublime. By first citing an impressive mass of material on the sublime, and then proclaiming a repudiation of all these structures, Pease's article offers a clear example of what I intend as the postmodern sublime, organized, indeed, on Hertz's paradigm of blockage and release. Not only does Pease confront something as overwhelming as the sublime, but he also *exceeds* it, thus "uplifting" postmodernism beyond the possibilities of what is usually known as "the sublime." In Pease's epistemolog-

ical displacement, the "sublime" reaches what Kant's conservatism represses: namely, the discontinuity between the given structures and the individual effort to transcend that given; Pease's sublime results in the *différance* between self and world, present and past, referent (the "sublime politics") and sign (a discourse exceeding that referent).

33. Dick Hebdige, in "The Impossible Object: Towards a Sociology of the Sublime," is more explicit than Pease in affirming the existence of a postmodern sublime based on the ironic rejection of previous theories of the sublime and on the disruption of totalities. Hebdige singles out what he calls "the pull towards the asocial sublime" in contemporary discourse: for Hebdige, the mode of the "asocial sublime" is a celebration of the "camp vision," the vision of waste, trash, and excrement – an indirect citation of Barthelme's "digging on the leading edge of the trash phenomenon." The ironic inversion of the sublime from Kant's and Lyotard's totalizing aestheticizations (a re-engagement of the excess as aesthetic work), to the new "camp vision," explicitly aims at both resisting unity and lo-cating the force of postmodern sublime within the realm of an anti-aesthetic *différance*. For Hebdige, one of the most remarkable strategies of the postmodern sublime consists in the simultaneous citation and combination ("double coding," in Umberto Eco's or Linda Hutcheon's terminologies) of texts belonging to high and camp culture. The result of this peculiar citational practice is complexly disruptive and constructive at once: at the same moment in which hierarchy (high vs. low culture) is disrupted, the postmodern subject is "uplifted" with a sense of complete mastery of both fields:

> Rather than surrender mastery of the fields, the critics who promulgate the line that we are living at the end of everything (and are all these critics men [sic]?) make one last leap and resolve to take it all – judgement, history, politics, aesthetics, value – out of the window. . . . The implication seems to be that if they cannot sit at the top of Plato's pyramid, then there shall not be any pyramid at all. (Hebdige 70)

34. As Fred Pfeil maintains, manipulation and digestion of culture in its entirety, from high to low, coincides with some sort of *jouissance*, of a pleasure that is, in the last analysis, the constitutive nature of postmodern subjectivity:

> *[the postmodern subject] finds him/herself an extraordinarily*
> *well-rounded, complete cultural consumer and connoisseur, emi-*
> *nently capable of taking pleasure in a spectrum of choices . . .*
> *ranging from just a step ahead of mass culture . . . to just a foot*
> *short of high.* (108)

35. At this point, we can start defining the specific features of a postmodern strategy of the sublime, which is – *on le sait!* – an anti-theory, a virtual subversion of all totalizing theories. Hebdige's sense of metaphoric inversion from art to anti-art, from aesthetics to anti-aesthetics, from the "beautiful" to the sublime "camp vision," and from "exhaustion" to "mastery," no longer stresses the drama of "ultimacies," or the disintegration of identity; instead, it shifts into the strategy for the *Bildung* of a new subject. This new subject confronts given structures to master them with some kind of Keat-sean negative capability.[14] In his book on *The Art of Excess: Mastery in Contemporary American Fiction*, Tom Le Clair argues:

> *Recognizing their dependence on their culture's system of dissemi-*
> *nation . . . novelists have two strategies to counter the homogeneity*
> *of mass-produced and institutionally controlled information. One*
> *strategy is to collect to excess and thus use against the dominant*
> *culture its own information. The other. . .* (16)

. . . But let us stay with the first of Le Clair's strategies of mastery: the postmodern sublime, to start with, is a strategy of "collection" and excess (etymologically: *ex cedere*, to give out), in which the givens of an "accumulation of writing" (Hertz), of a political embarrassment (Pease), or of "mass-produced and institutionally controlled infor-mation" (Le Clair), lead not so much to a rejection, but rather to an introjection (admission of the problem, commentary, citation, allusion), which poses a blockage suddenly overcome by a release, an ironic "excess" which turns the manipulator against cultural givens. This sublime strategy of ingestion, ironic blockage, and final release, has been defined by Arthur Kroker and David Cook as the privileged strategy of an "excremental culture": such a culture nour-ishes itself of the "pestilential spirit" of social and cultural entropic systems, to finally digest and drop out a fairly new message of disruption whose "psychological signs are those of . . . disaccumula-tion": "[postmodern art] exists at the edge of ecstasy and decay where the consumer culture of the passive nihilists does a reversal and in a catastrophic implosion flips into its opposite number" (10 ff.). Not altogether differently, John Barth's metaphor of disaccumulation in *Lost in the Funhouse* suggests that "The final possibility is to turn ultimacy, exhaustion, paralyzing self-consciousness and the adjective weight of accumulated history . . . Go on. Go on. To turn ultimacy against itself to make something new and valid" (109).

36. Ihab Hassan, as far as I know, is the first critic who has defined the postmodern sublime as ironic discharge of the "infinite powers" that impede expression. Hassan's metaphor is that of defecation overcoming the nausea brought about by constipation:

> Nathaniel West, writing at the edge of our contemporaneity, first comes to mind . . . The Dream Life of Balso Snell, *mock artist, proves to be a wet dream. More precisely, Snell imagines that he ascends into the bowels of the Trojan horse. This accords with his view of art as "sublime excrement." West seems to endorse this bilious irony: his own repugnance of life touches even his craft. His nausea, which no social dependency of the thirties can entirely explain, conceals itself in black comedy. A world of ugly doorknobs, dead dreams, and distressed loves, burns into the ash of parodic apocalypse. Thus West, turning violence into dubious merriment, is the new satirist laughing at the wound within his laugh. Thirty years after, William Burroughs carries the excremental vision even farther. A devilish mimic, he transposes a world ruled by entropy, waste, and disease into a film of metallic laughter.* (Dismemberment 249)

37. The vision of excremental sublime, as "parodic apocalypse" of a subject opposing "a world ruled by entropy," certainly emerges in many postmodern works. We might think of Pynchon's "defecation rites," or of the narrator of Gass's *The Heart of the Heart of the Country* who asserts that "I want to rise so high that when I shit I won't miss anybody." Federman's *The Voice in the Closet* provides the (autobiographical) example of a thirteen-year- old boy hidden in a closet to escape the Nazis: "I was scared. And on top of that, in the middle of the afternoon I had to take a crap. And why not? So I unfolded one of the newspapers and took a shit on it" (47). After defecation, fear is overcome; the boy finds courage to leave the closet, and embarks to America. Federman charges the scene with almost obvious allegori-

cal implications: the closet becomes the tomb and the womb for the coming-into-life of a new subject; defecation is the ironic release of the fear of death and annihilation. The same allegorical structure is at work in Coover's *Spanking the Maid*. The "teacher" of Coover's story has to realize that his Victorian ideal of *Bildung* – "feeding with spanking . . . that broad part preferred by him and Mother Nature for the invention of the souls" – is absolutely incorrect. For "that broad part" of the human body "seems more like a place for letting things out than putting things in." After a moment of apparent death, which is, in truth, only a digestive pause, the "invention of souls," the epiphany of the subject, happens in a water-closet, in a last heraldic effort to produce "spiritual" signs: "twitching amicably yet authoritatively like a damp towel, down a bottomless hole, relieving himself noisily" (102). Even more explicitly, Vonnegut's *Slaughterhouse Five* offers fecal signs as allegorical signs of authorial consciousness and as the epiphany of the radical writer opposing war and its horrors:

> Billy looked inside the latrine. The wailing was coming from there. The place was crammed with Americans who had taken their pants down. The welcome feast had made them as sick as volcanoes. The buckets were full or had been kicked over. An American near Billy wailed that he had excreted everything but his brains. Moments later he said, "There they go, there they go." He meant his brains. That was I. That was me. That was the author of this book. (125)

38. This is the price that the subject has to pay for its survival. Giving up any metaphysical consistency, this sort of subject becomes, quite literally, an excrement, a surplus that cannot be codified and inscribed in the fabricated notions of "reality." Its "resistance" to codification institutes at the same time its absolute superfluity in relation to the symbolic order. Its manipulation of codes and structures, in other words, cannot have any effectual consistency if not in establishing a *topos* in which subjectivity may exist, as a digestive process, in a sublime manipulation of pre-existing categories.

39. Examples of excremental sublime in postmodern American fiction could multiply almost endlessly. However, I should discourage my reader from thinking that the excremental sublime is limited to the (many) cases in which fecal signs explicitly appear in the literary space; rather, excremental sublimity consists of a *narrative practice* which I have defined as a movement from blockage to re-

lease, and from Longinian citation or Kantian representation to sublime digestive transformation. As such, it encompasses a more general postmodern trend: it includes any strategy of incorporating social myths and given plots – we might say: history and/as literary tradition – to finally release new stories and new modes of being. This new mode of being is the postmodern radical subject, who has survived the menaces of death and has "uplifted" him/herself with "joyful pride" in an act of ultimate *poiein*. In this sense, we might well conceive of the postmodern subject as a sphincter muscle performing its daily activity of retention, manipulation, and ex-pression; Altieri seems to endorse this idea when he argues, rather aphoristically, that "as organ, the [postmodern] ego has its own rhythms of expansion and contraction . . . it is not a place to store experience, but a *way* of experiencing" (627; Altieri's emphasis).

40. However, some mysteries are still unsolved: how can postmodern irony overcome the moment of blockage? And *how* can a subject be reconstituted – in his/her "way of being" – in spite of a power aggressively trying to "objectify" him/her? The postmodern answer to both questions is that the blockage – the "impossibility" – is not "real"; power is only a fiction. Put like this, the answer may seem too blunt, and it certainly exacts sharpening in order to prevent excessive optimism. It is my assumption that the achievements of Marcuse's *Eros and Civilization* (1962) and Norman O'Brown's *Life against Death* (1964) must be taken as defining features of the American postmodern sublime. For it is in these works that, through an alliance of Marx and Freud, the inevitable confrontation of subject and power takes place in a radically new fashion. Exemplified (maybe at the excess) by Theodore Roszack's "The Dialectics of Liberation," the problem of "making a counter culture" during the sixties could be put like this:

> While both Marx and Freud held that man is the victim of a false consciousness from which he must be freed to achieve fulfillment, their diagnoses were built on very different principles. For Marx, that which is hidden from reason is the exploitive reality of the social system. Culture – "ideology" [. . .] – intervenes between reason and reality to mask the operation of invidious class interest. . . . For Freud, that which is hidden from reason is the content of the unconscious mind. Culture plays its part in the deception not as a

mask concealing social reality, but rather as a screen on which the psyche projects itself in a grand repertory of "sublimations." [. . .] There we have the issue. Is the psyche, as Marx would have it, a reflection of "the mode of production of material life"? Or is the social structure, as Freud argued, a reflection of our psychic contents? (84-85)

41. What is power, then? Social superstructure, or father figure projected by the unconscious? Philosophically, the issue raises the question of the locus of reality; politically, it poses the question of how liberation is to be achieved: by social or psychic revolution? Marcuse's answer to these questions is that power is both a reality and a fiction: accordingly, he tries to develop a radical social critique out of the psychoanalytic assumption that power may be, after all, a projection, a myth. Significantly enough, this Freudian turn moves American radicalism away from Marxist de-subjectification and, in a very Emersonian way, puts the accent upon those "tendencies that have been attenuated in the post-Marxian development of his critique of society [Marx's, in his first writings], namely, the elements of communistic individualism."[15]

42. Marcuse's social critique hinges on the notion of "alienation." For Marcuse, "alienation" does not have any of Marx's (or Hegel's) connotations. Alienation is no longer a locus between labor and exploitation, but rather a disease that is rooted inside human beings. What the psychiatrist knows is that alienation results from acts of repression: the patient "forgets" his/her own construction of symbolic structures that the analytic anamnesis should re-present. Marcuse emphasizes the primacy of consciousness in social changes: the subject must be conscious of his/her own projections; s/he must recognize, in other words, that "power" is nothing else than the re-presentation of an Oedipal complex (*Eros* viii ff.). The impossibility, or blockage, is only a psychic construction, a story.

43. I will discuss the Oedipal strategy of the postmodern sublime, based on Freud's notion of "anal character," in the next section. To bring the current section to a conclusion, let me notice how Marcuse's social critique bears powerfully on postmodern narrative. Larry McCaffery's *The Metafictional Muse* provides a neat summary of how postmodern narrative can produce an anamnesis of the artificial construction of overpowering structures of "reality":

In examining the concept of man-as-fiction-maker, [postmodern works] deal with characters busily constructing systems to play with or to help them deal with their chaotic lives. Some of these systems are clearly fictional in nature: we observe writers trying to create stories, men struggling to break the hold of mythic patterns, desperate people inventing religious explanations for a terrible catastrophe. . . . Yet, [postmodern narrative] is filled with hints that other, less obviously artificial systems – such as mathematics, science, religion, myth, and the perspectives of history and politics – are also fictional at their core. . . . [T]here exists a tension between the process of man creating his fictions and his desire to assert that his systems have an independent existence of their own. . . . [T]his tension typically results in man losing sight of the fictional basis of his systems and eventually becoming trapped within them. (25-26)

44. The postmodern subject is thus the *locus* (maybe all-too literally a rhetorical *topos*) of consciousness; consciousness of the fictional nature of overpowering structures will finally allow the subject to imagine new plots, new stories, new lives to be told. Let us think, in this context, of Coover's maneuver in "Aesop's Forest": the imaginative power of the narrator is here absolutely impaired by the presence of his grand precursor – Aesop. Facing such an overpowering presence, the narrator can only cite the stories already told by the genius – Aesop. But, as the scholar well knows, "Aesop" is only "a fictional construct . . . [a] biography . . . reconstructed to satisfy the Greek requirement, according to which all genres should have an inventor" (Chénetier 97). The overpowering presence that impairs the subject turns out to be a mere fiction! As Borges would put it, "[t]he fact is that every writer *creates* his own precursor."[16] The blockage – the death – may be overcome by consciousness, thus uplifting the subject as the true crafter of his/her own narration. In this moment of sublime release, the *dejecta membra* are re-composed into subjective expression: "Orpheus, dismembered, continues to sing" (Hassan, *Dismemberment* 45).

45. . . . You see, dear reader, how, step by step, singing along, citing, arguing, implying, yawning, digesting what has been already said, apologizing, we go on together from section to section! We are already at the end of the second section, and one hour ago the first

one did not even exist yet. You see, this is the mystery and joy of the excremental sublime. There was a great silence, nothing that we could say to each other, no new story we could entertain each other with. In truth, you did not even exist, and neither did I. There was nothing, not even the excremental sublime. Maybe only the embarrassing feeling of something that we wanted to say. And then, in this silence, a voice is heard, a voice that I want to compare to the growling of the bowels after a meal long retained, and the voice becomes stronger, and the story bigger, and nothingness a logorrhea. . . . Maybe it was in this way that the world we live in was created – from the unintentional digestion of an apple. . . .

46. . . . Well, I was happy to find ourselves at the end of the second section, but now I am losing myself in superfluous details. And so, let us jump into our third section. . . .

the postmodern subject: an epiphany of sorts

I think of myself as a lyrical socialist, which makes about as much sense, given the world we live in, as being an anal-retentive anarchist with a bomb in his hand. – Robert Coover, *Whatever Happened to Gloomy Gus of the Chicago Bears?*

47. "All aesthetics has its root in repressed anal erotism," the psychoanalyst says (Ferenczi 325). All writing, *on le sait!*, engages in some sort of coprophiliac activity. Yet the paradigm of blockage and release that we have followed so far seems to suggest that the process – *the movement* from retention to release – is far more important, for the postmodern Muse, than the final excremental result. It is this process, after all, that structures the intensity of postmodern narrative – a process of digestion of old and mythical structures that will indefinitely defer the production of an ultimate (fecal) meaning. In this sense, even the postmodern subject will be, as Altieri has already told us, a "process," rather than a simple excremental left-over of our times.[17] It is a subject, as Kathy Acker's *Don Quixote* has it, that resists "capitulation to social control.... [t]o letting our political leaders locate our identities in the social" (18), and that continually refuses to end its manipulations and digestion into visible social signs. It is a subject, in other words, that finds in the process defined above as excremental sublime its locus and only *raison d'être*.

48. Another way to define this process, and thus identify our subject, is of course through Freud's notions of "anal retentiveness" and "anal character":

> they [anal characters] seem to have been among those who *refuse to empty the bowel when placed on the chamber, because* they derive an incidental pleasure from the act of defecation. ("Character" 28; emphasis mine)

Anal retention aims at finding "an incidental pleasure" in the moment of eventual defecation. Pleasure is "incidental" to actual defecation, since it belongs more properly to the *process* of retention and release. Such process is also, as the quoted passage suggests, an Oedipal strategy, that is, a refusal of the Law imposed by authority. If defecation is a pleasure, this pleasure cannot accept any external imposition or constraint: the subject must decide when, where, and how, this pleasurable activity shall take place. Freud supplements the passage quoted above with a footnote which better highlights the Oedipal *refusal* of a super-imposed Law (i.e., the wish of the nurse) which tries to regulate defecation according to social (i.e., non-pleasurable) norms; the footnote runs like this:

*It is one of the best signs of later eccentricity or nervousness if an
infant obstinately refuses to empty his bowel when placed on the
chamber, that is, when the nurse wishes, but withholds this function at his own pleasure. Naturally it does not matter to the child if
he soils his bed; his only concern is not to lose the pleasure incidental to the act of defecation.* ("Character" 29; emphasis mine)

49. The fact that Freud confers on the anal character the quality
of an "obstinacy [which] may amount to defiance, [and] with which
irascibility and vindictiveness may easily be associated" ("Character"
28) should not pass unnoticed. The most distinctive traits of the anal
character seem therefore to be those of a rebellious, almost anarchic
energy; its main qualities, much more than "parsimony" and "order,"
seem to be, as Freud's essay on "Character and Anal Erotism" has it,
"obstinacy," "vindictiveness," and "eccentricity." Dispositions, in
other words, which defiantly refuse social order. It is worth noting
that Freud, in *Civilization and its Discontents*, singles out in anal retention a "most remarkable" strategy for the "sublimation" of a particular kind of subjectivity, that is, an "original personality, which is still
untamed by civilization and may thus become the basis ... of hostility
to civilization" (43). Thus, an "anal character" is the sublimation of an
anti-social impulse, and the anal-retentive character might well be
identified with Coover's "anal-retentive anarchist with a bomb in his
hand": s/he who survives a repressive society by disrupting its order,
and by transforming its Law into pleasurable fecal signs.

50. In this ironic negativity, in this reduction to a metabolic process, Lentricchia's "radical subject" and "disappointed intellectual"
seems to have been re-membered and brought back to life after a
digestive nap; social reality has been redeemed from Debord's consumer conformism, Jameson's schizophrenia, and Habermas's indifference.

51. "But," the fairy-tale reads, "there's always a 'but'". . . . Like
Barthelme's "angel," my reader might be overtaken, at this point, by
some fundamental questions (the question of angels in postmodern
discourse has a considerable history, from Barthelme to Wim Wenders): Is redemption a mere narrative practice? Is the sublimation of
the subject a mere *narrative* freedom resulting from the disruption of
notions such as "essence," *arche*, and "representation"? Furthermore: what kind of hopes can we draw from a narrative that resolves

any signification to excrementality? Will digestion resist the inevitable commodification of our lives? Will we prevent society from reducing our selves to excremental left-overs? Henry Kariel, in *The Desperate Politics of Postmodernism*, woefully remarks that "we resist . . . by telling a story, by producing narratives that elaborately depict the drift of events as the sublime unfolding of the inevitable" (117). But what besides these stories and ephemeral resistance? What changes in "real life," or in the real life of our postmodern subjectivities – those wonderful entelechies of creation? However puzzling the term "real" may sound in the context of a postmodern condition, the doubt cannot be repressed; the angel, unaccustomed to doubt, falls into despair: "Redemption is a fucking fiction anyway," *Gravity's Rainbow* admonishes us; "It's all shit anyway," Coover's forest resounds. Maybe Cornelius Castoriadis is right in his jeremiad on "Post-Modernism as Generalized Conformism": even this allegory of the post-modern subject as excremental practice may be the, albeit sublime, manifestation of "the pathetic inability of the epoch to conceive of itself as something positive" (14). Moreover, as Yúdice admonishes, it is difficult to discern any political relevance – if not Coover's anal-retentive "anarchism" – in these narratives of *subjective* redemption:

> The aesthetics accompanying current analyses of eating disorders tend to celebrate the individual body, thus not posing any challenge to the Right or Liberalism. We need an aesthetics that instills the values of the social body. ("Transcendent Body" par. 36)

Undoubtedly, angels should start looking forward for a more "concrete" strategy of survival, a radical praxis that does not act only in the sacred wood of literary theory and in the groves of subjectivity, but also in the doomed world of production. Until then, postmodern theory and narrative will play the role of praxis while praxis has no more role to play.

52. Today that postmodernism, as Hassan pontificates (in *Selves At Risk*) is at its dusk – or is it an ironic dusk preparing for another rebirth?; today that postmodernism seems on the verge of its ultimate exhaustion; it is likely that we should surrender to the ultimate impossibility of reconstituting radical politics according to excremental practices. Probably, the postmodern sublime is today an untenable strategy even for real subjects' survival. Linda Hutcheon, among many, advocates the necessity of going beyond postmod-

ernism, of "using" it to "exceed" it: "Postmodernism manipulates, but does not . . . (re)construct the structures of subjectivity . . . [we] may *use* postmodern strategies of parodic inscription and subversion in order *to initiate* the deconstructive *first step*, but [we] *do not stop there*" (*Politics* 168; emphasis mine). Postmodernism is dead! Long live postmodernism! (But isn't there a sense of *déjà vu* in Hutcheon's forest? What is this initiation about?). Today, failure faced, one feels that new doors must be opened, new strategies found, new steps taken, new paths trodden. Let us finally digest postmodernism!

53. With a sense of deep elegy, a feeling of nausea and an unbearable burden in my constipated stomach, I conclude this paper with Robert Coover, postmodern Virgil, with whom my own quest began:

THIS ACT IS CONCLUDED

THE MANAGEMENT REGRETS THERE WILL

BE NO REFUND

(*Pricksongs* 256)

N O T E S

1. See Max F. Schulz, *Radical Sophistication*, esp. 198 ff.

2. See Franco La Polla, *Un posto nella mente: il nuovo romanzo americano*.

3. Frank Lentricchia, *Ariel and the Police: Michel Foucault, William James, Wallace Stevens*, 96-97; on the notion of postmodernism as "aesthetic of self-formation" see also George Yúdice, "Marginality and the Ethics of Survival."

4. Robert Coover, "Interview with Larry McCaffery," 68. In a slip of the tongue Coover seems to echo Sigmund Freud:

> *Life, as we find it, is too hard for us; it brings to us too many pains, disappointments, and impossible tasks. In order to bear it we cannot dispense with palliative measures. "We cannot do with auxiliary constructions," Theodor Fontane tells us. . . . But one can do more than that; one can try to re-create the world, to build up in its stead another world in which its most unbearable features are eliminated and replaced by others. . . .* (Sigmund Freud, *Civilization and its Discontents* 22 and 28)

5. Robert Coover, "Aesop's Forest" 82; see also Hassan's metaphorization of postmodernism in the terms of the Orpheus myth, in *The Dismemberment of Orpheus*.

6. Coover's active participation in Aesop's lynching cannot pass unnoticed in the shift from "They'll be here soon" (75), referring to the Delphians, to the final "We set him [Aesop] on his bendy legs and stepped back, blocking any possible escape" (81).

7. On the centrality of Bentham's notion of "necessary fiction" in American narrative, see Guido Carboni, *La finzione necessaria*; see also Fred Pfeil, *Another Tale to Tell*.

8. Maxine Hong Kingston, *The Woman Warrior: Memories of a Girlhood among Ghosts*, 88 and 90. For the symbology of the ghosts as essence of patriarchy, see Sidonie Smith, "Maxine Hong Kingston's Woman Warrior: Filiality and Woman's Autobiographical Storytelling." Notably within feminism, "big eating" seems to counteract what Kim Chernin has called "the tyranny of slenderness" imposed on women by patriarchy; on this issue, see Kim Chernin, *The Obsession. Reflections on the Tyranny of Slenderness*, and Susan Bordo, "Reading the Slender Body."

9. Jean Baudrillard, "The Obese," *Fatal Strategies*; on the way food industry may re-code gastronomic excess into consumerism, see Warren Belasaco, *Appetite for Change: How the Counterculture Took On the Food Industry, 1966-1988*.

10. In postmodern narrative, "[c]haracters become the passive receptors of phenomena from outside; they become all ears, listening to the sounds of voices, noises from the street, literary parodies and emulations, music . . . compulsion to repeat" (Poirier 9); anticipating for a moment, I would like to paraphrase Lacan, in order to individuate in the "repetition compulsion" an ironic ("reversal") mode of affirmation of the subject *in* history but as difference *from* history:

> [*the repetition compulsion*] *has in view nothing less than the historizing temporality of the experience of transference, so does the death instinct essentially express the limit of the historical function of the subject. This limit is death—not as an eventual coming-to-term of the life of the individual, nor as the empirical certainty of the subject, but, as Heidegger's formula puts it, as that "possibility which is one's ownmost, unconditional, unsupersedable, certain and as such indeterminable (unüberholbare)" . . . This limit represents the past in its real form, that is to say, not the physical past whose existence is abolished, nor the epic past as it has become perfected in the work of memory, nor the historic past in which man finds the guarantor of his future, but* the past which reveals itself reversed in repetition. ("The Function and Field of Speech and Language in Psychoanalysis" in *Ecrits* 103; emphasis mine).

11. Bové, *Destructive Poetics* 37. Examples of this break with genealogy: the abortion at the beginning of Kathy Acker's *Don Quixote*; the illegitimate child at the beginning of Maxine Hong Kingston's *The Woman Warrior.*

12. References are to Immanuel Kant, *The Critique of Judgement* 90-94.

13. See Hayden White, "The Politics of Historical Interpretation: Discipline and Desublimation."

14. Charles Altieri, in "From Symbolist Thought to Immanence," stresses the importance of Keats's notion of "negative capability" in the context of American postmodern poetics; he traces a genealogy from Keats to Olson.

15. Herbert Marcuse, *Reason and Revolution*, 294-295; another exemplary case of the psychoanalytic turn of Marxism into "Marxist Humanism" is certainly Erich Fromm, *Marx's concept of Man.*

16. Jorge Luis Borges, "Kafka and his Precursors," 201; Borges's own emphasis. Also Tony Tanner: "[postmodern writers suggest that] the plots men see may be their own inventions" (*City of Words* 156).

17. Charles Altieri, "From Symbolist Thought to Immanence"; but is this idea of self-as-process a novelty of postmodernism? Identity as a process of self-creation is, after all, a Jungian idea. James Olney confirms: "Like the ele-

ments, individual man never is but is always becoming: his self, as C.J. Jung will say some twenty-five hundred years after Heraclitus—nor did man change much in the interim—is a process rather than a settled state of being" (James Olney, *Metaphors of Self* 27). And so, postmodernism is once again repeating the old, isn't it? And yet, John Paul Russo comments on Olney's passage, "[i]t is hard to reconcile the two sides of this sentence: on one hand man is 'always becoming.' On the other, man has not changed 'much' in two and a half millennia" (John Paul Russo, "The Disappearance of the Self" 22).

W O R K S   C I T E D

Acker, Kathy. *Great Expectations*. New York: Grove Press, 1986.

Alter, Robert. *Partial Magic: The Novel as a Self-Conscious Genre*. Berkeley: U of California P, 1975.

Altieri, Charles. "From Symbolist Thought to Immanence." *boundary* 2, 3 (1985).

Barth, John:

Lost in the Funhouse. New York: Doubleday, 1968.

"The Literature of Exhaustion." *Atlantic Monthly* 220 (August 1967).

Barthelme, Donald:

"The Explanation." *City Life*. New York: Simon and Schuster, 1968.

Snow White. New York: Athenaeum, 1967.

Baudrillard, Jean:

"Consumer Society." *Selected Writings*. Ed. Mark Poster. Stanford: Stanford UP, 1988.

"The Obese." *Fatal Strategies*. Trans. P. Beitchman and W.G.J. Niesluchowski. New York: Semiotexte, 1990.

Belasaco, Warren. *Appetite for Change: How the Counterculture Took On the Food Industry. 1966-1988*. New York: Pantheon, 1989.

Bersani, Leo. *A Future for Astyanax: Character and Desire in Literature*. Boston: Little Brown, 1976.

Bordo, Susan. "Reading the Slender Body." In *Women, Science, and the Body*

Politic: Discourses and Representations. Eds. M. Jacobus, E. Fox Keller, and S. Shuttleworth. New York: Methuen, 1988.

Borges, Jorge Luis. "Kafka and his Precursors." *Labyrinths.* Ed. Donald A. Yates. New York: New Directions, 1964.

Bové, Paul A. *Destructive Poetics: Heidegger and Modern American Poetry.* New York: Columbia UP, 1980.

Carboni, Guido. *La finzione necessaria.* Torino: Tirrenia Stampatori, 1984.

Castoriadis, Cornelius. "The Retreat from Autonomy: Post-Modernism as Generalized Conformism." *Thesis Eleven,* 31 (1992).

Chénetier, Marc. "Ideas of Order at Delphi." *Facing Texts: Encounters Between Contemporary Writers and Critics.* Durham: Duke UP, 1988.

Chernin, Kim. *The Obsession. Reflections on the Tyranny of Slenderness.* New York: Harper and Row, 1981.

Cook, David, and Arthur Kroker. *The Postmodern Scene: Excremental Culture and Hyper-Aesthetics.* New York: St. Martin's Press, 1986.

Coover, Robert:

"Interview with Larry McCaffery." In *Anything Can Happen: Interviews with Contemporary American Novelists.* Eds. Larry McCaffery and Tom Le Clair. Urbana: U of Illinois P, 1983.

Pricksongs and Descants. New York: New American Library, 1969.

"Aesop's Forest." *Facing Texts: Encounters between Contemporary Writers and Critics.* Ed. Heide Ziegler. Durham: Duke UP, 1988.

Spanking the Maid. New York: Grove Press, 1982.

The Public Burning. New York: Viking, 1976.

DeLillo, Don. *Mao II.* New York: Viking, 1991.

Elkin, Stanley. *A Bad Man.* New York: Random House, 1967.

Federman, Raymond. *The Voice in the Closet.* New York: Grove Press, 1979.

Ferenczi, S. "On the Ontogenesis of the Interest in Money." *Sex in Psycho-analysis.* Trans. E. Jones. New York: Norton, 1950.

Ferguson, Frances. "A Commentary on Suzanne Guerlac's 'Longinus and the Subject of the Sublime.'" *New Literary History* 2 (1985).

Fiedler, Leslie. "The New Mutants." *Partisan Review* 32 (1965).

Freud, Sigmund:

Civilization and Its Discontents. Trans. and ed. James Strachey. New York: Norton, 1961.

"Character and Anal Erotism." *Character and Culture*. Ed. Philip Rieff. New York: Macmillan, 1963.

Fromm, Erich. *Marx's concept of Man*. New York: Ungar, 1961.

Guerlac, Suzanne. "Longinus and the Subject of the Sublime." *New Literary History* 2 (1985).

Harpham, Geoffrey Galt. *The Ascetic Imperative in Culture and Criticism*. Chicago: U of Chicago P, 1987.

Hassan, Ihab:

The Dismemberment of Orpheus: Toward a Postmodern Literature. Madison: U of Wisconsin P, 1982.

Selves at Risk: Patterns of Quest in Contemporary American Letters. Madison: U of Wisconsin P, 1990.

The Postmodern Turn: Essays in Postmodern Theory and Culture. Columbus: Ohio State UP, 1987.

Hebdige, Dick. "The Impossible Object: Towards a Sociology of the Sublime." *New Formations* 1 (1987).

Hendin, Josephine. *Vulnerable People: A View of American Fiction since 1945*. Oxford: Oxford UP, 1978.

Hertz, Neil. "The Notion of Blockage in the Literature of the Sublime." *Psychoanalysis and the Question of the Text*. Ed. Geoffrey H. Hartman. Baltimore: Johns Hopkins UP, 1978.

Hutcheon, Linda:

A Poetics of Postmodernism. New York: Routledge, 1988.

The Politics of Postmodernism. New York: Routledge, 1989.

Kant, Immanuel. *The Critique of Judgement*. Trans. J.G. Meredith. Oxford: Clarendon Press, 1957.

Kariel, Henry S. *The Desperate Politics of Postmodernism*. Amherst: U of Massachusetts P, 1989.

Kesey, Ken. *One Flew over the Cuckoo's Nest*. New York: American Library, 1962.

Kingston, Maxine Hong. *The Woman Warrior: Memories of a Girlhood among Ghosts*. New York: Vintage, 1989.

Klinkowitz, Jerome. "The Death of the Death of the Novel." *Literary Disruptions: The Making of Post-Contemporary American Fiction*. Urbana: U of Illinois P, 1980.

Kristeva, Julia. "Stabat Mater." In *The Female Body in Western Culture*. Ed. Susan Rubin Suleiman. Cambridge: Harvard UP, 1986.

Lacan, Jacques. "The Function and Field of Speech and Language in Psycho-analysis." *Ecrits: A Selection*. Trans. Alan Sheridan. New York: Norton, 1977.

Laing, Ronald D. *The Divided Self: An Existential Study in Sanity and Madness*. London: Pelican, 1969.

La Polla, Franco. *Un posto nella mente: il nuovo romanzo americano (1962-1982)*. Ravenna: Longo, 1983.

Lauretis, Teresa de. *Alice Doesn't: Feminism, Semiotics, Cinema*. Bloomington: Indiana UP, 1984.

Le Clair, Tom. *The Art of Excess: Mastery in Contemporary American Fiction*. Urbana: U of Illinois P, 1989.

Lentricchia, Frank. *Ariel and the Police: Michel Foucault, William James, Wallace Stevens*. Madison: U of Wisconsin P, 1988.

Lyotard, Jean-François. *The Postmodern Condition: A Report on Knowledge*. Trans. Geoff Bennington and Brian Massumi. Manchester: Manchester UP, 1984.

Marcuse, Herbert:

Eros and Civilization. New York: Vintage Books, 1962.

Reason and Revolution: Hegel and the Rise of Social Theory. Oxford: Oxford UP, 1941.

McCaffery, Larry:

The Metafictional Muse: The Works of Robert Coover, Donald Barthelme, and William H. Gass. Pittsburgh: U of Pittsburgh P, 1982.

"Three Checklists (Coover, Barthelme, Sukenick)." *Bulletin of Bibliography* 31 (1974): 112.

McHale, Brian. *Postmodernist Fiction*. London: Methuen, 1987.

Olderman, Raymond M. *Beyond the Waste Land: A Study of the American Novel in the Nineteen-Sixties*. New Haven: Yale UP, 1972.

Olney, James. *Metaphors of Self: The Meaning of Autobiography*. Princeton: Princeton UP, 1972.

Orbach, Susie. *Hunger Strike: The Anorectic's Struggle as a Metaphor for our Age*. New York: Norton, 1987.

Pease, Donald E. "Sublime Politics." *boundary* 2.3 (Spring/Fall 1984).

Pfeil, Fred. *Another Tale to Tell: Politics and Narrative in Postmodern Culture*. London: Verso, 1990.

Poirier, Richard:

The Performing Self. New York: Oxford UP, 1971.

"Thomas Pynchon's *V.*" *New York Times*, 1 May 1966.

Pynchon, Thomas. *Gravity's Rainbow*. Harmondsworth: Penguin, 1987.

Roszack, Theodor. "The Dialectics of Liberation: Herbert Marcuse and Norman Brown." *The Making of a Counter Culture: Reflections on the Technocratic Society and its Youthful Opposition*. New York: Doubleday, 1969.

Russo, John Paul. "The Disappearance of the Self: Some Theories of Autobiography in the United States, 1964-1987." *Tuttamerica* 29-30-31 (1986-87).

Sayres, Sohnya. "Glory Mongering: Food and the Agon of Excess." *Social Text*, 16 (Winter 1986-87).

Schulz, Max F. *Radical Sophistication: Status in Contemporary Jewish-American Novelists*. Athens: Ohio UP, 1969.

Sloterdijk, Peter. *Critique of Cynical Reason*. Trans. Michael Eldred. Minneapolis: U of Minnesota P, 1987.

Smith, Sidonie. "Maxine Hong Kingston's Woman Warrior: Filiality and Woman's Autobiographical Storytelling." *A Poetics of Women's Autobiography*. Bloomington: Indiana UP, 1987.

Sypher, Wylie. *Loss of the Self in Modern Literature and Art*. New York: Random House, 1962.

Tanner, Tony. *City of Words: American Fiction 1950-1970)*. New York: Harper and Row, 1971.

Tatham, Campbell. "Mythotherapy and Postmodern Fiction." *Performance in Postmodern Culture*. Eds. Michel Benamou and Charles Caramello. Madison: Coda Press, 1977.

Trilling, Lionel. *Sincerity and Authenticity*. Oxford: Oxford UP, 1972.

Vonnegut, Kurt, Jr. *Slaughterhouse Five*. New York: Dell, 1969.

White, Hayden:

"The Culture of Criticism." *Liberations: New Essays on the Humanities in Revolution*. Ed. Ihab Hassan. Middletown: Wesleyan UP, 1971.

"The Politics of Historical Interpretation: Discipline and Desublimation." *Critical Inquiry* 9 (September, 1982).

Wilson, Edmund. *The Cold War and the Income Tax*. New York: Signet, 1964.

Yúdice, George:

"Feeding the Transcendent Body." *Postmodern Culture* 1.1 (September 1990).

"Marginality and the Ethics of Survival." *Universal Abandon? The Politics of Postmodernism*. Ed. Andrew Ross. Minneapolis: U of Minnesota P, 1988.

Thousand Plateaus by Gilles Deleuze and Fe[l]
For the purposes of this paper, the clie[nt]
presumed to be a man and the mod[el]
presumed to be
woman. We are not trying to provide a
account of all aspects of the terrain of prostitution, [or]
even of escort agencie[s]
Cross-referenced terms are in upper cas[e]

THECALLTHEMODELTHECLIENTTHEAGENCYCYBO
G A S S E M B L A G E
ODYWITHOUTORGANSTIMESPACETHETELEPHON
V A L U E / E X C H A N
EDESIREFACIALITYTOOLSFETISHISMDET
R R I T O R I A L I Z A T I O

$ $ $ $ $ $ $ $ $ $ $ $ $ $ $ $ $ $ $

T H E C A L L

THE CALL is the interaction of THE MODEL and TH[E]
CLIENTwithin a particular spatial an[d]
temporal frame (see SPAC[E]
and TIME). THE MODEL is a student, an actress,
nurse'saide, a teacher, or a secretary..
THE CLIENT is
businessman, a dentist, a banker, a construction worker, o[r]
a computer programmer.... The temporal borders o[f]
THE CALLare delineated by THE TELEPHONE
which connects THE CLIEN[T]
THE MODEL, and THE AGENCY), i[n]
conjunction with the watch
or instrumental TIME. The arm of authority behind TH[E]
TELEPHONE and instrumental TIME i[s]
THE AGENCY. THE MODE[L]
gets ready for THE CALL, prepares to become a 'fantas[y]
girl,' by imitating (media) representations of women a[s]
objects of DESIRE: she wears garters and hose and hig[h]
heels; the nails of both
fingers and toes are painted
These are signifiers on a fragmented
coded body, signifier[s]
that THE CLIENT will be draw[n]
to (through DESIRE), that wi[ll]
reinforce his FETISHIS[M]
and in turn contribute to the
construction of his BODY WITHOUT ORGANS
(BwO). THE CLIENThas a BwO which he is drawn t[o]

FUCKING

WITH THEORY FOR

MONEY

< w k 1 1 + @ a n d r e w . c m u . e d u > (Ecstavasia)

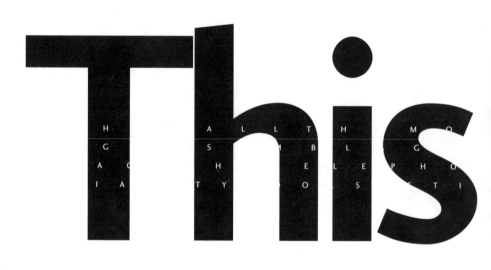

FUCKING (WITH

THEORY) **FOR** MONEY TOWARD AN INTRO-

DUCTION OF ESCORT PROSTITUTION

Audrey Ecstavasia

paper is intended as an introductory interrogation of the terrain of escort prostitution mobilizing terms from both *The Telephone Book* by Avital Ronell and *A Thousand Plateaus* by Gilles Deleuze and Felix Guattari. For the purposes of this paper, the client will be presumed to be a man and THE MODEL presumed to be a woman. We are not trying to provide a comprehensive account of all aspects of the terrain of prostitution, or even of escort agencies.

Cross-referenced terms are in SMALL CAPITALS

C   O   N   T   E   N   T   S

THECALLTHEMODELTHECLIENTTHEAGENCYCYB

ORGASSEMBLAGEBODYWITHOUTORGANSTIMES

PACETHETELEPHONEVALUEEXCHANGEDESIREFA

CIALITYTOOLSFETISHISMDETERRITORIALIZATION

$ $ $ $ $

THE CALL

THE CALL is the interaction of THE MODEL and THE CLIENT within a particular spatial and temporal frame (see SPACE and TIME). THE MODEL is a student, an actress, a nurse's aide, a teacher, or a secretary. . . . THE CLIENT is a businessman, a dentist, a banker, a construction worker, or a computer programmer. . . . The temporal borders of THE CALL are delineated by THE TELEPHONE (which connects THE CLIENT, THE MODEL, and THE AGENCY), in conjunction with the watch, or instrumental TIME. The arm of authority behind THE TELEPHONE and instrumental TIME is THE AGENCY. THE MODEL gets ready for THE CALL, prepares to become a "fantasy girl," by imitating (media) representations of women as objects of DESIRE: she wears garters and hose and high heels; the nails of both fingers and toes are painted. These are signifiers on a fragmented, coded body, signifiers that the client will be drawn to (through desire), that will reinforce his FETISHISM and in turn contribute to the construction of his CYBORG (BwO). THE CLIENT has a BwO which he is drawn to construct, which has an already written set of rules/conditions by which it must be constructed, conditions which include the fetishized system of signifying effects with which THE MODEL has attempted to encode her body (and which already encode her body as woman). THE MODEL goes to the CLIENT's hotel or motel or private home or apartment or to a bar or restaurant or hot tub spa. . . . When THE MODEL enters the SPACE of THE CALL, THE CLIENT gives her a substantial fee in EXCHANGE for an opportunity to spend a designated amount of time with her, an opportunity to interact with her cyborg subject-position "fantasy girl" (a subject-position which is composed of both fact and fantasy), an opportunity to construct his BwO. After she has been paid, THE MODEL calls THE AGENCY on THE TELEPHONE to announce that the EXCHANGE has been initiated and that it is now time to begin measuring the length of THE CALL. THE MODEL and THE CLIENT now interact together, their bodies intermingling with DESIRE, FETISHISM, representation, the SPACE of the room, the TIME measured by the MODEL's watch as well as the TIME elusively marked by THE CLIENT's memories, fantasies, and anticipation of orgasm (which is not the object of his DESIRE but a fetishized signifier which masks the perpetually deferred BwO, the plane of consistency of his DESIRE). When the end of THE CALL is announced by instrumental TIME (or by a telephone call from THE AGENCY if THE CALL has transgressed the boundaries marked by instrumental TIME), THE MODEL telephones THE AGENCY, says goodbye to THE CLIENT, and exits the   SPACE   of   THE   CALL.

$ $ $ $ $

THE MODEL

AdrienneAlannaAlexandraAlexisAllisonAman
daAngelaAnyaArdenArianaAshleyAudreyAvery

She will become part of the CYBORG ASSEMBLAGE which you are purchasing (you want to purchase the fulfillment of your CYBORG, to draw her into its logic, to name her through your DESIRE which is based on representations of women, on fetishization), after you have picked up THE TELEPHONE, after you have called her. What will you call her? You must first call her a partner in the EXCHANGE in which you are about to take part; you must call her the producer of the commodity for which you will give her $ (in an amount purportedly based on equivalence but in fact VALUE is measured by, determined by FETISHISM, DESIRE, and taboo. . .). I hear you're looking for some company tonight. . .

CameronCamilleCaroleCarolynCeceliaChantal
CharlottaCherylChristyClarissaColbyCorinne

She is called the call-girl: she is connected to both THE CLIENT and THE AGENCY by THE TELEPHONE.

> Claudette embodied a sophisticated, elegant New York look, so she always had a more fashionable hairstyle and very chic accessories. Tricia represented the girl next door, and she tended to wear dresses rather than suits – especially dresses with a Peter Pan collar or puffy sleeves. Michelle was a model. She was very tall, and her clothing would be slightly trendy, with more dramatic hair and make-up. Colby represented the healthy, outdoorsy

type, with a wind-swept, off-the-farm look. Marguerite was exotic and tended to wear tight skirts.

THE MODEL works as an independent contractor for an agency.

> We are very particular about the young ladies who work for us. They must work or go to school during the day, or be actively pursuing a career in the arts or in modeling.

THE MODEL, like THE CLIENT, has a BwO; her BwO is deterritorialized though, onto the commodity form money.

> DanieleDarleneDeidreDevinElaineEileenEliseElizabethEricaGabrielaGingerHeatherHelenaIrene

> You must always wear a skirt or a dress. Please don't wear anything very short or very trendy. . . you'll need at least one suit. . . you'll also need a dress, which should be lady-like and tailored, with no frills or ruffles.

THE MODEL can never fulfill the CLIENT's BwO – there will always be a gap. . .

> JaimeJanineJenniferJessicaJerriJoannaJulia SeverineShawnaShelbyShelleyShevaunSophia

$ $ $ $ $

THE CLIENT

THE CLIENT becomes a potential client when he picks up THE TELEPHONE.

> When you talk to friends about your work, you're going to end up talking about the weird clients and the mean clients and the bad clients, because they make hilarious stories. But even weird clients are usually nice people.

THE CLIENT becomes a client when the EXCHANGE is initiated.

> Some of our clients are made of gold, and you'll meet your share of them. But that's not true for

everybody. In some cases, the evening he spends
with you will be his biggest treat of the year.

theclientisafashionphotographerbusinessmancab
inetmakerdentistconstructionworkerbankercomp
uterprogrammerpestcontroltechniciandoctorcons
ultantmusicindustryprofessionalhousepainterle
verybodyInsomecasestheeveninghespendswithyou
willbehisbiggesttreatoftheyear.theclientisafashion
photographerbusinessmancabinetmakerdentistcon
structionworkerbankercomputerprogrammerpest
controltechniciandoctorconsultantmusicindustry
professionalhousepainterlawyeraccountantreale
statedeveloperarchitecttheclientisshortthinbald
averagelookingoldmarriedattractivefatsingletallug
lydivorcedtheclientisalegmanboobmanassmanthec
lientisafashionphotographerbusinessmancabinet
makerdentistconstructionworkerbankercomput
erprogrammerpestcontroltechniciandoctorconsult
antmusicindustryprofessionalhousepainterlawyer
accountantrealestatedeveloperarchitecttheclientis
shortthinbaldaveragelookingoldmarriedattractivef
atsingletalluglydivorcedtheclientisalegmanboob
manassmantheclientisafashionphotographerbusi
nessmancabinetmakerdentistconstructionwor
kerbankercomputerprogrammerpestcontroltechni
ciandoctorconsultantmusicindustryprofessional
housepainterlawyeraccountantrealestatedevelop
erarchitecttheclientisshortthinbaldaveragelook
ingoldmarriedattractivefatsingletalluglydivor
cedtheclientisalegmanboobmanassmantheclient

THE CLIENT is paying to interact with his "fantasy girl," his object of
DESIRE; he is paying to construct his CYBORG (BwO).

> I guess I'd like to know if there's any way to tell in advance
> what strange sex acts will turn a particular person on. . .
> absolutely anyone can be turned on by absolutely any-
> thing. . . part of my job is to respond to these people. . . .

THE CLIENT has a BwO which has an already-written set of rules, system of logic, by which it is to be constructed.

> We did all of the usual sucking and fucking. Then he put me in the Muslim prayer position so familiar to me, at the edge of the bed. Then he knelt on the floor and licked my asshole for a while . . . he started sticking his tongue in my ass. He stuck it in very deep, so deep I could feel it moving around inside me . . . then he really surprised me. He blew air into my ass and then inhaled deeply as the air came back out. He did it over and over, more times than I could count.

Integral to the logic of THE CLIENT's BwO is the fetishization of representations of women (by the media, by his memory, etc.) as objects of DESIRE. It is the signifying system, the codes inscribed on THE MODEL's body which is being fetishized, rather than woman *qua* woman.

> Remember, you're a fantasy for these guys. If someone asked you to sit down and spell out your description of what a high-class New York call girl would be like, you'd probably say, "Well, she'd have a beautiful hairdo, gorgeous makeup, she'd be very pretty and elegantly dressed, and sophisticated." That's exactly who our clients expect you to be. You just can't walk in there looking like the women he sees every day at work, like his secretary, or the wife he goes home to, or the girls he passes by on the street.

$ $ $ $ $

THE AGENCY THE AGENCY THE AGENCY

THE AGENCY serves as the arm of the law, sets up the boundaries/limits of (and is part of) the CYBORG ASSEMBLAGE which constitutes THE CALL, which in turn effects the possibilities of the logic of the BwO which may be fulfilled.

> Sometimes he might want to touch you back there.
> Technically it's known as Greek, and we don't allow
> it at all. We do not touch them there and they do
> not touch us there. . . .

THE AGENCY is headed by an agent, who is the personification of these limits.

> Now when you're talking to the client, please don't
> refer to us as the office or the agency. . . . Every
> man has a fantasy that he's calling a private
> madam . . . and we try to foster that image.

THE AGENCY is responsible for screening THE CLIENTS, which means screening out unwanted DESIRES, unwanted BwO's.

> For the man who asked, "Whaddya got tonight?"
> the answer was a dial tone.

THE AGENCY receives a percentage of THE MODEL's earnings from THE CALL. THE AGENCY is not a partner in the primary exchange with THE CILIENT; rather, the exchange between THE MODEL and THE AGENCY is a separate agreement based on different terms, different standards of VALUE. THE AGENCY is paid to function as protection, both before – through the screening procedure – and during THE CALL.

> Once you're in the room, ask if you could use the
> phone. . . . Call the office at the special number. . . .
> If you do want to leave . . . if you're not comfort-
> able, then we'll take care of it for you.

$ $ $ $ $

CYBORG ASSEMBLAGE

It is neither THE MODEL's body which is being purchased nor is it THE MODEL's TIME. What is being purchased is an opportunity to interact with the subject-position "fantasy girl," a subject-position which is constituted by THE MODEL, technology, fiction, SPACE and TIME: we would describe this subject-position as "cyborg space-time" and the assemblage which contributes to the subject-position's creation –

see below for elements of this assemblage – as a "CYBORG ASSEM-
BLAGE."
> A cyborg is a cybernetic organism, a hybrid of
> machine and organism, a creature of social reality
> as well as a creature of fiction.[1]

The CYBORG ASSEMBLAGE surrounding the subject-position "fantasy
girl" is composed of fiction as well as the material or concrete.
Fiction: representations of beauty, fetishization of signifiers than encode the body (= lines to media), etc.. The ASSEMBLAGE is also composed of the circuit of THE TELEPHONE, of TIME, of SPACE, of the escort
AGENCY (= the Law), of the EXCHANGE (= lines to capitalist system).

There has been much criticism of Haraway's cyborg myth as romantic – Mary Anne Doane: "What is missing in this account – and
seemingly unnecessary in the advanced technological society described here – is a theory of subjectivity"[2] – but we would argue for
the importance of the myth of the cyborg in that it is a similar myth
which forms the commodity in prostitution: it is formed through
both the concrete and the abstract, through the organic and the
technological. The cyborg myth is also, we think, important in that it
breaks down binary oppositions – the breaking down of oppositions such as public/private and smooth SPACE/striated SPACE is crucial to the enterprise of the escort agency and to the VALUE of the
commodity which is being sold.

We would want to think cyborg as articulation (using Stuart Hall's
concept of "articulation" here, with its connotations of gaps, con-
structedness, provisionality) of human subject and technology –
the cyborg subject necessarily foregrounds fragmentation, gaps,
partial/incomplete identity.[3]

For our project – and any project, we would argue – a theory of
subjectivity is necessary in order to discuss power relations, to make
distinctions and show relations between/among subject-positions;
indeed, in order to distinguish cyborgs.

Cyborg theory must be able to discuss power, DESIRE, interest.
Gayatri Spivak criticizes Deleuze and Guattari for not being able to
do this: "The failure of Deleuze and Guattari [in *A Thousand Plateaus*] to consider the relations between desire, power, and subjectivity renders them incapable of articulating a theory of inter-

est."[4] Conceptualizing CYBORG ASSEMBLAGE through a concept of articulation which accounts for provisional identity makes it possible to think subjectivity, interest, DESIRE, power. . . .

callgirltelephonevisaagenthotelcashmemoryfantasyclientmodel
taxiprivatehomeamexlingeriespacemastercardtimecondomsvice
squadmotellubevibratorvenerealdiseasewineyellowpages

CALLGIRLTELEPHONEVISAAGE

NTHOTELCASHMEMORYFANTASY

CLIENTMODELTAXIPRIVATEHO

MEAMEXLINGERIESPACEMASTE

RCARDTIMECONDOMSVICESQUA

DMOTELLUBEVIBRATORVENERE

ALDISEASEWINEYELLOWPAGES

callgirltelephonevisa
agenthotelcashmemoryf
antasyclientmodeltaxi
privatehomeamexlinger
iespacemastercardtime
condomsvicesquadmotel
lubevibratorvenereald
iseasewineyellowpages

CALLGIRLTELEPHONEVISAAGENTHOTELCASHMEMORYFANTASYCLIENTMO
DELTAXIPRIVATEHOMEAMEXLINGERIESPACEMASTERCARDTIMECONDOMS
VICESQUADMOTELLUBEVIBRATORVENEREALDISEASEWINEYELLOWPAGES
(CYBORG ASSEMBLAGE)

$ $ $ $ $

BODIESWITHOUTORGANS

The BwO is the commodity being sold by escort agencies. It is enacted by THE CLIENT, THE MODEL, the parameters of SPACE and TIME (which are permeable), THE TELEPHONE, representations of women through the media, the EXCHANGE (commodification of the BwO), TOOLS/paraphernalia – in short, by the CYBORG ASSEMBLAGE. The BwO is a program, a limit which marks the edges of the plane of DESIRE – it can never be reached, fulfilled. The BwO is both inside and outside the concrete, both inside and outside the abstract.

"The BwO is desire; it is that which one desires and by which one desires. . . There is desire whenever there is the constitution of a BwO under one relation or another."[5] Desire is the motor of the BwO, the driving force and predication of the logic of the BwO. "The BwO is the field of immanence of desire, the plane of consistency specific to desire. . . " (D&G 154)

The BwO is an assemblage of various bodies: "The masochist constructs an entire assemblage that simultaneously draws and fills the field of immanence of desire; he constitutes a body without organs or plane of consistency using himself, the horse, and the mistress" (D&G 156). The BwO is THE CLIENT, THE MODEL, the words, and the absent presence(s) upon which the conditions/logic of the BwO is based: girlfriend, mother, ex-girlfriend, girl next door, girl in magazine, stripper, etc. . . . .

Let me be your little boy.

". . . the BwO is not a scene, a place, or even a support, upon which something comes to pass" (D&G 153). What it is is a limit. . . it can never be achieved. "The BwO is what remains when you take everything away. What you take away is precisely the phantasy, and significances and subjectifications as a whole" (D&G 151).

The BwO is a program, with its own rules and logic and conditions. . . .

Let me be your slave.

"The masochist is looking for a type of BwO that only pain can fill, or travel over, due to the very conditions under which that BwO was constituted" (D&G 152). THE CLIENT is looking for – and paying for – a BwO which has already been scripted, already has a specific set of conditions within whose framework it must function. This set of conditions determines, too, THE CLIENT'S DESIRES:

"You can't desire without making [a BwO]" (D&G 149).

I want to give you all my money and all my cum.

> "You never reach the Body without Organs, you can't reach it, you are forever attaining it, it is a limit" (D&G 150).

> Re: the masochist: "Legs are still organs, but the boots now only determine a zone of intensity as an imprint or a zone on a BwO" (D&G 156). Like the object of DESIRE of the masochist, so too the fragments of the body of THE MODEL becomes for THE CLIENT "an imprint or a zone on a BwO." That is, she as signifying system (see FETISHISM) is part of the assemblage that constitutes the BwO, the plane of consistency of DESIRE. . . .

Do you like to see men jack off?

> THE MODEL is your invitation to build a BwO, as your invitation to interact with her [cyborg] subject position – that is, to have her become part of your BwO, to help you build it, to be built into it. . . .

Tell me what to do. Tell me who's boss.

> THE MODEL can never fulfill THE CLIENT'S CYBORG . . . even COCK RINGS, even TANTRIC SEX . . . only suspend the inevitable. . . . "Orgasm is a mere fact, a rather deplorable one, in relation to desire in pursuit of its principle" (D&G 156). "It is not a question of experiencing desire as an internal lack, nor of delaying pleasure in order to produce a kind of externalizable surplus value, but instead of constituting an intensive body without organs" (D&G 157).

Let me worship you.

$ $ $ $ $

TIME

> So you get in the elevator and you go on up. Before you knock on the client's door, be sure to look at your watch, because it's important to

> know what time you arrived – and nobody likes a
> clock watcher. Incidentally, it's helpful to wear a
> watch that's especially easy to read in a dim light
> with just a glance.

TIME becomes VALUE: THE MODEL's rate is based on hourly increments;
after an hour has passed, THE CLIENT must pay more if he wants THE
MODEL to stay for the next hour, and so on.

> "I took a look at my watch while I was in the bath-
> room, and I couldn't believe what time it was. . . . I
> don't want to rush you, but I do have to call Sheila
> in a little while and tell her if I'll be staying or
> leaving."

For THE CLIENT, TIME often functions as a dialectic between memory
and anticipation – "You never know what just happened, or you
always know what is going to happen" (D&G 193) – his DESIRES revolve
around memories and fantasies, past and future. . . . The BwO comes
from the past and is aimed at the future – it never comes into being,
never exists now.

Orgasm marks anticipatory (goal-oriented) TIME. Often THE CLIENT
will treat THE CALL as over if he has come and not over if he has not yet
come, regardless of the instrumental time as measured by THE
MODEL's watch. [See agency as arm of the law. . . .]

> Although escort services are techni-
> cally legal, they are at times raided by
> the police and forced to shut down –
> if only temporarily. To protect our-
> selves from being arrested under the
> prostitution laws, we always make it
> clear to our clients that we are charg-
> ing for the girls' time.

Think, a person moves from here (space/man/time) through here
(space/man enters into negotiation/time) to here (space/client
meets fantasy girl/time) and through (space/client enters fantasy
girl/time) to exit (space/man and model leave/time) — similar
scenario for model, first they are separate, then intersect, then
separate. . . .

$ $ $ $ $

SPACE

THE CALL: it is a public SPACE that gives the illusion of being a private SPACE. It is this illusion which THE CLIENT is paying for, this illusion which is produced and regulated by THE AGENCY, the capitalist system, THE TELEPHONE – e.g. public (social) SPACE. The physical SPACE of the room is criss-crossed by THE TELEPHONE, room service, beepers, etc..

> "In this space [of sex/pleasure/leisure], things, acts and situations are forever being replaced by representations. . . . "[6] [See FETISHISM]

> "For these bodies, the natural space and the abstract space which confront and surround them are in no way separable. . . . The individual situates his body in its own space and apprehends the space around the body" (Lefebvre 213).

BwO and SPACE: "It is not space, nor is it in space; it is matter that occupies space to a given degree . . ." (D&G 153).

privatehomehotelmotelofficehottubspa

> For some of these men, an hour or an evening with an escort was their only opportunity all week to drop their guard, be themselves, and relax.

The SPACE within THE CALL is [illusionarily] smooth SPACE – it is the illusion of smooth SPACE which THE CLIENT is paying for.

Striated SPACE is SPACE gridded by boundaries: constructed by VALUES of THE AGENCY, circuits of THE TELEPHONE, standards of U.S. Treasury, logic of BwO, etc. Marks the edges of illusion of smooth SPACE.

$ $ $ $ $

THE TELEPHONE

Okay. So there you are, sitting at home. Your makeup is on, you hair is done, your bag is packed, and you're ready to go. Suddenly the

TELEPHONE rings. Your picking it up means THE CALL has come through. It means more: you're its beneficiary, rising to meet its demand, to pay a debt. You don't know who's calling or what you are going to be called on upon to do, and still, you are lending your ear, giving something up, receiving an order.[7] But you **do** know who's calling. You are on call; it's your agent calling about a potential client. You get the following information: who he is, where he is, how old he is, and some other details about him, perhaps his profession, perhaps a little about his personality. You do know what you are going to be called upon to do, what you are going to be called upon to be. You are meeting a demand, receiving an order but you understand the demand, know the order. You will be THE CLIENT's fantasy girl in EXCHANGE for a substantial fee. THE TELEPHONE rings and you are part of the ASSEMBLAGE of escort prostitution.

theclientopensthetelephonebookfindstheadinthe
yellowpagesandcallstheagencytheagentcallsthem
odelthemodelcallstheclienttheclientcallsth
eagentbacktheagentcallsthemodeltoconfirmthe
modelcallstheagentonarrival(aftertheclientgivesthe
modelmoney)themodelcallstheagentagainbe
foreleaving(afterthemodelgivestheclientac
cesstoherbody)andagainwhenthemodelgetshome

Pager/beeper – some girls find it more convenient to use a beeper, which leaves them free to go shopping or out to a movie while they're waiting for us to call ... if you do use a beeper, you have to be all dressed and ready to go from wherever you are. Call-waiting – naturally, you'll want to keep your phone free. Most of the girls have call-waiting, and I strongly recommend it. Car phone – the car phone, if you can afford it, is the escort's best friend. It gives you access to the agency when you are out on the road (you wouldn't believe how many girls are on the way to the movie or somewhere else when their beeper goes

off), and it gives you more flexibility
when calling in to the agency after
you've been on a call.

$ $ $ $ $

VALUEVALUEVALUEVALUE

"Exchange is only an appearance: each partner or group assesses
the value of the last receivable object (limit-object), and the apparent equivalence derives from that" (D&G 439). In terms of the terrain
of escort "limit-object" is not determined solely by rational assessment but rather must be processed through the logic of THE CLIENT'S
BwO – VALUE is a derivation of DESIRE.

> I keep hearing from men who want to know if we
> have any girls who are more expensive, and pre-
> sumably more beautiful, than the others.

VALUE is not based on use value: "[Use value] is always concrete and
particular, contingent on its own destiny. . . . "[8] Use value is determined only after the EXCHANGE has taken place, and is, itself, "a
fetishized social relation" (Baudrillard 131). VALUE is the fetishization
of commodity's sign system; in escort prostitution, of the sign system encoded on THE MODEL's body. The fetishization of this sign
system is reinforced during THE CALL (see FACIALITY).

> A working girl doesn't really sell her body . . . she
> gives the client access to her body for a certain
> period of time and at a certain price.

The VALUE of the commodity before the EXCHANGE – in order for the
EXCHANGE to take place – is determined by the fetishization of the
commodity. "[F]etishism is not the sanctification of a certain object,
or value. . . . It is the sanctification of the system as such, of the
commodity as system: it is thus contemporaneous with the generalization of exchange value and is propagated with it" (Baudrillard 92).

> Reading woman repeatedly as the object of male
> exchange constructs a victim's discourse that
> risks reinscribing the very sexual politics it osten-
> sibly seeks to expose and change.[9]

THE MODEL has a dual register, as both object of and subject of –
partner in – EXCHANGE.

> Reading women as objects exchanged by male
> desiring subjects partakes of a degraded positiv-
> ism that relies on an outmoded, humanist view of
> identity characterized by a metaphysics of pres-
> ence; it assumes an unproblematic subjectivity
> for 'men' as desiring subjects and concomitantly
> assumes as directly accessible woman-as-object.
> (Newman 47)

The terrain of escort prostitution, like the terrain of sex/gender
relations, is problematic, in terms of the "traffic in women" paradigm.
Women working as escorts are not simply victims of some "pornographic mind" as Susan Griffin claims in *Pornography and Silence*,
where she equates the "mindset" (read unified, stable, subject position) of pornography producers with that of Nazis and the Marquis
de Sade.[10] Griffin's argument, as well as many other feminist arguments which want to label prostitutes and other women working in
the sex industry as "innocent victims" fallen prey to "false consciousness," presumes a unified subject and thus needs to be reexamined in
the light of post-structuralist theories of subjectivity. As both producer of commodity and embodiment of that commodity, the escort
participates in disruption of the "traffic in women" paradigm.

$ $ $ $

EXCHANGE↔EXCHANGE↔EXCHANGE

When each party has something the other wants, and they're able to
make a deal, that constitutes a fair EXCHANGE.

> The priest did not turn to the west. He knew that
> in the west lay a plane of consistency, but he
> thought that the way was blocked by the columns
> of Hercules, that it led nowhere and was unin-
> habited by people. But that is where desire was
> lurking, west was the shortest route east, as well
> as to the other directions, rediscovered or deter-
> ritorialized. (D&G 154)

You go into the bathroom to
spiff-up, to fix your face but
this is harder than it sounds.
You look in the mirror and see
that your eye makeup has run
onto your face, your lipstick
has disappeared and your hair
is completely disheveled. In
addition to fixing your face you
have to wipe your crotch for
wetness and odor, put on your
underwear, bra, hose, and garters, all without spending too
much time in the bathroom.
You panic.

$ $ $ $ $

FACIALITY

facialityfacialityfacialityfacialityfacialityfacialityfaciality
facialityfacialityfacialityfacialityfacialityfacialityfaciality
facialityfacialityfacialityfacialityfacialityfacialityfaciality

THE MODEL's face is part of THE CLIENT's BwO (see FETISH-
ISM). It is a signifier marking the boundaries of the object of
his DESIRE. Her face envelops the face of the prom queen
from his high school, of the girl in the centerfold of his
magazine, of his mother. . . .

Tell me who's boss.

"All faces envelop an unknown, unexplored landscape; all
landscapes are populated by a loved or dreamed-of face,
develop a face to come or already past" (D&G 173). To
come. . . .

Tell me what you like.

"The signifier is always facialized. Faciality reigns materially
over that whole constellation of significances and interpretations." (D&G 115)

Tell me how much you like it.

> When THE CLIENT says, "tell me how it feels" or some other such thing, it's not just about the words (he could say them himself) but about FACIALITY, watching the words being spoken by THE MODEL, watching the significance process through FACIALITY.

> After you knock on the door, stand back a couple of feet. A face is such a subjective thing. It's important that the client gets the full image of you when he first opens the door – the total you, rather than just your face. If you stand too close to the door, your face is all that he sees. And you might not be exactly what his fantasy was, because, let's face it, there's almost no way you could be.

(The BwO contains gaps and ruptures, never to be closed. . . see CYBORG.)

$ $ $ $ $

TOOLS

CONDOMSLIPSTICKVIBRATORSTOCKINGSBEEPERBREATHMINT
SLUBESMALLCHANGECREDITCARDSLIPBUSINESSCARDSEYELINER

> Some men are frightened by the sight of the vibrator. It's about fourteen inches long and you always keep a nine-foot extension cord attached to it. Sometimes a man will say, "What the hell is that?" or "Are you going to use that on me?" You say, "It's a vibrator, and I wouldn't think of using it on you. Not a chance. Don't you wish I would?" Then you use it on yourself while they watch.

TOOLS exist only in relation to the interminglings they make possible or that make them possible. (D&G 90)

> You start telling him what a bad boy he has been. He says "Yes Mistress." You go to the dresser in your five-inch heels and pick up a wooden hair-

brush. You tell him to stand up and bend over the
bed. You pull down his panties, to expose his
cheeks, and smack each cheek a few times. In between smackings you tell him what a bad boy he
has been.

TOOLS and DETERRITORIALIZATION: "there is an entire system of horizontal and complementary reterritorializations, between hand and
tool" (D&G 174).

suitbriefcasejewelrycocktaildressgartersstockin
gsbrasbustierslatexglovesbubblebathmassageoil

TOOLS form the appendages of the CYBORG ASSEMBLAGE. . . .

$ $ $ $ $

FETISHISM

Two kinds of FETISHISM occur during THE CALL – that of the commodity as VALUE and that of THE MODEL as object of DESIRE. The
fetishization is not of use VALUE or meaning; rather it is about being
drawn to the system of signification, it is a generalization of the
structural code of the object: "it is thus not a fetishism of the signified, a fetishism of substances and values (called ideological), which
the fetish object would incarnate for the alienated subject. Behind
this reinterpretation (which is truly ideological) it is a fetishism of
the signifier. That is to say that the subject is trapped in the factitious, differential, encoded, systematized aspect of the object"
(Baudrillard 92). This entrapment can be called DESIRE.

> people who want me to wear costumes, people
> who want me to sit with them while they watch
> dirty movies and jerk off, people who want to be
> tied up, people who want to wear diapers and be
> given a bottle. . . .

Beauty as FETISHISM: we are "bound up in a general stereotype of
models of beauty . . . the generalization of sign exchange value to
facial and bodily effects" (Baudrillard 94). Thus for clients FETISH-
ISM is being drawn to media representations of women, fascination
with the system of encodement represented on women's bodies

through images in magazines, porn movies, television, advertising, etc.

> After *Mommie Dearest*, suddenly there were guys
> who wanted to be hit with wire coat hangers.

FETISHISM is integral to logic of, to construction of, THE CLIENT'S CY-BORG: "the boots now only determine a zone of intensity as an imprint or a zone on a BwO" (D&G 156).

> The only concession we make to overt sexiness is
> the highest heels you can manage to walk in with-
> out falling over. In our experience, men just adore
> high heels.

"Tattoos, stretched lips, [etc.]: anything will serve to rewrite the cultural order on the body; and it is this that takes on the effect of beauty" (Baudrillard 94). For THE MODEL, it is not usually tattoos but rather, high heels, garters, bustiers, lipstick, eyeliner, mascara, painted toenails, long fingernails. . . .

> When these men were young the first naked
> women most of them had ever seen were usually
> dressed in frilly undergarments in a magazine like
> Playboy. As a result, seeing a woman dressed only
> in lingerie would create a powerful, nostalgic
> yearning that many men found irresistible. [See
> TIME] This made the experience more pleasant for
> the girls, because the more excited the man was
> as the evening became intimate, the easier things
> would be when it came down to the nitty-gritty.

> If he likes it I like it. That's part of his fantasy. It
> isn't even a question of whether I like it or not.

$ $ $ $ $

DETERRITORIALIZATION

THE MODEL performs a DETERRITORIALIZATION on her BwO during THE CALL, reterritorializes it onto the commodity form money (via cash, check or plastic), which stands in for her own DESIRE.

> Your BwO is my physical activity: fucking, sucking,
> spanking, bending, straddling, arching, moaning,
> gasping, etc. I am a material girl.

The impossibility of the BwO being ever reached is reterritorialized by THE CLIENT onto DESIRE, onto orgasm, onto THE MODEL as object of DESIRE.

"The more the system is systematized, the more the fetishist fascination is reinforced" (Baudrillard 92). DESIRE (for the object of DESIRE) is reterritorialized onto [see FETISHISM] the coded female body, through the system of media representations then again through the escort system. (Escorts are fetishized as "live" versions – but are in fact part of a further systematization – of the system of media.)

"Act like you're enjoying it."

N O T E S

1. Donna Haraway, "A Manifesto for Cyborgs," in Elizabeth Weed, ed., *Coming to Terms: Feminism, Theory, Politics* (New York: Routledge, Chapman and Hall, Inc., 1989), 149.

2. Mary Ann Doane, "Commentary: Cyborgs, Origins, and Subjectivity," in Weed, ed., *Coming to Terms*, 210.

3. Stuart Hall, "Signification, Representation, Ideology: Althusser and the Post-Structuralist Debates," in *Critical Studies in Mass Communication*, vol. 2, no. 2 (June 1985): 93.

4. Gayatri Chakravorty Spivak, *In Other Worlds: Essays On Cultural Politics* (London: Methuen, Inc., 1987), 273.

5. Gilles Deleuze and Felix Guattari, *A Thousand Plateaus* (Minneapolis: U of Minnesota P, 1987), 165. Cited in the text hereafter as D&G.

6. Henri Lefebvre, *The Production of Space* (Oxford: Basil Blackwell, 1991), 311.

7. Avital Ronell, *The Telephone Book: Technology, Schizophrenia, Electric Speech* (Lincoln: U of Nebraska P, 1989), 2.

8. Jean Baudrillard, *For a Critique of the Political Economy of the Sign* (Saint Louis: Telos, 1981), 130.

9. Karen Newman, "Directing Traffic: Subjects, Objects, and the Politics of Exchange," in *Differences*, vol 2 (Summer 1990): 47.

10. Susan Griffin, *Pornography and Silence: Culture's Revenge Against Nature* (New York: Harper and Row, 1981).

W O R K S   C I T E D

[Some unreferenced portions of this paper contain reworked material from *Mayflower Madam* (Sidney Biddle Barrows), *Working* (Dolores French), and the journals of the author.]

Barrows, Sidney Biddle with William Novak. *Mayflower Madam*. New York: Ballantine Books, 1986.

Baudrillard, Jean. *For a Critique of the Political Economy of the Sign*. Saint Louis: Telos, 1981.

Doane, Mary Ann, "Commentary: Cyborgs, Origins, and Subjectivity." In Elizabeth Weed, ed., *Coming to Terms: Feminism, Theory, Politics*. New York: Routledge, Chapman and Hall, 1989.

French, Dolores with Linda Lee. *Working*. New York: Windsor Publishing, 1988.

Griffin, Susan. *Pornography and Silence: Culture's Revenge Against Nature*. New York: Harper and Row, 1981.

Hall, Stuart. "Signification, Representation, Ideology: Althusser and the Post-Structuralist Debates." In *Critical Studies in Mass Communication*, vol 2, no 2 (June 1985).

Haraway, Donna. "A Manifesto for Cyborgs." In Elizabeth Weed, ed., *Coming to Terms: Feminism, Theory, Politics*. New York: Routledge, Chapman and Hall, 1989.

Lefebvre, Henri. *The Production of Space*. Oxford: Basil Blackwell, 1991.

Newman, Karen. "Directing Traffic: Subjects, Objects, and the Politics of Exchange." In *Differences*, vol 2 (Summer 1990).

Ronell, Avital. *The Telephone Book: Technology, Schizophrenia, Electric Speech*. Lincoln: U of Nebraska P, 1989.

Spivak, Gayatri Chakravorty. *In Other Worlds: Essays On Cultural Politics*. London: Methuen, 1987.

I would like to extend special thanks to Tessa Dora Addison for contributing a generous amount of her time and energy toward this project.

ELIZABETH A. WHEELER

BULLDOZING THE SUBJECT

ONE | MUDANZAS

Hoboken, New Jersey 1985

WHEN I HEAR the word "postmodernism" I see white people moving into the neighborhood and brown people having to move out.

My friend Tinkerbell from Tustin and I used to live in an apartment building wedged between a condominium and a tenement. We went to an open house in the condominium; the units sold for $275,000-$300,000 apiece. It looked like the QEII. The architect had added portholes, interior vistas, and pink balustrades. I went out on the balcony of the penthouse. Through the pink railings I saw a moving truck below, a small local one with "Mudanzas" painted on the side, the kind that carries Puerto Rican families further out from the city where they can still afford to live.

When I hear postmodernism I see pink balustrades in the foreground with a gray truck behind them. Not the balustrades alone, but also the changes – the mudanzas.

[1]   It is no accident that the Brooklyn Academy of Music, showcase for the latest postmodern compositions, defines one edge of a neighborhood called Park Slope, a neighborhood formerly working-class but now home to young professionals. It is no accident that the Temporary Contemporary museum of art in Los Angeles is housed in a renovated factory a block from Skid Row. It is no accident that postmodern architecture imprints itself most firmly on the urban landscape in the form of upmarket shopping malls. Postmodernism and gentrification are partners in joint venture.

[2]   "... the *scenario* of work is there to conceal the fact that the work-real, the production real, has disappeared," writes Jean Baudrillard (*Simulations* 47). Production has not vanished from the face of the earth; it has instead moved to the Third World. However, Baudrillard is right in touching on the unreality of life in postindustrial cities.

> It is thus extremely naive to look for ethnology among the Savages or in some Third World – it is here, everywhere, in the metropolis, among the whites, in a world completely catalogued and analysed and then artificially revived as though real . . . (16)

[3]   I write this essay towards an ethnology of postmodernism. It concentrates on the gentrification of Los Angeles in the 1980s, and finishes with a postscript on the 1992 insurrection. It starts on a city street.

TWO | THE DAY OF THE DEAD

Melrose Avenue, West Los Angeles 1987

> On Melrose, a district of stylish boutiques, there is a store painted in Day-Glo colors and stenciled with skulls like the Mexican images used in celebrating el Día de los Muertos, the day of the dead. The store is extremely successful and has counterparts in many American cities. It specializes in 'kitsch' artifacts: sequin picture frames, pink flamingoes, Barbie lunch boxes, but particularly inexpensive Mexican religious articles. As Baudrillard says, consumer culture needs to "stockpile the past in plain view" (19). The store has a day-of-the-dead quality: when the plastic dashboard Virgins go up on the shelves next to the plaster Elvises, pop nostalgia renders every icon equivalent. In Baudrillard's terms, the experience of shopping there has the power to cancel out the real experience of growing up Chicano/a and Catholic.

"For ethnology to live, its object must die" – *". . . the sign as reversion and death sentence of every reference."* (13, 11)

[4]   I feel a guilty fascination for the store because it looks very much like my own aesthetic. I have always loved bright colors, colors that looked garish in my parents' suburban home with its white walls, white curtains, white dishes. And for years I have collected Mexican religious articles, sneaking into *botanicas* where no one spoke English, hoping they wouldn't divine the irreligious, "inauthentic" uses to which I planned to put such items. When I walk into the store on Melrose, I see my own secret life as a kitsch consumer exposed.

[5]   I like to think, however, that there is something else going on between me and my Virgins of Guadalupe than my making fun of them. With their angels and showers of roses, I find them beautiful and redemptive. They speak to my Protestant longing for a spirituality that has festive colors and a Mother in it. My taste also carries an element of defiance: when I was growing up in Southern California, Mexicans were regarded as lower than us whites, and with the exception of "genuine" folk art, so was their culture.

[6]   Postmodernism is all about theft and transformation, as for instance my "inauthentic" use of the Virgin of Guadalupe. Here are the successive phases of the postmodern image:

> – the image is part of a culture, and
>   used by that culture with straight-
>   forward enjoyment;

> – the image is rejected as tacky, part
>   of an outmoded past to be left behind;

> – the image is resuscitated and used
>   defiantly, ironically, self-consciously,
>   often as part of a new chic.

[7]   Imagine the store on Melrose again. Now there is a low rider cruising down the avenue, carrying a Chicano couple dressed in the latest youth fashion. The car has a beautiful turquoise and red metallic paint job. It has a plastic Virgin on the dashboard. But there is a crucial difference between the car and the store.

[8]   Unlike Baudrillard, I believe that postmodern thefts and transformations do not have to kill the culture to which they refer. A Mexican-American can fragment, reappropriate, reconstruct "Mexicanness" for herself or himself, and help to define what it means to be Mexican. This variety of postmodernism maintains a relationship with a living community; it is not an autopsy on dead referents. In this paper I will describe two postmodernisms, one informal and personal, one heavily capitalized and imposed from outside. I will spend much of my time criticizing the ways French postmodern theory reinforces the cynical logic of kitsch consumerism.

[9]   Intolerance is the hallmark of dogma. While postmodern theory, particularly of the French sort, claims to have no "metanarrative," it reveals its dogmatism by only tolerating certain readings of itself. If Baudrillard refuses to ask or answer moral questions, then perversely I want to view him as a moralist. In *Simulations: The Precession of Simulacra*, he describes the death of the referent:

> – it is the reflection of a
>   basic reality
>
> – it masks and perverts
>   a basic reality
>
> – it masks the absence
>   of a basic reality
>
> – it bears no relation to
>   any reality whatsoever:
>   it is its own pure simula-
>   crum. (11)

[10]   What if we read Baudrillard's scale not as descriptive but as proscriptive, as a hierarchy of values? Those of us who still believe in realities, however fragmented, contested, and multiple, can then be dismissed as unprogressive, as "naive and cognitively immature" (Gilligan 30).1

[11]   How could this postmodern scale of values inform the ethnology of a particular city: Los Angeles? Baudrillard begins with the idea that "what draws the crowds" to Disneyland is not so much the entry into fantastic worlds as the "miniaturised and *religious* revelling

in real America" (23). He immediately moves beyond ideological analysis to a far more sweeping commentary:

> Disneyland is presented as imaginary in order to make us believe that the rest is real, when in fact all of Los Angeles and the America surrounding it are no longer real, but of the order of the hyperreal and of simulation. It is no longer a question of a false representation of reality (ideology), but of concealing the fact that the real is no longer real, and thus of saving the reality-principle . . .
>
> Los Angeles is encircled by these "imaginary stations" which feed reality, reality-energy, to a town whose mystery is precisely that it is nothing more than a network of endless, unreal circulation – a town of fabulous proportions, but without space or dimensions . . . this town, which is nothing more than an immense script and a perpetual motion picture, needs this old imaginary made up of childhood signals and faked phantasms for its sympathetic nervous system. (25, 26)

[12]   Anyone who has ever tried to get around Los Angeles without a car knows how real it is, how mired in "space and dimensions," how cruel to the poor. In promoting the unreality of Los Angeles, Baudrillard does the cops' dirty work. Because it is the most segmented of American cities, it was possible for Mayor Tom Bradley to instruct the police to round up homeless people with bulldozers and drive them into camps without shade or adequate sanitation. It is possible to grow up middle-class a few miles from Skid Row and never see a homeless person. The myth of Los Angeles as a fabulous unreality justifies the quiet elimination of its less-than-fabulous, all-too-real aspects.

[13]   Richard Rorty speaks of the "strand in contemporary French thought" that "starts off from suspicion of Marx and Freud, suspicion of the masters of suspicion, suspicion of 'unmasking'" (161). By itself, an ideological analysis of Los Angeles would remain impoverished. However, without the intellectual tool of unmasking, there is no suffering to uncover. Without awareness of power, it is the powerless who disappear.

THREE | BULLDOZING THE SUBJECT

Downtown Los Angeles, March 1987

> *Postmodern architecture plays a concrete role in the disappearance of the unwanted "referent." At 515 EAST 6TH STREET on SKID ROW, there is a soup kitchen and shelter called the WEINGARDT CENTER. Elegantly renovated in postmodern style, the building has WPA gargoyles and goddesses of work augmented with medieval banners and tastefully framed reproductions of modern art. When the building first opened, Maxine Johnston, director of the Center, did not allow her patrons to form a soup line in front of the building. It would spoil the look. Instead, they lined up around the corner, in front of the ugly building where my friend Tinkerbell worked.*

[14]   Johnston's penchant for postmodern decor and her harshness towards homeless people are more than individual eccentricities. They form part of a pattern. In the 1980s the City of Los Angeles devoted well over twenty million dollars to a redevelopment agency called SRO, Inc., which agency purchased Single Resident Occupancy hotels, renovated and postmodernized them. At 5th and San Julian, the hardest corner of Skid Row, a flophouse has been elaborately double-coded. It has neon signs in Old West, Victorian style. It has yuppie colors of mauve, pale green and beige. It has security guards everywhere.

[15]   On the morning of its rededication in 1987, Andy Robeson, director of SRO, Inc., stood outside the hotel with Mayor Tom Bradley. Robeson waved his hand across the panorama of 5th and San Julian, the street life, the raw deals, the people sleeping on the sidewalk. He turned to the mayor. "This has gotta go," he said. Soon bulldozers were sweeping 5th and San Julian three times a week. Since then, bulldozer sweeps have become an accepted part of

downtown life, sometimes more frequently, sometimes less. As of this writing, they come through twice a week.

[16]   How can it be said that the palest icon, the smallest neon-Victorian curlicue, enables and justifies the displacement of real people? Jochen Schulte-Sasse writes that to comprehend postmodernism we have to examine the "flow of capitalized images" (130). While modernism depends upon ideologically-charged, closed narratives, postmodernism relies on "the immediately transparent visual situation. Owning such images is capital, and the capital they represent reflects the capital that is invested in them. Every political campaign reveals the situation anew" (Schulte-Sasse 139).

[17]   In this well-financed, officially sanctioned SOLUTION TO HOMELESSNESS, the transparency of the neon sign makes it an excellent mask. The sign resembles Reaganism's image of the family — glowing, oversimplified, easy to read. Its readability distracts us from lived experience. It steals from our mouths the vocabulary we need to describe anger, family breakdown, the failure of all solutions to homelessness.

> Henceforth, it is the map that precedes the territory — PRECISION OF SIMULACRA — it is the map that engenders the territory and if we were to revive the fable today, it would be the territory whose shreds are slowly rotting across the map. (Baudrillard 2)

[18]   Postmodern architecture suits Los Angeles well. Its pastels and fanciful details talk back to the thousands of stucco bungalows built in Los Angeles in the 1920's and 1930's. Both architectural forms represent certain middle- class dreams, but they also differ in worldview.

[19]   Although built to look like a miniature castle, hacienda, mosque or Tudor cottage, the stucco bungalow can be called modernist. Families shut the doors of their dreamhouses and imagine themselves into a narrative, a tale of their freedom out West, their escape from an extended family and messy history back East.

[20]   In contrast, a postmodern residence is not a fictive universe. It is a surface, oddly two-dimensional, meant to be scanned rather than lived in. "It seems to me that the essay (Montaigne) is

postmodern, while the fragment (*The Athaeneum*) is modern," Lyotard writes (81). A postmodern building bears a very strong resemblance to an essay, with "quotations" from past architectures inserted into a grid format.

[21]   The art of quotation serves many purposes. Particularly characteristic of postmodernism is a blank parody, where it is impossible to determine the attitude of the citer towards the citation (Jameson 118). Despite this frequent indeterminacy, quotation in postmodern architecture often serves the same function as in the essay: it invokes authority. Strangely enough, Linda Hutcheon sees the quotation of classical motifs as a populist gesture.

> Like all parody, postmodernist architecture can certainly be elitist, if the codes necessary for its comprehension are not shared by both encoder and decoder. But the frequent use of a very common and easily recognized idiom – often that of classicism – works to combat such exclusiveness. (200)

[22]   Hutcheon goes so far as to valorize postmodern architects as "activists, the voices of the users" (8). However, as Mike Davis points out, rhapsodic critics have tended to overlook the obvious. A casual walk through downtown Los Angeles (if such were possible) would show you the new buildings' authoritarian attitude. "Public" spaces are openly hostile to certain publics, and combine architecture with surveillance. Whether discussing Frank Gehry's militarized library or the invention of the "bumproof" bus bench, Davis shows the complicity of postmodern L.A. architects in creating what he calls "spatial apartheid" (Davis 1992, 230):

> Yet contemporary urban theory, whether debating the role of electronic technologies in precipitating "postmodern space," or discussing the dispersion of urban functions across poly-centered metropolitan "galaxies," has been strangely silent about the militarization of city life so grimly visible at the street level. (Davis 1992, 223)
>
> . . . .
>
> Today's upscale, pseudo-public spaces – sumptuary malls, office centers, culture acropolises, and so on –

*are full of invisible signs warning off the under-
class "Other." Although architectural critics are usually oblivious to how the built environment contributes to segregation, pariah groups – whether poor
Latino families, young Black men, or elderly homeless white females – read the meaning immediately.
(Davis 1992, 226)*

FOUR | IT WILL BE "WHITE" LIKE ONE OF MALEVITCH'S SQUARES

*I was talking with my friend Paul Lopes about the
postmodern fragmentation of the "subject," the concept of the individual human doer or creator in Western philosophy. Paul said it reminded him of cults. The
first job of a cult is to break down your previous
identity and make you distrust it. "But they don't
leave it fragmented," he said. "They give you a new
identity to take its place – one they choose for you."*

[23]   While Baudrillard and Lyotard may genuinely believe in the death of the subject, most people do not. Maxine Johnston and Andy Robeson, for example, still believe in a referent. There is a reality out there they wish to manage into submission, and they use postmodern architecture cynically to help them do so. To invoke conspiracy theory, the death of a homeless "subject" creates a vacuum that can be filled by a "subject" with a better credit rating.

[24]   Returning to the cult analogy, identity does not stay fragmented – another identity rushes in to take its place. "We have seen that there is a way in which postmodernism replicates or reproduces – reinforces – the logic of consumer capitalism; the more significant question is whether there is also a way in which it resists that logic. But that is a question we must leave open" (Jameson 125).

[25]   In 1988 Cynthia Hamilton made a similar argument not about Skid Row but about the ghettoes of South Central. Hamilton compares South Central to a South African bantustan, explaining

how "containment zones," to use the LAPD term, function within the logic of urban capital:

> Much like the bulldozing of black encampments on the fringe of Johannesburg or Durban, it can be argued, South Central is inevitably slated by the historical process to be replaced without a trace: cleared land ready for development for a more prosperous – and probably whiter – class of people. . . This "bantustan," like its counterparts in South Africa, serves now only as a holding space for blacks and browns no longer of use to the larger economy.

[26]   In "What is Postmodernism?" Lyotard describes his ideal aesthetic of sublime painting. Again, if we view him as moralist as well as narrator, this process of "making it impossible to see" reads as deliberate erasure of the subject. The critic learns to look the other way when he hears bulldozers coming. Since those most likely to be erased are people of color, when Lyotard says his ideal is "white" I take him at his word.

> It will be "white" like one of Malevitch's squares; it will enable us to see only by making it impossible to see; it will please only by causing pain. (78)

[27]   French postmodern theorists in general, Lyotard and Baudrillard in particular, embrace the role of pain in knowledge. The impulse is paralleled by the sadomasochism in much postmodern literature and film. Both Baudrillard and Lyotard describe terror with a steady indifference. Richard Rorty comments on this philosophical "dryness" which descends from Foucault:

> It takes no more than a squint of the inner eye to read Foucault as a stoic, a dispassionate observer of the present social order, rather than its concerned critic. . . . It is this remoteness which reminds one of the conservative who pours cold water on hopes for reform, who affects to look at the problems of his fellow-citizens with the eye of the future historian. Writing "the history of the present," rather than suggestions about how our children might inhabit a bet-

ter world in the future, gives up not just on the notion of a common human nature, and on that of "the subject," but on our untheoretical sense of social solidarity. It is as if thinkers like Foucault and Lyotard were so afraid of being caught up in one more metanarrative about the fortunes of "the subject" that they cannot bring themselves to say "we" long enough to identify with the culture of the generation to which they belong. (172)

Baudrillard observes in a dispassionate footnote:

From now on, it is impossible to ask the famous question:
 "From what position do you speak?" –
 "How do you know?" –
 "From where do you get the power?," without immediately getting the reply: "But it is of (from) you that I speak" – meaning, it is you who speaks, it is you who knows, power is you. A gigantic circumlocution, circumlocution of the spoken word, which amounts to irredeemable blackmail and irremovable deterrence of the subject supposed to speak. (77-78)

[28] My first reaction to the above passage is an untheoretical and wordless rage. It is the anger every woman must have experienced, the feeling of being charged with our own victimization. ("Let's rape his daughter and see how he talks then," Tink says as she passes through the room.) In this explication Baudrillard calls for the end of dualistic thought, a central postmodernist project: "The medium/message confusion, of course, is a correlative of the confusion between sender and receiver, thus sealing the disappearance of all the dual, polar structures which formed the discursive organization of language, referring to the celebrated grid of functions in Jakobson. . . ." (76).

[29] The critique of dualism was a feminist project before it was a postmodern one. Adrienne Rich:

The rejection of the dualism, of the positive-negative polarities between which most of our intellectual training has taken place, has been an undercurrent of

*feminist thought. And, rejecting them, we reaffirm the
existence of all those who have through the centuries
been negatively defined: not only women, but the "un-
touchable," the "unmanly," the "nonwhite," the "illit-
erate": the "invisible." Which forces us to confront
the problem of the essential dichotomy: power/pow-
erlessness. (48)*

[30]   Ironically, Baudrillard uses the critique to an opposite end.
While the feminist wants to reveal the "invisible," to expose the
power relations inherent in dualism – white over black, male over
female, gentry over homeless – Baudrillard maintains that without
dualism power relations simply disappear. That is, if a conversation
is not organized in binary oppositions, it becomes completely dis-
ordered. However, there are other ways to critique the dualism
of structural linguistics. For instance, in "The Problem of Speech
Genres," Mikhail Bakhtin maintains that a conversation is ordered
not in sentence parts à la Roman Jakobson, but according to the
shifts in speaking subjects. Therefore it is still possible to ask, "From
what position do you speak?" Speaking "*of*" me does not mean
speaking "(from)" me.

[31]   We cannot sufficiently counter the dryness of Baudrillard's
logic without invoking the category of experience. When Baudrillard
speaks through the voice of the media or of the nuclear arms race,
he speaks of "the inconsequential violence that reigns throughout
the world, of the aleatory contrivance of every choice which is made
for us." Violence is inconsequential unless it happens *to you*. Baudrillard's indifference reveals the comfort of his own position. When
Baudrillard writes that "prisons are there to conceal the fact that it is
the social in its entirety, in its banal omnipresence, which is carceral"
(25), we know for certain he has never been to jail.

[32]   Baudrillard's mission seems to be to make us accept the
blank fact of terror. His work contains seeds of contempt for those
who refuse to accept the horror of the world. This rubric marks out a
diverse group, from people who desire the comfort of realist art, to
those who fight for political change. For Baudrillard, to insist on the
category of reality is to be in collusion with the powers-that-be.
Lyotard's contempt for the realist is even more blatant. His sublime

painting will "impart no knowledge about reality (experience)"; he disparages realist art forms like commercial photography and film, whose job is "to stabilize the referent" and to "enable the addressee . . . to arrive quickly at the consciousness of his own identity": "The painter and the novelist must refuse to lend themselves to such therapeutic uses" (78, 74).

[33]   Beneath his contempt lies the assumption that people cannot detect the harshness of their own experience and must have it explained to them. When Lyotard uses the word "therapeutic" disparagingly, he dismisses the role of the artist as healer. It never occurs to him that the viewers, the "patients," may have experienced more horror than he will ever know.

[34]   While realism is the dominant style of commercial media, the media do not have the deep stake in reality– effects both Lyotard and Baudrillard attribute to them. Television eats up postmodernism along with any other style available to it. Therefore, parody is not intrinsically subversive, as Baudrillard would claim. A postmodern segment of "Mighty Mouse," with fragments of 1940s episodes cut out of their narratives, edited by visual and rhythmic analogy, and set to a 1960's soul song, is no more or less subversive than any other kiddie cartoon.

[35]   Jochen Schulte-Sasse makes an important refinement on the realism argument in pointing out the "simultaneity of the non-simultaneous" between modernism and postmodernism. He remarks that neoconservative politics uses both modes, making a modernist call for "authority" and "values" while engaging in a brilliant postmodern manipulation of images. Schulte-Sasse sees this vacillation as a weakness, "one reason why neoconservatism is likely to remain a transitory phenomenon." I see it as neoconservatism's strength: it won on both fronts, appealing to the conscience while "colonizing the id" (145). The avant-garde, the State, or the television network can use either mode to any purpose.

[36]   Lyotard's championship of the avant-garde sounds curiously outdated: an anxious Baudelaire in his day made an almost identical argument for painting against photography. Lyotard assumes that there is no creativity outside the artistic bohemia and that the vernacular is by nature reactionary. This is a common aca-

demic failing. In *Rocking Around the Clock: Music Television, Postmodernism, and Consumer Culture*, E. Ann Kaplan sees only two options: either commercial mass media generated by corporations, or the avant-garde. Similarly, for Laura Mulvey there is only the dominating "male gaze" of Hollywood movies, or a quite unwatchable Brechtian cinema.

[37]   Lyotard decries the contemporary process of increasing eclecticism and kitsch: "...one listens to reggae, watches a western, eats MacDonald's food for lunch and local cuisine for dinner, wears Paris cologne in Tokyo and "retro" clothes in Hong Kong; knowledge is a matter for TV games...But this realism of the 'anything goes' is in fact that of money; in the absence of aesthetic criteria, it remains possible and useful to assess the value of works of art according to the profits they yield" (76).

[38]   Lyotard helps to promote the process he decries. "The desire for the sublime makes one want to cut free from the words of the tribe," Rorty writes (175). To deny the identity of a creative community is to help the media steal its products without acknowledgment. "Local tone" is one of the reality-effects Lyotard likes to see undermined by avant-garde art (79). "Local tone" is the first quality stripped away by the commercial media.

[39]   A rap song by the African-American group Salt'n'Pepa is postmodern in form – a montage of cuts from past musics – and very New York in feeling. When the same beat occurs in a candy commercial on TV, there is nothing black or local about it. In the age of cannibalization, "to cut free from the words of the tribe" is to cut the tribe free of its *own* words.

[40]   In seeking to "activate the differences and save the honor of the name," Lyotard apparently desires the inclusion of new and varied voices in the definition of culture (80). However, if he rejects narratives of struggle and liberation, much of Third World writing goes out the window again. For instance, Cherrie Moraga's *Loving in the War Years* could be and has been called a postmodern autobiography, because of the montage of genres within the text; the ways sexuality and race are always constructed, never taken as givens; and her constant play between fragmentation and a unified self. Nonetheless, Moraga is also a self-declared "movement writer," a Chicana

lesbian feminist who keeps faith with the ideals of liberation (Moraga, v). To use her image without her ideas is a reprehensible theft.

[41]   Furthermore, current postmodern theory could never come to terms with Moraga's insistence on experience, emotion, and direct speech. As bell hooks argues, if postmodernism "decenters authority," theorists must prove that claim by combatting elitism in writing style and attitudes.

> *Radical postmodernist practice, most powerfully conceptualized as a "politics of difference," should incorporate the voices of displaced, marginalized, exploited, and oppressed black people. It is sadly ironic that the contemporary discourse which talks the most about heterogeneity, the decentered subject, declaring breakthroughs that allow recognition of Otherness, still directs its critical voice primarily to a specialized audience that shares a common language rooted in the very master narratives it claims to challenge. If radical postmodernist thinking is to have a transformative impact, then a critical break with the notion of "authority" as "mastery over" must not simply be a rhetorical device. It must be reflected in habits of being, including styles of writing as well as chosen subject matter. (hooks, 25)*

[42]   In postmodernity it is indeed possible, as Lyotard writes, "to assess the value of works of art according to the profits they yield" (17). Price is the only difference between a plastic Virgin of Guadalupe for sale on Melrose Avenue or in a *botanica* in East Los Angeles. There is a 50 percent markup for ironic distance. If pop culture becomes art, the critic will have to work harder to redifferentiate herself or himself from the vulgar masses. Hence the writing style of a Lyotard: the invocation of classicism, the return to Kant, the resuscitation of Longinus' sublime and the traditional genre of the defense of poetry. The "lower" the culture, the "higher" the theory.

[43]   The anxious intellectual puts theory ahead of artistic practice; in fact, he or she attempts to make all of human experience look like an *example* of postmodern theory. This is evident in postmodern

approaches to Third World and/or feminist discourses. It is not only a matter of claiming such discourses for postmodernism; it is a matter of approving such discourses *because they are postmodern.* This somehow establishes their worth. Craig Owens:

> Still, if one of the most salient aspects of our post-modern culture is the presence of an insistent feminist voice (and I use the terms presence and voice advisedly), theories of postmodernism have tended either to neglect or to repress that voice . . . I would like to propose, however, that women's insistence on difference and incommensurability may not only be compatible with, but also an instance of postmodern thought. (61-62)

William Boelhower:

> This new ethnic pragmatics . . . in the very act of reflecting on its own limits, will discover the very strategies that make the ethnic verbum a major filter for reading the modern and so-called postmodern experience not as a universal condition but as a historical construct. (120)

George Lipsitz:

> But ethnic minority cultures play an important role in this postmodern culture. Their exclusion from political power and cultural recognition has enabled them to cultivate a sophisticated capacity for ambiguity, juxtaposition, and irony – all key qualities in the postmodern aesthetic. (159)

[44]   As Richard Rorty points out, this intellectual anxiety has to do with the difficulty of being part of one's own generation. The middle-class members of the post-World War II generation grew up in splendid isolation. In the United States we lived in suburban utopias, deliberately shielded from urban strife and any kind of past. In Europe, especially in Germany, cities were rebuilt out of concrete and the past was paved over. Suburbanization made us stupid. I think of Dustin Hoffman in the film *The Graduate* (1968), floating aimlessly in his parents' pool. Barbara Ehrenreich:

> A generation ago, for example, hordes of white peo-
> ple fled the challenging, interracial atmosphere of
> the cities and settled in whites-only suburbs. . . .
> Cut off from the mainstream of humanity, we came
> to believe that pink is "flesh-color," that mayon-
> naise is a nutrient, and that Barry Manilow is a
> musician. (20)

[45]   In Wim Wenders' 1974 film *Wrong Move*, Rudiger Vogler
wanders through the concrete wasteland of a bedroom town outside Frankfurt:

> Statt verzweifelt zu werden spürte ich nur, daß ich
> immer dummer wurde, und daß ich die wirklich
> verzweifelten um mich herum nur dumm anschauen
> konnte. Trotzdem bewegte ich mich durch die zube-
> tonnierte Landschaft als sei ich noch immer der, der
> alles erlitte – der Held. [Instead of becoming des-
> perate, I sensed that I was becoming stupider, and
> that I could only stare dumbly at the really desper-
> ate people around me. In spite of this, I moved
> though the concrete landscape as if I were still the
> one who suffered everything – the hero.]

[46]   By the mid-seventies the critique of suburbanized culture
was in full swing. In the face of feminism and immigration of ethnic
groups, the white male subject becomes worried that he is not the
hero of the story anymore. 1980s gentrification increased this anxiety. When members of the suburban middle class moved back into
the city, into areas such as Kreuzberg in West Berlin and downtown
Los Angeles, which had been home to working-class immigrants and
other minorities, we learned to negotiate a multi-cultural reality.

[47]   Many critics before me have pointed out the irony that,
just as previously-silenced, darker-skinned, non-Western, female
subjects begin to make themselves heard, the white European male
declares "the death of the subject."[2] I do not want to dwell on that
irony here, particularly since I want to affirm that postmodernism is
not a sham but a real process, a central part of our creative lives. It is
its theoretization and some of its official uses which are inadequate
and destructive.

FIVE | "THE LAWRENCE WELK SHOW SALUTES FREE ENTERPRISE"

Ludington, Michigan   February 1988

> *Deep in the heart of the Midwest, I am watching a rerun of "The Lawrence Welk Show." I experience the deep spinal tingle of the "certification effect," as that most Midwestern of television shows doubles for and validates the Midwest itself.*

> *I try to shove down my hilarity in front of my grandfather. It strikes me that the show isn't "realist" at all; it suffers from a mannerism so extreme it makes Parmigianino look like Norman Rockwell. Simulated faces à la Baudrillard:*

> *". . . they are already purged of death, and even better than in life; more smiling, more authentic, in light of their model, like the faces in funeral parlors" (23).*

> *My grandmother, now in a nursing home, was wildly in love with Lawrence Welk. My parents and I used to watch the show to make fun of it. Although we kept up our running ironic patter in front of the screen, over the years the show became a weirdly affirmative bonding ritual for the three of us. As I watch now, it scares me to realize how much of this Midwestern ethic I have absorbed: the sentimentality, the enforced niceness, the determination not to "go over anybody's head."*

> *When my parents moved out to Los Angeles after World War II, much of their Michigan past got erased. The more plebeian parts in particular got untold night after night at the dinner table. I have had to reconstruct them for myself with the help of this horrendous videotape.*

> *However, this is not a simulation; Lawrence Welk does*
> *not replace or erase me or my family. This odd arche-*
> *ology, this true-and-false process of calling myself a*
> *Midwesterner, exists in a set of relationships. There is*
> *my desire to remember what my grandmother liked,*
> *and was like, before her strokes. There is the smarta-*
> *leck sense of humor I share with my parents. Out of*
> *the tacky pieces of my family, out of the worst of*
> *American culture, I am building a self.*

[48]   I propose a double model for postmodernism. The official variety, the postmodernism of the development corporation and the dead referent, I call *classical* postmodernism. I name the variety after its reliance on classical motifs in architecture and in the essay; however, I also have in mind Bakhtin's distinction between the classical and the grotesque (in *Rabelais and His World*). For me as for him, classical art suffers because it is polished and finished off, denying its origins in unofficial popular art. A TV commercial or avant-garde monologue could be equally classical in their denial of origins. I see postmodernism as a creativity that begins in people's living rooms and automobiles and *then* makes its way to *Documenta* and the Brooklyn Academy of Music.

[49]   The second variety I call *messy, vital* postmodernism after Robert Venturi, who wrote the first postmodernist manifesto: "I am for messy vitality over obvious unity" (16). This postmodernism is not ashamed of its relationship to popular culture and the vernacular. George Lipsitz is quite right in commenting that pop music leads high art in the use of postmodern forms:

> *It is on the level of commodified mass culture that*
> *the most popular, and often the most profound, acts*
> *of cultural bricolage take place. The destruction of*
> *established canons and the juxtaposition of seeming-*
> *ly inappropriate forms that characterize the self-*
> *conscious postmodernism of "high culture" have long*
> *been staples of commodified popular culture.* (161)

[50]   While Lipsitz is writing on Chicano rock'n'roll, I know the truth of his statement through my own work on hiphop music. A three-minute hiphop track epitomizes the postmodern art of quota-

tion. In a high-speed electronic theft the DJ may combine cuts from Funkadelic, Kraftwerk, Mozart, Evelyn "Champagne" King, spaghetti Westerns and Senate testimony. Usually this is the low-affect quotation characteristic of postmodernism. Sometimes, however, you can discern an attitude towards the material quoted, which leads us to some of the differences between classical and messy, vital postmodernism.

[51]   Richard Rorty writes of the Habermas-Lyotard debate:

> We could agree with Lyotard that we need no more
> metanarratives, but with Habermas that we need less
> dryness. We could agree with Lyotard that studies of
> the communicative competence of the transhistorical
> subject are of little use in reinforcing our sense of
> identification with our community, while still insisting
> on the importance of that sense. (173)

[52]   A community feeling still reverberates in the urban popular musics we can call postmodern. For instance, the beats of James Brown are ubiquitous in hiphop music; the form would not exist without him. Brown even recorded a rap song, "I'm Real," to call attention to his continued existence in the face of so many copies. When the hiphop composer quotes James Brown, his or her attitude is always reverent. However, the listener cannot detect this reverence from the song alone. It is community-based knowledge. One has to hear people from the Bronx or South Central talk about Brown and his status in Black music history.

[53]   Lipsitz stresses the postmodernism of Chicano rock'n'roll, but also its grounding in the culture's experience: ". . . this marginal sensibility in music amounts to more than novelty or personal eccentricity; it holds legitimacy and power as the product of a real historical community's struggle with oppression" (175). Similarly, L.A. writer Ruben Martinez offers a catalogue of transnational consumerism like Lyotard's, but to a different end: to affirm that it still matters what color people are and why they're angry.

> One can spy on multilingual store signs in New York
> or Los Angeles, eat food from all over the world, listen
> to the rhythms of every culture and time on the air-

> *waves, but the fires of nationalism still rage, and in*
> *the cities of the United States, blacks and Koreans*
> *and Latinos and Anglos live in anything but a multi-*
> *cultural paradise. (Martinez, 1992)*

[54]   The individual subject, resistant to racism, still rules in popular urban arts. Here we glance back at Jochen Schulte-Sasse's "simultaneity of the non-simultaneous" in the combined use of modern
and postmodern forms:

> *The forms of cultural reproduction in modernity were*
> *closely linked to a mode of socialization intended to*
> *produce strong super-egos, which in turn favored*
> *the development of agonistic, competitive individuals*
> *with clearly delimited, ideological identities. (126)*

[55]   This sounds very much like the aggressive stance of the
pachuco or the rapper, proclaiming a resolute identity over a postmodern beat. While these figures often topple over into *machismo*,
the same idea of mixed modes could also apply to the feminist
Cherrie Moraga. She makes an uneasy, wrenchingly honest attempt
at a unified self because she needs to. While fragmentation plays an
important role in her work, she does not exalt it. Her subjectivity, her
community, have already been fragmented enough.

SIX | EL CERRITO, CALIFORNIA

April 29, 1992   My 33rd birthday

> *Before we moved to the suburbs in 1963, my*
> *family lived just a few blocks from the cor-*
> *ner of Florence and Normandie, epicenter*
> *of the 1992 riots. The day after the verdict,*
> *my father pointed to the television and*
> *said, "Look, Phyllis, there's our old super-*
> *market up in flames."*

[56]   The rage I saw frightened but did not surprise me. In a way it made me feel less crazy than usual. It gave concrete form to a (for me) often hard-to-nail reality. At tollbooths and checkout counters, with African-Americans I didn't know, I felt the cards go out on the table. We'd look each other straight in the eye – you-know-and-I-know – then transact our business with extra courtesy. For a brief window of time, it became possible to talk about racism and injustice with any other white person I met – not just with certain friends or in certain circles. Gradually that option closed back down again.

[57]   The process reminded me of a frantic phone call we received in 1965, during the Watts riots. My aunt still lived downtown and wondered if she should try to get in her car and come stay with us in the suburbs. That was the first time I remember knowing there was another reality, within driving distance of my world but with no visible correlative to it.

[58]   I have been thinking about ways to become responsible to my birthplace. However, as I write I feel uneasy with my personal stance. I'm not "the one who suffered everything – the hero." Experiencing something is not the same as seeing it on television.

[59]   The weeks after April 29, 1992 showed L.A.'s uneven balance of reality: some people had too little and some too much. At least three levels of knowledge exist about racist brutality. Some people experience it firsthand. Others know it happens all the time, if not to them. Yet others don't have a clue. With the videotape of Rodney King's beating, it seemed the knowledge of brutality could become widespread and generally accepted. In the not-guilty verdict, official language refused to mirror inner-city truth.

> *With those acquittals, for one shocking moment we all knew what it meant to feel something, to know it like the back of your hand, the bruise on your jaw, and then to have it denied. No, what you saw, experienced, suffered was really something other than what you saw, experienced, suffered. (Lisa Kennedy, "Blow by Blow," Institute 72)*

[60]   Such denial makes one feel crazy. If the basic reality could not be acknowledged in official words, Angelenos set out to burn it

on the landscape, while acquiring a few consumer products along the way. An anonymous man, who had looted a computer and then wished to return it, gave an important interview to *Mother Jones*'s David Weir. He described the destructiveness of life in South Central, his own efforts to stay human, and the craziness of living in a world soundless and invisible to the "dreamworld" of whites:

> When I saw white people being beaten in the street on TV, I smiled ear to ear and jumped up and down with glee, because it told me that I'm not crazy. I hate to say I did that, because I have white friends, but I've been screaming for a long time and nobody has been listening. . .
>
> . . . .
>
> I've been thinking for a long time that I'm crazy. There was one day, about a year ago, that I felt like going out and killing somebody. The denial in this country about what's really going on is so deep. For black men, we thought we were going crazy. But this event convinced me I was not nuts. . .
>
> . . . .
>
> The envelope was turned inside out for us, and we could see the seams. The riots straightened everything out. If the powers-that-be don't do something, if they don't pick up the ball and run in the right direction, there's no reason for us not to do it again. If you're not going to let us live, then nobody is going to live. Listen to me! That scared me! But I'll be there. I don't have any options.
>
> . . . .
>
> One day my brother, when he was 27, came home wearing only boxer shorts and one sock, and he had tire tracks, car-tire tracks, across his chest. When I asked him what happened, he said he didn't know. He didn't know what happened to him. Later on, he was shot in the arm, and he lost the use of his arm. That's what it's

like to live in South Central. My sister was
raped by nine guys. It's that desperate a situa-
tion. That's what happens there every day. I'm
gone from there, but I carry it with me. I see
white people, and they're living in a different
world, man, a dreamworld. (David Weir, "No-
body Listens," Institute 103)

[61]   Meanwhile, back in the Simulacrum, Mayor Bradley placed the rebuilding firmly in the hands of big capital. Peter Ueberroth's "Rebuild L.A." task force needs not answer to the public. "This Prophet of Profit immediately warned there would be 'no handouts' and that it would be not the state or federal government, God forbid, but the private sector that would reconstruct the ghetto. But it is that same private sector that has, under Bradley's stewardship, systematically retreated from, abandoned and ultimately strangled South Central Los Angeles" (Marc Cooper and Greg Goldin, "Some People Don't Count," Institute 46).

[62]   "Rebuild L.A." has acheived its greatest success to date by reducing its name to "R.L.A." and imprinting it on nice T-shirts. The "R.L.A." icon replaces and displaces pain in a couple of ways. In characteristic L.A. style, it manages chaos through chic. "R.L.A." read as "Our.L.A." erases the biggest problem, that of consensus, by regarding it as solved. As the anonymous speaker described above, "I've been screaming for a long time and nobody has been listening." There is no conversation, no common world, no "Our.L.A."

[63]   In 1993, Richard Riordan ran for mayor of Los Angeles against Councilman Michael Woo, and won on promises of law and order and more big-business solutions. In the suburban San Fernando Valley, the Riordan campaign circulated a leaflet showing a photograph of an African-American homeless person with the slogan: "Welcome to Michael Woo's Los Angeles." In another context, one could view this statement as a compliment, testimony to Councilman Woo's willingness to grasp the city's problems. In Riordan's context, such willingness is weakness. Riordan's vision acknowledges the city as a site of contested realities – but only one reality can win at a time. The message carries a science-fiction fear of contamination: Vote for me or you will become one of Them.

[64]   In this campaign leaflet as often in popular culture, the ghetto bears the burden of representing the city's reality – in condensed and essentialized form. Note the movie poster tag line for the summer of 1993's South Central gang film *Menace II Society*: "This is the truth. This is what's real." Critics often judge representations of the inner city by strict realist guidelines, guidelines they might consider outmoded for other subject matter. Sometimes they confuse realism with real life. As Heather Mackey writes, "Rap music tries to get a message out about the frustrating realities facing blacks today; mainstream media interprets that message as a threat" (Mackey, "I Told You So," Institute 128). In an interview concerning Ice-T's song "Cop Killer," actor Charlton Heston turned back into an irate Moses. When asked about the movie *The Terminator*, in which the Austrian actor Arnold Schwarzenegger kills L.A.P.D. members, Heston responded, "That's not real. It's a movie. Arnold Schwarzenegger doesn't really want to kill cops. Ice-T really wants to kill cops" (MacNeil-Lehrer Newshour, July 23, 1992).

[65]   If Cynthia Hamilton is right and South Central "serves now only as a holding space for blacks and browns no longer of use to the larger economy," maybe reality itself is just another outmoded product dumped downtown, a kind of postindustrial waste. South Central is a holding tank for suppressed truth, a switchboard programmed to dial America a periodic wake-up call. "If the powers-that-be don't do something, if they don't pick up the ball and run in the right direction, there's no reason for us not to do it again."

N   O   T   E   S

Grateful thanks to Rabbi Margaret Holub and Ms. Margarete Baum, Legal Aid Foundation of Los Angeles, for their insight, information, and fierce loyalty to homeless people.

1. I am thinking here of Carol Gilligan's feminist critique of Lawrence Kohlberg's scale of moral development, which moves from a stress on concrete human relationships upward to an increasing level of abstraction.

2. See for example Barbara Christian, "The Race for Theory," Cultural Critique 6 (Spring 1987), 51-63, as well as bell hooks, "Postmodern Blackness," cited below.

3. See Walker Percy, *The Moviegoer* (New York: Knopf, 1960).

W O R K S   C I T E D

Bakhtin, Mikhail. *Rabelais and His World.* Trans. Helene Iswolsky. Bloomington: Indiana UP, 1984.

Bakhtin, Mikhail. "The Problem of Speech Genres." In *Speech Genres and Other Late Essays.* Trans. Vern McGee. Austin: U of Texas P, 1986.

Baudrillard, Jean. *Simulations: The Precession of Simulacra.* Trans. Paul Foss, Paul Patton, and Philip Beitchman. London: Foreign Agents, 1984.

Boelhower, William. *Through a Glass Darkly: Ethnic Semiosis in American Literature.* New York: Oxford UP, 1987.

Davis, Mike. *City of Quartz: Excavating the Future in Los Angeles.* New York: Vintage, 1992.

Ehrenreich, Barbara. "The Unbearable Whiteness of Being." *This World.* San Francisco Chronicle 10 July 1988: 20.

Gilligan, Carol. *In a Different Voice: Psychological Theory and Women's Development.* Cambridge, MA: Harvard UP, 1982.

hooks, bell. "Postmodern Blackness." *Yearning: Race, Gender and Cultural Politics.* Boston: South End Press, 1990, 23-31.

Hutcheon, Linda. "The Politics of Postmodernism: Parody and History." *Cultural Critique* 5 (Winter 1986-87). 179-207.

Institute for Alternative Journalism, ed. *Inside the L.A. Riots: What Really Happened – and Why It Will Happen Again.* Institute for Alternative Journalism, 1992.

Jameson, Fredric. "Postmodernism and Consumer Society." *The Anti-Aesthetic: Essays on Postmodern Culture.* Ed. Hal Foster. Port Townsend, WA: Bay Press, 1983. 111-125.

Kaplan, E. Ann. *Rocking Around the Clock: Music Television, Postmodernism, and Consumer Culture.* New York: Methuen, 1987.

Lipsitz, George. "Cruising Around the Historical Bloc – Postmodernism and Popular Music in East Los Angeles." *Cultural Critique* 5 (Winter 1986-87). 157-177.

Lyotard, Jean-François. "What is Postmodernism?" 1982. *The Postmodern Condition: A Report on Knowledge.* Trans. Geoff Bennington and Brian Massumi. Minneapolis: U of Minnesota P, 1984.

Martinez, Ruben. *The Other Side: Fault Lines, Guerrilla Saints and the True Heart of Rock'n'Roll.* London and New York: Verso, 1992.

Moraga, Cherrie. *Loving in the War Years*. Boston: South End, 1983.

Mulvey, Laura. "Visual Pleasure and Narrative Cinema." *Women and the Cinema: A Critical Anthology.* Eds. Karyn Kay and Gerald Peary. New York: 1977. 412-428.

Owens, Craig. "The Discourse of Others: Feminism and Postmodernism." *The Anti-Aesthetic: Essays on Postmodern Culture.* Ed. Hal Foster. Port Townsend, WA: Bay Press, 1983. 57-77.

Rich, Adrienne. *Of Woman Born: Motherhood as Experience and Institution.* New York: W. W. Norton, 1976.

Rorty, Richard. "Habermas and Lyotard on Postmodernity." *Habermas and Modernity*. Ed. Richard J. Bernstein. Cambridge, MA: MIT, 1985. 161-175.

Schulte-Sasse, Jochen. "Electronic Media and Cultural Politics in the Reagan Era: The Attack on Libya and *Hands Across America* as Postmodern Events." *Cultural Critique* 8 (Winter 1987-88). 123-152.

Venturi, Robert. *Complexity and Contradiction in Architecture*. 1966. New York: Museum of Modern Art Papers on Architecture, 1977.

THE

MAR-

GINAL-

IZATION-

OF POETRY

-

-

-

bob

per –

el –

man

If

poems are eternal occasions, then
the pre-eternal context for the following

was a panel on "The Marginalization
of Poetry" at the American Comp.

Lit. Conference in San Diego, on
February 8, 1991, at 2:30 P.M.:

"The Marginalization of Poetry" – it almost
goes without saying. Jack Spicer wrote,

"No one listens to poetry," but
the question then becomes, who is

Jack Spicer? Poets for whom he
matters would know, and their poems

would be written in a world
in which that line was heard

though they'd scarcely refer to it.
Quoting or imitating another poet's line

is not benign, though at times
the practice can look like flattery.

In the regions of academic discourse,
the patterns of production and circulation

are different. There, it – again – goes
without saying that words, names, terms

are repeatable: citation is the prime
index of power. Strikingly original language

is not the point; the degree
to which a phrase or sentence

fits into a multiplicity of contexts
determines how influential it will be.

"The Marginalization of Poetry": the words
themselves display the dominant *lingua franca*

of the academic disciplines and, conversely,
the abject object status of poetry:

it's hard to think of any
poem where the word "marginalization" occurs.

It is being used here, but
this may or may not be

a poem: the couplets of six
word lines don't establish an audible

rhythm; perhaps they haven't, to use
the Calvinist mercantile metaphor, "earned" their

right to exist in their present
form – is this a line break

or am I simply chopping up
ineradicable prose? But to defend this

(poem) from its own attack, I'll
say that both the flush left

and irregular right margins constantly loom
as significant events, often interrupting what

I thought I was about to
write and making me write something

else entirely. Even though I'm going
back and rewriting, the problem still

reappears every six words. So this,
and every poem, is a marginal

work in a quite literal sense.
Prose poems are another matter: but

since they identify themselves as poems
through style and publication context, they

become a marginal subset of poetry,
in other words, doubly marginal. Now

of course I'm slipping back into
the metaphorical sense of marginal which,

however, in an academic context is
the standard sense. The growing mass

of writing on "marginalization" is not
concerned with margins, left or right

– and certainly not with its own.
Yet doesn't the word "marginalization" assume

the existence of some master page
beyond whose justified (and hence invisible)

margins the panoplies of themes, authors,
movements, general objects of study exist

in all their colorful, handlettered marginality?
This master page reflects the functioning

of the profession, where the units
of currency are variously denominated prose:

the paper, the article, the book.
All critical prose can be seen

as elongated, smooth-edged rectangles of writing,
the sequences of words chopped into

arbitrary lines by typesetters (Ruth in
tears amid the alien corn), and

into pages by commercial bookmaking processes.
This violent smoothness is the visible

sign of the writer's submission to
norms of technological reproduction. "Submission" is

not quite the right word, though:
the finesse of the printing indicates

that the author has shares in
the power of the technocratic grid;

just as the citations and footnotes
in articles and university press books

are emblems of professional inclusion. But
hasn't the picture become a bit

binary? Aren't there some distinctions to
be drawn? Do I really want

to invoke Lukács's antinomies of bourgeois
thought where rather than a conceptually

pure science that purchases its purity
at the cost of an irrational

and hence foul subject matter we
have the analogous odd couple of

a centralized, professionalized, cross-referenced criticism studying
marginalized, inspired (i.e., amateur), singular poetries?

Do I really want to lump
The Closing of the American Mind,

Walter Jackson Bate's biography of Keats,
and Anti-Oedipus together and oppose them

to any poem which happens to
be written in lines? Doesn't this

essentialize poetry in a big way?
Certainly some poetry is thoroughly opposed

to prose and does depend on
the precise way it's scored onto

the page: beyond their eccentric margins,
both Olson's Maximus Poems and Pound's

Cantos tend, as they progress, toward
the pictoral and gestural: in Pound

the Chinese ideograms, musical scores, hieroglyphs,
heart, diamond, club, and spade emblems,

little drawings of the moon and
of the winnowing tray of fate;

or those pages late in Maximus
where the orientation of the lines

spirals more than 360 degrees – one
spiralling page is reproduced in holograph.

These sections are immune to standardizing
media: to quote them you need

a photocopier not a word processor.
In a similar vein, the work

of some contemporary writers associated more
or less closely with the language

movement avoids standardized typographical grids and
is as self-specific as possible: Robert

Grenier's *Sentences*, a box of 500
poems printed on 5 by 8

notecards, or his recent work in
holograph, often scrawled; the variable leading

and irregular margins of Larry Eigner's
poems; Susan Howe's writing which uses

the page like a canvas – from
these one could extrapolate a poetry

where publication would be a demonstration
of private singularity approximating a neo-Platonic

vanishing point, anticipated by Klebnikov's handcolored,
single-copy books produced in the twenties.

Such an extrapolation would be inaccurate
as regards the writers I've mentioned,

and certainly creates a false picture
of the language movement, some of

whose members write very much for
a if not the public. But

still there's another grain of false
truth to my Manichean model of

a prosy command-center of criticism and
unique bivouacs on the poetic margins

so I'll keep this binary in
focus for another spate of couplets.

Parallel to such self-defined poetry, there's
been a tendency in some criticism

to valorize if not fetishize the
unrepeatable writing processes of the masters

– Gabler's *Ulysses* where the drama of
Joyce's writing mind becomes the shrine

of a critical edition; the facsimile
of Pound's editing-creation of what became

Eliot's *Waste Land*; the packets into
which Dickinson sewed her poems, where

the sequences possibly embody a higher
order; the notebooks in which Stein

and Toklas conversed in pencil: having
seen them, works like *Lifting Belly*

can easily be read as interchange
between bodily writers or writerly bodies

in bed. The feeling that three's
a crowd there is called up

and cancelled by the print's intimacy
and tact. In all these cases,

the particularity of the author's mind,
body, and situation is the object

of the reading. But it's time
to dissolve or complicate this binary.

What about a work like *Glas*?
– hardly a dully smooth critical monolith.

Doesn't it use the avant-garde (ancient
poetic adjective!) device of collage more

extensively than most poems? Is it
really all that different from,

say, the *Cantos*? (Yes. The *Cantos*'s
incoherence reflects Pound's free-fall writing situation;

Derrida's institutional address is central. Derrida's
cut threads, unlike Pound's, always reappear

farther along.) Nevertheless *Glas* easily outstrips
most contemporary poems in such "marginal"

qualities as undecidability and indecipherability – not
to mention the 4 to 10 margins

on each page. Compared to it,
these poems look like samplers upon

which are stitched the hoariest platitudes.
Not to wax polemical: there've been

plenty of attacks on the voice
poem, the experience poem, the numerous

mostly free verse descendants of Wordsworth's
spots of time: first person meditations

where the meaning of life becomes
visible after 30 lines. In its

own world, this poetry is far
from marginal: widely published and taught,

it has established substantial means of
reproducing itself. But with its distrust

of intellectuality (apparently indistinguishable from overintellectuality)
and its reliance on authenticity as

its basic category of judgment (and
the poems exist primarily to be

judged), it has become marginal with
respect to the more theory-oriented sectors

of the university, the sectors which
have produced such concepts as "marginalization."

As an antidote, let me quote
Glas: "One has to understand that

he is not *himself* before being
Medusa to himself. . . . To be oneself

is to-be-Medusa'd. . . . Dead sure of self. . . .
Self's dead sure biting (death)." Whatever

this might mean, and it's possibly
aggrandizingly post-feminist, man swallowing woman, nevertheless

in its complication of identity it
seems a step toward a more

communal and critical reading and writing
and thus useful. The puns and

citations lubricating Derrida's path, making it
too slippery for all but experienced

cake walkers are not the point.
What I want to propose in

this anti-generic or over-genred writing is
the possibility, not of some pure

genreless, authorless writing, but instead, a
polygeneric writing where margins are not

metaphors, and where readers are not
simply there, waiting to be liberated.

For all its transgression of local
critical decorum, *Glas* is still, in

its treatment of the philosophical tradition,
decorous; it is *marginalia*, and the

master page of Hegel is still
Hegel, and Genet is Hegel too.

But a self-critical poetry, minus the
short-circuiting rhetoric of vatic privilege, might

dissolve the antinomies of marginality that
broke Jack Spicer into broken lines.

MARXIST PLEASURE

JAMESON &

EAGLETON

STEVEN HELMLING

MARXIST PLEASURE

JAMESON &

EAGLETON

As reading matter, contemporary Marxist criticism is pretty heavy ⟨1⟩
going, first and most obviously because it inherits a long, rich and
adventurous tradition not only of political and sociological but also
of philosophical argument – the breadth of Marx's own interests
insured that: he aimed, and so have all Marxisms after him, to synthe-
size all sciences, to make Marxism the key to all mythologies, or (in
Fredric Jameson's now-famous phrase) the "untranscendable horizon" of all cultural, political, and social inquiry. (Marxism obliges
itself to reckon with, say, deconstruction; whereas deconstruction
regards dealing with Marxism as discretionary.) But Marxism takes
on other difficulties, other burdens besides the intellectual ones; it
carries the torch of a moral tradition as well, of concern, even an-
guish about the plight of the oppressed. And its burdens are "moral"
in another sense, too, the sense that connects less with "morality"
than with "morale"; for it is the very rare Marxist text that is without
some sort of hortatory subtext – though usually, it is true, expressed
polemically (often most fiercely against other Marxists). And here,
too, Marx himself is the great original: he asks to be read as a
scientist, not a moralist, but we do not readily credit any Marxism
that is deaf to the moralist (and ironist) in Marx's potent rhetoric.

So "doing Marxism" is not easy. To join in the Marxist conversa- ⟨2⟩
tion, even just as a reader, requires an *askesis* that cannot be casual,
an experience of initiation that involves extraordinary "difficulty" of
every possible kind: difficult texts, difficult issues, difficult problems,
a (very) difficult history, difficult political conditions. Yet the initiation into Marxism is not without its pleasures, too: pleasures, indeed, not punctually marked off from, but rather continuous with,
the satisfactions of the adept – and even more conflictedly, pleasures somehow deriving from, even constituted precisely by, the
very "difficulties," both moral and intellectual, that Marxism obliges
its initiates to shoulder.

I want in this essay to consider Fredric Jameson and Terry Eagle- ⟨3⟩

ton, the two leading Marxists writing in English, with an eye to the contrasting ways each negotiates the contradictions of this mix of intellectual pleasure with intellectual-moral difficulty. (A salient topos will be "Left puritanism," with some sidelights from Roland Barthes.) I hope to stage the contrasts between these two very different prose styles as a way of access to how each writer handles "pleasure" as an issue – a problem, desire, or object of critique – to see how (or whether) what each says *about* "pleasure" squares with the pleasures (or however else we are to name the satisfactions) of their writing.

4   The eminence of Jameson and Eagleton makes them the obvious choices for such an essay in contrasts. Their substantive differences are as well known as the warmth with which they avow common cause, but in what follows I want to shift the emphasis from their "positions" to the ground where the contrasts between them are the sharpest, namely to their prose styles. That a subculture so devout as the academic about splitting fine ideological hairs nevertheless seems agreed on accepting as indispensable two writers so different – Jameson with his melancholy hauteur warmed occasionally by erudite despair, Eagleton with his impetuous, energetic hope – attests that their manifest differences as stylists, and in their stances as writers, make them virtually polar terms, "representative," between them, of the limits, the possibilities and the predicaments, of the rhetorical or libidinal resources available to Marxist criticism in our historical moment.

5   That my focus on "textual" effects intends no renunciation of more substantively "thetic" interests should go without saying – but "in our historical moment" it had better not. The necessity of saying it, as well as the language I'm saying it in ("textual," "thetic") are recognizably symptomatic of (the theme of this volume) "the postmodern" Jameson, of course, has devoted much energy to this theme; Eagleton very little, dismissing it as "ideological" in his contempt for "*post-histoire*," "the end of history," etc. "The postmodern" is too large a topic to deal with more than glancingly in this essay; at its close, though, I will suggest some of the ways that "our" changing awareness of the relation of content to form, substance to style, "thetic" to "textual," can help focus the contrasts between Jameson and Eagleton, and perhaps the questions facing any future project, Marxist or otherwise, of "critique."

So, then: "pleasure." A convenient place to begin, as it happens, 6
is with Eagleton's essay, "Fredric Jameson: The Politics of Style"
(1982), in which Eagleton avows the "profound pleasure" he experiences reading Jameson. Tactically, consider what a very strange
move Eagleton makes in speaking this way. Though I no longer find
Jameson as vexing to read as I once did, "pleasure" seems a calculat-
edly provocative word for whatever it is that keeps me reading him –
and lest we miss the point, Eagleton even takes care to remind us
that "'pleasure' is not the kind of word we are accustomed to encountering in Jameson's texts" (*Against the Grain*, 66). Indeed, not.
Quite apart from its notorious difficulty, Jameson's writing is fastidi-
ously pained, "stoic," even "tragic," in its evocation of the ordeals
Utopian desire must suffer through what he calls "the nightmare of
history as blood guilt."[1] Most readers sense from the tone and
sound of Jameson's work, long before they get a grip on the complexities of its content, that the best motto it supplies for itself is the
famous "History is what hurts" passage, the often quoted perora-
tion to the opening chapter of *The Political Unconscious*. The passage
begins in reflection on the genre of "dialectical" analysis to which
Jameson obviously aspires to contribute:

the most powerful realizations of Marxist historiography . . . remain
visions of historical Necessity . . . [and of] the inexorable logic involved in
the determinate failure of all the revolutions that have taken place in
human history . . . [they adopt] the perspective in which the failure or the
blockage, the contradictory reversal or functional inversion, of this or
that local revolutionary process is grasped as "inevitable," and as the
operation of objective limits. (The Political Unconscious, 101-102)

As visions go (and "visions" is Jameson's own word here), this one –
the failure of all revolutionary action as "inevitable" after the fact – is
about as bleak as any vision (Marxist or otherwise) could possibly
be. (In other Marxist writers, Jameson warns that such a vision risks
"post-Marxism," and this is obviously an anxiety close to the quick
for Jameson himself.)[2] This bleak vision bears a patent family resemblance to many other critically powerful pessimisms – Michel Foucault's "total system," Paul de Man's "aporia," and Harold Bloom's
"Gnosticism," to name three whose "defeatism" Eagleton has particularly vilified.

Contempt for "defeatism" is a constant in Eagleton's work, a ges- 7 ture (symptomatically) much against the grain not only of Marxist "critique" but of culture-criticism generally. So in testifying to the "profound pleasure" of reading Jameson, Eagleton is playing a deep game, seeming to praise Jameson but also, with typically British (not to say Marxist British) puritanism, subtly indicting Jameson in terms that echo Eagleton's repudiation of the "frivolous" counter-culture (and **French**!) hedonism of Barthes and the *Tel Quel* group. Eagleton means it as a sign in Jameson's favor when he specifies that he derives "pleasure" from Jameson's work, but **not** "*jouissance.*"[3] Evidently, "pleasure" may be tolerable in contexts of righteous revolutionary effort, but "*jouissance*" would be going too far. (Insofar as Eagleton's own pugilistic wit invites us to pleasures that feel distinctly masculine, his aversion to Barthesian "*jouissance*" might seem almost a residual, unwitting homophobia: the revolutionary band of brothers, apparently, is to enjoy collective pleasures, but not collective ecstasies.)

8   Perhaps Eagleton's double-edged praises of the "pleasure" of reading Jameson express the embarrassments of meeting so potent a version of the "defeatist" vision under the Marxist banner. But my point is that Jameson's peculiar eloquence has been of that ascetic, despairing, facing-the-worst type familiar, and according to some (Leo Bersani and Richard Rorty, as well as Eagleton, **and** Barthes), over-familiar, in nineteenth-and twentieth-century culture-criticism. It is a rhetoric that cuts across the ideological spectrum: beside Foucault, de Man, and Bloom, whom I have already named, one might place Adorno, one of Jameson's particular culture-heroes, and T. S. Eliot, one of his particular *bêtes noirs*. But what Jameson especially admires in a writer like Adorno, he has said repeatedly, is a "dialectical" quality in the writing: a power to render unflinchingly the awfulness of our present condition, but also to sustain some impulse toward utopian hope.

9   But this utopian impulse must not offer any solace; to do so would make it liable to a post-Althusserian, Levi-Straussian definition of "ideology": "an imaginary solution to a real contradiction," i.e., a kind of "false consciousness" – and the more so in that it here appears as a textual effect, an achievement of style. Yet just this, but (ironically?) as "praise" rather than indictment, is the implication of Eagleton's judgment that "Style in Jameson. . . both compensates for and adumbrates pleasures historically postponed" (*Against the*

Grain, 69). Such "compensation," such "adumbration" of how things will be after the revolution, is for Jameson, sheer "ideological" indulgence in "the Imaginary," and as such a particular pitfall or temptation that Marxist writing must avoid.

On the contrary, what Jameson calls "the dialectic of ideology [the capitalist present] and utopia [the socialist future]" should aggravate, rather than soothe, our discontent with the way we live now.[4] Jameson is trying for a rhetoric, a tone, that will not be a profanation of its subject matter, an eloquence appropriate to the plight of capitalism's victims, and to the hour of Marxism's time on the cross. In a time (ours) of near-total "commodification" or "reification," this task gets harder and harder, as you can hear in Jameson's grim joke that Adorno's question about whether you can write poetry after Auschwitz "has been replaced with that of whether you could bear to read Adorno . . . next to the pool" (*Late Marxism*, 248). The point of such a joke is not "pleasure," but laceration; you might even call it a moral-intellectual masochism.[5]

And this seems a model for Jameson's effect generally. As a writer, as a stylist, Jameson is committed to a bleak "vision" of near-total desperation, and to praise the effects of his prose, as Eagleton does, in terms of "profound pleasure" seems a shrewdly pointed missing of the point. True, Jameson himself earlier commended the "purely formal pleasures" of Adorno's prose, but Jameson's language sounds sober – even "purely formal"? – whereas Eagleton's praise of the "intense libidinal charge" of Jameson's prose sounds like transport, not to say (the word Eagleton specifically rules out) *jouissance*.[6] And Eagleton's "defense" (or mock-defense?) of Jameson's style is couched not only in terms of pleasure, but of Jameson's **own** pleasure: "weighed down" as he is with the "grave burdens" and "historical responsibilities" he has assumed, writes Eagleton,

[Jameson] must be allowed a little for himself, and that precisely, is style. Style in Jameson is the excess or self-delight which escapes even his own most strenuously analytical habits. . . . (Against the Grain, 66)

I lack the space here to rehearse Jameson's aversion to all discussion of literary, cultural, social, political, or even psychological issues in terms of "self"; any reader of Jameson will have noticed that after his 1961 book on Sartre, hostility to the category of "the subject" is the most consistent of his presuppositions. So Eagleton's reinscription of "pleasure" here in terms of a stylistic self-consciousness, and a "self-delight" that is Jameson's due as a sort of allowance or indulgence (like Lenin's penchant for Beethoven, or Freud's cigars) compounds Eagleton's sly "mis-taking" of Jameson's point. (When Jameson, asked in an interview about the difficulty of his prose, replies in terms of "my own pleasure in writing these texts" – "I wouldn't write them unless there were some minimal gratification in it for myself" – it sounds more like a confession of self-indulgence than a boast of "self-delight" ["Interview," 88].) Eagleton is raising issues as ancient as Aristotle on tragedy: how do we derive pleasure (if it **is** pleasure) from works that visit unpleasure upon us? Eagleton seems "materialist" in the British tradition of Hobbes and Bentham rather than Marx when he unmasks the "pleasure" of reading Jameson in this way.

12   Eagleton's remarks originally appeared in a 1982 issue of *Diacritics* devoted to Jameson. It was in the following year (1983) that Jameson published an essay that not only mentioned the word "pleasure," but took it as its title, "Pleasure: A Political Issue." I do not argue that Eagleton's remarks prompted Jameson's essay, but reading it "as if" it did makes its centerpiece, Jameson's elaboration of Barthes's *plaisir/jouissance* distinction, seem a kind of defense against, correction of, or better, a dialectical out-leaping of, Eagleton's implied strictures, as well as a tacit program or apologia for Jameson's own writing as far as its literary "effects" are concerned.

13   "Pleasure: A Political Issue" argues against what Jameson calls "Left puritanism" of just the sort that I have identified with Eagleton (IT2, 66-7); and its vehicle is a reconsideration of Barthes, a much more positive one than Jameson had offered, for example, in "The Ideology of the Text" (1976). The treatment of Barthes is, as usual in Jameson, quite unstable; he passes over, for example, Barthes's wobble over the relation of *"jouissance"* to "significance" ("bliss" as liberation from the tyranny of "meaning," versus "bliss" as restoration of a "meaning" utopia); and one of the most simply pleasurable parts of the essay, the opening jeremiad against the commodification of "pleasure" in our mass culture, ascribes this theme to *The Pleasure of the Text*, where it nowhere appears. (Jameson is conflating *plaisir/ jouissance* with *S/Z*'s *lisible/scriptible*.)[7] Eagleton took care to absolve Jameson of any taint of Barthes's "perversity"; but Jameson mounts a defense of the Barthesian "perverse" that resonates with

his homage to Lacan.[8] And where Eagleton reviles Barthesian *jouissance* as a flight from politics into a cerebral-sensual wetdream, Jameson avers that

> the immense merit of Barthes's essay [*The Pleasure of the Text*] is to restore a certain politically symbolic value to the experience of *jouissance*, making it impossible to read the latter except as a response to a political and historical dilemma. . . (IT2, 69)

"Impossible"? As usual when Jameson offers a judgment for or against a writer's politics, this seems an eye-of-the-beholder situation, Jameson's construction of a "political" Barthes attesting Jameson's ingenuity more than Barthes's politics; but I want to pass to the next, most interesting phase of Jameson's argument, in which Jameson reads Barthes's binary of "pleasure" and "*jouissance*" as a contemporary avatar of Edmund Burke's "beautiful" and "sublime." It seems a master stroke, until you reread Barthes. Jameson invokes Barthes's epigraph from Hobbes about "fear," and quotes Barthes quoting Hobbes in the section of *The Pleasure of the Text* called "Fear." My own reading of Barthes is that by "fear" he means something like "shame":

> Proximity (identity?) of bliss and fear. What is repugnant in such nearness is obviously not the notion that fear is a disagreeable feeling – a banal notion – but that it is not a very worthy feeling . . . (Barthes's emphasis; *Pleasure of the Text*, 48)

This unworthiness is a particular in which "fear" resembles "pleasure"; only two pages earlier Barthes protests the "political alienation" enforced by

> the foreclosure of pleasure (and even more of bliss) in a society ridden by two moralities: the prevailing one, of platitude; the minority one, of rigor (political and/or scientific). As if the notion of pleasure no longer pleases anyone. Our society appears to be both staid and violent: in any event: frigid.[9]

But Jameson tilts Barthes's invocation of "fear" away from the disquiets of prudery and the miseries of a closeted Eros in a very different direction: towards a Burkean sublime of terror, an effect that "threatens, diminishes, rebukes individual human life" (IT2, 72). Jameson initially treats this as an effect merely aesthetic, and therefore "ideological," a mystification (Burke, he notes, makes the end-term of the sublime God Himself), and he jeers the hunger for such an effect – "choose what crushes you!" (IT2, 72) – but the valence changes when he goes on to posit an end-term of his own, namely that "unfigurable and unimaginable thing, the multinational apparatus" of late capitalism itself. Jameson alludes to the work of "the capital-logicians," who invert Hegel's providential world-historical metanarrative so that "what Hegel called 'Absolute Spirit' was simply to be read as the transpersonal, unifying, supreme force of emergent Capitalism itself"; it is "beyond any question," he continues, that some such apprehension attaches to "the Barthesian sublime" (IT2, 72-73). Granted Barthes's good-leftish politics, an *écriture* ("sublime" or not) that "threatens, diminishes, rebukes individual human life" is not only very un-Barthes-like, but actually valorizes Barthes in terms of that very "Left puritanism" Jameson affects to defend Barthes against.

15   Jameson has remade Barthes's *jouissance,* in short, in the image of his own "sublime," a passion of "fear" prompted by "History," by "what hurts": it is not Barthes who has chosen what crushes him; Barthes is willing to confess (or boast) that at least parts of him are not crushed; it is Jameson who insists on being crushed, by a "sublime" villain, late capitalism. The measure of that "crush" is of course the effect of the prose in which Jameson projects his "vision of Necessity" and its inverted Hegelian-Marxist metanarrative in which "the subject of History" proves to be not the proletariat but capitalism. "Pleasure: A Political Issue" invites a redescription of what Eagleton named the "pleasure" of Jameson's prose as, on the contrary, a type of "the sublime."

16   "The sublime" is a theme that has much preoccupied Jameson in the '80s, a decade in which, it seems to me, his prose has undergone a change. It is as allusive and inward as ever, but its emotional charge is much larger and more accessible than before. Eagleton in 1982 chided Jameson's "regular, curiously unimpassioned style" (*Against the Grain,* 74), and here his judgment is avowedly adverse: he is calling in fact for a more "impassioned" Jameson. But the formula of 1982 no longer fits the Jameson of 1992, as a even a cursory reading of, for example, the short meditations on diverse topics gathered as the "Conclusion" to *Postmodernism* will show. Moreover, "the sublime" is a frequent theme in this writing, and Jameson unfailingly

characterizes it (as in the passage quoted above) in terms of unrepresentability, unfigurability, unsymbolizability. To evoke the nightmare of history as beyond the intellect's grasp is to present a vision of "fear." But another frequent theme in Jameson is the ambition to write a "dialectical prose," like Adorno's, that resists or escapes what Jameson calls "thematization." Jameson nowhere speaks of this condition "beyond thematization" as a "*jouissance*," but insofar as it, too, involves a transit beyond a linguistic-semantic entrapment, this ambition of Jameson's rewrites the fear of the sublime as a kind of desire, and thus projects the terror of the sublime as a kind of utopia.

I want to mention one more portent in the later Jameson's evocation of "the sublime": if "the sublime" is the unfigurable, it must necessarily defeat any project of interpretation. From long before his 1971 essay "Metacommentary," through *The Political Unconscious* (1981), with its programmatic opening chapter, "On Interpretation," Jameson presented his effort as a hermeneutic project, opposed to that of "anti-hermeneuts" from Susan Sontag to Foucault, Barthes and Derrida. In his work since then, "postmodernism" itself figures as the unfigurable, insofar as it is (to use a paleoMarxist shorthand whose terms Jameson disapproves) the "superstructural" concomitant of changes in the "base" wrought by a "late" or (in Ernest Mandel's terms) "third-stage" capitalism whose modes of production have undergone a decisive world-historical alteration since, roughly, the '60s. Hence Jameson's more recent rhetoric in which, ominously, the center does not hold: as if, to use the terms of the eleventh thesis on Feuerbach, our impotence to "change" the world must be expressed as an impotence also to "understand" it, in accordance with ("Left puritanism" indeed) the "vision of Necessity" in which the "failure" of revolution appears as "inevitable after the fact" – and must further entail the "vision" of the "inevitable failure" of "dialectical historiography" itself, along with any hermeneutic labor tributary to it. Hence the agitation of Jameson's recent prose, particularly the later pieces in *Postmodernism*, in which "the sublime" is not only a prominent theme, but also a frequent effect.[10]

I have suggested that "Pleasure: A Political Issue" be read "as if" it responds directly to Eagleton's ambiguous praise of the "pleasure" of reading Jameson, "as if" it aims to propose another ethos, a literary "effect" ("the sublime") more creditable than "pleasure" for culture-criticism generally, and for Jameson's own work in particular. I want now to turn to Eagleton's writing, which, beyond ideological affinities, seems diametrically opposed to Jameson's rhetorically, in its effects as writing. Where Jameson enlarges every problem, problematizes every solution, insists on "inevitable failure," and proposes both for his prose and for his readers an *askesis* of facing the worst (what Geoffrey Galt Harpham has called "the ascetic imperative"), Eagleton writes a prose full of jokes and irreverences, bronx cheers and razzberries, polemical piss and ideological vinegar, every clause lighting a ladyfinger of wit, almost as if under the compulsion of a kind of high-theory Tourette's syndrome. It is a style with affinities to "counter-culture" journalism, as if James Wolcott had gone to graduate school instead of *The Village Voice*. With obvious and naughty relish, Eagleton transgresses the decorums of academic prose, setting (for example) a clever bit of baby-talk on Derrida's name (labelled "Oedipal Fragment") as epigraph to a chapter on "Marxism and Deconstruction," or concluding a book of essays with a doggerel busker-ballad in the broadside style ("Chaucer was a class traitor,/ Shakespeare hated the mob," etc., to be sung to the tune of "Land of Hope and Glory"), or launching his essay on Jameson's style with a parody of Jameson, or indulging a parody of Empson in his essay on Empson, "The Critic as Clown," or sending up **everything** academic-critical in a parody of the academic handbook manner in "The Revolt of the Reader." (Equally un- or anti-academic, but in the other direction, is the poem at the end of Eagleton's book on Benjamin; compare the poem dedicating *Criticism and Ideology* [1976] to his father.) [11]

19   As for the pained, mournful, obligatory pessimism of "the ascetic imperative," Eagleton consistently jeers it as a kind of false consciousness. Here, for example, he is setting the stage for a recuperation of Walter Benjamin (whose "melancholy" he readily concedes) under the sign of "carnival"; and with characteristic brass, he makes the very implausibility of such a move his opening gambit:

> the suffering, Saturnine aspects of Benjamin, the wreckage of ironic debacles and disasters that was his life, have been seized upon with suspicious alacrity by those commentators anxious to detach him from the vulgar cheerfulness of social hope. Since political pessimism is a sign of spiritual maturity . . . Benjamin offers a

> *consolingly familiar image to disinherited intellectuals everywhere,*
> *downcast as they are by the cultural dreariness of a bourgeoisie*
> *whose property rights they would doubtless defend to the death.*
> (*Walter Benjamin,* 143)

Two pages later, enter Bakhtin, and the theme of "carnival," which the prose not only describes but enacts:

> *In a riot of semiosis, carnival unhinges all transcendental signifiers*
> *and submits them to ridicule and relativism. . . power structures are*
> *estranged through grotesque parody, 'necessity' thrown into satir-*
> *ical question and objects displaced or negated into their oppo-*
> *sites. A ceaseless practice of travesty and inversion (nose/phallus,*
> *face/buttocks, sacred/profane) rampages throughout social life,*
> *deconstructing images, misreading texts and collapsing binary*
> *oppositions into a mounting groundswell of ambiguity into which*
> *all articulate discourse finally stutters and slides. Birth and death,*
> *high and low, destruction and renewal are sent packing with their*
> *tails in each other's mouths. . . A vulgar, shameless, materialism of*
> *the body – belly, buttocks, anus, genitals – rides rampant over*
> *ruling-class civilities; and the return of discourse to this sensuous*
> *root is nowhere more evident than in laughter itself, an enunciation*
> *that springs straight from the body's libidinal depths.* (Walter
> Benjamin, 145, 150)

These passages are from the chapter of *Walter Benjamin* called "Carnival and Comedy: Bakhtin and Brecht," and I want to consider this essay at length here: it provides the program projected in the book's subtitle ("Towards a Revolutionary Criticism"), and the place of "pleasure" in this program is large and important – both as an aim proposed by the argument and, more immediately, as an effect of the writing. The energy of these passages is not the only kind of energy to be found in Eagleton – space forbids sampling the rabble-rousing wisecracks, the downright, matey metaphors, the sheer gusto for combat and polemical hurly-burly, the insouciantly highbrow laying about amid Heidegger, Althusser, Hegel, or whomever. But the fluency of Eagleton's rant makes a sharp contrast with Jameson: while Jameson's notoriously "difficult" prose enacts the difficult (indeed impossible) position of Marxism today, the sheer brio of Eagleton's prose in all its guises, its "riot of semiosis," seems to address a political situation whose solution ought to be as simple as getting everyone to admit what they already know, if only by springing jokes so cunningly as to enable us to catch them laughing despite themselves. "A vulgar, shameless materialism of the body – belly, buttocks, anus, genitals – rides rampant over ruling-class civilities": is there a straight face to be seen? The transgressions seem a test to see who will laugh, and who will scowl – good fun, and pointed, of course, at the latter.

20   Surely this is Eagleton's dominant effect: it is why graduate students idolize him, and part of why he is recommended for anyone wanting an introduction to "theory." He can, quite simply, be fun to read, and in that regard, more than any other contemporary highbrow Marxist, he can remind you of some passages in Marx himself. You can, indeed, **almost** imagine a coal miner or a factory worker reading him, as, in labor movement myth, some of them used to read Marx. I highlight this effect of Eagleton's prose because it is an effect of **pleasure.** Even Eagleton's darker notes, the moments of righteous anger, generally assume or imply (indeed, they aspire to **create**) a political situation in which righteous anger can readily find its proper effectivity – a situation, to put it another way, in which righteous political anger is felt as a pleasure in its own right. Eagleton's prose means to yield such pleasure as an **effect**, as well as proposing it as a **theme** or **program**.

21   Over the course of Eagleton's career, indeed, the effect of pleasure is far more consistent than the theme; about the theme, Eagleton has often, especially when younger, expressed doubts – as in the caveat above about Jameson, for example: "pleasure," yes; "*jouissance*," no. *Jouissance* is a Barthesian word, and although Eagleton does on occasion resort to it as a positive term, his reservations about Barthes remain everywhere in force. *Pace* Jameson, Eagleton regards Barthes's *plaisir* and *jouissance* as privatistic, apolitical, and corrupted with the (to Eagleton) irredeemably contemptible bourgeois pathology of guilt-as-added-thrill; Barthesian pleasure is "guilty pleasure," enacted behind closed doors in controlled environments, whereas Eagleton's rabble-rousing implies gleeful sacrilege in public places, and not with guilt, but with whoops of righteous laughter.

22   "Carnival and Comedy" proposes such effects, such styles of revolutionary laughter and humor, not only in its practice (in the

style of its prose), but also as a program for a "Marxist theory of comedy" (*Walter Benjamin*, 159), which Eagleton sketches out, with Brecht's help, as properly answering to something like the movement of history itself. For Brecht, the Marxist "dialectic of history" is "comic in principle": "a source" – quoting Brecht now – "of enjoyment" heightening "both our capacity for life and our pleasure in it."[12] Hence, explains Eagleton, the redemptive move from pessimism to "the vulgar cheerfulness of social hope": "What for Walter Benjamin is potentially tragic . . . is for Brecht the stuff of comedy." But what of history's horrors? Eagleton seemingly bids defiance to all obligatory handwringing on that score: "Hitler as housepainter yesterday and Chancellor today is thus a sign of the comic, because that resistible rise foreshadows the unstable process whereby he may be dead in a bunker tomorrow" (*Walter Benjamin*, 161). (Note the verb tenses, and especially the "may" in that last clause: even in this "comic" moment, Eagleton is conjuring with the prospect of future Hitlers, warning that we must not be complacent because the last one was vanquished.)

But against Auschwitz, a paragraph later, Eagleton knows that his 23 comic bravura will not stand, and he acknowledges that there is "always something that escapes comic emplotment . . . that is non-dialectizable" (*Walter Benjamin*, 162). This last nonce-word seems a little too impromptu; it would be a mistake to hold Eagleton to all its implications against "dialectic" itself. It is better taken as a symptom of how Eagleton's improvisational afflatus can tread Marxist toes as readily as bourgeois ones. But Eagleton means the word to acknowledge that the "comic" critique he projects here has its limit, comes up against things in history that can **not** be "emplotted" in a "comic" mode. If "comedy" can mean Dante, or the Easter Passion, it may seem that Eagleton has confused the "comic" with the "funny"; immemorially august Western conceptions of "the comic" certainly have claimed to encompass brutality, suffering, injustice. Perhaps Eagleton regards these as in bad taste, or perhaps he wants to avoid the assimilation once again of Marxism to religion.

However that may be, what happens next in "Carnival and Come- 24 dy" provides a far more surprising tack away from revolutionary laughter toward something like the "melancholy" the essay began by protesting. And it does so, more remarkably still, by way of a reading of a passage from the *Eighteenth Brumaire*, perhaps the first among

Marx's texts one might have cited as exhibiting just the sort of "carnivalesque" angers and "comic" pleasures (ridicule and mockery) Eagleton had seemed to project. But Jeffrey Mehlman, in *Revolution and Repetition*, reads the passage this way, and it is as a refutation of Mehlman's reading that Eagleton stages his own. What apparently prompts Eagleton's ire is Mehlman's reference to the "anarchism" of Marx's prose, which Eagleton finds complicit with "those ruling ideologies that have an interest in abolishing dialectics and rewriting Marxism as textual productivity" (*Walter Benjamin*, 162). Mehlman argues that Marx's rhetorical excesses overflow his supposed thesis; Eagleton scorns such a notion, but goes on to make an argument not much different.

25   Eagleton's fulcrum-point is the first-time-as-tragedy-second-time-as-farce motif, for Marx specifies "Caussidière for Danton, Louis Blanc for Robespierre . . . the Nephew for the Uncle," quite as if the Revolution's giants were first-timers, and did not themselves dress up in Roman togas (conveniently requiring little restyling when the signified changed from "Republic" to "Empire"). Yet precisely this revolutionary repetition – both heroic **and** farcical – quickly becomes Marx's main theme. Eagleton interrogates the resulting "semiotic disturbance" (inconsistent metaphors, etc.) over several pages of "close reading," much too lengthily to quote here; but its surprising premise is that "Marx's text is symptomatically incoherent" (*Walter Benjamin*, 163). But where Mehlman found this carnivalesque, and thus a strength and an interest, Eagleton, avowedly promoting "carnival and comedy," is pained at Marx's "unwitting" loss of control over his language, and finds himself talking back to Marx, correcting him, unmixing his metaphors for him. He recovers himself at last by the threadbare critical move of transferring the "symptomatic incoherence" from Marx to his object (bourgeois revolution), thus at the final bell transforming what had been Marx's unwitting "symptom" into his masterful critical "negation." But the passage ends weakly, and the essay moves to a coda lamenting Western Marxism's loss of Marx's comic strength (as if forgetting Brecht, Eagleton's initial sponsor). There is irony here, insofar as Eagleton has just (by imposing a monologic of his own on Marx's figurally dialogic text) sapped the very strength he now professes to mourn; and there is pathos in this wistful statement of irrecoverable loss, since recovering a comic possibility for Marxist critique had

been, just a few pages earlier, Eagleton's boldly stated ambition. The essay ends this way:

> Benjamin, like Gramsci, admired the slogan "Pessimism of the intellect, optimism of the will," and in what Brecht called "the new ice age" of fascism one can see its point. But Marxism holds out other strategic slogans too. Having taken the point of the first, it might then be possible to say, without voluntarist or Kautskyist triumphalism: "Given the strength of the masses, how can we be defeated?" (*Walter Benjamin*,172)

Tentative ("it might then be possible to say"), and with the taunts of the shibboleth-meisters ("Voluntarist!" "Kautskyist!") rising in his inner ear, Eagleton's final flourish cannot, for once, deliver the pleasurable Eagletonian "triumphalism" that is his usual stock in trade. The final "slogan," indeed, ending on a question mark, sounds more like a real question than a rhetorical one. Here the "optimism of the will" is too willful to convince, the "pessimism of the intellect" too much more than merely intellectual not to. For once, "pessimism of the intellect" really seems to win the agon in the arena of Eagleton's prose.

So a guerilla foray, driven by "carnival" energies, into a "Marxist theory of comedy" loses momentum at the name of the eponymous master. A gallant defense of Marx turns into a subtle assault on Marx –"anxiety of influence"? – and suddenly all Eagleton's fight (and fun) have gone out of him: this failure tempts the sort of lit-crit "psychoanalysis" indicated when, say, the word "balls" sends Stephen Dedalus's chastely passionate villanelle off the rails. But of course we had better push in the direction of that transindividual "libidinal apparatus" that assigns the "objective limits" (Jameson's phrase) determining such failures – and in fact to "allegorize" the trajectory of Eagleton's essay as enacting the fate of pleasure in our present "conjuncture," is to assimilate Eagleton to Jameson. Jameson, as we have seen, makes a "vision" of "necessary failure" an imperative for Marxist criticism, and Eagleton, despite his bravely avowed aim of rebutting all such "pessimism" here ends by bowing to it. Jameson, inscribing a failure imperative, compels from it his tortured, ambivalent, "difficult" success; Eagleton, in brash defiance of all pessimisms and confident of Marxism's inevitable, eventual success, here "enacts" the Jamesonian "vision" of "necessary failure"

26

the more movingly for all his "optimism of the will" against it. This may sound like scoring points against both of them, especially against Eagleton – but if pressed to admit that Eagleton's failure, at least, does seem a "symptom" rather than a "negation," I would want to add that both writers, by putting their expository "mastery" at risk, challenge the whole ethos of "critique" that gives the "symptom"/"negation" binary its significance. The ensuing gain is that we can see how two writers so different enact differing consequences of the same "contradiction," must probe and come up against different reaches of the same "objective limits."

27   Today, any such limits must involve the question of "the postmodern," and specifically for us here the question whether the contrasts I've drawn between Jameson and Eagleton can be usefully articulated with their different stances toward postmodernism or postmodernity. Jameson takes "the postmodern" very seriously, as nothing less than "the cultural logic of late capitalism"; Eagleton, as I noted above, usually identifies it with the ideological pipedream marketed most recently under the trademark "the end of history." In *On Ideology* (1991), Eagleton makes "postmodernism" a prop of that "enlightened false consciousness" that Peter Sloterdijk has called "cynical reason."[13]

28   It is over-simple, but I hope not too grossly so, to say that "postmodernism" functions in Jameson's discourse as an apocalyptic theme (or rhetorical/libidinal resource), in Eagleton's as a satiric object. Without venturing a typological scheme in the manner of Northrop Frye or Hayden White, nor deploying, Jameson-like, a Greimassian "semantic rectangle," I offer this simplification for what it suggests about what White calls the "historical emplotments" and "modes of ideological implication" of these two potent critical stylists: Eagleton's "pleasure" easily aligns with "satire," Jameson's "sublime" with "the apocalyptic." Eagleton would doubtless dismiss as "ideological" distraction such readings of, or responses to, avowedly "political" texts; we've already seen him spurning Mehlman and others who reduce Marx's writing to "textual productivity." For Eagleton, such "aestheticization" is "postmodern" in the bad sense, the, as it were, permanent or chronic sense that (for the sufficiently privileged) the "ideology of the aesthetic" has always functioned – this, indeed, is its express purpose, according to Eagleton – as an evasion of hard political realities, or hard-hitting political polemics. What,

Eagleton might indignantly ask, is "new" (or "postmodern") about such moves? There have always been those ready to find Voltaire a "pleasure," or Isaiah "sublime." Eagleton writes as one for whom the situation, or the mission, of "critique" is pretty much what it has always been; his enemies are different, or have different names, from Isaiah's or Voltaire's, but the situation his prose projects remains an us/them, friends/foes confrontation. Eagleton reflects very little, if at all, on his own project--which is not to say his prose is without the interest of self-consciousness (on the contrary, the "self-delight" Eagleton ascribes to Jameson is a characterization more apt for his own work; some might complain of it as a kind of narcissism), only that in Eagleton's work "the postmodern" remains a mere topic; it never passes to a suggestive model for Eagleton's own project, or a fresh way of access to it.

Jameson, by contrast, is polemical only by-the-way – his larger   29
ambitions are for subtlety and complexity to which the imperatives of polemic are inimical – and his constructions of "the postmodern" invariably implicate, reflexively, not only the thematics, but the methods and the ambitions of his own work. And Jameson writes with – indeed, derives many of his most potent effects from – a sense that the challenges facing critique now are unprecedented; hence, for him, "the emergence of that new type of discourse called theory" (*Signatures of the Visible*, 68; cf. *Postmodernism*, 391-9) is itself an important sign of "the postmodern." Critique now must be something it never was before – a "textual *genre*" (IT2, 40) whose difficult, perhaps impossible, ambition is to escape the intellectual reification Jameson calls "thematization," and whose exemplars for Jameson's own writing practice include (as we've seen) the "dialectical" prose of Adorno, Lacan's "discourse of the analyst," and Barthes's "writing with the body."

Such post-expository, post-"thetic" effects can be referred to no   30
other category than "the aesthetic." Jameson, for all his suspicion of "the aesthetic," remains an aesthete in the sense that he never forgets that the pleasure of Voltaire is calculated, that the sublime of Isaiah is passionately achieved – and that such effects, and such calculations and passions no less, are meaningful, even determinately so. Like Eagleton, Jameson scorns the aesthete who would disjoin aesthetics from politics, but his practice also reproves the politically committed reader who – thinking to obey Walter Benjamin's admo-

nition that communism must politicize aesthetics as antidote to fascism's aestheticization of politics – would enforce the very same disjunction. "The postmodern," "the aesthetic" – for Eagleton, these are objects of satiric attack, to be externalized, pilloried, purged, and eventually overcome, vanquished. But for Jameson such features of the reified world are not to be confronted as subject confronts object, but *suffered* "homeopathically," in a condition in which the subject/object distinction is (ideally) superseded, and in which "critique" must always, simultaneously, be "self-critique." Hence the "stoic," even "tragic" tone (see note 1) – and "the sublime" – of so much of Jameson's writing, especially his recent writing, in *Postmodernism* particularly.

31   This last point suggests one further way of posing the question of the "pleasures" of these two writers' very different kinds of "textuality": in terms of "subject positions." Eagleton indicts the subject/object binary as readily as anyone, but his (virtually always) polemical stance, unlike Jameson's "homeopathic" critique, maintains it in his writing practice. He is always the "subject" of his own writing, and so insistently that you, reading him, must also be the "subject" of that reading; you are a specatator, enjoying the show as Eagleton demolishes his (and your) polemical "objects," or else (as happens when his polemic simplifies things about which you have your own ideas), you resist or rewrite as you read; both positions are "pleasurable" ones (unless perhaps your identification is with Eagleton's targets). His prose is always pressing the reader to a pro or con, "with us" or "against us" position.

32   Jameson's "homeopathic" prose puts you in very different places. There are "polemical" moments (Jameson often signals them by hoping that they are not "moralizing"), but they afford none of Eagleton's demolition-derby kind of fun. Their tone is melancholy, world weary, and such as to implicate "us" (writer *and* reader, and people of the left generally, in line with the imperative that "critique" must entail "self-critique") in the co-optations and predicaments, the false consciousness and reifications – the "what hurts" – that they protest. Hence Jameson's "difficulty": next to his, Eagleton's prose seems an affair of almost indecently *easy* pleasures. Eagleton's wit dazzles, but it never makes me feel stupid or inadequate: my very appreciation of it, my very pleasure in it, warrants my (at least intellectual) worthiness to read it. By contrast, Jameson's notoriously

complicated prose (itself a limit-point of any instrumental disjunction of "style" from "content"), frequently daunts. You cannot read it without a degree of involvement or participation that I at least cannot call "spectatorial"; nor, most of the time, does it allow you any self-congratulation on your "mastery" of it. Indeed, a frequent experience of my own reading Jameson is of a kind of cerebral overload, of more going on than I can keep track of – an experience I would call a reader's, or hermeneutic, sublime, in line with Jameson's own characterization of "the sublime" as a congestion exceeding representational capacities and overflowing into "unsymbolizabity" and "unfigurability." Jameson's avowed resistance to "thematization" is among the "motivations" of this effect, and disables any such rewriting or talking back, arguing back while you read, as Eagleton invites. Jameson constructs no argument, but rather suspends arguments, mobile-like, in the airstream of the postmodern "*vécu*," to see or test what rotations and tangles will result. His prose less offers an argument *about* our postmodern condition, than it enacts, or suffers, a widely informed, deeply felt participation *in* it – a moral-intellectual pathos different in almost every possible way from Eagleton's.

As for the question how to name the complex satisfaction of 33 reading such writers as Eagleton and Jameson, the very difficulty of calling it "pleasure" raises problems whose force is worth looking into in its own right. What Jameson's discomfort with "pleasure," his need to sublimate it into "the sublime," tells us about the fate of pleasure in our historical moment converges with Eagleton's seemingly opposed embrace of pleasure (with, nevertheless, his reservations about "bliss" on the one hand and the more obscurely motivated "failure" enacted at the close of "Carnival and Comedy" on the other).

Which returns us to the question of "Left puritanism." Both 34 Eagleton and Jameson seem shadowed by the "minority (political) rigor" whose affinities with the more majoritarian moralisms we saw Barthes uncovering. Each seems to find some sorts of enjoyment (however they differ on which ones) tainted by (Barthes again) "unworthy [bourgeois] feelings." Neither, of course, wants to be tarred as a "Left puritan"; Jameson's embrace of Barthes (and Lacan) bespeaks his desire to escape that label, and Bakhtin serves as a similar alibi for Eagleton. As I have argued above, though, Jameson's construction of Barthes seems motivated by a very un-Barthes-like, and very "Left puritan," distrust of *"plaisir,"* and his reinscription of *"jouissance"* into "the sublime" sublimates it into something very far from enjoyment (in anything other than, say, the Žižekian sense).[13] As for Eagleton's appropriation of Bakhtin, it is to be read in opposition to, not as a version of, Barthesian *"jouissance."* It constructs "carnival" as **social**, and thus an affair less of Eros than of its collective sublimate, Agape. Sex, in Eagleton's "carnival," is comically **deflationary** – "A ceaseless practice of travesty and inversion (nose/phallus, face/buttocks)" (*Walter Benjamin*, 145) – rather than a unique, privileged, grand (or grandiose) access to the transport and exaltation of "the sublime."

35

Barthes, I suspect, would see in both of these writers more than a few symptoms of that "frigidity" he protests, "As if the notion of pleasure no longer pleases anyone" (*Pleasure of the Text*, 46-7). Barthes writes as one for whom the *"promesse de bonheur"* that Marxists so frequently denounce as "ideological" has already been in some measure cashed; his superego has apparently fought free of that "categorical imperative" that would have him deny his own pleasure in the name of the possibly counter-revolutionary effects of corrupt ideas of "pleasure" **on others**. But insofar as the resistance to "pleasure" involves the worry of "false consciousness," the fear of being falsely consoled by "an imaginary solution to a real contradiction," it will doubtless remain a potent source of moral trouble for Marxists and others who would direct the energies of "critique" to the tasks of making a more just society. The example, though, of Eagleton's "optimism of the will" (and, most of the time, of his optimism of the intellect, too) prompts me at least to the pleasurable speculation whether "false consciousness" might not equally involve the temptation of responding to real contradictions with imaginary aggravations.

N   O   T   E   S

1. "Stoic" and "tragic" are terms of praise in Jameson's essay "Imaginary and Symbolic in Lacan" (1978), in *The Ideologies of Theory, Volume* 1 (hereinafter IT1), 98, 112; and it is manifest that part of Lacan's fascination for Jameson is Lacan's achievement of an ethos at once ("dialectically") Hegelian *and* pessimistic, and to that extent a model for Jameson's own. For "the nightmare of

history as blood guilt," see "Architecture and the Critique of Ideology" (1985), in *The Ideologies of Theory, Volume* 2 (hereinafter IT2), 43, and "Pleasure: A Political Issue" (1983), *ibid.*, 68.

2. See, for example, Jameson's account of the Italian architectural historian Manfredo Tafuri in "Architecture and the Critique of Ideology" (1985), in IT2, 35-60; the caution about "post-Marxism" is on 38. See also remarks on Tafuri in *Postmodernism*, 61. Jameson scorns any suggestion of his own putative "post-Marxism" in the opening pages of the "Conclusion" to *Postmodernism*.

3. *Against the Grain*, 68. Eagleton similarly praises Jameson in "The Idealism of American Criticism," in *ibid.*, 49-64.

4. "The Dialectic of Ideology and Utopia" is the title of the last chapter of *The Political Unconscious* (pp. 281-99), but the motif recurs throughout Jameson's work, from the chapters on Marcuse (pp. 83-115) and Ernst Bloch (pp. 116-59) in *Marxism and Form* to the section of the "Conclusion" of *Postmodernism* called "The Anxiety of Utopia" (pp. 331-40).

5. Cf. Jameson's most unequivocal praise for Paul de Man: that no one has been more "self-punishing" in pursuit of a moral-intellectual *askesis* (*Postmodernism*, 239).

6. Eagleton quotes Jameson on Adorno (from *Marxism and Form*, xiii) in "The Politics of Style" (*Against the Grain*, 66); on the same page he quotes himself, on Jameson's "intense libidinal charge," from "The Idealism of American Criticism" (*Against the Grain*, 57).

7. "Commodification" is a frequent topos in both Eagleton and Jameson, as well as in many other Marxist (and not-so-Marxist) writers. (Eagleton even images Jameson's encyclopedic range of reference as a shopping cart wheeling through "some great California supermarket of the mind" collecting Hegel, Deleuze, Croce, et al., like so many designer-products [*Against the Grain*, 70]). Indeed, anxiety about the commodification of highbrow "theory" like his own – Barthes, Lukács, Macherey, and whoever else as status-acquisitions in some flash-card degradation of intellectual life – frequently appear in Jameson himself, and in just such consumerist terms – as, for example, when he deplores hearing figures like Althusser, Gramsci, et al. turned into "brand-names for autonomous philosophical systems" ("Interview," 78).

8. For Eagleton exempting Jameson from Barthesian "perversity," see *Against the Grain*, 66; for Jameson on Barthes and Lacan, compare "Pleasure: A Political Issue" (IT2, 69) with the closing paragraph of "Imaginary and Sym-

bolic in Lacan" (ITI, 115).

9. *Pleasure of the Text*, 46-7. One of Jameson's more dazzling insights is the linkage of Barthes with Lionel Trilling's *Sincerity and Authenticity* on the grounds that both associate what they despise with the left – student radicals for Trilling, "Left puritanism," as in the quoted passage, for Barthes (IT2, 65).

10. This hermeneutic despair, surprisingly, lightens in work Jameson has published since *Postmodernism*. See the (previously unpublished, and presumably recent) essay, "The Existence of Italy," in *Signatures of the Visible*, 155-229, where hermeneutic satisfactions again compensate for the reifications accounted for; and *The Geopolitical Aesthetic: Cinema and Space in the World System*, in which third world cinema's reinvention of narrative and realism and its sense of "totality as conspiracy" offer a prospect of the world system once again rendered intelligible to the terms of a politically committed (mass) art form. See my review of these two books in *Kritikon Litterarum* (forthcoming).

11. "Oedipal Fragment," *Walter Benjamin, Or, Towards a Revolutionary Criticism*, 131; "The Ballad of English Literature," *Against the Grain*, 185; the parody of Jameson, *ibid*, 65; of Empson, *ibid*, 151; "The Revolt of the Reader, *ibid*, 183-4. For the homage to Benjamin, see *Walter Benjamin*, 183-4. This is also the place to mention Eagleton's play, *Brecht and Company* (1979) and his novel, *Saints and Scholars* (1987).

12. *Brecht on Theatre*, 277; qtd. *Walter Benjamin*, 160.

13. In *The Ideology of the Aesthetic* [1990], Eagleton's view is more complicated, as his closing chapter, "From the Polis to Postmodernism," assimilates "the postmodern" to the book's interestingly ambivalent rehabilitation of "the aesthetic" itself; this chapter's 48 pages make, interestingly, only one (glancing) reference to Jameson. *The Ideology of the Aesthetic* seems to me Eagleton's best and most important book, an instantiation of the point that Eagleton is at his best when the monologic drive--or pleasure principle!--of his ferocious polemical wit entertains competing impulses, whether of intellectual scruple, as in *The Ideology of the Aesthetic*, or of passional ambush, as in "Carnival and Comedy."

14. I am thinking, of course, of (Slavoj) Zizek's *Enjoy Your Symptom: Jacques Lacan In Hollywood and Out*, but readers of Zizek know that they will find this and Zizek's other central themes rehearsed in virtually any of his books they pick up.

WORKS CITED

Barthes, Roland. *The Pleasure of the Text.* 1973. Trans. Richard Miller. Hill and Wang: New York, 1975.

Eagleton, Terry:

Against the Grain: Selected Essays. Verso: New York and London, 1986.

Walter Benjamin, Or, Towards Revolutionary Criticism. Verso: New York and London, 1981.

Jameson, Fredric:

The Geopolitical Aesthetic: Cinema and Space in the World System. Bloomington/London: Indiana UP/British film Institute, 1992.

The Ideologies of Theory, Volume 1: Situations of Theory. U of Minnesota P: Minneapolis, 1988.

The Ideologies of Theory, Volume 2: The Syntax of History. U of Minnesota P: Minneapolis, 1988.

"Interview," *Diacritics* 12, 3 (Fall 1982)

Late Marxism, Or, Adorno: The Persistence of the Dialectic. Verso: New York and London, 1990.

Marxism and Form. Princeton UP: Princeton, NJ, 1971.

The Political Unconscious. Cornell UP: Ithaca, NY, 981.

Postmodernism, or The Cultural Logic of Late Capitalism. Duke UP: Durham, NC, 1991.

Signatures of the Visible. New York and London: Routledge, 1992.

Mehlman, Jeffrey. *Revolution and Repetition.* U of California P: Berkeley, 1977.

Žižek, Slavoj. *Enjoy Your Symptom: Jacques Lacan In Hollywood and Out.* Routledge: New York and London, 1992.

NEIL LARSEN

POST MODERNISM AND IMPERIALISM

THEORY AND POLITICS IN LATIN AMERICA

My remarks here[1] concern the following topics of critical discussion and debate: **1)** the ideological character of postmodernism as both a philosophical standpoint and as a set of political objectives and strategies;
2) the development within a broadly postmodernist
theoretical framework of a trend advocating a critique
of certain postmodern tenets from the standpoint of
anti-imperialism; and **3)** the influence of this trend
on both the theory and practice of oppositional culture in Latin America. So as to eliminate the need for
second-guessing my own standpoint in what follows,
let me state clearly at the outset that I will adhere to
what I understand to be both a Marxist and a Leninist
position as concerns both epistemology and the social and historical primacy of class contradiction. Philosophically, then, I will be advancing and defending historical and dialectical materialist arguments. Regarding questions of culture and aesthetics, as well as those
of revolutionary strategy under existing conditions –
areas in which Marxist and Leninist theory have either
remained relatively speculative or have found it necessary to rethink older positions – my own thinking
may or may not merit the attribution of "orthodoxy,"
depending on how that term is currently to be understood.

2 **1** One typically appeals to the term "postmodern" to characterize a broad and ever-widening range of aesthetic and cultural
practices and artifacts. But the concept itself, however diffuse
and contested, has also come to designate a very definite current of
philosophy as well as a theoretical approach to politics. Postmodern
philosophy – or simply postmodern "theory," if we are to accept
Jameson's somewhat ingenuous observation that it "marks the end
of philosophy"[2] – arguably includes the now standard work of post-
structuralist thinkers such as Derrida and Foucault as well as the
more recent work by ex-post-Althusserian theorists such as Ernesto
Laclau and Chantal Mouffe, academic philosophical converts such
as Richard Rorty and the perennial vanguardist Stanley Aronowitz.
The latter elaborate and re-articulate an increasingly withered poststructuralism, re-deploying the grandly dogmatic and quasi-mysti-
cal "critique of the metaphysics of presence" as a critical refusal of
the "foundationalism" and "essentialism" of the philosophy of the
Enlightenment. These two assignations – which now come to replace the baleful Derridean charge of "metaphysics" – refer respec-
tively to the Enlightenment practice of seeking to **ground** all claims
regarding either truth or value in terms of a self-evidencing standard
of Reason; and to the ontological fixation upon being as **essence**,
rather than as relationality or "difference."

3 Postmodern philosophy for the most part adopts its "anti-
essentialism" directly from Derrida and company, adding little if
anything to accepted (or attenuated) post-structuralist doctrine.
Where postmodernism contributes more significantly to the honing
down and re-tooling of poststructuralism is, I propose, in its indictment of foundationalism – in place of the vaguer abstractions of
"presence" or "identity" – as the adversarial doctrine. It is not all
"Western" modes of thought and being which must now be discarded, but more precisely their Enlightenment or *modern* modalities,
founded on the concept of *reason*. Indeed, even the charge of "foundationalism" perhaps functions as a minor subterfuge here. What
postmodern philosophy intends is, to cite Aronowitz's forthright
observation, a "rejection of reason as a foundation for human affairs."[3] Postmodernism is thus a form, albeit an unconventional one,
of *irrationalism*.

4 To be sure, important caveats can be raised here. Postmodernist

theoreticians often carefully stipulate that a rejection of reason as foundation does not imply or require a rejection of all narrowly "reasonable" procedures. Perhaps it is possible to *act* "reasonably" without the need to *prove* that that is what one is doing. Postmodernity, at any rate, is not to be equated with an anti-modernity. Aronowitz, for example, has written that "postmodern movements" (e.g., ecology and "Solidarity" type labor groups) "borrow freely the terms and programs of modernity but place them in new discursive contexts" (UA 61). Chantal Mouffe insists that "radical democracy" – according to her, the political and social project of postmodernity – aims to "defend the political project [of Enlightenment] while abandoning the notion that it must be based on a specific form of rationality."[4] Ernesto Laclau makes an even nicer distinction by suggesting that "it is precisely the *ontological status* of the central categories of the discourses of modernity and not their *content*, that is at stake [. . . .] Postmodernity does not imply a *change* in the values of Enlightenment modernity but rather a particular *weakening* of their absolutist character."[5] And a similarly conservative gesture within the grander irrationalist impulse can, of course, be followed in Lyotard's characterization of "paralogy" as those practices legitimating themselves exclusively within their own "small narrative" contexts, rather than within the macro-frames of modernist meta-narratives of Reason, Progress, History, etc.[6]

Two counter-objections are necessary here, however. The first is that any thoughtful consideration of claims to locate the attributes of reason within supposedly local or non-totalizable contexts immediately begs the question of what, then, acts to set the limits to any particular instance of "paralogy," etc.? How does the mere adding of the predicate "local" or "specific" or "weakened" serve to dispense with the logic of an external ground or foundation? Cannot, for example, the ecology movement be shown to be *grounded* in a social and political context outside and "larger" than it is, whatever the movement may think of itself? If reason is present (or absent) in the fragment, does not this presence/absence necessarily connect with the whole on some level? If, as one might say, postmodernism wants to proclaim a rationality of means entirely removed from a rationality of ends, does it not thereby sacrifice the very "means/ends" logic it wants to invoke, the very logical framework in which one speaks of "contexts"? I suggest it would be more precise to describe the measured, non-foundationalist "rationalism" of postmodernism as simply an evasive maneuver designed to immunize from critique the real object here: that is to preserve "Enlightenment" as merely an outward and superficial guise for irrationalist content, to reduce "Enlightenment," as an actual set of principles designed to govern consciously thought and action, to merely the specific mythology needed to inform the project of a "new radical imaginary" (Laclau, UA77).

6   Clearly, there is a complete failure – or refusal – of *dialectical* reasoning incurred in postmodernism's attempted retention of an Enlightenment "micro"-rationality. And this brings up the second rejoinder: postmodern philosophy's practiced avoidance on this same score of the *Marxist*, dialectical materialist critique of Enlightenment. Postmodern theory, seemingly without exception, consigns something it calls "Marxism" to the foul Enlightenment brew of "foundationalism." Marxism is, in effect, collapsed back into Hegelianism, the materialist dialectic into the idealist dialectic – or, as Aronowitz somewhat puzzlingly puts it, the "form of Marxism is retained while its categories are not" (UA 52). But in no instance that I know of has a postmodern theorist systematically confronted the contention first developed by Marx and Engels that "this realm of reason was nothing more than the idealized realm of the bourgeoisie."[7] I think perhaps it needs to be remembered that the Marxist project was and is not the simple replacement of one "universal reason" with another, but the practical and material transformation of reason to be attained in classless society; and that this attainment would *not* mean the culmination of reason on earth à la Hegel but a raising of reason to a higher level through its very de-"idealization." Reason, then, comes to be grasped as a time-bound, relative principle which nevertheless attains an historical universality through the social universality of the proletariat (gendered and multi-ethnic) as they/we who – to quote a famous lyric – "shall be the human race."

7   But again, postmodern irrationalism systematically evades confrontation with *this* critique of Enlightenment. It typically manages this through a variety of fundamentally dogmatic maneuvers, epitomized in the work of Laclau and Mouffe who, as Ellen Meiksins Wood has shown,[8] consistently and falsely reduce Marxism to a "closed system" of pure economic determinism.

8   Why this evasion? Surely there is more than a casual connection

here with the fact that the typical postmodern theorist probably never got any closer to Marxism or Leninism than Althusser's left-wing structuralism and Lacanianism. One can readily understand how the one-time advocate of a self-enclosed "theoretical practice" might elicit postmodern suspicions of closure and "scientism." Indeed, Althusser's "Marxism" can fairly be accused of having pre-programmed, in its flight from the class struggles of its time and into narrowly epistemological speculation, the subsequent turn-about in which even the residually rationalist categories still formally upheld by Althusser are themselves rejected for their inconsistency.[9]

But this is secondary. What I would propose is that postmodern-[9] ism's hostility towards a "foundationalist" parody of Marxism, combined with the elision of Marxism's genuinely dialectical and materialist content, flows not from a simple misunderstanding but, objectively, from the consistent need of an ideologically embattled capitalism to seek displacement and pre-emption of Marxism through the formulation of radical-sounding "third paths" (i.e., "neither capitalism nor socialism"). That postmodern philosophy normally refrains from open anti-communism, preferring to pay lip service to "socialism" even while making the necessary obeisances to the demonologies of "Stalin" may make it appear as some sort of a "left" option. But is there really anything "left"? The most crucial problem for Marxism today – how to extend and put into practice a critique *from the left* of retreating "socialism" at the moment of the old communist movement's complete transformation into its opposite – remains safely beyond postmodernist conceptual horizons.

Postmodernist philosophy's oblique but hostile relation to Marx-[10] ism largely duplicates that of Nietzsche. And the classical analysis here belongs to Lukács' critique of Nietzschean irrationalism in *The Destruction of Reason*, a work largely ignored by contemporary theory since being anathematized by Althusserianism two decades ago. Lukács identifies in Nietzsche's radically anti-systemic and countercultural thinking a consistent drive to attack and discredit the socialist ideals of his time. But against these Nietzsche proposes nothing with any better claim to social rationality. Any remaining link between reason and the emancipatory is refused. It is, according to Lukács, this very antagonism towards socialism – a movement of whose most advanced theoretical expression Nietzsche remained fundamentally ignorant – that supplies to Nietzschean philosophy its point of departure and its principal unifying "ground" as such. "It is material from "enemy territory," problems and questions imposed by the class enemy which ultimately determine the content of his philosophy."[10] Unlike his more typical fellow reactionaries, however, Nietzsche perceived the fact of bourgeois decadence and the consequent need to formulate an intellectual creed that could give the appearance of overcoming it. In this he anticipates the later, more explicit "anti-bourgeois" anti-communisms of the coming imperialist epoch – most obviously fascism. This defense of a decadent bourgeois order, based on the partial acknowledgement of its defects and its urgent need for cultural re-newal, and pointing to a "third path" "beyond" the domain of reason,[11] Lukács terms an "indirect apologetic."

11   Postmodern philosophy receives Nietzsche through the filters of Deleuze, Foucault and Derrida, blending him with similarly mediated versions of Heidegger and William James into a new irrationalist hybrid. But the terms of Lukács' Nietzsche-critique on the whole remain no less appropriate. Whereas, on the one hand, postmodernist philosophy's aversion for orthodox fascism is so far not to be seriously questioned, its basic content continues, I would argue, to be "dictated by the adversary." And this adversary – revolutionary communism as both a theory and a practice – assumes an even sharper identity today than in Nietzsche's epoch. Let it be said that Lukács, writing forty years ago, posits an adversarial Marxism-Leninism more free of the critical tensions and errors than we know it to have been then or to be now. If, from our own present standpoint, *The Destruction of Reason* has a serious flaw, then it is surely this failure to anticipate or express openly the struggles and uncertainties within communist orthodoxy itself. (Lukács' subsequent allegiance to Krushchevite positions – by the, perhaps, inevitable – marks his decisive move to the right on these issues.) But the fact that postmodern philosophy arises in a conjuncture marked by capitalist restoration through out the "socialist" bloc and the consequent extreme crisis and disarray within the theoretical discourse of Marxism, while it may explain the relative freedom from genuinely contestatory Marxist critique enjoyed by postmodern theorists, in no way alters the essence of this ideological development as a reprise of pseudo-dialectical, Nietzschean "indirect apologetics."

12   This becomes fully apparent when one turns to postmodernism's

more explicit formulations as a politics. I am thinking here mainly of Laclau and Mouffe's *Hegemony and Socialist Strategy*, a work which, though it remains strongly controversial, has attained in recent years a virtually manifesto-like standing among many intellectuals predisposed to poststructuralist theory.[12] *Hegemony and Socialist Strategy* proposes to free the Gramscian politics linked to the concept of "hegemony" (the so-called "war of position," as opposed to "war of maneuver") from its residual, Marxian "foundationalism" in recognition of what is held to be the primary efficacy of discourse itself and its "articulating" agents in forming hegemonic subjects. And it turns out of course that "socialist strategy" means dumping socialism altogether for a "radical democracy" which more adequately conforms to the "indeterminacy" of a "society" whose concept is modeled directly on the poststructuralist critique of the sign.

The key arguments of *Hegemony and Socialist Strategy* – as, in addition, the serious objections they have elicited – have become sufficiently well known to avoid lengthy repetitions here. What Mouffe and Laclau promise to deliver is, in the end, a revolutionary or at least emancipatory political strategy shorn of "foundationalist" ballast. In effect, however, they merely succeed in shifting the locus of political and social agency from "essentialist" categories of class and party to a discursive agency of "articulation."[13] And when it comes time to specify concretely the actual articulating subjects themselves, *Hegemony and Socialist Strategy* resorts to a battery of argumentative circularities and subterfuges which simply relegate the articulatory agency to "other discourses."[14]

Ellen Meiksins Wood has shown the inevitable collapse of *Hegemony and Socialist Strategy* into its own illogic as an argument with any pretense to denote political or social realities[15] – a collapse which, because of its very considerable synthetic ambitions and its conceptual clarity, perhaps marks the conclusive failure of poststructuralism to produce a viable political theory. But the failure of argument has interfered little with the capacity of this theoretical tract to supply potentially anti-capitalist intellectuals with a powerful dose of "indirect apologetics." The fact that the "third path" calls itself "radical democracy," draping itself in the "ethics" if not the epistemology of Enlightenment, the fact that it outwardly resists the "fixity" of any one privileged subject, makes it, in a sense, the more perfect "radical" argument for a capitalist politics of pure irrational-

13

14

ist spontaneity. And we know who wins on the battlefield of the spontaneous.[16] While the oppressed are fed on the myths of their own "hegemony" – and why not since "on the threshold of postmodernity" humanity is "for the first time the creator and constructor of its own history" (Laclau, UA 79-80)? – those already in a position to "articulate" the myths for us only strengthen their hold on power.

15 **2** In my remarks so far I have emphasized how contemporary postmodern philosophy's blanket hostility towards the universalisms of Enlightenment thought may in fact serve to pre-empt Marxism's carefully directed critique of that *particular universal* which is present day capitalist ideology and power. Does not the merely theoretical refusal of the (ideal) *ground* serve in fact to strengthen the *real* foundations of *real* oppression by rendering all putative knowledge of the latter illicit? When Peter Dews rebukes Foucault for his attempt to equate the "plural" with the emancipatory, the remark applies to more recent postmodern theory with equal force: "the deep naivety of this conception lies in the assumption that once the aspiration to universality…is abandoned what will be left is a harmonious plurality of unmediated perspectives."[17] In light of this perverse blindness to *particular* universals, postmodernism's seemingly general skepticism towards Marxism as *one* possible instance of "foundationalism" would be better grasped as a specific and determining antagonism. Is there an extant, living – i.e., *practiced* – philosophy *other* than Marxism which any longer purports to ground rational praxis in universal (but in this case also practical-material) categories? I am saying, then, that postmodern philosophy and political theory becomes objectively, albeit perhaps obliquely, a variation of anti-communism.

16 It might, however, be objected at this point that postmodernism encompasses not only this demonstrably right-wing tendency but also a certain "left" which, like Marxism, aims at an actual transcendence of oppressive totalities but that diverges from Marxism in its precise identification of the oppressor and of the social agent charged with its opposition and overthrow. Under this more "practical" aegis, the axis of postmodern antagonism shifts from the universal versus the particular to the more politically charged tension between the "center" and the "margin." Such a shift has, for example, been adumbrated by Cornel West as representing a particularly

American inflection of the postmodern. "For Americans," says West,

> are politically always already in a condition of postmodern frag-
> mentation and heterogeneity in a way that Europeans have not
> been; and the revolt against the center by those constituted as
> marginals is an oppositional difference in a way that poststructur-
> alist notions of difference are not. These American attacks on
> universality in the name of difference, these "postmodern" issues of
> otherness (Afro-Americans, Native Americans, women, gays) are
> in fact an implicit critique of certain French postmodern discourses
> about otherness that really serve to hide and conceal the power of
> the voices and movements of Others. [18]

Among instances of a "left" postmodernism we might then include
certain of contemporary feminisms and the theoretical opposition
to homophobia as well as the cultural nationalisms of ethnic minority groups. The category of the "marginal" scarcely exhausts itself
here, however. Arrayed against the "center" even as also "concealed"
by its discourses and "disciplines" are, in this conception, also the
millions who inhabit the neocolonial societies of the "third world."
Hence there might be a definite logic in describing the contemporary anti-colonial and anti-imperialist movements of the periphery
as in their own way also "postmodern."

It is this "marginal" and "anti-imperialist" claim to postmodernity   17
which I now wish to assess in some depth. In particular I propose to
challenge the idea that such a "left" movement within postmodernism really succeeds in freeing itself from the right-wing apologetic
strain within the postmodern philosophy of the "center."

The basic outlines of this "left" position are as follows: both   18
poststructuralism and postmodernism, as discourses emergent in
the "center", have failed to give adequate theoretical consideration
to the international division of labor and to what is in fact the uneven
and oppressive relation of metropolitan knowledge and its institutions to the "life-world" of the periphery. Both metropolitan knowledge as well as metropolitan systems of ethics constitute themselves upon a prior exclusion of peripheral reality. They therefore
become themselves falsely "universal" and as such ideological rather
than genuinely critical. The remedy to such false consciousness is
not to be sought in the mere abstract insistence on "difference" (or
"unfixity," the "heterogeneous," etc.), but in the *direct* practical in-

tervention of those who *are* different, those flesh and blood "others" whom, as West observes, the very conceptual appeal to alterity has ironically excluded. As a corollary, it is then implied that a definite epistemological primacy, together with a kind of ethical exemplariness, adheres to those subjects and practices marginalized by imperialist institutions of knowledge and culture.

19   Among "first world" theorists who have put forward this kind of criticism perhaps the best known is Fredric Jameson. In his essay "Third World Literature in the Era of Multinational Capitalism" Jameson argues that "third world texts . . . necessarily project a political dimension in the form of national allegory: the story of the private individual destiny is always an allegory of the embattled situation of the public third world culture and society."[19] Third world texts, then – and by extension those who produce them and their primary public – retain what the culture of postmodernism in the "first world" is unable to provide, according to another of Jameson's well-known arguments: a "cognitive map"[20] equipped to project the private onto the public sphere. As such, these peripheral practices of signification consciously represent a bedrock political reality which, for the contemporary postmodern metropole, remains on the level of the political unconscious. (It should be pointed out of course that Jameson's schema is largely indifferent in this respect to the modernism/postmodernism divide.) What enables this is the fact that the third world subject, like Hegel's slave, exhibits a "situational consciousness" (Jameson's preferred substitute term for materialism). As "master," however, the metropolitan consciousness becomes enthralled to the fetishes which symbolize its dominance.

20   An analogous but weaker theory of the marginal as epistemologically privileged is to be found in the writings of Edward Said. In *The World, the Text and the Critic*, for example, Said chastises contemporary critical theory, especially poststructuralism, for its lack of "worldliness" – by which he evidently means much the same thing designated by Jameson's "situational consciousness." What is needed, according to Said, is "a sort of spatial sense, a sort of measuring faculty for locating or situating theory"[21] which Said denotes simply as "critical consciousness." *The World, the Text and the Critic* ultimately disappoints in its *own* failure to historically or "spatially" situate such "critical consciousness," but given Said's public commitment to

Palestinian nationalism it wouldn't seem unreasonable to identify in his call for "worldliness" a prescription for "third-worldliness."

Both Jameson and Said – the former far more openly and forth- 21
rightly than the latter – violate central tenets of postmodernism, of course, insofar as they posit the existence of a marginal *conscious-ness* imbued with "presence" and "self-identity." That is, they appear to justify an orthodox postmodernist counter-accusation of "essentialism." But should this be thought to constitute a final incompatibility of postmodernism for an anti-imperialist, post-colonial standpoint, however, it suffices to mention here the work of Gayatri Chakravorty Spivak. Foreseeing this difficulty, Spivak has (in her critical reading of the work of a radical collective of Indian historians known as the "subaltern studies group") sought to justify such "essentialism" as a strategic necessity, despite its supposed epistemological falsity. The radical, third world historian, writes Spivak, "must remain committed to the subaltern as the subject of his history. As they choose this strategy, they reveal the limits of the critique of humanism as produced in the west."[22] Spivak, that is to say, poses the necessity for an exceptionalism: a conceptual reliance on the "subject of history," which as a poststructuralist she would condemn as reactionary and "humanist," is allowed on "strategical" grounds within the terrain of the "subaltern." It begins to sound ironically like the old pro-colonialist condescension to the "native's" need for myths that the educated metropolitan city-dweller has now dispensed with – but more on this below.

Even if the "marginal" cannot be proved to enjoy an epistemolog- 22
ical advantage, however, its very *reality* as a "situation" requiring direct action against oppression can be appealed to as politically and ethically exemplar. Thus, in her very poignant essay entitled "Feminism: the Political Conscience of Postmodernism?"[23] the critic and video artist Laura Kipnis proposes that feminism, seemingly entrapped between the "textualist" (i.e., modernist) aestheticism of French poststructuralist critics on the order of Cixous, Irigaray, etc., and North American liberal reformism (another case of "essentialism"), adopt "a theory of women not as class or caste but as colony" (UA 161). The efforts of a Rorty or a Laclau to salvage "Enlightenment" by ridding it of foundationalism and leaving only its "pragmatic" procedures would, in this view, be too little too late. For Kipnis, as for Craig Owens,[24] postmodernism denotes what is really

the definitive decline of the "West" and its colonial systems of power. If those marginalized within the center itself, e.g., women, are to rescue themselves from this sinking ship they must model their opposition on the practice of non-Western anti-colonial rebels. Referring to the 1986 bombing of Libya, Kipnis writes: "When retaliation is taken, as has been announced, for 'American arrogance,' *this* is the postmodern critique of Enlightenment; it is, in fact, a decentering, it is the margin, the absence, the periphery rewriting the rules from its own interest" (UA 163).

23   An analogous proposal for third world revolt within the conceptual terrain of postmodernism has been issued by George Yúdice. Against the postmodern "ethics" formulated by Foucault as an "aesthetics of existence" – manifesting itself, e.g., in the liberal comforts of pluralism – Yúdice suggests finding an ethical standard "among the dominated and oppressed peoples of the "peripheral" or underdeveloped countries."[25] As a mere "aesthetic" the postmodern "explores the marginal, yet is incapable of any solidarity with it" (UA 224). Yúdice terms this marginal ethic an "ethic of survival" and points to the example set by Rigoberta Menchú in her role as an organizer for the Christian base-community movement against genocidal repression.[26] "Menchú, in fact, has turned her very identity into a 'poetics of defense.' Her oppression and that of her people have opened them to an unfixity delimited by the unboundedness of struggle" (UA 229). In Menchú's ethical example we thus have, so to speak, the subversive promise of "unfixity" à la Mouffe-Laclau made flesh.

24   Yúdice is not the first to attempt this particular inflection with specific reference to Latin America. The "liberation theology" which guides Menchú's practice as a militant might itself lay some claim to represent an indigenously Latin American postmodernism – "avant la lettre" insofar as Foucault and his followers are concerned. The philosophical implications of liberation theology have been worked out by the so-called "Philosophy of Liberation," a intellectual current which developed in Argentina in the early 1970s. As recounted recently by Horacio Cerutti-Guldberg,[27] "Philosophy of Liberation" set out explicitly to formulate a uniquely Latin American doctrine of liberation which would be "neither a liberal individualism nor a Marxist collectivism" (LAP 47). Rather, it would set itself the goal of "philosophizing out of the social demands of the most needy, the mar-

ginalized and despised sectors of the population" (LAP 44). This in turn requires, according to exponent Enrique Dussel, a new philosophical method – known as "analectics" – based on the logical priority or "anteriority" of the exterior (i.e., the marginal, the Other) over totality.[28] "Analectics" are to supplant the "Eurocentric" method of dialectics. As Cerutti-Guldberg observes:

> Dialectics (it doesn't matter whether Hegelian or Marxist, since analectical philosophy identifies them) could never exceed "intra-systematicity." It would be incapable of capturing the requirements of "alterity" expressed in the "face" of the "poor" that demands justice. In this sense, it would appear necessary to postulate a method that would go beyond (ana-) and not merely through (dia) the totality. This is the "analectical" method which works with the central notion of analogy. In this way, analectical philosophy would develop the "essential" thinking longed for by Heidegger. Such thinking would be made possible when it emerges out of the cultural, anthropological "alterative" Latin American space. This space is postulated as "preliminary in the order of Being" and "posterior in the order of knowledge" with respect to the "ontological totality." It is constituted by the poor of the "third world."
> (LAP 50)

In Dussel's *Philosophy of Liberation* the logic of going "beyond" the totality ultimately leads to explicit theology and mysticism. "What reason can never embrace – the mystery of the other as other – only faith can penetrate"(Dussel, 93). But the "analectical" method has received other, non-theological formulations in Latin America, most notably in the case of the Cuban critic Roberto Fernández Retamar, whose theoretical writings of the early 1970s[29] were aimed at refuting the possibility that a "universal" theory of literature could truthfully reflect the radical alterity of "Nuestra América." This is argued to be so not only as a result of the unequal, exploitative relation of imperial metropolis to periphery – a relation which is historically evolved and determined and thus subject to transformation – but because all notions of universality (e.g., Goethe's, and Marx and Engels' idea of a *Weltliteratur*) are fictions masking the reality of radical diversity and alterity.

One should point out here that Retamar's philosophical authority is José Martí and certainly not Derrida, Deleuze or Foucault, whom, had he been aware of them at the time, Retamar would almost surely have regarded with skeptical hostility. Dussel and the various Latin American philosophers associated with "Philosophy of Liberation" have obvious debts to European phenomenology and existentialism, especially to Heidegger and Levinas. But here, too, a philosophical trend in which we can now recognize the idea of postmodernity as a radical break with Enlightenment develops out of what is perceived at least as a direct *social and political* demand for theory to adequately reflect the life-world of those who are, as it were, both "marginal" and the "subject of history" at once. One can sympathize with the general impatience of Latin American critics and theorists who see in the category of the "postmodern" what appears to be yet another neo-colonial attempt to impose alien cultural models. (Such would probably be Retamar's conscious sentiments.) But the example of the "analectical" critiques of Dussel and Retamar show, in fact, that the intellectual and cultural gulf is overdrawn and that all roads to postmodernism do not lead through French poststructuralism.

27   **3** Do we then find a *Latin American culture* of postmodernism linked to these particular conceptual trends? I would argue – and have argued elsewhere[30] – that the recent proliferation in Latin America of so-called "testimonial" narratives like that of Rigoberta Menchú, as well as the fictional and quasi-fictional texts which adopt the perspective of the marginalized (see, inter alia, the works of Elena Poniatowska, Eduardo Galeano and Manlio Argueta), give some evidence of postmodernity insofar as they look for ways of "giving voice" to alterity. Significant here is their implicit opposition to the more traditional (and modernist) approach of "magical realism" in which the marginal becomes a kind of aesthetic mode of access to the ground of national or regional unity and identity. One could include here as well the general wave of interest in Latin American popular and "barrio" culture as an embodiment of "resistance."

28   But our direct concern here is with the ideological character of the conceptual trend as such. Does the move to, as it were, *found* post-modernism's anti-foundationalism in the rebellious consciousness of those marginalized by modernity alter orthodox postmodernism's reactionary character?

29   I propose that it does not. Basing themselves on what is, to be

sure, the decisive historical and political reality of unequal development and the undeniably imperialist and neo-colonialist bias of much metropolitan based theory, the "left" postmodernists we have surveyed here all, to one degree or another, proceed to distort this reality into a new irrationalist and spontaneist myth. Marginality is postulated as a condition which, purely by virtue of its objective *situation,* gives rise to the *subversive particularity* upon which postmodern politics pins its hopes. But, one must ask, where has this been shown actually to occur? Where has imperialism, and its attendant "scientific" and cultural institutions, actually given way and not simply adapted to the "new social movements" founded on ideals of alterity?

Jameson, whose argument for a third world cognitive privilege 30
gestures openly towards an anti-imperialist nationalism as the road to both political and cultural redemption from postmodern psychic and social pathologies, speaks to us of Ousmane Sembene and Lu Hsun, but leaves out the larger question of where strategies of all class national liberation have ultimately led Africa and China – of whether, in fact, nationalism, even the radical nationalism of cultural alterity, can be said to have succeeded as a strategy of anti-imperialism. As Aijaz Ahmad remarked in his well-taken critique of Jameson's essay, Jameson's retention of a "three worlds" theoretical framework imposes a view of neo-colonial society as free of class contradictions.[31]

Spivak's move to characterize the "subaltern" as what might be 31
termed "deconstruction with a human face" only leads us further into a spontaneist thicket – although the logic here is more consistent than in Jameson and Said, since the transition from colonial to independent status itself is reduced to a "displacement of function between sign systems" (Spivak 198).

Kipnis, whose attempt to implicate *both* textualist and reformist 32
feminisms in a politics of elitism and quietism has real merits, can in the end offer up as models for an "anti-colonial" feminism little more than the vague threat of anti-Western counter-terror from radical third world nationalists such as Muammar Khadafy. One recalls here Lenin's dialectical insight in *What is to be Done?* regarding the internal link between spontaneism and terrorism. Yúdice's counter-posing of a third world "ethic of survival" to a postmodern ethic of "self-formation" possesses real force as itself an ethical judgment and one can only concur in arguing the superior moral example of a

Rigoberta Menchú. But where does this lead us *politically?* Those super-exploited and oppressed at the periphery thus become pegged with a sort of sub-political consciousness, as if they couldn't or needn't see beyond the sheer fact of "survival."

33   Are these lapses into the most threadbare sorts of political myths and fetishes simply the result of ignorance or bad faith on the part of sympathetic first world theorists? I do not think so. Regarding current political reality in Latin America, at least, such retreats into spontaneism and the overall sub-estimation of the conscious element in the waging of political struggle merely reflect in a general way the continuing and indeed *increasing* reliance of much of the autochthonous anti-imperialist left on a similar mix of romantic faith in exemplary violence and in the eventual spontaneous uprising of the "people," whether with bullets or with ballots. Although both *foquismo* and the strategy of a "peaceful road to socialism" based on populist alliances are recognized on one level to have failed, the conclusions drawn from this by the mainstream left have on the whole only led to an even more thorough-going abandonment of Marxist and Leninist political strategies in favor of a "democratic" politics of consensus.

34   Here I would refer the reader to the survey of recent intellectual-political trends in Latin America undertaken by James Petras and Michael Morley.[32] These authors note how, after the fascist counter-revolutions of the 1970s and the ensuing normalization of counter-revolutionary policy under the guise of the "return to democracy" in the 1980s, a new type of intellectual replaces the Latin American "organic" intellectual – the Martís, Mariáteguis, Guevaras, etc. – that typified previous periods of revolutionary and radical ferment. This they term the "institutional intellectual," alluding to the latter's frequent dependence on research-funding from liberal and social-democratic foundations based in the metropolis. Writing in *US Hegemony under Siege*, Petras and Morley note the involvement of the new "institutional intellectuals" in various successive "waves" of research agenda, emanating from the funding agencies themselves. These focused, in turn, on a critique of the economic model and human rights violations of the military dictatorships and on an assessment of the "new social movements" emerging in the wake of the dictatorships. Concerning this latter focus, Petras and Morley note how

Studies [. . .] of the social movements claimed that [these] were counterposed to class politics, that the class structure from which they emerged was "heterogeneous," and that the struggles of the social movements were far removed from older ideological politics. The political line in regard to social movements was in the first instance that they should separate themselves from the ideological (radical) political parties; later, with the rise of liberal electoral parties, the political line shifted and the movements were advised to channel their attention toward the "struggle for democracy." The "autonomy of social movements" was promoted when the researchers sought to separate them from the revolutionary left; "participation" in "broad democratic fronts" became the formula the researchers promoted when liberal electoral politics came to the fore. (149)

Unfortunately, Petras and Morley provide few specific names of "institutional intellectuals" or their host foundations – something that considerably weakens their otherwise highly valuable efforts. But it will not be difficult, for the reader of recent, "postmodern" social and political theory in Latin America, to recognize in the above description of "social movement" research, the work of theorists such as Arditi, Argumedo, Borón, Brunner, Escobar, García Canclini, Lechner, Nun and others.[33]

This entire political trend within Latin America can, I think, be correctly grasped only as a consequence of the failure of Marxists, in particular the established Communist Parties and allied organizations, to carry out a self-criticism from the left, and of the resulting shift rightward into political positions which merely compound the errors of the past. As Petras and Morley put it in *Latin America in the Time of Cholera*, the "internal crisis of the political parties of the popular classes has severely weakened the political, organizational, and ideological capacities of the oppressed majorities to respond to the prolonged decay of social life: double negativity has not yet generated a positive outcome" (20). The response of traditional Latin American Marxism to the evident failure of populism (with or without a foco component) as a variation on the orthodox "two-stage" model (democratic capitalism first, then socialism) has typically been to jettison the second stage entirely. One could argue with a certain justice that this collapse was inevitable, given the political mistakes already embedded in the older line. As Adolfo Sánchez Vásquez has recently pointed out,[34] Latin Americans inherited the Marxism of the Second International, the Marxism which regarded revolution in the Western centers of capitalism as the necessary precondition for even national liberation, much less socialism or communism on the periphery. The Marx who, after studying British colonialism in Ireland, concluded that the liberation of Irish workers from imperialism was key to the political advance of an increasingly reformist and conservative British working class; the Marx who speculated that peasant communes in Russia might make feasible a direct transition to socialism: this Marx was largely unknown in Latin America. Thus when the Communism of the Third International adopted the "two stage" model for neocolonial countries, Latin American revolutionaries had scarcely any theoretical basis upon which to dissent. (This, according to Sánchez Vásquez, held true even for so original a Marxist thinker as Mariátegui, who, perhaps because he had to go outside Marxism for theories sensitive to factors of unequal development, was ultimately led in the direction of the irrationalism of Bergson and Sorel.) Latin America is in no way unique in this, needless to say. Everywhere the dominant trend is to compound past errors with even greater ones, thus reaching the point of renouncing the very core of Marxism as such in preference for liberal anachronisms and worse.

37   I dwell on this because I think a truly critical assessment of an "anti-imperialist" postmodernism, as of orthodox postmodernism, requires a prior recognition of the essentially parasitical dependence of such thinking on Marxism and particularly on the *crisis within Marxism* – a dependence which, as we have repeatedly observed, postmodernism systematically tends to erase. The very insistence on a politics of spontaneism and myth, on the tacit abandonment of conscious and scientific revolutionary strategy and organization, is, I am suggesting, the derivative *effect* of developments within Marxism itself, of what amounts to the *conscious political* decision to give up the principle of revolution as a scientifically grounded activity, as a praxis with a rational foundation. The contemporary emphasis on "cultural politics" which one finds throughout intellectual and radical discourse in Latin America as well as in the metropolis, while useful and positive to the degree that it opens up new areas for genuinely political analysis and critique, is symp-

tomatic, in my view, of this theoretical surrender, and more often than not simply ratifies the non-strategy of spontaneism. One might almost speak these days of a "culturalism" occupying the ideological space once held by the "economism" of the Second International revisionists. To adopt the "postmodern" sensibility means, in this sense, to regard the "culturalization" of the political as somehow simply in accordance with the current nature of things – to so minimize the role of political determination as to eliminate it altogether. And yet, this sensibility itself is *politically* determined.   38

Spontaneism, however it may drape itself in populist slogans and admiration for the people's day to day struggle for survival, etc., rests on an intellectual intellectual distrust of the masses, a view of the mass as beyond the reach of reason and hence to be guided by myth. The Latin American masses have a long history of being stigmatized in this way by both imperial and creole elites. This elitism begins to lose its hold on the intelligentsia in the writings of genuine "radical democrats" such as Martí and is still further overcome in the discourses of revolutionary, "organic" intellectuals such as Mariátegui and Guevara, although even here vestiges of the old viewpoint remain. (Mariátegui, who saw the Quechua-speaking indigenous peasants of Peru as beings with full historical and political subjecthood, maintained ridiculously archaic and racist views regarding Peru's blacks and Asian immigrants.) And, of course, sexism has been and remains a deadly obstacle.

But in the era of "postmodernity" we are being urged, in exchange   39
for a cult of alterity, to relinquish this conception of the masses as the rational agents of social and historical change, as the bearers of progress. Given the increasing prevalence of such aristocratism, however it may devise radical credentials for itself, it becomes possible to fall short of this truly democratic vision, to be seduced by the false Nietzschean regard for the masses as capable only of an unconscious, instinctual political agency.

In this respect, it is important to consider what was, during the   40
1980s, the role of the Nicaraguan revolution, and especially the theory and practice of *sandinismo*, in supplying to radical, or "anti-imperialist" postmodernism a species of historical warrant. As Greg Dawes has recently observed in *Aesthetics and Revolution* (see, especially, chapter one, "Sandinismo and Postmodernism"), "terms such as *pluralism, unfixity, différance,* and *totality*" were "frequently evoked

when historians, political scientists, and literary theorists . . . turned their gaze toward Nicaragua." Dawes asserts the existence of a definite "correlation between a certain type of postmodern theoretical language . . . and the "post-Marxist" revisions incarnated in the politico-aesthetic alterations that have taken place in Nicaragua since 1979."[35] Inspired, in part, by *sandinista* theoreticians themselves,[36] but above all by the great explosion of cultural energy unleashed by the revolution, not a few intellectuals claimed to see in the evident freedom of *sandinismo* from orthodox, Marxist notions of class, and the former's seemingly successful attempts to utilize culture itself as a primary means of constructing a popular-revolutionary subject, a corroboration in practice of certain basic tenets of postmodern political theory.

41   The clearest example of this is, I think, to be found in John Beverley and Marc Zimmerman's *Literature and Politics in Central American Revolutions*, as well as in Beverley's subsequently written essay, "Postmodernism in Latin America."[37] In the former work, the authors, in effect, argue two fundamental theses. The first is that, due to the effects of dependent, export-oriented capitalism in the region, and the resulting absence of a well developed scientific and technical culture, it is literature, and above all poetry that takes on the role, in Central America, of producing the "subject position of a radicalized intelligentsia" (L&P 9). Here, it seems to me, Beverley and Zimmerman make a highly compelling case. Their second thesis complicates matters, however. Invoking both the Althusserian theory of ideology as an unconscious process of subject formation and the Laclau-Mouffe theory of society as "not some essence that is prior to representation but rather the product of struggles over meaning and representation" (L&P ix) – i.e. society as itself the supreme ideological construct – *Literature and Politics* implicitly attributes to Central American revolutionary poetry as "ideological signifier" the power to, as it were, constitute the revolutionary society itself. True, this is revolutionary society in its subjective dimensions only; but following the Laclau/Mouffe logic, one is forced to conclude that society *has* no other dimension. Beverley and Zimmerman cite the example, here, of Carlos Fonseca, founder of the FSLN, whose basically literary invention of Sandino as revolutionary theorist in the so-called *Ideario* supplied a needed "ideology of armed national liberation struggle specific to Nicaragua's cultural and political experience" (L&P 32).

That is, if literature in Central America is a "model for politics" (L&P xiii), *sandinismo* itself, as formulated by the basically literary intelligence of Fonseca (over which the poetry of Darío exercised a decisive influence) represents such a "model" in truly practical form. *Sandinismo*, and not "Marxism-Leninism," becomes the "necessary and sufficient ideological signifier for all social forces in the country capable of being mobilized against dictatorship and U.S. domination" (L&P 32). Explicit efforts to rouse class-*consciousness* become unnecessary – and even, perhaps, counter-productive. By coming at the subject on the level of culture – that is, *unconsciously* and, as it were, from behind – *sandinismo* becomes a formula for a spontaneous revolutionary will.

What then to make of the FSLN's fall from power, after their electoral loss in February 1990? In *Literature and Politics* – caught virtually in press by this unexpected turn of events – Beverley and Zimmerman concede that the "identification achieved in the period of insurrection and reconstruction between a radicalized intelligentsia . . . and the popular sectors" had "at least in part, broken down" (111). They hold out the possibility, however, that a "continued radicalization and democratization at the cultural level might have produced a stronger bond between the revolution and the popular sectors, and that this, in turn, might have offset some of the ideological damage caused by the economic crisis and the war" (112). In Beverley's "Postmodernism in Latin America." this same hope is expressed in stronger language:

> Even in defeat (and precisely because of their commitment to implement and respect democratic processes in the face of massive foreign aggression and interference) it seems to me the Sandinistas are exemplary of the emergence of a postmodern but still explicitly socialist political agency in Latin America: I believe their political project is by no means exhausted. (26)

If we take off our postmodern spectacles, however, and look at what – on the level of *sandinismo* as *economic and social policy* rather than "ideological signifier" – preceded the electoral debacle of 1990, a rather different picture emerges: that of a *conscious* decision to seek accommodation with the revolution's enemies, both in Washington and within Nicaragua itself, leaving the masses of Nicaraguan workers and peasants to suffer the consequences. As Petras and Morley report in *Latin America in the Time of Cholera* (see chapter

6, "The Electoral Defeat of the Sandinistas: Critical Reflections"),
the FSLN response to the combined pressure of the contra war and
the economic embargo was, among other things, to implement massive, IMF style austerity measures, resulting in catastrophic economic
hardships for the poor; to send in the police to break the resulting
strikes and protests; to agree to elections *while* the contra war was
still being actively pursued by Washington; to permit massive foreign funding of the pro-US opposition parties coalesced in UNO; and
to conduct a glitzy, US-style electoral campaign, in the hopes that
this sort of "ideological signifier" and "struggle over meaning" might
persuade those it had betrayed that the FSLN was still their best
hope for the future. As FSLN *comandante* Tomás Borge himself de-
clared, "we sacrificed the working class in favor of the economy as
part of a strategic plan."[38] Unfortunately for Borge, Ortega and the
FSLN leadership, however, this strategy failed, leaving the revolution
to, as Petras and Morley put it, "fall between two chairs" – unable to
sell itself to the imperialists in Washington and the capitalist elites in
Nicaragua itself, after having first sold out the Nicaraguan masses
who had supplied the "political agency" – in the form of armed
insurrections – that brought the FSLN to power in the first place. And
as for the "exhaustion" of their "political project," about which Beverley expresses a cautionary optimism: Petras and Morley report
that *after* the election of UNO candidate Violeta Chamorro in 1990,
Ortega and the FSLN directorate have, while threatening "government from below," actively facilitated Chamorro's "free market,"
neo-liberal "reforms" – even, in the person of former FSLN vice-
president Sergio Ramirez, travelling to Washington to help Chamorro's representatives offer up the latest round of sacrifices to the
World Bank and other prospective lenders (139).

44   The lesson here, *qua* the question of "postmodern . . . political
agency," would seem to be that there is no magical, cultural route –
no matter how poetically inspired – around the stubborn political
problem of class consciousness as such. Re-"articulate" and re-"signify" the social text as it would, when *sandinismo* made the calcula-
tion that a good dose of "revolutionary" culture would enable it to
re-negotiate its identity with the popular sector while its leading
representatives re-negotiated the economic pact with imperialism,
this problem came back to haunt them with a vengeance. While the
FSLN trusted to the spontaneous power of its ideological signifiers to

generate a mass revolutionary will, the masses responded by spontaneously turning them out of power. Of course, in doing so, the latter demonstrated its own grievous lack of consciousness. But even to suggest, as Beverley and Zimmerman do, that this was somehow a result of insufficient "radicalization and democratization at the cultural level," is to trade in reality itself for a pair of postmodern spectacles.

Ultimately, it may be only revolutionary practice, the *activity* of   45
strategy and organization, that can successfully trouble the political reveries of postmodernism. But just the sheer history of such practice, particularly in Latin America, makes risible any theory which considers politics (in the Leninist sense) to be either too abstract to matter, or – in what finally amounts to the same thing – to be "self-produced," as Aronowitz has phrased it.

Perhaps the most eloquent refutation of spontaneist faith in   46
"new social movements" is recorded in Roque Dalton's "testimonial classic" *Miguel Mármol*, in which the legendary Salvadoran revolutionary named in the title recounts a life as a communist militant in Central America. It is impossible, by citing excerpts, to do justice to the combined practical wisdom and theoretical profundity of this narrative (by which I mean Mármol's own; I leave it to subtler intellects than my own to decide whether Dalton's editorial participation in this narrative may somehow serve to render it a postmodern "historiographic metafiction"). But one in particular speaks poignantly to the question at hand: in the third chapter of the text, Mármol discusses his return in 1930, shortly before he participates in founding the Salvadoran Communist Party, to his home town of Ilopango. His task is to organize a union of rural workers. At first, as he tells it, the workers reject him, suspicious of his being anti-Catholic. He is led to recall the failure of previous union organizing efforts carried out by a local teacher and a railroad engineer. "However, we suspected they had always worked outside reality, that they hadn't based their organizing work on the actual problems of people and, on the contrary, had created an impenetrable barrier between their "enlightenment" and the "backwardness" they ascribed to the people."[39]

Mármol, however, persists in "finding out what the people   47
thought" (M 119) – that is, he refuses to take their initially backward reaction (defense of church authority) to mean that they lack "en-

lightenment." Meetings are called, and as the people begin to talk about working conditions, Mármol recalls, "it wasn't hard to hear, over and over again, concepts that sounded to me just like the 'class struggle,' the 'dictatorship of the proletariat,' etc." (M 135-136). Mármol's task, then, is not that of "enlightening" the "backward" masses, nor is it simply to acknowledge "what the people thought" as sovereign. Rather, it is to collect these isolated concepts, to *articulate* them, and to lead the masses in drawing the logically necessary conclusions.

48   Of course, the eventual armed insurrection of 1932, towards which the practice of Mármol and the Salvadoran Communists were ultimately directed, proved a miscalculation, and was drowned in blood. But the fact that it could be planned at all must be considered, as it is by Mármol, a significant step forward. If, as the present situation in Central America suggests, the positive culmination of such practice still remains distant, this, it seems to me, is not a reflection of Mármol's "sectarianism" (as Dalton had, and, no doubt, the postmoderns would have it) but of his precociousness. Here, in so many words, Mármol demonstrates his profound, dialectical grasp of the contradictory relation of theory to practice, of concept to reality, of culture to class, of the conscious to the spontaneous, of the "from without" to the "from within." Postmodernism, meanwhile, even at its most "left," political and self-critical, remains cut off from the dialectical truths discovered in the practice of Mármol and of the millions of others in Latin America and across the planet who prepared it and will follow it through.

N   O   T   E   S

1. An original version of this paper was presented as a lecture, entitled "Postmodernism and Hegemony: Theory and Politics in Latin America," at the Humanities Institute at SUNY Stony Brook on March 2, 1989. A Spanish translation appeared in *Nuevo Texto Crítico* año III, segundo semestre de 1990, no 6, pp 77-94.

2. Fredric Jameson, "Postmodernism and Consumer Society," in *The Anti-aesthetic: Essays on Postmodern Culture*, ed. Hal Foster (Port Townsend, WA: Bay Press, 1983) 112.

3. Stanley Aronowitz, "Postmodern and Politics," in *Universal Abandon?: the*

Politics of Postmodernism, ed. Andrew Ross (Minneapolis: University of Minnesota Press, 1988), 50. *Universal Abandon?* cited hereafter in text and notes as UA.

4. Chantal Mouffe, "Radical Democracy," in UA 32.

5. Ernesto Laclau, "Politics and the Limits of Modernity," in UA 66-67.

6. Jean-François Lyotard, *The Postmodern Condition*, trans. Geoff Bennington and Brian Massumi (Minneapolis: University of Minnesota Press, 1984)

7. Frederick Engels, *Socialism: Utopian and Scientific* (Beijing: Foreign Languages Press, 1975), 46.

8. See Ellen Meiksins Wood, *The Retreat from Class: a New "True" Socialism*, (London: Verso, 1986) chapter 4, "The Autonomization of Ideology and Politics."

9. See, for example, Laclau and Mouffe, *Hegemony and Socialist Strategy: Towards a Radical Democratic Politics* (London: Verso, 1985), 97-105.

10. Georg Lukács, *The Destruction of Reason,* trans. Peter Palmer (Atlantic Highlands, NJ: Humanities Press, 1981), 395.

11. "The two moments – that of reason and that of its other – stand not in opposition pointing to a dialectical *Aufhebung*, but in a relationship of tension characterized by mutual repugnance and exclusion." Habermas, "The Entry into Postmodernity: Nietzsche as Turning Point" in *The Philosophical Discourse of Modernity,* trans. Frederick Lawrence (Cambridge: MIT Press, 1987), 103.

12. In the area of Latin American studies these include, *inter alia*, George Yúdice, John Beverley, Marc Zimmerman, Howard Winant and Doris Sommer.

13. See the introductory chapter to my *Modernism and Hegemony: a Materialist Critique of Aesthetic Agencies* (Minneapolis: University of Minnesota Press, 1989).

14. ". . . [T]he exterior is constituted by other discourses." *Hegemony and Socialist Strategy,* 146.

15. Op. cit.

16. See Lenin, *What is to Be Done?: Burning Questions of Our Movement* (Moscow: Progress Publishers, 1973): "...*all* worship of the spontaneity of the working class movement, all belittling of the role of the "conscious element," of the role of Social-Democracy, *means, quite independently of whether he who belittles that role desires it or not, a strengthening of the influence*

of bourgeois ideology upon the workers (39). "Since there can be no talk of an independent ideology formulated by the working masses themselves in the process of their movement, the *only* choice is – either bourgeois or socialist ideology. There is no middle course (for mankind has not created a 'third' ideology, and, moreover, in a society torn by class antagonisms, there can never be a non-class or an above-class ideology). Hence to belittle the socialist ideology *in any way, to turn aside from it in the slightest degree* means to strengthen bourgeois ideology. There is much talk of spontaneity. But the *spontaneous* development of the working class movement leads to its subordination to bourgeois ideology. . ." (40-41).

17. Peter Dews, *Logics of Disintegration* (London: Verso, 1987), 217.

18. "Interview with Cornel West," in UA 273.

19. Fredric Jameson, "Third-World Literature in the Era of Multinational Capitalism," *Social Text* 15 (Fall) 1986: 69.

20. See Fredric Jameson, "Postmodernism, or, the Cultural Logic of Late Capitalism," *New Left Review* 146 (July-August 1984).

21. Edward Said, *The World, the Text and the Critic* (Cambridge: Harvard University Press 1983), 241.

22. Gayatri Chakravorty Spivak, *In Other Worlds: Essays in Cultural Politics* (New York, London: Methuen, 1987), 209.

23. UA, 149-166.

24. See "The Discourse of Others: Feminism and Postmodernism" in Foster, 57-82.

25. George Yúdice, "Marginality and the Ethics of Survival," UA 220.

26. See Rigoberta Menchú, *Me llamo Rigoberta Menchú ... y así me nació la conciencia* (Mexico: Siglo veintiuno, 1983).

27. See "Actual Situation and Perspectives of Latin American Philosophy for Liberation," *The Philosophical Forum* 20. 1-2, (Fall-Winter 1988-89): 43-61. Cited hereafter in text as LAP.

28. See Enrique Dussel, *Philosophy of Liberation* trans. Aquilina Martínez and Christine Morkovsky (Maryknoll, NY: Orbis Books, 1985), 158-160.

29. Roberto Fernández Retamar, *Para una teoría de la literatura hispano-americana* (Habana: Casa de las Américas, 1975).

30. Neil Larsen, "Latin America and Postmodernity: a Brief Theoretical Sketch," unpublished paper; and *Modernism and Hegemony*.

31. Aijaz Ahmad, "Jameson's Rhetoric of Otherness and the 'National Allegory'," *Social Text* 17 (Fall 1987): 3-27.

32. See *US Hegemony Under Siege; Class, Politics and Development in Latin America* (London: Verso, 1990), especially chapters 1, 5; and *Latin America in the Time of Cholera* (New York; Routledge, 1992), especially chapters 1, 7.

33. See, for example, Benjamín Arditi, "Una gramática postmoderna para pensar lo social," *Cultura, política y democratización*, ed. Norbert Lechner (Santiago de Chile: FLACSO/CLASCO/ICI, 1987), 169-187; Alcira Argumedo, *Los laberintos de la crisis, América Latina: Poder transnacional y comunicaciones* (Buenos Aires: ILET/Punto Sur, 1984); Atilio A. Borón, *Estado, Capitalismo, y Democracia en América Latina* (Buenos Aires: Ediciones Imago Mundi, 1992); José Joaquín Brunner, "Notas sobre la modernidad y lo posmoderno en la cultura latino americana," *David y Goliath* 17. 52 (septiembre 1987): 30-39; Arturo Escobar, "Imagining a Post-Development Era? Critical Thought, Development and Social Movements," *Social Text* 31/32 (1992): 20-56; Arturo Escobar and Sonia E. Alvarez, eds. *The Making of Social Movements in Latin America: Identity, Strategy, and Democracy* (Boulder: Westview Press, 1992); Néstor García Canclini, *Culturas híbridas: Estrategias para entrar y salir de la modernidad* (Mexico: Grijalbo, 1990); Norbert Lechner, *La conflictiva y nunca acabada construcción del orden deseado* (Madrid: Siglo Veintinuno and Centro de Investigaciones Sociológicas, 1986); José Nun, *La rebelión del coro: estudios sobre la racionalidad política y el sentido común* (Buenos Aires: Editores Nueva Visión, 1989). See also David Slater, ed. *New Social Movements and the State in Latin America* (Amsterdam: CEDLA, 1985).

34. Adolfo Sánchez Vásquez, "Marxism in Latin America," *The Philosophical Forum* 20. 1-2 (Fall-Winter 1988-89): 114-128.

35. Greg Dawes, *Aesthetics and Revolution: Nicaraguan Poetry, 1979-1990* (Minneapolis: University of Minnesota Press, 1993), 25.

36. See, for example, Orlando Núñez and Roger Burbach, *Democracia y revolución en las Américas* (Managua: Editorial Vanguardia, 1986).

37. John Beverley and Marc Zimmerman, *Litreature and Politics in the Central American Revolutions* (Austin: University of Texas Press, 1990) [hereafter cited in text as L&P); and John Beverley, "Postmodernism in Latin America," unpublished manuscript, forthcoming in *boundary* 2, special issue on "The Postmodernism Debate in Latin America."

38. Quoted in *Latin America in the Time of Cholera*, 134.

39. Roque Dalton, *Miguel Mármol*, trans. Kathleen Ross and Richard Schaaf (Willimantic, CT: Curbstone Press, 1982), 119. Cited hereafter in text as M.

POSTMODERN **ISM**

ETHNICITY AND UNDERGROUND

REVISION **ISM**

IN **ISH** MAEL REED

DAVID MIKICS

ismishismish ismish ismish ismishismish
ismishismish ismishismish ismishismish
ismishismish ismishismish ismishismish
ismishismish ismishismish ismishismish
ismishismish ismishismish ismishismish
ismishismish ismishismish ismishismish
ismishismish ismishismish ismishismish
ismishismish ismishismish ismishismish
ismishismish ismishismish ismishismish
ismishismish ismishismish ismishismish
ismishismish ismishismish ismishismish
ismishismish ismishismishismishismish
ismishismish ismishismish ismishismish
ismishismish ismishismish ismishismish
ismishismish ismishismish ismishismish
ismishismish ismishismish ismishismish
ismishismish ismishismish ismishismish
ismishismish ismishismish ismishismish
ismishismish ismishismishismishismish
ismishismish ismishismish ismishismish
ismishismish ismishismish ismishismish
ismishismish ismishismish ismishismish
ismishismish ismishismish ismishismish
ismishismish ismishismish ismishismish
ismishismish ismishismishismishismish
ismishismish ismishismish ismishismish

I. ish and ism

Ishmael Reed is a postmodern writer; he is also an African- American 1
writer. The purpose of this essay is to reflect on the conjunction
between these two roles in Reed's work – and the somewhat surprising fact that they are in conjunction more than in conflict. Postmodernism, with its definition of the contemporary world as a realm of
fragmentation, disassociation, and the post-personal, seems to dissolve the cultural continuities of community and individual ego to
which earlier artistic eras remained loyal. Postmodernism, in other
words, declares the death of cultural authenticity. African-American
literature, by contrast, often seems to value cultural authenticity as a
means of ensuring communal and individual self-assertion in the
black diaspora.[1] Reed's work suggests how African-American tradition, which generally – not always, but generally – wants to depict
the survival of a people and a culture in its original, authentic
strength, can be reconciled with postmodernism, which destroys
the notions of origin, authenticity and tradition itself.

Since the African-American tradition is posited by Reed as a 2
definitive cultural value often repressed or distorted by modern
mass culture, a value that can in some sense act as a critique of
capitalist modernization, an allied question (one subject to much
recent debate) will be whether Reed's postmodernism damages the
critical capacity of his project.[2] Can postmodern techniques be the
vehicle for a cultural critique, or must they be "affirmative," acqui-
escing in the deterioration of art and political speech into commodities under late capitalism?

I have found the theory of Jürgen Habermas useful in posing 3
these questions. In particular, Habermas' distinction between a "lifeworld" of everyday experiential practice and a systemic, administrative complex that embodies the managerial necessities of late capitalism, and continually encroaches upon or threatens the lifeworld,

seems to be replicated in Reed's distinction (in his novel *The Terrible Twos*) between African-American subcultural experience and a destructive mass culture ruled by the commercial system. Habermas' work is a sustained attempt to seek a means of resuscitating the lifeworld that has been impoverished by the managerial priorities of the welfare state (priorities that Reed aptly sees encoded in the pacifying, tepid character of many mass cultural forms).[3] In this attempt, Habermas champions aesthetic modernity, with its emphasis on the unique, autonomous individual, as a more helpful lifeworld response to modernization processes than the postmodern dissolution of the individual as a category.

4   For Habermas, postmodernism is "affirmative": that is, it tends to mimic the purely negative dispersal of subjective freedom enforced by modernization (the ability to consume what one wants) instead of asserting the critical potential implied by the more positive side of such modernization (the ability to think what one wants). Modernization's corrosive effect on traditional cultural continuities also entails a democratic emphasis on individuality within intersubjective relations, and therefore, Habermas claims, any critical response to modernity must capitalize on its positive aspect, the promise of more intellectual autonomy for the individual, who now judges culture and its prejudices from a distance. According to Habermas' argument, criticism within aesthetic modernity takes its most legitimate and useful form when it secures the rights of the individual subject to reevaluate and revise culture in a way that champions the power of the lifeworld while acknowledging the lifeworld's confrontation with the social rationalization process. The need to acknowledge the effects of rationalization and modernization means that this advocacy of the lifeworld must not take the neoconservative form of an attempt to revive a cultural tradition in an unreconstructed way, for such an attempt would have to ignore the dangerous effects that modernization has already had on the lifeworld, its destabilizing of tradition.[4]

5   As I will suggest, Reed is certainly in accord with Habermas' idea of a critically self-revising tradition, in Reed's case African-American tradition, as the necessary form of an effective contemporary invocation of the lifeworld. But his work challenges Habermas' assumption that such critical use of tradition must be coupled with the assertion of an autonomous modernist self. Reed suggests a subcul-

tural rather than an individualist answer to the destructive effects of modernization. The postmodern aspect of Reed's work, his attack on the notions of character and individual consciousness, does not invalidate its critical potential, as Habermas' argument would imply. Instead, the subcultural practice of "neohoodooism" acts as a subversive force that seizes mass cultural phenomena and reuses them for the purpose of resistance. Habermas' prejudice in favor of the individual not only compels him to deny the reality of the Freudian unconscious as a social formation that defeats the wish for self-possession central to his neo-Kantian notion of the individual,[5] it also blinds him, along with other leftist critics of postmodernism, to the force of postmodern subversions, like "neohoodooism," that do not base themselves on envisioning autonomous selves exercising political judgment.

Reed's lack of desire for the autonomous self accounts for another, more obstreperous leftist objection to the discerning of a critical project in his work. Reed's fiction, which is often hermetic in texture, does not pursue the definition of politics as a matter of attaining the self-empowering judgment (however difficult it may be to achieve such judgment) that is the goal of Brecht's or Baraka's radical theater. One answer to this objection would draw on Habermas' terms. In his Adorno prize lecture, Habermas notes that in order for critical art to succeed in the contemporary moment, it must be supported by changes in the lifeworld: the burden of critique must not be placed on aesthetics alone without considering its reception in everyday life. Change cannot be legislated by authors, and given this fact, authors must not be faulted for not aiming to produce social change in an *immediate* way, for example through populist style or overtly revolutionary rhetoric. The prescriptive moralizing on the part of critics who insist on such features has at times been an inhibiting factor in contemporary African-American writing, since what such critics want cannot be readily delivered by writers intent on exploring the artistic implications of their material in the context of an ever more complex late capitalist society.

I would extend this answer to the demand for an autonomous political art beyond Habermas' idea of attending to institutional and everyday contexts before individual literary works. Habermas cannot convey a nearly full enough picture of everyday life because he retains the goal of an empowered self freed, as much as possible, from alienation and false consciousness – his legacy from Kant and Marx. Reed's artistic technique, by contrast, exposes the unconscious dimensions of ordinary existence, our styles of being, and it therefore necessarily gravitates away from injunctions toward clarifying one's consciousness in preparation for political judgment. Reed's work is more, not less, political because of his recognition that clarification is always an aspect of what *Mumbo Jumbo* calls the Wallflower Order, an attempt to repress and avoid the dense, Dionysian "Work" that an African-American form like jazz tries to acknowledge: "Jes Grew, the Something or Other that led Charlie Parker to scale the Everests of the Chord . . . the manic in the artist who would rather do glossolalia than be 'neat clean or lucid.'"[6] Reed's novels aim at the recognition of the improvisatory changes that are always happening, and always repressed by, ruling culture, rather than (the way we usually think of political art) the gearing up for a change in or replacement of the consciousness that rules.

8   The utopian demand that the text be a lever, in and of itself, for such a decisive change in consciousness, without regard for its function within a larger social and institutional discourse, has often influenced current debates on the politics of literary study (for example, the ongoing revisions of the literary canon). Such utopianism must be regarded as an inevitable symptom of an era in which the relative absence of radical thought about institutions themselves is all too clear.[7] In particular, the requirement that texts unequivocally declare their wholesome political uses, thus single-handedly transforming institutional contexts of reading, has weighed heavily (and, I believe, harmfully) on the choice of "black literature" for the new curriculum. For example, the common assumption that black writers should display an attractive, easily accessible communal optimism militates for the selection of *For Colored Girls* . . . or *The Color Purple* in introductory core courses that have room for only one African-American text. Such bias necessarily excludes the work of writers like Adrienne Kennedy, Andrea Lee, James MacPherson, David Bradley, Jay Wright – and Reed. The demand that African-American literature incarnate a positive representative function, praising the strength of cultural continuity and communal values, has dogged Reed throughout his career. The charge frequently made by both black and white critics that Reed is not properly representative of African-American literature seems to rest on the dangerous assumption that the black

writer is bound to a representative goal: bound, that is, to present encouraging or correct portraits of his/her culture. This need for African-American literature to perform a representative function has complex historical roots, often involving the burdensome obligation imposed on black writers to legitimate black life for a white audience.[8] In the 1990s, however, the wish for the representative is an anachronism, a symptomatic reaction against postmodern conditions in which, despite the continuing social and economic racism of American society, late capitalism has produced a diversity of intra- and interracial roles that erodes cultural uniformity in black America, as elsewhere.[9] Since multifarious and contradictory modes of African-American life now exist on an unprecedented scale, any demand for representative description is bound to fail. I do not wish to claim Reed as a representative of a new postmodern strain in African-American life; that would simply be inverting the criticisms of those who deny Reed's legitimacy. Reed's work, because it is a partial (in every sense of the word) rather than a grandly unified vision of African-American experience, cannot be representative in any way. Rather, he creatively and successfully exploits a particular African-American subculture in order to invent his own brand of critical postmodernism.

As he rejects the idea of a representative or unified vision of black life, Reed also shies away from the easy acceptance of totality in affirmative postmodernism, which is another example of a representative strategy, one that says: this is our new world, from which no escape, or even critical distance, is possible. By indifferently combining the fragments of various traditions and histories, affirmative postmodernism sets even fragmentation under the sign of Baudrillard's homogeneous, uniform "society of the spectacle." By contrast, Reed *via* his subcultural strategy sets the plural cultural forces of postmodern society in conflict, propounding an aesthetics of resistance or social tension rather than reconciliation.[10] Thus Reed "mobilizes a sense of a particular history of subject positions that will not be subsumed under the apparently seamless master text."[11]

Before discussing Reed's African-American critical postmodernism in more detail, I want first to differentiate him from postmodernists who do not oppose lifeworld to rationalization systems but who, instead, see postmodernity as the inevitable colonization of lifeworld by system. Frank Lentricchia has recently proposed Don DeLillo's *Libra* as an example of critical postmodernism in its treatment of mass culture, of "an everyday life . . . utterly enthralled by the fantasy selves projected in the media."[12] DeLillo does not offer any escape from a media-absorbed world that has replaced the first-person self with third-person fantasies of the self. In DeLillo as in Pynchon, there are no local, popular cultural forces that would provide resistance to modernization; there is only an oppressive totality. In DeLillo, phenomena of resistance (*The Names'* terrorism) or esoteric revisionism (*White Noise*'s "Hitler studies") are simply mirror images of the increasingly systematized society that they rebel against. No route is possible back to the authenticity desired by the modernists, since authenticity has itself become a mass cultural icon. (Thus DeLillo's Lee Harvey Oswald in *Libra* wants to "be somebody," an ambition that can only be realized within the confines of the mass media image.) Yet it is important to remember, as Lentricchia stresses, that DeLillo's attitude toward this fragmented and imprisoning system, his image of postmodern America, is critical rather than celebratory. Postmodernist critique does not need to invoke adversarial forces like the high-modernist self or the utopian vision of a radically different society in order to avoid the pitfalls indulged in by the affirmative, pastiche-ridden, unreflective postmodernisms that are now shared by the advertizing world and a large sector of the visual arts community. What makes the difference in critical postmodernism is its reflective capacity, its dwelling on current social and aesthetic contradictions, rather than the dissolving of contradiction into easy juxtaposition dictated by the affirmative postmodern. Such contradictions often involve the survival of earlier aesthetic and cultural forms alongside or within postmodernity: thus the desperate desire for existential self in DeLillo's Oswald, Barthelme's protagonists, or Mailer's Gary Gilmore (in *The Executioner's Song*) – or the survival of premodern, subcultural secret society traditions in Reed.

11   Oddly enough, the critical edge provided by a subcultural survival like Reed's vodoun has its near-counterpart in high modernism. Lionel Trilling, for example, praises Freud's image of the "other culture," the secret traditions Freud chose to ally himself to as counters to the dominant values of Austrian society. One of Freud's other cultures was England; another was ancient Greece; and still another, Hebraic tradition.[13] But Reed's postmodernism again generates a key difference from the modernist Freud. For Reed, unlike Trilling's

Freud, the subculture or other culture is interwoven, despite its esotericism, with the imagery of mass culture, imagery that the subculture both mimics and, through its mimicry, resists. The jazz style celebrated in *Mumbo Jumbo* is, after all, a mass cultural form.

A similar attachment to mass-cultural image is at work in the 12 postmodern treatment of character, again marking a difference from modernism. For Reed, as for DeLillo, the self is a caricature, a stylistic move determined by cultural stereotype rather than a modernist dream of individual authenticity. But the stereotypes are not, in his work, only the property of a mechanized mass culture, as in DeLillo. Their mass-cultural face may also stem from, or be appropriated by, African-American counterculture. Reed's aesthetic of "sampling,"[14] of inventively assembling snippets from the tradition with which he identifies (Neohoodooism) as well as the cultural syndrome he opposes (the Wallflower Order), thus presents itself as sustained dialogic satire.[15]

The sort of reconciliation between an African-American tradition 13 and postmodernism that I have hinted at has been offered in the context of Reed's work by Henry Louis Gates, Jr., and the late James Snead, both of whom speak of Reed as demonstrating affinities between his own postmodern technique and the techniques of "signifying" in black culture. Snead specifically points to sudden rhythmic juxtaposition and syncretism, two features of African religion and music that are echoed in Reed's work.[16] Gates and Snead, by making their connection between Africa and Reed, imply that postmodernism can be rooted, even if only by analogy, in a specific cultural tradition, such as that of the African-American. Reed himself seems to concur in this analysis, identifying his own authorial practice with the Africa-derived folk tradition of vodoun.

Gates and Snead reading Reed are brilliantly helpful, and I will 14 finally agree with their assessment of Reed. But I would like to introduce a possible objection to their readings that hinges on the ideological implications of presenting an element of the African-American lifeworld like vodoun alongside modernist and postmodernist artistic practice. The objection would go something like this: both Gates and Snead seem to imply that Reed claims an identity between vodoun and his own work because he perceives a natural, implicit analogy between modern and postmodern European aesthetics and black culture. One might argue against Gates and Snead by reminding oneself that such an analogy is not natural, but instead an ideological construct of twentieth-century European modernism's attraction to "primitive" forms. In contrast to mass culture, which is made possible by the dissolution of traditional communal ties under advanced capitalism – the meeting hall or fête replaced by a million TV sets – popular or folk culture is by definition premodern: its premise must be an assumed community of style and cultural symbolism rather than the alienated perspective of the individual artist. From this perspective, the twentieth-century European or Euro-American artist's frequent invoking of African and African-American popular cultural practice as an analogy to his or her own efforts, from Picasso's interest in "primitive" art to Norman Mailer's White Negro to the later albums of the American pop music group Talking Heads,[17] is significantly problematic. The high culture/"primitive" analogy is motivated by nostalgia for the (supposed) immediacy or palpable, experiential knowledge that the alienated artist perceives in either colonized nations or the underclass of his or her own nation. As such, it is inevitably a colonial gesture. By failing to address this cultural-historical basis for the comparison that modern and postmodern European Euro-American art habitually makes between itself and the premodern aspects of African/African-American culture, both Snead and Gates imply that such comparisons describe a natural or neutral similarity, instead of themselves enacting ideologically freighted gestures.[18] In these two critics' analogies between African-American art and the European modernist/postmodernist tradition, ideology disappears.

15   Reed's identification of his art with vodoun shares something with the European modernist's colonialist gesture: he desires to restore to his work a dimension of authenticity that has been lost in much of the modern world.[19] In other words, Reed reacts against social modernization by allying himself to vodoun. After all, vodoun is communal folk culture, a survival of an era untouched by the atomizing, alienating effects of the modern mass media. There is, then, no precise fit between popular tradition and postmodern strategy, as Gates and Snead tend to suggest in their praises of Reed. The unique, eccentric character of Reed's postmodernism, its antinormative nature, suggests that the popular is, in part, invoked as a way of grounding the postmodern in its very opposite, the force of folk tradition, as a counterbalance against its potentially uncon-

trolled, antitraditional mirroring of the fragmenting effects of late capitalism.[20]

The objection to Reed's appropriation of the supposed authenticity of folk culture that I have just outlined is a serious one, but I believe one can acknowledge its seriousness while also making it defer to the gaiety of Reed's work, which ultimately undercuts the proclamation of authenticity that one aspect of Reed still wants to make. Reed's delight in subversive traditions, which is so well evoked by Gates and Snead, extends to the self-mockery of folklore itself, which becomes the madly esoteric and writerly venture of neohoodooism. In practical terms, Reed does not seem to be hamstrung by any gap between tradition and postmodern subversion. Instead, he aims, largely successfully, at a coherence of folk and postmodern expression in which neither element serves or counterbalances the other, in which they form a crazy whole. In other words, Reed wants to show the ways in which the popular uncannily anticipates and redeems what we thought were the properties of contemporary mass culture alone by being, so to speak, always-already postmodern, postmodern from way back. By presenting us with a partial or eccentric claim to contemporary mass culture, a creative appropriation of its reifying tendencies, he negotiates the Scylla and Charybdis of twentieth-century art: the stale modernist opposition between the reified and the creative, and the affirmative postmodern claim that reification subsumes all contemporary narratives into an undifferentiated whole. In contrast to the centrifugal atmosphere of affirmative postmodernism, in which traditional elements are used as mere decorative fragments,[21] the premodern subculture that Reed celebrates provides an *ad hoc*, self-ironizing center of gravity for his work by endowing aesthetic eccentricity with the lure of tradition. Traditional culture has been irreversibly transfigured by the new aura of postmodern technological reproduction, but it still retains an otherness, a mark of difference.

II. Reed, Baraka, Pynchon: Postmodernism and Community

Well, and keep in mind where those Masonic Mysteries came from in the first place. (Check out Ishmael Reed. He knows more about it than you'll ever find here.) – Thomas Pynchon, *Gravity's Rainbow* [23]

It is also significant that most of the [vodoun] houngans who claim the patronage of Ogoun belong to the Masonic Order. – Maya Deren, *Divine Horsemen* [23]

17   In his career as a novelist, Ishmael Reed has frequently occupied himself with the images produced by American mass culture. Some of these images are the travesties of black life produced by white America – the antebellum stereotypes of Mammy and Uncle Tom invoked in *Flight to Canada* (1976), Reed's parodic takeoff on slave narrative; or the Amos and Andy routines in *The Last Days of Louisiana Red* (1974), a satirical pseudo-thriller. Some, on the other hand, are not specific to Afro-America, like the Wild West parodied in *Yellow Back Radio Broke Down*, Reed's "Western" written in 1969. In *The Terrible Twos* (1982), which I will focus on in the remainder of this essay, Reed centers his analysis on a mass-produced and mass-marketed image of general import in American culture, that of Santa Claus. In particular, the novel has as its subtext the standard movie myth of American Christmas, *Miracle on 34th St.* As I hope to show, the ossified, stereotypical mythology embodied by this film is undermined by Reed's radically unorthodox mode of narration – a mode that has itself been called filmic. Reed counters the ideologically dominant images of *Miracle* with his own subversive quasi-filmic techniques, unravelling one filmic mode by means of another.

18   As James Snead points out, Reed's work, like much postmodern writing, has important correlations with the aesthetics of movie-making in its use of sudden and suggestive juxtaposition (montage),

as well as with the similar principles of creative juxtaposition (which Snead calls "cutting") active in African religion and music: "Reed elides the 'cut' of black culture with the 'cutting' used in cinema. Self-consciously filmable, *Mumbo Jumbo* ends with a 'freeze frame'... underscoring its filmic nature."[24] My aim in this essay is to explore some of the ways in which Reed uses familiar images from American film, and in fact opposes these official, mass-cultural images to an alternative culture of the "cut" or radical juxtaposition, which has affinities both with Euro-American postmodernism and with the African-American belief system of vodoun. As I have noted, Reed's final aim is a therapeutic criticism of the numbing, homogenizing effects of modernization. Far from exulting in the culture of the mass media as the "affirmative postmodernist" would do, Reed in *The Terrible Twos* opposes the mass culture of Hollywood movies and TV to an underground folk tradition that partakes of vodoun habits of mind, specifically in its occult revisionary reading of St. Nicholas, otherwise known as Santa Claus. Reed's hermetic St. Nicholas revolts against the official or established culture represented in *The Terrible Twos* by commercial capitalism's image of Christmas.

Reed criticizes not only the late capitalist system itself; he also criticizes the most common reception of African-American culture within that system. African-American tradition has been taken as an offer of escape from official culture into a viable marginal one – now that the alienated, solipsistic subjectivity of European modernism, or the fantasies of postmodernism, which decenter subjectivity without offering a communal alternative to the now-defunct self, seem less than comfortably livable. For contemporary critical ideology, black writing seems to represent a potential for communal authenticity that has long been excluded from the Euro-American avant-garde. A drama like *Slave Ship*, as Kimberly Benston convincingly argues, achieves precisely what the Euro-American modernists cannot: a depiction of oppositional community based in an existing cultural reality.[25] This escape from modernist alienation into black cultural authenticity is the pattern of Baraka's career, as well as the goal of the "Black Aesthetics" movement of the 1960s and '70s in which Baraka, along with Addison Gayle, Hoyt Fuller, Larry Neal, and others, played a prominent role.

As Gates has shown in his reading of *Mumbo Jumbo*, Reed criticizes such attachment to authenticity by attacking the essentialist aspect of the Black Aesthetics/Black Arts movement (and, before it, the Negritude movement). Reed opposes the notion of blackness as a "transcendental signified," an authoritative, static and univocal symbolic presence.[26] Instead, Reed reveals black discourse to be, in postmodern fashion, decentered and polyvocal. Where does this postmodern aesthetic strategy leave Reed in terms of the communal emphasis of African-American culture? Houston Baker has cited Reed's fiction as a return to "the common sense of the tribe"[27]: but how can such a collective or tribal orientation coexist with the atomizing, depersonalizing effects of postmodernist technique also evident in Reed?

21   One approach to a definition of Reed's decentered communalism, his subversive interest in the lifeworld's subcultural traditions, is by way of a contrast with Baraka. Though both Baraka and Reed move from avant-garde alienation in early works like Baraka's *Preface to a Twenty Volume Suicide Note* and Reed's *The Free-Lance Pallbearers* to an emphasis on the power of African-American cultural continuity, there are important differences. Reed's "neohoodooist" aesthetic, as we shall see, is syncretic and assimilative, whereas Baraka's black consciousness attempts the monolithic and univocal. In Reed, vodoun does not need to reject European influence in order to safeguard its purity; instead, it translates this influence into the terms of a newly indigenous New World culture.

22   In other respects as well, Reed's vision of African-American culture should not be conflated with Baraka's (or, say, June Jordan's) equally powerful, but very distinct, definition of that culture. Throughout his work, Reed consistently rejects the invocation of ethnic community on a grand scale, opting instead for the investigation of the esoteric cultural practices, like vodoun, that appear as sect, secret society, or personal obsession rather than as mass movement. Reed's choice of the occult and dispersed, rather than the fully public, continuities in African-American culture suggests that eccentric or idiosyncratic rewritings of culture are valuable precisely because they are idiosyncratic – and that such stylistic quirks may constitute the only existential rebellion still viable. The later work of Baraka, by contrast, like that of many other politically committed African-American artists, strives for community through its normative and explicit approach, the plain force of a quintessentially public rhetoric. Baker's phrase "the common sense of the tribe" is a

better description of Baraka's mode in its willed commonness than it is of Reed's willful peculiarity.

Having clarified his differences from Baraka's more normative ap- 23 proach to African-American tradition, I now want to pursue a comparison between Reed and Pynchon,[28] which will reveal an equally telling difference. To return to Habermas' terms: Reed is interested in upholding the lifeworld and its traditions against the modernization process, whereas for Pynchon the lifeworld is merely an attenuated reflection of the systemic aspect of modernization.

Pynchon is a natural parallel for Reed; especially, Pynchon's 24 flaked-out whimsy in *The Crying of Lot 49* bears a remarkable tonal resemblance to some of Reed's work.[29] There's also a thematic resemblance between Pynchon and Reed: they both participate in the postmodernist polemic against authenticity by creating, for the most part, caricatures rather than "realistic" characters. Reed has his hardboiled detectives and monomaniacal radicals, Pynchon his male-bonded post-adolescents and *femmes fatales*. The sense that these figures, by-products of modernity's obsessions, suffer or play out their stereotypical identities, instead of actively controlling them, is characteristic of postmodernism.[30]

Pynchon's defiant authorial eccentricity imagines the rebellion 25 against modernity, not as a viable cultural alternative, but as an intricate fantasy that rewrites the way of the world in a language of conspiratorial oddity. In Pynchon, as in DeLillo, subversive fantasies usually turn out to be as chillingly claustrophobic as official reality.[31] The notion of escape from a hegemonic culture occupies Reed's work as it does Pynchon's, but the difference, I will argue, is Reed's effort to ground the escape in an actual alternative – African-American – aesthetic, that of vodoun.

There is a striking passage in Pynchon's *The Crying of Lot 49* that 26 dramatically evokes the possibility of subversive or alternative community as, at the same time, the threat of an utterly private world of paranoid self-delusion – a world that ironically and horrifyingly mirrors the oppressive totality of the increasingly rationalized contemporary universe. Pynchon's Oedipa Maas, as she discovers the massive underground postal network called W.A.S.T.E. seemingly everywhere she turns, speculates to herself that

Either you have stumbled indeed, without the aid of LSD *or other indole alkaloids, onto a secret richness and concealed density of*

dream; onto a network by which X number of Americans are truly communicating whilst reserving their lies, recitations of routine, arid betrayals of spiritual poverty for the official government delivery system; maybe even onto a real alternative to the exitlessness, to the absence of surprise to life, that harrows the head of everybody American you know, and you too, sweetie. Or (here comes the second alternative) you are hallucinating it . . . in which case you are a nut, out of your skull. [32]

27   Oedipa's potentially paranoid fantasy may, this passage from *Lot 49* suggests, be the only possibility for a rebellious collective imagination that remains in American life. Reed shares Pynchon's distaste for what Oedipa Maas describes as the "exitlessness" of American life, the overwhelming pressure of a bland and univocal day-to-day rationality. The transhistorical Wallflower Order in *Mumbo Jumbo*, which tries to stamp out jazz dancing and all other forms of collective imaginative improvisation, is an openly malevolent version of such oppressive blandness.

28   Pynchon leaves us in the dark as to whether the secret community that Oedipa envisions actually exists; but if it does, it is invigorating only to the degree that it is also scary and sinister. [33] Reed, by contrast, is able to depict the counterforce to Wallflower oppression not as an ontologically dubious fantasy, like Oedipa Maas' underground postal-cum-waste-disposal system, but as an actual cultural phenomenon, what *Mumbo Jumbo* calls Jes Grew: black music, dance and verbal "signifying." [34]

III. The Filmic Double

29   We are now ready to deal with the importance of mass culture in *The Terrible Twos* by way of its major filmic subtext, the "classic" Christmas movie *Miracle on 34th Street*. First, though, this is an appropriate time to briefly and somewhat violently summarize the novel's plot: it begins with "a past Christmas" – the Christmas just following Reagan's 1980 electoral victory, when charity has been abandoned in favor of Lucchese boots and Gucci handbags. A top male model

named Dean Clift, represented by Reed as a know-nothing automaton sunk in infantile dependency on his wife, whom he calls "Mommy," is running for Congress from the "silk stocking district" in Manhattan. By the novel's second section, set during "a future Christmas," Dean Clift – a composite portrait of Ronald Reagan and Dan Quayle – has become president. Meanwhile, Santa Claus has become even bigger business than he was in the 1980s: a character named Oswald Zumwalt, head of a company called the North Pole Development Corporation (or Big North for short), has secured "exclusive rights" to Santa. (A class action suit is filed by thousands of rival Clauses, "black, red and white," but they lose.) Zumwalt establishes a Christmas Land at the North Pole "to which consumers all over the world [will] fly, Supersaver, to celebrate Christmas" (TT, 64).[35] Meanwhile, President Clift has signed a bill giving Adolf Hitler posthumous American citizenship. The economy's in trouble – a loaf of bread costs fifty dollars. The hungover president's eyes "look like two Japanese flags."

In the midst of this dangerous atmosphere of crisis, a sect called the Nicolaites has sprung up, determined to rescue Santa Claus from his position as avatar of mass media commercialism. The Nicolaites are dedicated to the original image of the fourth-century St. Nicholas as a forthright defier of imperial authority, a populist whose miracles rivalled Christ's, causing the Vatican to declare him moribund in the '60s in the face of popular enthusiasm for Nicholas' cult. The Nicolaites succeed in kidnapping Big North's official Santa Claus and momentarily replacing him with their own spokesman, a black dwarf known as Black Peter. (As we shall see, Black Peter is St. Nicholas' somewhat sinister accomplice in some versions of the Nicholas legend.) The flamboyant and persuasive Black Peter, projecting his voice ventriloquist-style into a false Santa Claus, delivers a condemnation of the hardheartedness of American commercial capitalism and, in particular, capitalism's exploitation of Santa. Finally, President Clift, after being taken on a Dantesque tour in which he meets the damned souls of dead American presidents, realizes the error of his ways and, like Jacob Marley in *A Christmas Carol*, suddenly overflows with charitable Christmas cheer, passing out Redskins tickets and championing disarmament. At the novel's end, President Clift has been placed in a sanatorium by his shocked former supporters and a manhunt is on for Black Peter.

31   President Dean Clift is not only like Jacob Marley but also like Claude Rains in *Mr. Smith Goes to Washington*, another conversion narrative, in which Rains as the supposedly populist, but actually cynically self-interested, congressman finally breaks down and admits his own corruption, thus becoming dangerous to the corporate interests that support him. But the major subtext of The Terrible Twos is *Miracle on 34th St.* (1947; written and directed by George Seaton). In this film, Kris Kringle, the real Santa Claus hired by Macy's to play Santa Claus, represents a critique of commercialized Christmas and a polemic in favor of Christmas charity, which is ideologically defined by *Miracle* as both the antithesis and the salvation of corporate commercialism. By the end of the movie Kringle, played by Edmund Gwenn, succeeds not only in converting hardnosed businesswoman Mrs. Walker (Maureen O'Hara), to his humanitarian gospel, but also her much harder-nosed child, played by the preteenage Natalie Wood. Kringle's most important convert, however, is Mr. Macy himself, who by the end of the film becomes a fervent supporter of his Santa's claim to be *the* Santa Claus. Though the film retains enough cynicism concerning Macy's profit-oriented motives for his support of Kris Kringle to save it from sentimental idealization of the American corporation, the point is nevertheless quite clearly made that Macy's is now a kinder, gentler store as a result of Kringle's presence. Kringle even unites Macy and Gimbel as, in the spirit of Christmas generosity, both begin referring customers to the competing store and vying for the privilege of rewarding Kris himself for his services. By being an authentic rather than a false, merely commercial Santa, *Miracle*'s Kris Kringle ameliorates the grasping commercialism of Macy's, infusing it with the heartwarmingly populist, anti- greed "true" spirit of Christmas. *Miracle*'s ideological goal is to claim that mass culture can become popular culture: to present the corporation in a newly beneficent, populist role by showing it embracing anti-commercialism. Kris may protest against the consumerist version of Christmas, but he nevertheless works happily at Macy's, advising its customers to buy Macy's toys. At the film's end, Kris's own populist beliefs are recognized and partially adopted by Macy's. The parallel to Macy's in Reed's novel is Zumwalt's Big North, which has secured exclusive rights to Santa Claus just as, in *Miracle*, New York's largest department store owns Santa in the person of Kris Kringle. The difference, of course, is that Reed's Big North,

unlike Macy's in the film, is openly malevolent and not at all liable to be affected by the "true" anti-commercial spirit of Santa Claus.

The three subtexts for Reed's novel that I've mentioned, *Christmas Carol*, *Mr. Smith*, and *Miracle*, all enfold the political in the personal, reducing a political situation to a matter of human character, and showing a generous personality winning out over a cynical one. Reed implicitly argues that a similar ideological effect is accomplished by Reagan's commercial success as the "likeable" President. Not for the first time in American history, but perhaps most remarkably, a President's politics are obscured by his transfiguration into a fictively endearing mass media personality. [32]

Reed's *The Terrible Twos* deliberately obstructs the kind of metamorphosis of politics into individual personality that is so emphatically present in his source text *Miracle on 34th St.* This is where Reed's postmodernist replacement of character with caricature comes in: Big North is a cold-blooded operation, and the "real" Santa Claus is a mere corporate stooge, not a kindly old gent like Miracle's Kris Kringle. There is no pretense that the "reality," the mimed authenticity, of this Santa Claus means anything more than the company's ability to buy the name: no one at Big North, including their Santa, even considers the idea that the personality of Santa might have symbolic efficacy – he is nothing but an ersatz, infinitely reproducible trademark for Christmas consumerism. [33]

The Terrible Twos presents not just a critique of commercialism and its lack of authenticity, but a revolt against it that takes the form of a hermetic inquiry into Church history – the "underground revisionism" alluded to in my title. As he becomes corporate property, the historical identity of Nicholas (known as Claus in northern Europe) as a populist Christian saint becomes more and more effaced. The self-imposed task of the Nicolaites, the secret society that opposes itself to Big North's official, corporate Santa Claus in *The Terrible Twos*, is to resurrect the forgotten radical historicity of St. Nicholas, to oppose the phoniness of mass culture by invoking the subversive reality of popular tradition. [34]

Like the *Mu'tafikah* in Reed's *Mumbo Jumbo*, the Nicolaites have formed a sect intent on returning a degraded symbol to its original, authentic power. In *Mumbo Jumbo*, the *Mu'tafikah* are a secret society that makes a career of "liberating" works of art from Western museums and returning them to their African, Asian or Native American [35] places of origin. The *Mu'tafikah* stand against the Atonist (Christo- and Eurocentric) effort to reduce all culture to a single Christianized meaning – or else destroy it. But the *Mu'tafikah* are oddly compara- ble to *Mumbo Jumbo*'s Atonists, who are equipped with their own secret societies, the Teutonic Knights and the Knights Templar, in their desire for singular and authentic cultural origins – origins with a racial basis.[36] Reed's purpose is not to engage in a moralizing comparison of the exclusionary essentialisms that sometimes in- habit radical critiques of a ruling ideology with the more palpa- ble destruction wrought by that ideology. Instead, Reed, in Nietz- schean fashion, implies the difficulty of achieving a truly radical break from any oppressive mode of thought without inadvertently duplicating its repressive need to exclude the other. Reed, like Ellison in his depiction of the Brotherhood in *Invisible Man*, asks whether a radical, conspiratorial alternative to the reigning culture is truly an alternative, if it is bound to reproduce some aspects of the oppres- sion it protests.[37]

36   Like the *Mu'tafikah*, the Nicolaites in *The Terrible Twos* are a thin- ly veiled allegory of 1960s radicalism: Black Peter takes over the Nicolaites as Black Power swayed white radicals in the '60s. These groups' efforts to establish an adversarial culture based on a faith in native origins are criticized by Reed in much the same terms he uses to attack essentialist definitions of "black aesthetics" and negri- tude.[38] Refusing the belief in an exclusivist and prescriptive, rather than a multicultural, black art that was sometimes featured in the Black Aesthetics movement, Reed proposes in place of this purism a multicultural synthesis derived from the syncretism of African and Asian religions, "Neohoodooism." In aligning his own critical princi- ples with the African New World belief system of vodoun, Reed proclaims his place in African-American tradition while refusing the essentialist definitions of this tradition that would reject syncretism or the multicultural as a contamination of origins.

37   PaPa LaBas, the sly, knowing old man in *Louisiana Red* and *Mumbo Jumbo* is, of course, a major deity in vodoun. In *Mumbo Jumbo*, LaBas invokes vodoun as both a refusal of the Atonists and an illuminating alternative to the monocultural purism of the *Mu'tafikah* and the Muslim editor, Abdul: LaBas speaks of "the ancient Vodun aesthetic: pantheistic, becoming, 1 which bountifully permits 1000s of spirits, as many as the imagination can hold."[39]

The vodoun aesthetics described by PaPa LaBas is centrally rele- 38
vant to the arguments that occur among *The Terrible Twos'* Nicolaites
over the true character and identity of St. Nicholas. On the one
hand, as I have said, the Nicolaites' quest for definitive origins, for
the *real* St. Nicholas, marks them as loyal to a univocality, a concept
of absolute and singular identity, that vodoun refuses. For this reason Reed links the Nicolaites to another African New World belief,
Rastafarianism, which fervently invests authority in a singular black
origin and destiny. When Black Peter proposes replacing St. Nicholas with Haile Selassie, the Nicolaites are "split down the middle"
over which deity to follow (44). Yet Brother Peter's argument for
Haile Selassie does partake of vodoun aesthetics in its oddball perception of cultural analogies; his logic is, finally, far more vodoun
than Rastafarian. Although Black Peter aims to replace Nicholas with
Selassie, the associationist logic of his argument is implicitly syncretic: it suggests a conflation of Nicholas and Selassie that is more
vodoun than Rastafarian. Black Peter states that Selassie and Nicholas are "one and the same" because they both ride on a white horse;
Nicholas punished a thief as Selassie punished "the teef Mussolini,"
Nicholas flew and so does Selassie (by airplane), and so on (46).
Like the African religions from which it derives, vodoun routinely
synthesizes deities of different tribes, including the Christian saints.
For example, vodoun believers argued that since St. James is surrounded by red flags and carries a sword, he is essentially similar to
the martial Yoruba deity Ogun, who is also clothed in red. But instead of being replaced by Ogun, St. James is conflated with him to
become the vodoun spirit "Ogu-feraille."[40] Reed's "neo-hoodoo-
ism" likewise blends Nicholas and Selassie in *The Terrible Twos* into
"Selassie-Nicholas," or, alternatively, "Nicholas-Selassie" (177), so
that the syncretism of Europe and Africa is in its technique a distinc-
tively African combination. In Reed's earlier novel, *Yellow Back Radio
Broke Down*, the Pope himself speaks of Europe's unsuccessful attempt to Christianize the African slaves in the New World, an attempt thwarted by the capacity for multicultural juxtaposition implicit in the "elastic" discourse of vodoun: "the natives merely placed
our art alongside theirs."[41]

The vodoun religion syncretizes not only West African spirits 39
with Christian saints, but also the generally "cool" or peaceful West
African religions with the fiercer beliefs of the Kongo. In fact, many

scholars identify two seemingly opposed, but actually ambiguously combined aspects of vodoun, Rada and Petro: often a vodoun deity will have both a Rada and a Petro (that is, a good and a cruel) side. Petro, the aggressive, malevolent aspect of vodoun, derives its name from the legendary magician figure Dom Pedro (or Pètre).[42] Dom Pedro, of course, is Reed's shady and mysterious Black Peter, present in some versions of the St. Nicholas legend as Nicholas' sidekick or opposite number, his "blackamoor servant." If Nicholas is benevolent and devoted to saving children, Black Peter, by contrast, is a kidnapper.[43] The religious scholar Charles Jones notes that the pairing of the kindly Nicholas and the cruel Peter derives from an earlier ambiguity in the character of Nicholas himself, who is seen as both gentle and violent, a bearer of both gifts and switches.[44] Gradually, as the Nicholas legend shifts to Northern Europe, Nicholas' evil traits are exorcised and projected onto the figure of a black servant. Similarly, European Christianity projects its sins onto the Africans that it enslaves; the sins return, in Reed's novel, *via* the image of Black Peter literally taking possession of Santa Claus, inflecting the ersatz, commercialized "innocence" of Christmas with the harsh truth of his satire. Reed thus restores the ethical ambiguity or doubleness of the original Nicholas, as well as the subversive power of this saint who openly criticized the Emperor Constantine,[45] by allowing Black Peter to speak through him. It is interesting in this connection that, as Herskovits notes, St. Nicholas is regarded in Haitian vodoun as protector of the *marassa*, the spirits of twins.[46]

40   The ambiguous combination of good and evil in Nicholas, so similar to the equivocal, mixed nature of vodoun gods like Ogoun and the *marassa*, is replicated in the character of childhood itself, at once innocent and terrible. (Thus the double-edged title, *The Terrible Twos*.) Reed describes the severe, perplexing nature of this dualism in a passage I shall cite at length:

> *Two-year-olds. In mankind's mirific misty past they were sacrificed to the winter gods. Maybe that's why some gods act so young. Ogun, so childish that he slays both the slavemaster and the slave.*
>
> *Two-year-olds are what the id would look like if the id could ride a tricycle. That's the innocent side of two, but the terrible side as well. A terrible world the world of two-year-olds. . . . Someone is constantly trying to eat them up. The gods of winter crave them –*

the gods of winter who, some say, are represented by the white horse that St. Nicholas, or Saint Nick, rides as he enters into Amsterdam, his blackamoor servant, Peter, following with his bag of switches and candy. Two-year-olds are constantly looking over their shoulders for the man in the shadows carrying the bag. Black Peter used to carry them across the border into Spain. (28)

Just as Ogoun is both a healer and a warrior – and as the champion of the Haitian Revolution, a slayer of both master and slave[47] – so Nicholas/Peter are both gift-givers and conniving thieves. By reinjecting paganism's vivid spiritual dualism into Christianity, Reed incarnates a world of shockingly energetic contrasts; a world that stands against the bland, homogenized commercialism of Big North's, and Macy's, corporate Santa. Part of this energy derives from the esoteric nature of Reed's vision here, his zest for an off-the-wall hermeneutics that is, finally, too peculiar to be popular in the sense of "popularity" that Macy's and Big North, and *Miracle on 34th St.*, seem to have coopted. For Reed, Macy's is mass culture as rootless, best-selling hype, despite its self-disguise as popular culture in *Miracle*. Reed presents, as a pointed contrast to the film's duplicitous claim to folk status, a popular tradition just as strange as it is true, one that resists, and revises, mass culture through both its strangeness and its truth. Reed's eccentricity finds its thematic roots in the popular culture of vodoun just as the bemused and outrageous improvisational comedy of his prose, the wry, crisply logical way with a joke that is so uniquely his, draws on the rhythms of African-American discourse. The result is a postmodernism in which Reed's style perfectly illustrates his syncretic and subversive argument. If Reed does not invoke his connections to tradition in the service of an easily communal utopian optimism, but instead remains skeptical about the possibility of a full-scale alternative to the Atonists,[48] he also insists on the historical presence of a secret, underground alternative to Wallflower culture, a revolt that is always occurring, in one scene or another.

N O T E S

1. Since the 1960s, the academy and the world of publishing have tended to favor those African-American writers who seem most overtly to invoke the communal inheritance of traditional African-American values. Writers like Andrea Lee who exhibit skepticism about the survival of tradition in a postmodern world are stigmatized by the critical establishment.

2. See, among many other sources, Hal Foster, ed., *The Anti-Aesthetic* (Port Townsend, WA: Bay Press, 1983); Seyla Benhabib, "A Reply to Jean-François Lyotard," in Linda Nicholson, ed., *Feminism/Postmodernism* (New York: Routledge, 1990); Jürgen Habermas, *The Philosophical Discourse of Modernity* (Cambridge, MA: MIT Press, 1990); Andreas Huyssen, *After the Great Divide* (Bloomington: Indiana UP, 1986); Fredric Jameson, *Postmodernism* (Durham, NC: Duke UP, 1991). Huyssen's delineation of the limitations in Habermas' championing of aesthetic modernity against postmodernity has influenced my own case for the critical capacity of postmodernism.

3. It is important to note, of course, that Habermas also emphasizes the gains in human freedom that have stemmed from the Weberian rationalization processes that enable the state to survive.

4. See Habermas' Adorno prize lecture, translated as "Modernity: An Incomplete Project," in Foster, ed., 3-15, and *The Philosophical Discourse of Modernity*.

5. As Paul Smith, Rainer Nagele, and others have pointed out: see Paul Smith, *Discerning the Subject* (Minneapolis, MN: U of Minnesota P, 1988), 163-64, and Rainer Nagele, "Freud, Habermas and the Dialectic of Enlightenment," *New German Critique* 22 (Winter 1981), 41-62.

6. *Mumbo Jumbo* (Garden City, NY: Doubleday, 1972), 211. Thus *Mumbo Jumbo*'s tongue-in-cheek genealogy of Jes Grew – whose contagious character means that it can never really be pinned down as lineage or inheritance – stretches from Isis and Osiris, to Dionysus, to Jethro, to vodoun.

7. On this point, see David Kaufmann, "The Profession of Theory," PMLA May 1990, 519-30.

8. On this issue of what DuBois called "double consciousness," see Robert Stepto's landmark *From Behind the Veil* (Champaign-Urbana, IL: U of Illinois P, 1979).

9. On this point I have benefitted from Lawrence Hogue's work in progress on African-American postmodernism, as well as a talk given by David Bradley at Trinity College (Hartford, CT), 1989.

10. Here as elsewhere in this essay, I am indebted to Hal Foster's analysis of the subcultural as a viable force in postmodernism: see "Readings in Cultural Resistance" in *Recodings* (Port Townsend, WA: Bay Press, 1985).

11. This is Charles Altieri's description of Paul Smith's position in Altieri's *Canons and Consequences* (Evanston, IL: Northwestern UP, 1990), 206. Altieri criticizes Smith for imagining a too easy transition from such practices of resistance to statements of political position, thus giving short shrift to those resistant modes, like Derrida's and the later Barthes', which do not add up to avowals of political responsibility. While agreeing fully with Altieri's brilliant and subtle critique of Smith, I also have major misgivings concerning Altieri's finding of deficiencies in Derrida's and Barthes's notions of responsiveness. For Altieri, the private, self-ironizing nature of Derrida's later style needs to be compensated for by a publicly responsible or official subject, who will stabilize (or perhaps repress?) what is risky about such intimate ironies (see *Canons*, 209; see also Altieri's essay on *Ecce Homo* in Daniel O'Hara, ed., *Why Nietzsche Now?* [Bloomington, IN: Indiana UP, 1985], 410-11). I think that the model of compensation/stabilization, along with the zero-sum picture of bargaining, negotiation and consensus that tends to accompany Altieri's official self, adds up to a dangerously limited way of conceiving the political. The invocation of the normative force of reasonable choice as a necessary supplement to aesthetics and private life is directly relevant to the antagonistic criticism of Reed. Instead of trying to make our private aesthetic obsessions publicly responsible by worrying that theorists like Nietzsche and Derrida, or writers like Reed, are not sufficiently interested in justifying liberal political judgment, I believe we ought to acknowledge – rather than look for ways of repressing – the gap between personal aesthetics and public responsibility, the unavoidable fact that defines (post)modern politics. Needless to say, my qualm here applies to Habermas, as well as Smith and Altieri.

12. Frank Lentricchia, *"Libra* as Postmodern Critique," *South Atlantic Quarterly*, 89 (1990), 431-53. (Essay originally published in *Raritan*, Spring 1989.) The passage cited is on 443.

13. Lionel Trilling, "Freud: Within and Beyond Culture," in *Beyond Culture* (New York: Viking, 1965). Freud, of course, was in fact Jewish, whereas the other "other cultures" cited in Trilling's great essay were located purely in Freud's imagination, not his biographical context. But, following a strategy which critical postmodernists might find appealing, Trilling tends to downplay this distinction: the adversarial use of the subculture/other culture takes precedence over the question of its literal historical presence.

14. I am indebted to Michael Jarrett for the analogy between Reed and sampling.

15. Lentricchia has noted the total absence of his own ethnicity from De-Lillo's work (in "The American Writer as Bad Citizen – Introducing Don DeLillo," SAQ 1990 [89, 2], 239-44); and Pynchon's prestigious New England ancestry is played as an elaborate self-exploding joke in *Gravity's Rainbow*. There is, of course, an analogy between Pynchon's "preterite" and Reed's "neohoodooism," but Reed claims a concrete cultural context (even if a slippery and self-displacing one) for his aesthetic slogan as Pynchon does not. It should be understood that I am not arguing that contemporary writers "ought" to use subcultural tradition in Reed's manner, nor that Reed is a better writer than Pynchon or DeLillo for their failure to do so.

16. See Henry Louis Gates, Jr., "The Blackness of Blackness: A Critique of the Sign and the Signifying Monkey," and James A. Snead, "Repetition as a Figure of Black Culture," in Gates, ed., *Black Literature and Literary Theory* (New York: Methuen, 1984).

17. The Talking Heads' *Speaking in Tongues* (New York: Sire, 1983), whose title humorously endows commodified pop with a quasi-religious aura borrowed from alien traditions, draws on Nigerian Juju music; their later record *Naked* (New York: Sire, 1988) is similarly indebted to Zairian soukous. For a very useful treatment of the analogy between modern art and "primitive" art as an attempt to construct "universalism," see James Clifford, "Histories of the Tribal and the Modern," in his *The Predicament of Culture* (Cambridge, MA: Harvard UP, 1988).

18. For a treatment of this issue of appropriation in the context of the Cuban Afro-Cubanismo movement, see Roberto González-Echevarría and Alejo Carpentier, *The Pilgrim at Home* (Ithaca, NY: Cornell UP, 1977).

19. Reed's status as an African-American writer who claims Africa-derived folk culture for his own just as Yeats claims Celtic folklore should prevent us from simply identifying his authorial ideology in respect to Africa with that of Picasso, Stravinsky et. al.; one might choose the claiming of African folk culture in Aimé Césaire, Jay Wright, Edward Brathwaite, Toni Morrison and Derek Walcott for an extremely various set of comparisons to Reed.

20. I am here arguing against the easy conflation of ethnicity, political opposition, and postmodernism in Linda Hutcheon, *A Poetics of Postmodernism* (New York: Routledge, 1988), 60-70. Hutcheon programmatically ignores the conflicts among modernist, postmodernist, and nostalgic or pre-modern desires in texts such as Morrison's *Tar Baby* in order to claim a (false) harmony between postmodernism and African-American self-assertion.

21. Lee Breuer's dreadful *Warrior Ant* comes to my mind here, but any reader will be able to supply his/her favorite examples.

22. Thomas Pynchon, *Gravity's Rainbow* (New York: Viking, 1973).

23. Maya Deren, *Divine Horsemen* (New Paltz, NY: Book Collectors Society, 1970 [1st ed. 1953]), 134.

24. James A. Snead, "Repetition as a Figure of Black Culture," in Henry Louis Gates, Jr., ed., *Black Literature and Literary Theory*, 72. See also 67: "In black culture, the thing (the ritual, the dance, the beat) is 'there for you to pick up when you come back to get it.' If there is a goal . . . it continually 'cuts' back to the start, in the musical meaning of 'cut' as an abrupt, seemingly unmotivated break. . . ." For a very helpful analysis of the technique of "cutting" in African music, see J.M. Chernoff, *African Rhythm and African Sensibility* (Chicago: U of Chicago P, 1979).

25. See Kimberly Benston, *Baraka: the Renegade and the Mask* (New Haven, CT: Yale UP, 1976).

26. See Henry Louis Gates, Jr., "The Signifying Monkey," in *Black Literature and Literary Theory*, 297.

27. Houston Baker, *Modernism and the Harlem Renaissance* (Chicago: U of Chicago P, 1987), 56; see 69.

28. See Cornel West, "Minority Discourse and the Pitfalls of Canon Formation," in *Yale Journal of Criticism* 1 (1987), 199. West's essay is a very important and persuasive statement, though I disagree locally with his view of Reed.

29. A comparison might also be drawn between Reed and Don DeLillo, whose recent *Libra* advances a conspiracy theory of the JFK assassination not unlike the conspiracies so doggedly pursued in Pynchon's and Reed's novels, though DeLillo's tone of dire, hard-boiled historicity differs from theirs. For remarks on Reed and Pynchon, see Reginald Martin, *Ishmael Reed and the New Black Aesthetic Critics* (New York: St. Martin's P, 1983), 2; see also 43.

30. This point is argued by Fredric Jameson in an interview in *Social Text* 17 (1987), 45, in which Jameson contrasts the passivity of the postmodern individual subject to the "collective subject" present in "third world literature." This "collective subject" is an interpretive construct similar to Baker's "common sense of the tribe," the communal emphasis of much African-American literature. See the related (and problematic) article by Jameson, "Third World Literature in the Era of Multinational Capitalism," in *Social Text* 15 (1986), and the response by Aijaz Ahmad, "Jameson's Rhetoric of Otherness," *Social Text* 17 (1987).

31. For two opposed points of view on this issue in Pynchon (whether his notion of the subversive is sinister and hopeless or liberating), see, respec-

tively, the essays by George Levine and Tony Tanner in Levine and David Leverenz, eds., *Mindful Pleasures* (Boston: Little, Brown, 1976).

32. *The Crying of Lot 49* (New York: Harper and Row, 1986), 170-71. (The passage is cited by Tony Tanner in Harold Bloom, ed., *Thomas Pynchon* [New York: Chelsea House, 1986], 188; see Tanner's commentary on 187.) The third alternative that Oedipa considers – that "a labyrinthine plot has been mounted against" her – exposes the negative potential of the secrecy whose positive side is the liberating "density of dream." Among the many remarkable features of this passage one might notice Pynchon's punning connection, in lamenting "exitlessness," between American failure and the sense of constriction, on the one hand, and American success and wide open spaces, on the other (cf. Latin *exitus* and Spanish *exito*) – a frontier ideology also dear to Reed (see, among other texts, his introduction to his anthology of California poetry, *Calafia* [Berkeley, CA: Y'Bird, 1979]). The dominant image conjured by Pynchon's "exitlessness" is that of a Southern California freeway like those driven so often by Oedipa, but without exits: the frontier as labyrinth or imprisoning web.

33. The possibility of subversively liberating moments does, as Levine insists, exist in Pynchon, but these are only moments, not full-scale traditions or communities. The radical or revolutionary movements in the book, even when grounded in community, are just as macabrely threatening as the establishment they combat (for example, the mass-suicidal Hereros of *Gravity's Rainbow* [315ff.]).

34. For a useful survey of Reed's adversarial relation to various "black aesthetic" critics, chiefly Addison Gayle, Houston Baker, and Amiri Baraka, see Martin's book. Reed asserts that he writes within an African-American aesthetic, but he identifies such an aesthetic with a stylistic and structural approach (similar to the concept of "cutting" described by Snead), rather than with revolutionary content, as does Baraka. See Martin, 2; see also Reed's important introductions to the anthologies *Yardbird Lives* (New York, 1978) and 19 *Necromancers from Now*, as well as his famous run-in with the socialist realist Bo Shmo in *Yellow Back Radio* (Garden City, NY: Doubleday, 1969), 34-35. A simplified critique of Reed's polemic in this passage is presented by Michael Fabre, "Postmodernist Rhetoric in Ishmael Reed's *Yellow Back Radio Broke Down*," in P. Bruck and W. Karrer, eds., *The Afro-American Novel Since 1960* (Amsterdam: Gruner, 1982), 177, who sees it as championing "art" against "commitment."

35. Page citations to *The Terrible Twos* are from the Atheneum edition (New York: Atheneum, 1982).

36. Despite the multiplicity of the cultures that the *Mu'tafikah* want to

liberate, their faith is in the singularity of each of these cultures, and in their own singularity as quarrelsome representatives of these cultures. A Mexican tells an Anglo revolutionary during a *Mu'tafikah* meeting that he suspects him because "you carry [Cortes and Pizarro] in your veins as I carry the blood of Moctezuma"; a Chinese attacks a black member by claiming that "you North American blacks were" – and are – "docile"--because "the strong [Africans] were left behind in South America" (*Mumbo Jumbo*, 86-87).

37. For recent remarks along these lines, see Valerie Smith, *Self-Discovery and Authority in Afro-American Narrative* (Cambridge, MA: Harvard UP, 1987), 102.

38. In his Preface to the 1975 anthology *Yardbird Lives* (ed. with Al Young; New York: Grove, 1978), Reed attacks the critics who "in 1970" (just before the publication of the volume edited by Addison Gayle, *The Black Aesthetic*) "were united in their attempt to circumscribe the subject and form of Afro-American writing." He goes on to announce that what he calls "the ethnic phase of American literature" is now over, "counterculture ethnic, black ethnic, red ethnic, feminist ethnic, academic ethnic, beat ethnic, New York School ethnic, and all of the other churches who believe their choir sings the best." Reed proclaims that "the multicultural renaissance is larger than the previous ones because, like some African and Asian religions, it can absorb them" (*Yardbird Lives*, 13-14).

39. *Mumbo Jumbo*, 35.

40. See R.F. Thompson, *Flash of the Spirit* (New York: Random House, 1983), 172-77, Deren, *Divine Horsemen*, and Melville J. Herskovits, *The New World Negro* (Bloomington, IN: Indiana UP, 1966), 324-25, which lists other vodoun syntheses of pagan and Christian.

41. *Yellow Back Radio*, 153.

42. See Thompson, 179ff. On the ethical ambiguity of vodoun deities and its relation to the twin modes Petro and Rada. On Dom Petro/Pètre, see Thompson, 179. It is interesting to note that the Bacchic or Satyrlike sexuality of Reed's Black Peter (revealed as a clever impostor in the sequel, *The Terrible Threes*, 40, 42) can be cross-referenced to the phallic energy frequently associated with the trickster figure in African legend via a pun concealed in his name (the "black snake" of blues tradition). On the "phallic trickster," see Houston Baker, *Blues, Ideology and Afro-American Literature* (Chicago: U of Chicago P, 1984), 183ff. Baker remarks that "the trickster is also a cultural gift-bearer" (like Peter/Nicholas!).

43. St. Nicholas was noted for rescuing children, usually in groups of three.

44. See Charles W. Jones, *St. Nicholas of Myra, Bari, and Manhattan* (Chicago: U of Chicago P, 1978), 43, 61, 307ff. See also 309: Nicholas "thinks in

dualities." (Reed evidently relied heavily on Jones' study in writing *The Terrible Twos*.) The duality persists, in diluted form, in the present-day Santa who may give lumps of coal as well as candy.

45. For Nicholas' defiance of the Emperor Constantine, see Jones, 34.

46. Herskovits, 324. On the marassa as representative of "man's twinned nature," see Deren, 38-41.

47. See Deren, 130-37.

48. Such skepticism is even more prominent in the sequel to *The Terrible Twos*, 1989's *The Terrible Threes*, which ends with the officially-sponsored kidnapping of the now-leftist Dean Clift.

post-soviet subjectivity

IN ARKADII DRAGOMOSHCHENKO AND ILYA KABAKOV

barrett watten

While it has often been said that since the purported
"fall of communism" the Soviet Union has become in
reality a collection of Third World countries with nu-
clear weapons and a subway system, this is an un-
truth. It is the "Second World" – and what is that?
(Watten, in Davidson, 23)

Subjectivity is not the basis for being a Russian per-
son. . . . "Protestants," said Arkadii, "go to church to
mail a letter to God, the church, it's like a post office.
The Orthodox church – the building is not symbolic
– it is considered to be the real body of God, and
Orthodox people too are God because they are to-
gether here, not alone, and speaking, by the way, has
nothing to do with it." (Hejinian, in ibid., 34-35)

●

1.The break-up of official culture in the Soviet Union, even the "offi-
cial/unofficial" dialectic that was a part of it, led to an intense,
utopian, and metaphysically speculative subjectivity in emerging art
and literature that I am going to call "post-Soviet" even if it had its
origins in earlier periods. Beginning in the 1960s with the optimistic
horizons prior to the invasion of Czechoslovakia in 1968, extending
through the Brezhnev "era of stagnation" of the 1970s with its increasingly articulated counterculture, through the opening to the
West and the influence of emigration in the 1980s, a series of these
developments anticipate their reception as "postmodern culture" in
the West. Identifying these "post-Soviet" developments with postmodernism would be to misunderstand them, however; as poet Dmi-
trii Prigov has said of the Moscow conceptual art of the 1970s, "When
[Western conceptualism] entered our part of the world, [it] discovered the total absence of any idea of the object and its inherent
qualities or of any hint whatsoever of fetishism" (12). The subsequent valorization of Andy Warhol by post-Soviet artists would have
yet-to-be-determined (though not unimaginable) consequences; so
the "Women Admirers of Jeff Koons Club" I encountered in Leningrad

in 1989 would be the sign of an emerging feminism as much as an acceptance of the Reagan-era consumerism of Koons's work. Even the culture of Russian modernism, refracted through Western connoisseurship, has been reinterpreted in the new post-Soviet context in a way discontinuous with its historical origins. In order to understand these developments as not simply a colonization of Western postmodernism (arriving fully formed with multinational capital and Xerox), it will be necessary to develop models for Second World discourses of subjectivity. A prospective conclusion is that contemporary post-Soviet culture, once it has expanded to integrate both unofficial and international influences, does not simply mean an uncritical embrace of Western postmodernism but reveals a post-Soviet subjectivity that is not simply reducible to the various national identities now contesting the ground of the former Soviet state. This subjectivity is not simply "decentered" in relation to the possibility of Western modernity's failed project, as if post-Soviet culture could understand such a failure to begin with. Rather, post-Soviet subjectivity involves a range of related responses to specific forms of identity that developed and devolved within the complex and shifting horizons of the Soviet Union in the period of its transition from a "stable," Second-World society to a social form that cannot now be predicted. I see aspects of this subjectivity in Moscow conceptual art, originating in the 1970s and producing internationally recognized figures such as Komar and Melamid, Erik Bulatov, and Ilya Kabakov; and in the 1980s "meta" literature from Moscow and Leningrad, now being translated in the West, exemplified by poets Arkadii Dragomoshchenko, Ivan Zhdanov, Alexei Parshchikov, Ilya Kutik, and Nadezhda Kondakova.

●

A METAPOETICS OF MEMORY

2. Arkadii Dragomoshchenko's poetry, it was said, "is unlike anything else being written in the Soviet Union today" (Molnar, 7), and direct observation bears this out. At the Leningrad "Summer School" of 1989 (a conference of American, French, and Soviet avant-garde writers sponsored by official cultural institutions as part

of a last-ditch effort to avert the political crisis of *perestroika*), Dragomoshchenko was unique in abandoning the often complex metrical
forms and performative theatricality of the dominant poetic tradition (both official and oppositional). That tradition's range of verse
practices, however inflected by skewed and difficult sound patterns
and semantics, may be said to look back to the precedent "classical
tradition . . . as in the Acmeism of Akhmatova or early Mandelstam,
[which] stood for heroically distanced emotion and a European
cultural intertext" but which often led to poetic norms reduced to
"ruthless metricality and relentless rhyming" (Molnar, 10). Dragomoshchenko read his poems as if they were written texts rather than
oral presentations of cultural memory embodied in the poet as much
as in the poet's rhymes – unlike Ivan Zhdanov, who declaimed the
highly wrought language of his richly textured and difficult lyrics as if
ab eterno, directly from memory, to great effect. One listener after-
ward complained to Dragomoshchenko, "What you are doing isn't
poetry" – because it lacked the generic markers by which poetry had
been set apart, in ways directly related to Osip Mandelstam's mem-
orization, interiorization, and embodiment of poetry as a standard of
truth set against ideological lies. While equally based in an internal-
ized self-consciousness, Dragomoshchenko's poetry tears a hole in
the lyrical fabric of tradition's modernist authority – not simply for
anti-authoritarian motives, whatever those might be in a culture
where oppositional poetics are as fully invested with authority as the
authority they contest, but to create a new poetics that challenges
conventional meaning and its entailments of common knowledge. It
would be hard to overestimate the radical effect of Dragomoshchenko's break with the overdeterminations of sound and sense that
provide the standards for Russian verse – and the resulting demand
it conveys for a redefinition of collective memory and objective truth.

3. A poetics of collective memory in opposition to official history
(often meeting at a middle ground in official/unofficial poets such as
Yevgenii Yevtushenko, Andrei Voznesensky, and Bella Akhmadulina)
has been one of the implicit goals of Russian modernism – the poet
(seen as survivor) becomes a living embodiment of cultural memory.
But in Dragomoshchenko's poem "Nasturtium as Reality," a poetics
of memory is fractured and refigured in its living embodiment by
means of a relentless epistemological critique toward a more complicated horizon. The poem begins by essaying "An attempt / to de-

scribe an isolated object / determined by the anticipation of the resulting whole – / by a glance over someone else's shoulder" (93). A verbal organization of diverging angles of approach specifies the dynamics of this "attempt," a series of spatial and temporal vectors predicated on a "missing X" that precedes the poem, presumably the nasturtium but also a grammatical "there exists." The poem's predicative address introduces the "nasturtium" itself in the second stanza as subsequent to the initial, abstract "attempt," both to be resolved as parallel and equivalent in the "resulting whole," now only anticipated, that will make either possible. Equally important, however, is the necessary opacity of the "glance over someone else's shoulder" in the approach to the nasturtium – that which interferes with vision equally motivates it. Transparency (clarity of address to the nasturium) and opacity (difficulty of the attempt) are mutually implicated, staged toward an eventual reconciliation that is prefigured by the language of the poem's initial complication of the visual. In language, the nasturtium is seen as if through a window that is both transparent and opaque, not to the nasturtium but to itself – the "window" an opaque analogy to transparent language through which a nasturtium normally would be described: "A nasturtium composed / of holes in the rain-spotted window – to itself / it's 'in front,' // to me, 'behind.'"

4. This "rain-spotted window" *is* the language of the poem, through whose constructed elisions occurs the possibility of description; on the surface of language, description is "in front," though from the point of view of subjectivity in the poem the nasturtium is "behind" language, anterior to it (from an easier perspective, of course, "in front" and "behind" mean the nasturtium's relation to the window). Where a window, like description, is conventionally transparent, here it is a shattered opacity of perspectives, interfering with and determining the gaze much like "someone else," leading to grounds of certainty and belief posed grammatically as a question: "Whose property is the gleaming / tremor / of compressed disclosure / in the opening of double-edged prepositions / in / a folded plane / of transparency which strikes the window pane?" Anything but transparently, we begin to see the nasturtium as if in double-edged language that predicts a "resulting whole" of description subsequent to "an isolated object." Because it is anterior to language and realized in language's unfolding, the prospective nastur-

tium aligns closely with memory – it becomes the unstable site of a memory configured in relation to a nature subject to an "attempt" as much as to any certainty. In the ensuing working through of the poem, description is displaced and refigured in and as memory; the poem demands a mutual construction of memory and knowledge sited between a past it embodies and a future it will reveal. Futurity will have accounted for the nasturtium that preceded the poem, making possible the "compressed disclosure" of an intensely subjective continuity

5. In stages of approach, the poem sharpens the edges of prospective meaning figured in the nasturtium, often defining the space where the nasturtium would exist by negation, in the central figure's absence from other spaces of description and memory: "A sign, inverted – not mirror, not childhood. // (A version: this night shattered apart / by the rays of the dragonflies' concise deep blue / drawing noon into a knot of blinding / foam" (94). Here, an eruption of what V. N. Voloshinov would have called ideological speech (as elsewhere in "A sign sweats over the doorway: 'Voltaire has been killed. Call me immediately'") shifts the poem away from its object. Similarly, the poem shifts "thematic" address to noncontiguous objects of a fractured nature such as the dragonfly (later a specific tree, a flight of "swifts"). These devices, however, cannot detract from the poem's expanding subjective truth: "the knowledge, which belongs to me, / absorbs it cautiously, tying it / to innumerable capillary nets: / the nasturtium – it is a section of the neuron / string" (96). This knowledge is presented not as a report to some transcendent observer – a comparison with Marianne Moore's aesthetics of natural grandeur in "An Octopus" would fail at this point – but through the materiality of language produced from a variety of sites. It is to the point of Dragomoshchenko's poetics of description that such shifts away from the ostensible subject of the poem are "only a continuation / within the ends' proximity" (97); the poem is free to expand, to include fragments of dialogue, self-reference ("Arkadii / Trofimovitch Dragomoshchenko describes / a nasturtium, inserts it in his head"; (99), along with its recording of spatial and temporal discontinuities. A developing axis of meta-commentary, based on a series of spatial predicates, is created by means of such semantic shifts: "The nasturtium / and anticipation rainy as the window and wind- / ow behind wind-/ ow / (he in it, it in him) / like meanings smashing each other /

[I don't say, metaphor . . .] / drawn / by emptiness / one of the distinct details – "; 100). In the extent of this effect, through the poem's insistent reduction of similarity to contiguity – description turning to language – poetry becomes virtually a kind of physics, itself a part of the natural world it describes ("The mechanism / of the keys, extracting sound, hovering over / its description // in the ear, // protracted with reverberation into the now").

6. This alignment of poetry with nature paradoxically depends, for its assertion of palpable reality, on a continual undermining of language by itself ("When? Where? / Me? Vertigo conceives / 'things'"; 101), but at issue is not simply a decentering of poetic voice. In the poem's vertiginously expanding horizon of meaning, sense is made "only / through another / multiplication tables, game boards, needles, a logarithmic / bird," i.e., anything presentable in language, "and the point isn't which kind" (103). The poem oscillates between intensely subjective moments and objective properties of description, attempting both in either's negation: "I contemplated the truth behind events listening to the vividness / of the erased words / ready to expound on the defects of precision," in a counterpoint to the poet's self-canceling voice: "And here in the 41st year of life / A pampered fool, whose speech continually / misses the point" (106). Subjectivity in "The Nasturtium" proceeds through such locative intensities of language: "I follow from burst to burst, from explosion to explosion, / faces, like magnesium petals floating by, which permit those who remain a misprint in memory / to be recognized" (108), but it offers no assumptions about the continuity of nature behind the poem as the basis for these effects. Nature cannot be assumed as a stable, encompassing reality which the poet's memorial condensations have arisen from and into which they devolve. Rather, the poem moves directly from negated description of objective reality to expanded systems of meaning encompassing it: "Conjecture is simple – / the nasturtium is not // necessary. It is composed from the exceptional exactness / of language / commanding the thing – 'to be' / and the rejection of understanding" (110-11). The poem locates the objective world by placing the language of description under erasure, opening itself to many languages and so determining what its relation to nature is going to be: "The nasturtium – it is the undiminished procession / of forms, the geological chorus of voices crawling, / shouting, disclosing each other" (112).

7. It is through this clash of languages tending toward future objectivity that a space for refigured subjectivity, seen in purely material strands of memory, can be located in the poem. In that futurity is connected here to a poetics of "many languages," it is important that Dragomoshchenko is by birth Ukrainian (born in postwar occupied Potsdam, raised in multilingual environs of Vilnitsa, now living in St. Petersburg), although he writes in Russian. He has, in other poems, shifted to Ukrainian as poetic counterpoint specifically to bring up a kind of archaic subtext under the surface of ordinary language, further allying epistemological concerns with those of cultural memory. In "The Nasturtium," such archaic subtexts are figured in two autobiographical, memorial narratives that emerge out of its nonnarrative continuum. In one such vignette, a typically cine-matic moment of self-knowledge, "tossing her skirt on the broken bureau / with wood dust in her hair / a neighbor girl, spreading her legs / puts your hand where it is hottest" (103) – which reveals, not quite as typically, an authorial solipsism in anxious spasms of linguis-tic cross-cutting. It is as if the eruption of the feminine demands a release of poetic authority; the poem is unable to maintain its ad-dress to the nasturtium's futurity at the moment the "meaning of her" intrudes. There is a disjunction here between prospective nature as ground for memorial condensation and the emergence of the femi-nine, as occurs likewise in the next section in a more measured way where an account of the death of a woman close to the poet, again in and of language, undermines the progressively unfolding horizons of the poem: "and all the more unbearable the meaning of 'her' ripened in you / while the quiet work went on revealing / thoughts / (you, her) from the sheath of feminine pain / the silent symmetry crumbling in the immense proximity of the end" (105). There is a difficult cultural fact to this admission of women only at the extremes of authorizing self-knowledge, but it is also here that the poetic convention of a stable, feminized, assumed nature (from waving fields of grain as meaning "poetry" in a Sovkino documentary of Yevtushenko to the Stalinist cathexis of "Mother Russia") as the basis of memorial effects is starting to be broken down in its assumptions.

8. This location of a poetics in a refiguring of memory through the limits of objectivity aligns Dragomoshchenko's work with related projects in post-1960s Soviet culture. So the films of Andrei Tar-kovsky, a prior reference point for the semantically shifting world of

Dragomoshchenko's writing, crop up in his recent article on poetic subjectivity. Making a figure for collective knowledge, Dragomoshchenko says that the poet may return, like a blind bee, to a "hive" of understanding, "but there is no hive. It disappears at the very moment when understanding comes close to being embodied in itself and its `things,' which to all appearances is really the 'hive.' We wander through a civilization of destroyed metaphors: road, home, language, a man on a bicycle, embraces, Tarkovsky's films, moisture, 'I,' memories, history, and so forth" ("I(s)," 130). For Dragomoshchenko, "the problem of subjectivization is tautological," fractally reproduced in the dispersion and refiguring of a collective center, "the hive," in culture's unreified objects. Wandering through this "civilization of destroyed metaphors," one can only figure the holistic tenor from its dispersed vehicles. Such a demetaphorization occurs similarly in a film such as Tarkovsky's *The Mirror* (by means of techniques intended as the opposite of Eisenstein's constructed film metaphors). Nonnarrative, intuitive sequences displace memory, continuity, futurity onto a fragmented world of objects comprising several registers of image. In one, the burning house in the countryside to which mother and son have been removed during the war stands as mnemonic placeholder for the future return of the father that is always to come (there is a question for the viewer if it "really" takes place). In another, the multiple, sidelong, disjunct views down corridors of the state publishing house where the mother worked in the 1930s as proofreader enacts the moment where the collective "hive" dissolves into "things"; millennial horizons become fragments of presence, as in the hinted propaganda poster barely glimpsed on the way to other rooms. Finally, the insertion of documentary footage of the Spanish Civil War asserts the film's overarching formal subjectivity against the intrusion of represented history, which can only take on memorial value as loss. Images in Dragomoshchenko have similar organizing dynamics; so "the nasturtium bearing fire" which closes Dragomoshchenko's poem is substituted in place of memory's anticipated return; the overlapping and mutually contradictory frames of descriptive language dissolve certainty into isolated moments addressed to futurity; and the interruptions of narrative displace subjectivity toward expanded horizons. Closure – the father's return or the nasturtium as realized object – is distributed through these registers as partial, prefigured resolution.

9. The relation between empirical reality and a deferred future that exceeds nature but in terms of which nature can only be known (figured here in the form of the poem) is also a central theme in recent discussions in Soviet (and post-Soviet) science. The opening invocation of our "Summer School" was to "be scientific," but what followed led rapidly away from any question of empirical verification toward a prospective, metaphysical hyperspace in which, for example, "futurist art [like that of Khlebnikov's post-Euclidean mathematics of world correspondence] has its own dominant in consciousness" (Watten, in Davidson, 43). So a recent article by Moscow philologist Mikhail Dziubenko describes a scientific project that would unite the problem of "new meaning" in poetry and art with an alternative branch of Soviet science known as the "Linguistics of Altered States of Consciousness" – a quest for a new approach to method characteristic of a wide range of Soviet science. For Dziubenko, "At deep levels of consciousness (which acquire primary meaning in the creative process) the ability to penetrate into the logic of other languages is established. Artistic creativity, then, involves a breakthrough into another language, which uses the characteristics and lacunae of the original" (27). Such a language, in addition, is based in material reality, but only for its future potential:

> We must understand that there is only one linguistic universum; uniting all world languages in the massive entity of their historical development and functional applications. This universum is not a scientific abstraction. It is manifested concretely, on the lowest, phonetic level, in naming, where moreover language differentiations do not play any definitive role, and on the highest, grammatical-syntactic level, in art, which is only possible by virtue of the existence of different languages and which is itself an unconscious borrowing of foreign language structures. (29-30)

For Dziubenko, "the knowledge of one language is knowledge of all languages," leading to a research program in which "there is no doubt that a Persian specialist could contribute a great deal to the study of Khlebnikov's works" (30-31). Creativity expands language into a utopian "linguistic universum" in a romantic philology that recalls Wilhelm von Humboldt's fantasy of whole nations thinking in each of their various languages. There are several points to this excursus into late-Soviet discussions of scientific method: the first is that creativity is thought to have ontological implications; the second is that as material reality, creative language extends, "through characteristics and lacunae," into a greater reality that contains it; and a third would be that, structuring language in the variety of its altered states as well as being structured by it, subjectivity is not permitted the transcendent distance of the observer but instead experiences loss due to an expanded suprasubjectivity whenever the grounds for language (altered states, presumably) historically change. So the importance of creativity for method is to open a space of loss of certainty in a romantic science that produces not stability of knowledge but expanded horizons of meaning elaborated against an unstable ground. Clearly this view of science has analogies with the form of Dragomoshchenko's poem, which interprets the relation between creativity and nature discussed by Dziubenko in a kind of vertiginous, open-ended hysteria. The poetics of embodied cultural memory with which we began – the "social command" of several generations of Soviet and post-Soviet poets – thus devolves in fragmentary, recombinant, and prospective form, given the lack of any stability of the objective world. Such an initial premise of anxiety and loss can only be resolved by a reconfigured memory realized in the impossible futurity of the poem, as with the final self-immolation of Dragomoshchenko's nasturtium. In this sense, "Nasturtium as Reality" is not only a demonstration of post-Soviet subjectivity but a parallel text to post-Soviet refigurings of collective memory and empirical truth. An "authoritarian complex" involving several strands in Soviet culture – lyric voice, embodied memory, and scientific objectivity – is being reconstructed as the occasion of poetic address.

●

THE FALL OF SOVIET MAN

10. The theatricality of Ilya Kabakov's conceptual albums, paintings, and installations is at a polar remove from Dragomoshchenko's prospective interiority. *Ten Characters*, a series of installations with accompanying narratives published as a book of the same name based

on the theme of the *kommunalka* or communal apartment, was presented by Kabakov at the Ronald Feldman Gallery in New York and the Institute for Contemporary Art, London, in 1988–89. These projects had been under development since at least the early 1980s, but one imagines their everyday materials to have been collected, and various components worked on, over the preceding decade. Installation itself, understood as one of the forms by which traditional genres such as painting and sculpture have become destabilized and augmented in postmodernism, takes on a culturally hybrid value in Kabakov's work as most of what was seen in the active Soviet underground of the 1970s was itself "installed" in some nongallery setting such as an apartment or open-air happening; the bulldozer art exhibition of the late Brezhnev era in this sense could be the outer social horizon for the form. The genre continued in Moscow conceptual art in what has been called "Aptart," which was characterized as uniting a social scale of presentation based in everyday life with a diverse and often aggressively dissonant range of issues, materials, and strategies. This work seems more a cultural breeding ground for new ideas than a finished product, while Kabakov's installations have all the finish and framing of the most professional work in the genre as it has developed as a component of museum programs over the last fifteen years in the West – witness his inclusion in the recent *Dislocations* show at the Museum of Modern Art. It would be interesting to chart Kabakov's movement from Soviet oppositional scale to that of Western postmodernism; this could be read thematically in his work as a movement from the simultaneously millennial and dystopian horizons of the Soviet context through to another kind of transcendence implied in Kabakov's showing, outside the Soviet Union, works that depict aspects of its deepest, most interior reality.

11. Subjectivity in Kabakov, rather than being read along some razor's edge of language in nonnarrative forms addressed to metaphysical horizons, is narratively defined in the life histories of disjunct, created personae configured around the communal apartment seen from a transcendent perspective (even if it is still linked to an immanent metaphysics as enabling point of reference for the work). Transcendence is really the only option for a social reality modeled on such living arrangements, which, from the Revolution through the Khrushchev housing boom and into the present, typically crammed

the urban working class into multi-family dwellings, often one family per room, where everyone shared the collective amenities and, according to Kabakov, life was open-ended verbal abuse. Given this premise, Kabakov has created a world of discontinuous, extreme personality types to be imagined as somehow, impossibly, sharing the same communal space while inventing wildly adventurous behaviors and systems of belief to accommodate them themselves to their world. The short narrative accounts that accompany Kabakov's meticulously detailed physical installations (generally typed and mounted on walls near them) are anything but anecdotal; rather, these narratives form a template through which the realities of Soviet systems of belief can be represented as they would be experienced in everyday life. ("Everyday life" translates as *byt* in the Soviet lexicon; it is a central term in Kabakov's work, and one that evinces from many post-Soviets an unutterable horror: "Our everyday life, you cannot imagine how boring it is!" remarked poet Alexei Parshchikov.) There is a system of interlocking, mutually supporting belief systems in Kabakov's *byt*, a structuring intersubjectivity that gives an accurate value to the represented world of May Day parades, the Moscow Metro, Soviet theme parks outside. "The *kommunalka* presents a certain collective image, in which all the ill-assortedness and multi-leveledness of our reality is concentrated and vividly revealed" for Kabakov (Tupitsyn, 50), a reality figured as an "autonomous linguistic organism," "an extended childhood," "a repressive sea of words," "the madhouse," and so on (51–54). Alternatives emerge: one can go into oneself ("Some of the inhabitants of the communal apartment lead a mysterious, even secretive existence"; Kabakov, 52) or "leap out of oneself," as Kabakov himself says he did ("While formally I haven't ceased to live inside myself, I observe what happens from repeatedly shifting positions"; Tupitsyn, 55). Beyond either possibility, "some powerful, lofty, and faraway sound is clearly audible. A higher voice" (54) for both artist and communal residents. Listening to the voice of the "beyond" will be one of the organizing metaphors of Kabakov's project – it is simultaneously the voice of collective life and the position of transcendence from which the *kommunalka*'s voices are heard. Kabakov's work raises the question of the interlocutor Slavoj Žižek calls "the Big Other" – whose absense Kabakov presents in terms of high-pitched frequencies of hysteria, deformed features of ideological projection, and blank voids of nihilism. All are operative in the emergence of post-Soviet horizons prefigured by Kabakov in the social space of the *kommunalka*.

12. So in "The Man Who Flew into His Picture," subjectivity is drawn as if by a magnet to a negating white space, a ground for pure projection: "He sees before him an enormous, endless ocean of light, and at that moment he merges with the little, plain figure that he had drawn." At this moment of self-undoing, however, "he comes to the conclusion that he needs some third person, some sort of witness [to be] present to watch him 'from the side'" (7). Such a witness is given embodiment as merely the case of delusions in the next room, where "The Man Who Collects the Opinions of Others," "standing behind the door, immediately writes down in his notebook everything which is said, no matter what" (9). This witness's quest for objectivity yields only another structured fantasy:

> According to his view, opinions are arranged in cir-
> cles. Beginning at any point, they then move centrifu-
> gally and as they move away from the centre they
> meet "opinions" moving from other centres. These
> waves are superimposed, one on top of another; ac-
> cording to him, the entire intellectual world is a gi-
> gantic network, a lattice of similar dynamic intersec-
> tions of these waves. He compared all this to the
> surface of a lake, where 10–20 stones are randomly
> and uninterruptedly thrown all at once. (9)

"In talking about this, it was as though my neighbour actually saw these magical, shining circles" (10); Kabakov visualizes them likewise in his installation of tidy mock-ups of the character's notebook pages arranged around the "objects" that gave rise to the "opinion waves." While this is clearly high satire of venerable Russian literary pedigree, there is an identification with these delusional modes of organizing reality that makes Kabakov's procedure unlike the realist mode of describing the subject positions of, say, the flophouse in Gorky's *The Lower Depths* (which Kabakov cites in an interview). Being an artist for Kabakov means to act in as delusional and obsessive manner as his "characters"; so the meticulous details of Kabakov's miniature mock-up and full-scale realization of the scene from "The Man Who Flew into Space from His Apartment" reveal a complicity with the urban space traveler's monumental obsessiveness, as do other characters' collections of objects and albums of kitsch post-cards. It is Kabakov himself who assembled these Soviet versions of Trivial Pursuit, reframing his activities through the various personae. In each of these works, the space of culture and everyday life is seen as the opposite of the transcendental perspective and monumental organization of Soviet society's official self-presentation (given in the dominant red of numerous cheap posters covering the walls). The corresponding explosion that rips a hole in the top floor of the communal apartment, sending its resident into orbit, creates a negative space out of the horizon of Soviet monumentalism, where the orbits of Yuri Gagarin and followers ironically mimed here stand for state-sponsored transcendence purveyed to the masses at large. The desire to substitute material reality for ideological abstraction created this negative space: "I asked him why there were metal bands attached to the model and leading upward from his future flight" (13). Such kitsch futurism – the mechanical predictability of "We are Going to Communism" – seems to have created, in this character, a highly developed metaphysics to explain how it will be:

> He imagined the entire Universe to be permeated by huge sheets of energy which "lead upwards somewhere." These gigantic upward streams he called "petals.". . . The Earth together with the sun periodically crosses through one of these enormous "petals." If you knew this precise moment, then you could jump from the orbit of the Earth onto this "petal," i.e., you could enter, join this powerful stream and be whirled upwards with it.

Fabricating a contraption made of rubber "extension wires" and explosive charges, the resident realizes his objective and blasts into orbit, thus creating a monumental gap in the explanatory fabric of everyday life which others rationalize in a characteristic way: "Maybe he really did fly away, that sort of thing happens." In the ideological space vacated by monumental trajectories and transcendent goals one can see a cultural breeding ground for rumors, speculations, and theologies of all sorts – a space to be filled with all manner of cultural detritus.

13. Such systems of belief, orbiting as it were around a vacant belief, are made equivalent, in yet another irony, to the material culture that was supposed to provide them with normative expecta-

tions. So a metaphorized collecting, a simple accumulation of bits and pieces of culture, becomes the activity of the artist; material reality replaces a more conventionally redemptive collective memory. In works like "The Short Man," "The Collector," "The Person Who Describes His Life Through Characters," and "The Man Who Never Threw Anything Away," Kabakov makes his art an inductive process whose compilation of oddments adds up to indeterminate, compensatory, but fascinating horizons that motivate his fractal characters. The "short man's" project of accumulation and re-presenting cultural detritus in fold-out albums is a parodic version of realism seen as representing the world "in little": "Everything that goes on in our communal kitchen, why, isn't that a subject, it's actually a ready-made novel!" (20); however, the only people who can stoop so low as even to read this little world are, like its author, little – others invited in to view the work merely step over it as an obstacle. (As the poet Louis Zukofsky wrote, "Strabismus may be of interest to strabismics; those who see straight look away!") The substratum of material culture, reinterpreted as past not present reality, initiates a process of individuation and recuperation in "The Man Who Never Threw Anything Away": "A simple feeling speaks about the value, the importance of everything. This feeling is familiar to everyone who has looked through or rearranged his accumulated papers: this is the memory associated with all the events connected with each of these papers" (44). So this character initiates a project of collecting, preserving, and labeling all the discarded items found in the *kommunalka*'s hallway in order to recover their memorial value: "An enormous past rises up behind these crates, vials, and sacks. . . . They cry out about a past life, they preserve it" (45). This collecting of material fragments here reverses the cultural demand for a stabilizing poetics of memory, invalidating sentimental retrospection at the outset and leaving subjects no option but to face the compelling voids of futurity without recourse to affective substitution.

14. "The Person Who Describes His Life Through Characters" continues this process of induction to uncover a principle of individuation through his collected, collective subjects: "that even these variegated fragments belonged not to his single consciousness, his memory alone, but, as it were, to the most diverse and even separate minds, not connected with each other, rather strongly different from each other" (34) – a speculation on the accumulated debris of

culture that produces what amounts to the delusional notion that there are, in fact, other people. "The Untalented Artist" modulates this effect of individuation through structures of the state that produced it; the paradoxical success of his paintings (in the actual installation an excessively beautiful group of large-scale, ideologically inflected works by Kabakov) is described as based equally in the artist's partly realized native talent and in the lacunae of official projects (various official notices and posters) he was commissioned to paint: "What results is a dreadful mixture of hackwork, simple lack of skill, and bright flashes here and there of artistic premonitions and 'illuminations'" (17) – a kind of suprasubjective intention realized in place of the unique signature of individual personality, yielding a socially paradoxical figure for the artist. In "The Collector" a similar suprasubjective horizon looms as the dissociation of identity by means of collective culture proceeds; arrangements of numerous color postcards on state tourist and memorial themes become "enormous, complex pictorial works which are worthy of a very great professional talent" (31), beyond that of the individual artist. Recombining disparate strands of the culture produces an effect of "the power of ORDER"; "This is the triumph of the victory of order over everything." There is a paradox here, however; while it is the artist who in fact created this order by making his arrangements of cultural materials, the voice of order points beyond individuality: "It seemed to me that in some terrible way, some kind of, how shall I say it, idea of COMMUNALITY, was expressed in [the arrangements], that very same thing which surrounded us all in our common overcrowded apartment" (32). This drawing out of the collective voice is pursued in "The Composer Who Combined Music with Things and Images," whose staged mass productions in the *kommunalka* hallway, like a miniature version of a Stalinist sports extravaganza, trades the sovereignty of the artist who arranges reality for a collective voice heard by all: "Gradually those who are reading the [arranged] texts begin to notice that beyond the sound of their voices is a faintly heard, special kind of sound" (27) – a transcendent moment reproducing a metaphysics of communality.

15. So we have come full circle, from an obsessively material collocation and implicit satire on Soviet collective life to the question of higher, transcendent, metaphysical perspectives. In "The Rope," a piece that serves as a comment on his "characters," Kabakov essays

the point at which materialism breaks off and spirituality begins: "So these empty ends of rope . . . represent the soul before and after 'our' life, and in the middle is depicted its life, so to speak, in its earthly segment" (48). Working out from these middles toward the open ends of the soul, Kabakov recuperates the multiple identities of his communal apartment in terms of a single, collective destiny – albeit otherworldly. His *kommunalka* project could not be less like George Perec's description of multiple lives in the same building in *La Vie mode d'emploi*, where each life means a separate history, a different outcome rendered in the reified space of owned or rented individual dwellings. Kabakov, in his ironic rejection of Soviet culture, still maintains a totalizing attitude toward history – at the risk of a virtual nihilism in regard to the things of this world, an attitude necessary, it would seem, to maintain the coherence of totality even it turns out to be entirely negative. In a short text on the status of the "beyond" in relation to material reality, Kabakov speaks of "emptiness" as a condition of his work: "First and foremost I would like to speak about a peculiar mold, a psychological condition of those people born and residing in emptiness. . . . Emptiness creates a peculiar atmosphere of stress, excitedness, strengthlessness, apathy, and causeless terror" (Ross, 55). In the negated space once occupied by a transcendent, materialized state, there is now the inescapable horizon of a totalizing "stateness":

> The stateness in the topography of this place is that which belongs to an unseen impersonality, the element of space, in short all that serves as an embodiment of emptiness. . . . A metaphor comes closest of all to a definition of that stateness: the image of a wind blowing interminably alongside and between houses, blowing through everything by itself, an icy wind sowing cold and destruction. . . . What sort of goals does this wind, this stateness, set for itself, if they exist at all? These goals always bear in mind the mastery of the scope of all territory occupied by emptiness as a SINGLE WHOLE. (58)

From this single whole of Soviet reality it is but one step to a profound nihilism (and one that is more socially significant than simply the attitude of an artist): "Nothing results from anything, nothing is connected to anything, nothing means anything, everything hangs and vanishes in emptiness, is born off by the icy wind of emptiness" (59). These collective emptinesses interpret the nonexistent fullnesses, the pasts and futures at both ends of Kabakov's individual, material rope. Ernst Bloch's millennial horizons of "hope," having devolved through the course of their progressive unfolding in the history of the Soviet state, here reach their antithesis in nihilism. (With evidence of similar phenomena in the West over the last two decades, this is not simply a post-Soviet phenomenon; what seems specifically post-Soviet is Kabakov's fear of the lack of any mediation for these compelling voids. What would constitute such social mediation for post-Soviet nihilism – mafia-based accumulation of property, soccer clubs, the Sotheby's auction would be prime candidates – remains to be seen.)

16. Values for transcendence in the project would thus seem to refer importantly to two diverse registers: the this-worldly perspective of the artist-as-character who organizes reality in some compensatory way, and the other-worldly vision of the collective/individual subject, who would seem to have no other option than to await the dystopian millennium. Kabakov, in his position outside beyond Soviet reality in commenting on his installation for the Museum of Modern Art, explicitly resolves these two versions of transcendence:

> The installation as a genre is probably a way to give new correlations between old and familiar things. By entering an installation, these various phenomena reveal their dependence, their "separateness," but they may reveal as well their profound connection with each other, which was perhaps lost long ago, which they at some time had, and which they always needed. And particularly important is the restoration of that whole that had fallen into its parts [the separation of art from the "mystical"] I had spoken of.

The "mystical" union of restored parts within a formal whole would be one that Kabakov had induced from the ideological horizons of his characters but which, as artist working as it were "outside" the *kommunalka*, he can realize in his chosen form. There is an explicit self-contradiction here; so when Kabakov says in an interview, "Upon discharge from the madhouse, I cease to exist. I exist only insofar as I am the resident of a *kommunalka*. I know no other self" (Tupitsky, 54), it is clear that his "outside" position as installation artist in the Museum of Modern Art, Kabakov's position as quasi-Soviet emigré (he maintains studios in France and in Moscow) can only be another version of the transcendence strategized from within the confines of collective life. Re-sited within the museum's horizon, however, this insistence on wholeness becomes reinterpreted as tragic separation and loss, as the Fall of Communism that so comforts the curatorial perspective of *Dislocations*:

> *Kabakov's reconstruction of the Tenants' Club of Moscow Housing Project No. 8 gives one a sense of the dreary mediocrity of Soviet society. . . . This unwelcome gathering place has been set up for an official lecture on the demerits of unofficial art, examples of which are propped against the drab gray walls between oxblood banners. Although the work of artists outside the system, the paintings nonetheless exemplify some of the bleakness and awkwardness of mainstream Soviet life to which they are the oppositional exception.* (Storr, 16–17)

Nothing in Kabakov's work could be construed as endorsing such a view of "opposition"; indeed, its explicit purpose is to induce a metaphysical wholeness that reinterprets "the unity of opposites we learned about in school." How then to understand the central conceit of Kabakov's MOMA installation, that "apparently, someone or something was to appear in the city that evening, and not just anywhere, but right in the middle of the club hall"? The appearance and disappearance of this person occurs: "There is no single description of what happened – the reports of various witnesses maintain the most adamant discrepancies"; but this leads to a negative vision of sorts: "After all the commotion had subsided, the entire floor in the center of the hall was littered with groups of little white people, constantly exchanging places." It is almost too easy to view this moment as an allegory for the collapse of central authority leading to a negative social space in which the masses circulate aimlessly, without direction. The too-availability of this reading does seem to indicate an influence of the Museum's interpretative horizons, trading on Soviet history in a representative installation of Kabakov's totalizing process. This is the crisis of emigration, of the literal materialization of the transcendent position outside a totality it organizes, and here it leads Kabakov's partial, metaphysically sited narratives to a grand narrative of somewhat lesser interest. However, it may be said here, as elsewhere, that nothing is lost even in translation, for the likewise evident effect of Kabakov's piece is to make each of the other installations in this mainstream extravaganza – by Adrian Piper, Chris Burden, David Hammons, Louise Bourgeois, Bruce Nauman, and Sophe Calle, indeed the entire permanent collection of MOMA used by Calle as the site for her work – interpretable as the compensatory projects of other residents of an expanded communal apartment on 53rd Street in New York called "The Museum of Modern Art." This sovietization of cultural horizons – an opening up from the oppositional politics of the Cold War to the reality of collective horizons – is a hopeful reason to reject Kabakov's integration into the MOMA show as an imperial trophy collected under the banner of Western postmodernism.

●

WHICH SUBJECT?

17. Two aspects of post-Soviet subjectivity are evident in the examples of Dragomoshchenko and Kabakov. In the former, authority is impossibly sited from immanent horizons that entail elements of lyric subjectivity, collective memory, and scientific objectivity. The entire activity of Dragomoshchenko's poem – its creation of new meaning in and of itself – is central to its implicit thesis that subjectivity, while everywhere in its own undoing, is produced in a movement toward the impossible horizons of a transcendental position. The formal dimensions of Dragomoshchenko's work – nonnarrative, fractal, predicative, and continually metaleptic – are an instance of a "world-making" poetics that organizes a continuity of fabricated worlds only as they will be superseded. Central to these constructions is their conveyance of futurity; the lyric voice will have been the authority of present address from a point in the distant future; both collective memory and objective truth will have been revealed in

similar ways. Simultaneously, it is exactly the authority invested in the creation of new meaning that cancels out the empirical ground against which stable condensations (of memory and culture) may occur. While Dragomoshchenko's work seems to argue for a stability of archaic subtexts (of the precedent collective body of the Orthodox church; of linguistic substrata such as Ukrainian; of individual memory), it is through a present skepticism, figured exactly in the problem of "description," that it argues the unstable positions of post-Soviet subjectivity. In order to understand the larger implications for post-Soviet culture, it will be necessary to develop an account of subjectivity in relation to the epistemological uncertainty and cultural loss of Dragomoshchenko's lyricism. Georg Lukács remarks that Stalin's greatest intellectual crime was to think of "social engineering" as "scientific"; the qualification of scientific knowledge by creative method in Dragomoshchenko clearly wants to undermine the authority of any such thing as a "scientific socialism" in canceling the ground of "nature" for prospective identity.

18. In Kabakov's constructions, a converse implication for the subject may be descried, one that is more amenable to the international horizons of postmodern culture simply because it dismantles transcendence in the process of post-Soviet emigration. These displacements of subjectivity and authority are literally enacted in Kabakov's shows in the high-rent collective apartments of the West, and in so doing take part in the process by which Soviet authority has been undermined through the foreign contacts that the Stalinist state did so much to prohibit. This new horizon is nothing if not ironic, and the emptying out of the "full presence" of the collective apartment into the nihilism of "stateness" illustrates an eerily dystopian moment. In Kabakov's *kommunalka*, every prospective unfolding of an individual's response to the interpellations of state culture involves a dystopian horizon in radical contradiction to any utopia at "the end of history." Rather than organizing a decentered subjectivity around the reifications of an effectively productive mass culture, post-Soviet subjects encounter a contradiction between the materiality of everyday life and the metaphysics of a higher reality that they must internalize and reproduce – in the absense of a stable interpellating voice. It is clear that such a moment of social reproduction can only yield an ideologically deformed result. The difference from Western discourses of the postmodern, with their invocation of rationality

and critique in relation to a dispersion of subject positions in mass culture, should be apparent here – even with the unforeseen result that the historical emergence of an unstable post-Soviet subjectivity makes Western postmodernism appear even more qualified by an imaginary totality that has come undone without the opposition of the Soviet state. Here the construction of the postmodern as an effect of Cold War antagonism – hinted at by Fredric Jameson's citing of it as consequence of the "era of national revolutions" and to that extent inflected by their lost horizons – shows a "cultural specificity" to the West when compared to the post-Soviet horizons of "Second-World" subjectivity. The "postmodern" thus is not universally applicable to forms of social organization at moments of devolution away from the organizing stabilities of modern society – pointing to the enormous differences between the First and Second Worlds. While the postmodern and the post-Soviet may have a great deal to say to each other, finally the historical conditions of their emergence mark them as incommensurate ●

W O R K S C I T E D

Bloch, Ernst. *The Utopian Function of Art and Literature*. Cambridge, MA, 1988.

Davidson, Michael, Lyn Hejinian, Ron Silliman, and Barrett Watten. *Leningrad: American Writers in the Soviet Union*. San Francisco, 1991.

Dragomoshchenko, Arkadii:

Description. Trans. Lyn Hejinian and Elena Balashova. Los Angeles, 1990.

"I(s)." Trans. Lyn Hejinian and Elena Balashova. *Poetics Journal* 9 (June 1991): 127–37.

"Syn/Opsis/Taxis." Trans. Lyn Hejinian and Elena Balashova. *Poetics Journal* 8 (June 1989): 5–8.

Dziubenko, Mikhail. "'New Poetry' and Perspectives for Philology." Trans. Lyn Hejinian and Elena Balashova. *Poetics Journal* 8 (June 1989): 24–31.

Jameson, Fredric. Introduction to *Postmodernism, or, The Cultural Logic of Late Capitalism*. Durham, NC, 1991.